THE OXFORD DIARIES OF
Arthur Hugh Clough

Arthur Hugh Clough is one of the most undervalued of Victorian poets. His importance is now being recognized, and the *New Oxford Book of Victorian Verse* assigns him his rightful position as a major poet. While an undergraduate at Balliol and a Fellow of Oriel Clough wrote a series of intensely personal diaries, which throw light not only on his own development as a poet, but on the Oxford education of the time and the religious sensibility of the early Victorian era.

Having been influenced by Thomas Arnold at Rugby, Clough felt the attraction at Oxford of the charisma of Newman. He was torn between the liberal and the catholic view of Christianity and began to raise the questions which led him eventually to agnosticism. In lighter moments the Diaries show Clough boating on the river and walking with Matthew Arnold through the countryside immortalized by *The Scholar Gypsy*.

ANTHONY KENNY was until recently Master of Balliol College, Oxford.

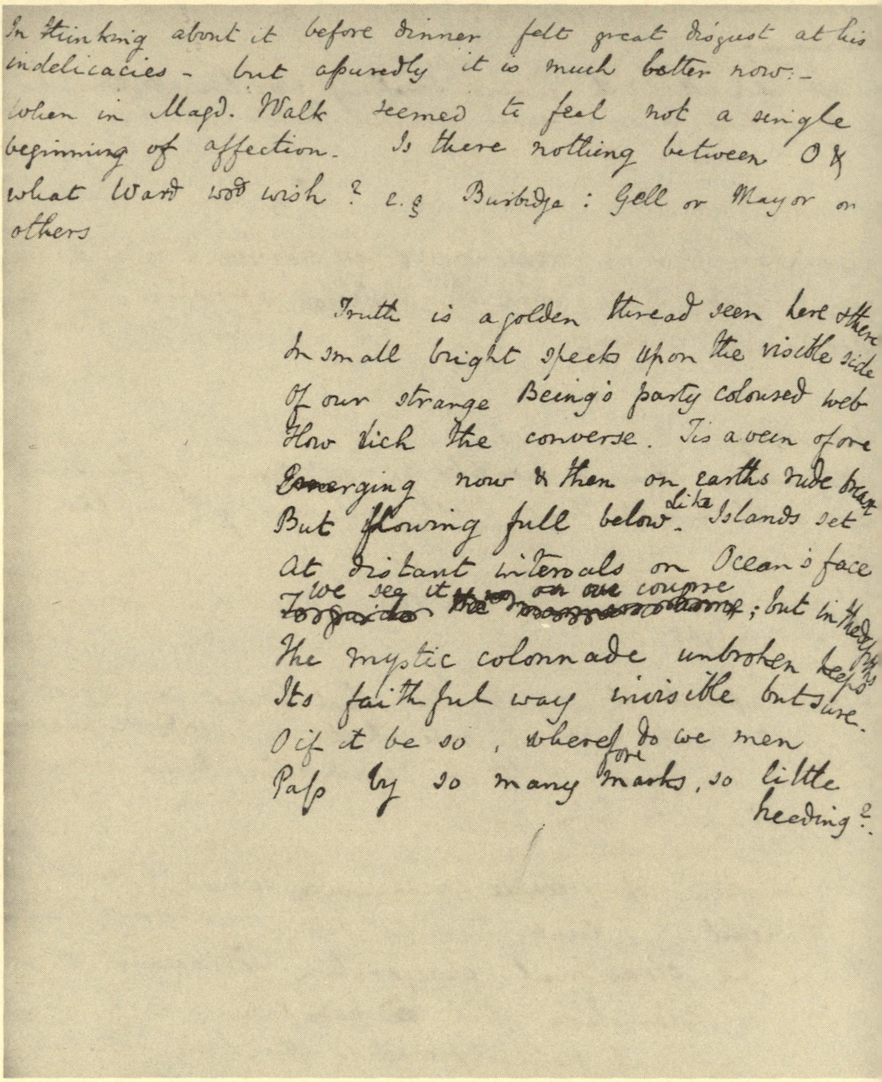

In thinking about it before dinner felt great disgust at his indelicacies — but assuredly it is much better now. — When in Magd. Walk seemed to feel not a single beginning of affection. Is there nothing between O & what Ward wod wish? e.g. Burbidge : Gell or Mayor or others

Truth is a golden thread seen here & there
In small bright specks upon the visible side
Of our strange Being's party coloured web
How rich the converse. Tis a vein of ore
Emerging now & then on earths rude breast
But flowing full below. Like Islands set
At distant intervals on Ocean's face
We see it ~~on our course~~ ; but in the deep
The mystic colonnade unbroken keeps
Its faithful way invisible but sure
O if it be so, wherefore do we men
Pass by so many marks, so little
                                    heeding?

Fig. 1 'Truth is a golden thread': 14 October 1838

THE
OXFORD DIARIES
OF
Arthur Hugh
Clough

EDITED BY
ANTHONY KENNY

CLARENDON PRESS · OXFORD
1990

Oxford University Press, Walton Street, Oxford OX2 6DP

Oxford New York Toronto
Delhi Bombay Calcutta Madras Karachi
Petaling Jaya Singapore Hong Kong Tokyo
Nairobi Dar es Salaam Cape Town
Melbourne Auckland
and associated companies in
Berlin Ibadan

Oxford is a trade mark of Oxford University Press

Published in the United States
by Oxford University Press, New York

British Library Cataloguing in Publication Data

Clough, Arthur Hugh, 1819–1861
The Oxford diaries of Arthur Hugh Clough.
1. Poetry in English. Clough, Arthur Hugh, 1819–1861
I. Title II. Kenny, Anthony, 1931–
821'.8

ISBN 0-19-811739-6

Library of Congress Cataloging in Publication Data
Clough, Arthur Hugh, 1819–1861.
The Oxford diaries of Arthur Hugh Clough | edited by Anthony Kenny.
p. cm.
Bibliography: p.
Includes index.
1. Clough, Arthur Hugh, 1819–1861—Diaries. 2. Poets,
English—19th century—Diaries. 3. University of Oxford—Students—
Diaries. 4. Oxford (England)—Intellectual life. 5. Oxford
movement. I. Kenny, Anthony John Patrick. II. Title.
PR4458.A426 1989
828'.803—dc20
89-9271

[B]

ISBN 0-19-811739-6

Set by Eta Services (Typesetters) Ltd., Beccles, Suffolk
Printed and bound in
Great Britain by Biddles Ltd.
Guildford and King's Lynn

Contents

Acknowledgements

I AM deeply grateful to Miss Katherine Duff, Arthur Hugh Clough's great-niece, for permission to publish these diaries, whose copyright she owns, and for friendly encouragement in the task.

Many of my colleagues have put me in their debt by their readiness in answering queries and their willingness to suggest lines of research to elucidate difficult passages. In particular I am grateful to R. H. Lonsdale, K. W. Garlick, Sir Keith Thomas, J. M. Prest, E. V. Quinn, Jasper Griffin, Miriam Allott, Norman McKenzie, and Cecil Lang.

In the Balliol library Dr P. Bulloch and Mr Alan Tadiello were unfailingly helpful. At the Oxford University Press I received most valuable assistance from Ms Kim Scott Walwyn and Mr Edwin Pritchard.

List of Illustrations

Abbreviations

A & C	E. Abbot and L. Campbell, *The Life and Letters of Benjamin Jowett* (London, 1897)
Allott & Super	M. Allot and R. H. Super (edd.), *The Oxford Authors: Matthew Arnold* (Oxford, 1986)
Bertram	J. Bertram (ed.), *New Zealand Letters of Thomas Arnold the Younger* (London, 1966)
C	*The Correspondence of Arthur Hugh Clough*, ed. F. L. Mulhauser (Oxford, 1957)
Davidson	R. T. Davidson and W. Benham, *Life of Archibald Campbell Tait, Archbishop of Canterbury* (London, 1981)
Greenberger	E. Greenberger, *Arthur Hugh Clough: Growth of a Poet's Mind* (Harvard, 1970)
Honan	P. Honan, *Matthew Arnold, a Life* (London, 1981)
Knight	W. Knight, *Principal Shairp and His Friends* (London, 1888)
Lake	K. Lake, *Memorials of William Charles Lake* (London, 1901)
L & D	*The Letters and Diaries of John Henry Newman*, ed. G. Tracey, vol. vi, *1837–8* (Oxford, 1984).
M	*The Poems of Arthur Hugh Clough*, ed. F. L. Mulhauser, 2nd edn. (Oxford, 1974)
Mulhauser	A numbered list of letters indicating those not reproduced in *The Correspondence of Arthur Hugh Clough*, referred to by entry number
PPR	Arthur Hugh Clough, *The Poems and Prose Remains*, ed. Blanche Clough (London, 1869)
PPS	J. H. Newman, *Parochial and Plain Sermons* (London, 1868–70)
Prothero	R. E. Prothero, *The Life and Correspondence of A. P. Stanley* (London, 1893)
Prothero 1895	R. E. Prothero, *Letters and Verses of A. P. Stanley* (London, 1895)
Rogers	R. H. Holden (comp.), *Reminiscences of William Rogers, Rector of St. Botolph's Bishopsgate* (London, 1888)
Sandford	E. G. Sandford (ed.), *Memoirs of Archbishop Temple by seven friends* (London, 1906)
Scott	P. Scott, *Arthur Hugh Clough: The Bothie* (St Lucia, Queensland, 1976)
Ward	Wilfrid Ward, *William George Ward and the Oxford Movement* (London, 1889)

Biographical Introduction

ARTHUR HUGH CLOUGH was the second son of James Butler Clough, a Liverpool cotton merchant of Welsh extraction, and of Anne Perfect, the strict and pious daughter of a Yorkshire banker. He was born on New Year's Day in 1819, and was just five months older than Queen Victoria. When Arthur was 4 years old, the Cloughs migrated to Charleston, South Carolina, so that James could preside over the American export side of the business. The family remained in America for thirteen years, but Arthur and his elder brother received their schooling in England.

Both boys entered Rugby in 1829. The new headmaster there was Dr Thomas Arnold, the reformer who more than any other man set the ideal for the nineteenth-century public school in England. He strove to establish a tone of moral earnestness, and insisted on the serious study of classics, mathematics, modern history, and science. He encouraged competitive sport in order to promote physical fitness, courage, and endurance. The schooling was set in the firmly religious context of a traditional Christianity which set before the boys the example of Christ and encouraged a life of obedience to God expressed in service to one's neighbour. Little emphasis was laid on the ritual and dogmatic aspect of the Christian tradition, much on critical self-examination and strict cultivation of conscience. The regime was austere and the discipline strict; but there was less arbitrary beating than elsewhere and the senior pupils were encouraged to take their part in the enforcement of the school ethos.

Clough entered fully into Arnold's programme: he worked hard in class, and performed brilliantly. Despite a frail constitution which hampered him throughout his short life, he achieved renown as a runner, a swimmer, and a rugby player. Though many of his school writings sound priggish to twentieth-century ears, he was popular with his schoolfellows, and was often consulted by the headmaster. He edited the Rugby Magazine, and in his senior years he played a significant part in student self-government.

Having no home in England Clough had to spend vacations with uncles and cousins. He was frequently entertained in the

Arnolds' private quarters at school and at their vacation residence in the Lake District. He looked up to them as second parents, and formed friendships which were to last a lifetime with their sons Thomas and Matthew. His devotion to Arnold refined an already sensitive conscience, and reinforced the sense of duty inculcated by his mother. At Rugby, and at his early days at Oxford, Clough regarded Arnold's influence as a great blessing.

The schoolboy friends whom Clough made at Rugby were important to him long after he had left the school. But some of the closest friends left in October 1835, two years before his own departure. Three to whom he had been particularly close, and to whom he had looked up, C. J. Vaughan, J. N. Simpkinson, and J. P. Gell, went to Trinity College, Cambridge. To Cambridge too went Thomas Burbidge, a somewhat scapegrace friend to whom Clough, in later life, would regularly send drafts of his poems and with whom he published a joint volume of verse in 1848 under the title *Ambarvalia*. With the departure of these Clough felt lonely in the sixth form, and he also believed that the general moral standard of the school—for which, as head of the School House, he felt partly responsible—had steeply declined. In the period March 1835 to December 1836 he kept a journal in which, among other things, he noted down remarks on his own sins and the wickedness, as he put it, of his schoolfellows, some of whom were given to drunkenness and brawling. In May 1836 he wrote to Simpkinson that much as he loved Arnold and his family, and members of the Rugby staff, he had not one real friend in the school, and no congenial company in the sixth; only some juniors, such as the brothers Henry and Theodore Walrond, in whom he felt 'a great and deep and loving interest' (C i. 46).

Clough's attempts to reform his wayward schoolfellows met with little success, but his academic career at Rugby was brilliant, and he won every prize that the school had to offer. In November 1836 he went to Oxford to sit for a scholarship to Balliol college. He explained to his mother that he wanted the scholarship 'not only for the honour's sake—though the honour is the greatest part of it—but for the £30 per annum, which with an exhibition will, I trust, all but pay my way at Oxford, as Balliol is £20 or £30 cheaper than any other College, I understand' (C i. 44).

Not only was Balliol cheap: it was one of the most academically distinguished colleges in the university. It had played a part in the academic reforms of the early part of the century, opening most of its scholarships to competitive examination, priding itself on the record of its scholars in the university class lists at the end of their course, electing to fellowships on merit, and imposing on its tutors a high standard of dedication to their pupils. Since 1819 the Master, or head, of the college had been Dr Richard Jenkyns, religiously and politically conservative, but with a keen and encouraging eye for academic talent.

Jenkyns was thus described by one of his junior colleagues, who eventually was one of his successors as Master, Benjamin Jowett.

He was a gentleman of the old school, in whom were represented old manners, old traditions, old prejudices, a Tory and a Churchman, high and dry, without much literature, but having a good deal of character. He filled a great space in the eyes of the undergraduates. 'His young men', as he termed them, speaking in an accent which we all remember, were never tired of mimicking his voice, drawing his portrait, and inventing stories about what he said and did . . . He was a considerable actor, and would put on severe looks to terrify Freshmen, but he was really kind-hearted and indulgent to them . . . He was short of stature and very neat in appearance; the deficiency of height was more than compensated by a superfluity of magisterial or ecclesiastical dignity. (Ward, 431)

Fellows as well as undergraduates were in awe of Jenkyns—in his presence. But he was the kind of person about whom anecdotes circulate and multiply.

One such anecdote concerned the scholarship examination which Clough sat in 1836: it was told by William Rogers, one of four Eton boys who competed.

The examination took place in the College Hall, and for some reason no Fellow presided and we were left to ourselves. There was at times a good deal of noise and laughing, and rightly or wrongly, I got credited with more than my share in making it. On the last day of the examination, when all the paper work was over, I was sent for by the Master, Dr Jenkyns to be taken in *viva voce*. When he had heard me, he said 'You will not return to the Hall', but gave no reason. I had however arranged to go out with Hobhouse [another of the Etonians] and wanted to communicate with him. I accordingly disobeyed the Master's instruction, opened the door of the Hall, just put my head in, and began my explanation by calling out 'That ugly little devil'—there I stopped. My remark was received with a death-like silence, in strange contrast to the hilarity of the previous days, but the reason was immediately apparent. Just behind the door stood the figure of one of the tutors, Mr Tait. I vanished into space and so did my chance of either scholarship or matriculation. Tait reported my evil words, and though the Master was willing to forgive me the Fellows objected, and I was refused admission to the College. (Rogers, 22)

At the end of this disorderly examination, Clough was elected to the scholarship. 'The examination concluded this morning about 12 o'clock', he wrote to his father on 26 November, 'I have got the Head [scholarship], which also includes an Exhibition, added to it to make it more valuable' (C i. 53). Clough and the other examinees went in a body to Jenkyns to plead for the unfortunate Rogers, and to assure him that they had not been disturbed by him. But it was several months before the fellows relented and allowed Rogers to resit the examination.

Clough returned to Rugby for the remainder of the academic year. He was much happier during these final months in school, partly because Burbidge, having got into some scrape, had returned to live in lodgings nearby under Arnold's supervision. 'It is a greater blessing to me than I can well describe to have him here, and see every day at least once', Clough wrote to Simpkinson (C i. 58). Even after the summer vacation Clough returned to Rugby for the beginning of the half-year, for the seven weeks before the Oxford term began in October.

'Behold I am in Oxford', he wrote to his sister Annie on 15 October 'safe and sound, capped and gowned, have attended Chapel twice, once with and once without surplice, have been to Hall (signifying dinner in Hall) also twice, to a wine party also, to call on the Master, and to the University Sermon this morning. So that by tomorrow evening, when I hope my books will be arrived and arranged on my shelves, and when, also I trust, I shall be furnished with a kettle and set of tea things (for as yet I have been dependent on the bountiful hospitalities of my friends) I shall be pretty completely settled' (C i. 64).

Clough had no lack of friends ready made in Balliol, for many of his schoolfellows had preceded him there. He came up with Arthur Stanley, son of the newly appointed bishop of Norwich, who had been at Balliol since 1834, and had recently distinguished himself by winning a coveted university prize, the Ireland scholarship (after having been falsely accused of cheating) and by winning the Newdigate prize for poetry with his verses 'The Gipsies'. Stanley was now due to take his final examinations in November (Prothero 121, 176, 187). A contemporary of Stanley's was Benjamin Brodie: he was rare among Clough's friends as having a mathematical and scientific bent. A year junior was William Lake, who had gone up from Rugby in 1835; Clough had been fond of him, but had heard rumours that he was too exclusive at Oxford, and he was to find him from time to time irritatingly pompous as they were thrown together. Contemporary with Lake as a scholar from Rugby was Edward Goulburn, whom Clough seems to have known better at Oxford than at school, and who eventually was one of its headmasters. Another Rugbeian who was just ahead of Clough at Balliol was William Fox (whom he had described as the only tolerable company in the sixth in 1836) (C i. 46).

Scholars at Balliol sat at a separate table in the dining hall (which is now the library). Besides the Rugby scholars Clough met there the Etonian James Lonsdale, just about to take Schools, and the Pauline Benjamin Jowett: both of these were to be elected fellows and move to a higher table a year after Clough's arrival. Charles Trower, a future fellow of Exeter and barrister, was immediately senior to him. Stafford Northcote, later Lord Iddesleigh, was elected with Clough, but was not intimate with him; he is mentioned only twice in his diary.

At Jesus college, across Broad Street and a few yards down Turl Street from Balliol, Clough had family connections. His uncle, Alfred B. Clough, was a fellow of the college. Dispatching Clough to Oxford, Arnold had written a glowing testimonial ('he has passed eight years without a fault . . . he has gone on ripening gradually in all excellence intellectual and spiritual . . . he has now gone to Oxford, not only full of honours, but carrying with him the respect and love of all whom he has left behind, and regarded by myself, I may truly say, with an affection and interest hardly less than I should feel for my own son.') The President of the college, Henry Foulkes, was also a family connection, and the young Edmund S. Foulkes ('E.S.F' often in Clough's diary) became in time a very familiar companion.

Clough's first term seems to have passed in an agreeable whirl. He kept no diary, and he was too busy to write even to old friends like Simpkinson and Gell. Writing to the former after the term was over he said, 'I like Oxford very much and hope to live there very comfortably from next term forward'. Of the undergraduates, it was Brodie and Lake with whom he most kept company during the term: but it was not an undergraduate, but a tutor, who had become his closest friend (C i. 66).

The tutorial system in Oxford in the 1830s was rather different from that familiar to recent generations. A college like Balliol had a dozen fellows, but only three or four would be tutors. Tutors, moreover, imparted instruction not primarily to single pupils or small groups, but in lectures to as many as twenty pupils at a time; these lectures resembled modern sixth-form classes much more than twentieth-century university tutorials. One-to-one sessions of instruction were known, but these were imparted by a 'coach' to his 'cub', and a coach was not provided as part of the normal college instruction, but had to be hired by an undergraduate who was anxious to win a university prize or do particularly well in the final Honour Schools.

Undergraduates had to pass two examinations in order to obtain the degree of Bachelor of Arts. The first was Responsions, nicknamed 'Little-Go', in which they were questioned orally in Greek and Latin, and in logic or geometry. The second public examination, held in the fourth year after matriculation, contained written papers in religion, in *literae humaniores* (that is to say, Greek and Latin literature and history, plus composition and logic), and, optionally, in the elements of mathematics and physics. Corresponding to the examination requirements, Balliol in 1838 had two classical tutors, Archibald Tait and Robert Scott, and one lecturer in mathematics and logic, William George Ward.

All three men were intellectually distinguished, and together they had the reputation of being the most effective tutorial team in Oxford. The three were very different from each other. Scott was a gentle, scholarly person, full of erudite information, too much given to punning, if Jowett is to be believed, but also famous for a number of *bons mots*. He was later to be Master of the college, between Jenkyns and Jowett, but he is best known to posterity for the massive Greek dictionary which he produced in collaboration with Dean Liddell of Christ Church.

Tait was less intellectual, but more vigorous. He was a Scotsman, shrewd and humorous, reputed one of the most devoted tutors in Oxford. Later he became archbishop of Canterbury. Jowett, who did not like bishops, said, 'He was one of the few by whom high preferment was never sought and to whom it did no harm'. One of Tait's rare gifts, which was to have full play in Balliol during Clough's Oxford career, was the ability to remain on close terms of friendship with those from whom he differed theologically. He was in his Balliol years a moderate low churchman, and suspicious of theological innovation.

Of the three tutors the most remarkable character, and the one who was to have the most influence on Clough, was William George Ward. Ward was highly intelligent, with a passion for abstract logic that went hand in hand with a cavalier attitude to historical fact. Like Tait, he too could be very devoted to his pupils; but he had favourites, and with these he would try to enter too much into their lives. He was a clumsy, Johnsonian figure, fat and ill-dressed, an eccentric about whom affectionate stories gathered almost as ripely as about Jenkyns. Jowett, at a time when Ward and himself had permanently parted company on religious topics, could still say, 'I cannot resist the charms of the fat fellow whenever I get into his company. You like him as you like a Newfoundland dog. He is such a large, jolly, shaggy creature.' He was a great expert on the theatre and the opera, for both of which he had a passion; the actor Macready was one of his heroes, and he used to sing the buffo arias from Mozart operas in the country lanes outside Oxford. His mathematics tutorials were notorious for ending with an animated discussion of current burlesque shows. He was in demand as a mimic, and was a great favourite with the college servants. His son describes how he would amuse his colleagues and pupils by sketching a *ballet d'action* on events of university interest:

Dr Jenkyns of Balliol was an especially favourite character in these performances, and Mr Ward would send his company into fits of laughter by a combined imitation of the peculiarities of the Master's manner, and the received movements of the ballerina—the pirouette and the various forms of step, fast and slow. (Ward, 40)

Ward would represent each of the characters in turn, accompanied by one of his colleagues on the piano. His listeners found extremely droll the contrast between his normal occupation of deep metaphysical discussion and these light-hearted performances. It was, one of them said, like watching Thomas Aquinas dancing a ballet.

On one of these occasions the performance was more vigorous than usual, and Ward was for the moment impersonating Cupid. Mr Chapman, one of the tutors, was unable to continue his reading in the room below, and sent his scout to ascertain the cause of the disturbance. The scout came back with the assurance, 'Its honly Mr Ward, sir. 'E's a hacting of a cherubym'. (Ward, 40)

Beneath the jovial farce of Ward's exterior there lay not only a passionate interest in metaphysics, but also a deeply depressive nature. The burlesque persona was only sustained by making enormous demands, in private, on those to whom Ward felt close. Clough was to learn this to his cost.

At the end of his first term Clough, with the other Balliol undergraduates, had to undergo an internal college examination called 'collections'. He was examined on the gospel of St Matthew, one book of Thucydides, three of Homer's Iliad, a play of Aristophanes, and some early Greek history; in Latin he had been studying Virgil's eclogues. During the term he had written three essays: on the effects of drama on taste and morals, on the effects of printing on literature, and on Venice. These essays were normally read by the Master and returned on Saturday mornings. At collection time Jenkyns summed up Clough's work as 'good, but deficient in elegance and neatness of style'. In morals, however, he was described as 'excellent' and 'uniformly diligent'.

Clough had been studying algebra and logic with Ward. He was not certain, he had told his sister, whether he would be able to take the final examination in mathematics 'as I do not believe myself to be over strong'. But Ward was quick to appreciate his pupil's gifts, and made much of him. But it appears that much of their talk was not of mathematics but of theology.

Clough had arrived in Oxford at a period of religious excitement. The university still saw itself as largely a religious institution: it was a necessary condition for matriculation to subscribe to the Thirty-nine Articles of the Church of England, so that not only atheists but Catholics and Dissenters were excluded. Attempts to modify or abolish subscription had been defeated both in the university and in Parliament in 1835. Hand in hand with academic reform in Oxford had gone a growth in the seriousness of

moral and religious attitudes. But there was no agreement where ·
true seriousness lay.

Three main currents of religious thought were powerful in the
Oxford of 1838 and were influential in the life of the young
Clough. The evangelical tradition which Clough had already
encountered through his mother laid stress on interior religious
sentiment, the sense of sin, and the experience of conversion. The
liberal tradition of Rugby saw morality in conduct and motive as
the essence of Christianity; it was not deeply concerned with the
dogmatic formulation of religious truth. The new but growing
Tractarian movement, centred in Oxford and led by John Keble,
John Henry Newman, and Edward Bouverie Pusey, fostered
within the Church of England a Catholic emphasis on the mystical
power of sacramental symbols and the necessity of a priesthood in
succession to the Apostles, to give authoritative interpretation of
Scripture and ecclesiastical tradition. The movement took its
name from the 'Tracts for the Times' which from 1833–41
propagated its tenets.

Clough's background would dispose him to suspicion of the
Tractarian movement. From Rugby he had observed the in-
tolerance which led its members, in alliance with the old-
fashioned Tory clergy, to censure in 1836 Renn Hampden, the
liberal Professor of Divinity nominated by the Whig government
of Melbourne (C i. 44). His admired Arnold had denounced the
Tractarians fiercely in an article 'The Oxford Malignants'. Yet in
his first letter to Simpkinson after going to Balliol he wrote, 'Have
you ever read Newman's Sermons? I hope you will soon if you
have not, for they are very good and I should think especially
useful for us' (C i. 66).

No serious young man in Oxford could be impervious to the
charisma of Newman. Many of Clough's contemporaries have left
descriptions of the parochial sermons which Newman preached in
the church of St Mary of which he was vicar—sermons which
made far more impact than the cycle of university sermons
preached by officially appointed academic grandees. The most
famous such description is that written by Matthew Arnold, who
was taken by Clough a few years later to hear Newman preach.
Writing in 1883 he said of Newman:

Forty years ago he was in the very prime of life; he was close at hand to us in Oxford; he was preaching in St Mary's pulpit every Sunday; he seemed about to transform and to renew what was for us the most national and natural institution in the world, the Church of England. Who could resist the charm of that spiritual apparition, gliding in the dim afternoon light through the aisles of St Mary's, rising into the pulpit, and then, in the most entrancing of voices, breaking the silence with words and thought which were a religious music,—subtle, sweet, mournful? (Allot and Super, 472)

Clough valued Newman's rhetorical gifts, but even more he admired his austerity of life. He was to become a regular attender at the lectures and seminars which Newman conducted in a vestry of the university church.

But more immediate and inescapable than the influence of Newman himself was that of Ward pulling in the same theological direction. Ward had before 1838 been, like Clough, a follower of Arnold: he had been converted to Arnoldism from an initially utilitarian and rationalist position, and on one famous occasion paid a special journey to Rugby to lay some theological problems before the headmaster. The visit had its embarrassing side, as Ward used later to relate:

Dr Arnold, busy all day with the routine of school-work came in the evening, pretty well tired out, to discuss as he could Mr Ward's sceptical difficulties and intellectual problems; while the younger man, who had sat on the sofa reading novels all day, brought to the discussion not only his special habits and endowments as a dialectician, but the freshness of an unexercised brain. The result was that Arnold not only failed to satisfy him, but was himself so exhausted that on Ward's departure he had to spend a day in bed. (Ward, 79)

None the less, when the time came for Ward to be ordained deacon he subscribed the Thirty-nine Articles in the liberal sense in which Arnold understood them. So suspicious was he at this time of Newman that he had to be tricked into attending his first sermon at St Mary's: 'Why should I go and listen to such myths?'

Still critical of Tractarianism, Ward began to take Stanley to Newman's seminars in St Mary's vestry. Goulburn later described the scene to Ward's son:

Your father and Arthur Stanley, who, though still an undergraduate, was his bosom friend and constant associate, the Pylades to his Orestes, used to sit side by side at these lectures, full in front of Mr Newman's desk, and drinking in with open ear and quick intelligence every word which fell

from his lips. Your good father was the most demonstrative of men—
wholly incapable of suppressing any strong emotion which for the time
got possession of him; and as these lectures awakened in him the strongest
emotions both of admiration for their power and (at that time) indignant
repudiation of their conclusions, he put the preacher somewhat out of
countenance by his steadfast gaze, his play of features as some particular
passage stirred him, his nudges of Stanley and whispered 'asides' to him
('What would Arnold say to that' etc. etc.) Your father's manner and
gestures were so pronounced that no one in the congregation could help
noticing them; and it was well known also that the criticisms, which the
demonstrations gave expression to, were at that time unfriendly. Mr
Newman, however, proved equal to the occasion, and at the lecture
immediately succeeding one at which Ward had been specially demonstrative, we found the benches of the congregation turned side-ways (as in
college chapels) so that he and Stanley could not, without turning their
heads askew, look the preacher in the face. (Ward, 83)

After 1837 Clough succeeded Stanley as Ward's closest associate
among the undergraduates. Indeed, Ward made preposterous
intellectual and emotional demands on his favourite pupil. Many
hours of almost every day he would keep Clough in his room,
arguing theology and craving for comfort and affection. Clough
tolerated with remarkable patience the possessiveness of his tutor,
and shared many of his intellectual and theological concerns, but
it is clear that the relationship placed severe strains on his sensitive
mind. The account of the progress and difficulties of their
relationship is one of the major themes of the diaries which Clough
began to keep at the beginning of the Lent Term of 1838.

He states his motive for keeping a diary in an entry for 2
February. 'I find from my exceeding irregularity and inconsistency, and hardness and I much fear profound self-deception, that
I must take to this work once more. All the enjoyment, and
attention, & be-praisement of this Place is too much as yet for me.'
The diary for the term is full of relentless self-examination, and
Clough kept a tally of tiny sins of speech and thought. The
external events which are noted—his first wine party, Arnold's
visit to preach in an Oxford church, the round of lectures and the
attendance at debating societies—are submerged in a mass of
introspection and self-reproach. The Balliol diaries, unlike the
Rugby diaries, are free from denunciations of the wickedness of
others; indeed he is astonishingly ready to make excuses for others
and to reject all palliation of his own misdeeds and mixed motives.

Clough's health was poor during this term, with headaches and stomach troubles, and he consulted more than one physician; he was inclined to take his illness as a punishment for his sins, and his doctors did not discourage him in this view. In addition to the twice daily services in the college chapel he would spend long periods each day in private devotions in his room. He also, from time to time, resolved to take up fasting; but this resolution, like his frequent resolutions about the times of rising and retiring, does not seem to have been regularly carried into action.

Academically, the term was not a successful one. Clough was competing for the Hertford scholarship, which, as he said, would bring 'great fame and glory and £30'. He had hired a Wadham coach, Massie, to supplement the lectures which he was receiving from Scott and Tait. Two other Rugby friends, 'Plug' Arnold at Balliol and Richard Congreve at Wadham, were also competing for the prize; Clough was deeply downcast to be told that Arnold had a better chance of winning, as he was when the Master thought little of an essay he had written in January on the Law of Nations. In the event none of the Rugby candidates won the Hertford, but Frederick Blaydes, 'an insignificant commoner of Christ Church'. However, in the Balliol examinations in early April Clough received nothing but praise from his tutors.

Clough attended Newman's services, and read his published sermons; indeed at the beginning of Lent he entertained Newman to dinner, but the occasion seems to have been a disappointing one. With Ward he discussed the relation between Scripture and ecclesiastical tradition, and the nature of baptismal regeneration; each week's sermon would be carefully dissected, mostly with Ward but sometimes with Stanley. The most important theological event of the term was the publication by Newman and Keble of the *Remains* of Hurrell Froude. These papers of a Tractarian colleague at Oriel who had died young revealed a devotion to asceticism, and a hostility to the Protestant reformation, which alienated some of Newman's moderate Anglican supporters while encouraging others, such as Ward, to look with a favourable eye on the Roman Catholic Church. Ward and Clough read Froude's *Remains* together, and they clearly had an influence on the style of Clough's own journals. At the end of the term he recommended them to Gell as one of the most instructive books he had ever read.

The Easter vacation marked the high point of Clough's

conversion to Newmanism. He stayed up in college and celebrated Holy Week as a spiritual retreat, reading each day the passages in the gospel relating the words and actions of Christ in the last week of his life, comparing together the versions of the different evangelists, and copying long Greek passages from the New Testament into his diary, along with verse passages from Keble's *The Christian Year*. He was deeply moved by Newman's reading of St Matthew's passion in St Mary's on Palm Sunday, and on the following day he noted in his diary

many persons of the most advanced piety and goodness are this week engaged in all sorts of self-denial, & mortification, fasting from food & sleep, amusement & society—Newman for instance, whose errors as we believe them to be must not make me ever forget how far he is above me in goodness and piety, and wisdom too, tho' in certain points we with less power may by our advantages be nearer the real truth, and though less wise have more wisdom.

But he was constantly distracted from his devotions. On Easter Eve he wrote, 'It has been indeed a poor week compared with my hopes', and on Easter Monday, 'I, who have kept no fast, must not now dare to keep feast'.

In the summer term Clough attended Newman's Tuesday evening lectures, which were on the sacramental system. He was impressed by the fairness of Newman's presentation, but he remained convinced that the High Church sacramental doctrine was incompatible with Scripture. His view here was very similar to Stanley's. At one time Stanley had been very attracted by Tractarianism, and at about the time of his first class in Schools in November 1837 Newman had thought he had made a convert of him. But by March of 1838 he could write to a friend, 'I am now more at peace about Newmanism. The opposition which it seems to meet from the Canonical Scripture seems so very strong that I am content to lay the question on the shelf for a time' (Prothero, 196).

Similarly, Clough wrote to Gell on 8 May:

One thing I suppose is clear—that one must leave the discussion of *Tὰ Nεανθρωπικά* [*Newmanist matters*] all snug and quiet for after one's degree. And it is no harm but rather good to give oneself up a little to hearing Oxford people, and admiring their good points, which lie, I suppose principally in all they hold in opposition to the Evangelical portion of society—the benefit and beauty and necessity of forms—the ugliness of feelings put on unnaturally soon and consequently kept up by artificial means, ever strained and never sober. I should be very sorry ever to be brought to believe their further views of matter acting on morals as a charm of sacramentalism, and the succession-notion so closely connected with it. All this, and their way of reading and considering Scripture— such a contrast to the German fashions—rests I suppose entirely on their belief in the Infallibility of the Church down to a certain period, to which they are led by a strong sense of the necessity of some infallible authority united with a feeling of the insufficiency of the New Testament. Indeed I think a good deal of what they say as to this latter point is stronger than anything I ever heard against it. Newman is now giving lectures on the Mystical Power of the Sacraments and seems to have stated the objections to it Scripturally in a very fair and candid manner. (C i. 71–2)

Clough's own diaries seem full of 'feelings put on unnaturally soon and kept up by artificial means': his constant lamentation of his sins, and second-order lamentation for being insufficiently miserable about his sins, seem to smack of the Evangelical unctuousness that he saw Newman correcting. But it was indeed Newman's insistence on austere moral standards, and constant call for self-denial, rather than his theories of church government or sacramental grace, which kept a hold on Clough. On 27 May, marked in his diary as the Sunday after Ascension Day, Clough noted, 'I seem to have lost all notion of sin. I must keep fast every day to the end of term except Sundays & Holydays or else I shall never keep right.'

But life during this term was not all self-absorbed self-reproach. He could sum up his activities to Gell as 'reading for little-go, and paying off wine-party scores'. Also his diary shows that he frequently went skiffing on the river, and on at least one occasion attended a boat-race. He was also active in two debating societies, the Union and the Decade. Both of them, though, became sources of self-rebuke; he accused himself of castle-building concerning the Union 'that I should come forward in it, & be a great personage, and develop my views & be the leader of a great party of disciples'; and after attending the Decade he would usually suffer a bad night and accuse himself of vanity and excitement.

The Decade was a more select group than the Union. It had been founded by Lake and Brodie shortly after they came to Balliol, to 'discuss rather graver subjects than were common at the

Union' (Lake, 38). Clough must have been asked to join it shortly after arriving in the college, and remained a member until his departure from Oxford in 1848. Members were elected without their knowledge, to preclude canvassing. Others who were members of it during his time were Stanley, Goulburn, Lake, Jowett, Coleridge, Prichard, Matthew and Tom Arnold, John Blackett, George Butler (the husband of Josephine), and John Conington, who was for a time its secretary (PPR 25–31; A & C i. 81). Its membership was predominantly liberal, and the topics of debate literary and political. The fullest account of Clough's appearances at the Decade in the years 1843–8, with an account of the motions which he supported, is given by Evelyn Greenberger in her book *Arthur Hugh Clough: Growth of a Poet's Mind*, pp. 68–72; but it is clear from the diaries that Clough was active in the society from his first Oxford days and not only after his election to a fellowship at Oriel.

At the end of the summer term of 1838 Clough was glad to escape from Oxford and what he called the 'hot-house atmosphere which destroys all strength and healthiness of genuine feelings in me'. At the end of June, having been examined and had his work declared 'good—deficient in polish and elegance', he travelled north by train, meeting Burbidge on the way. The two called on Arnold at Fox How near Grasmere and then settled for a number of weeks at Patterdale in company with Theodore Walrond. Clough wrote a number of joyous letters describing their expeditions over the fells around Ullswater (C i. 72–4, 78–80). Burbidge had recently published a book of verse; Clough's admiration for it was genuine but qualified. He thought that it showed greater promise than Tennyson's early verse (C i. 73); on the other hand he thought it was far too self-revelatory. It was, he wrote to Gell, surely quite wrong morally 'so writing as to expose peculiar circumstances of your own life or conduct or friends' (C i. 74). This did not prevent Clough from hugely enjoying his time with Burbidge, and writing to Ward full of his praise (C i. 80). During this happy summer the diary was laid aside, and was not taken up again until Clough was home in Liverpool in September.

At the end of September Clough spent some days at Rugby, again in the company of Burbidge; they talked about sacraments, free-will, and the problem of evil. Burbidge, like Stanley, seems to have confirmed Clough in his opinion that the Tractarian view of sacramental grace was contrary to the teachings of St Paul. Arnold was too busy to talk much to him; Theodore Walrond was preoccupied with his new duties as prefect; Clough left for Oxford reluctantly and in an unsettled state.

The problem which faced Clough at the beginning of his second year was above all how to relate to Ward. During the summer Ward had written him letters principally about theological matters (urging prophetically the view of a friend that 'there is no mean between Newmanism on the one side and extremes far beyond anything of Arnold's on the other') but also displaying a great possessiveness with regard to his pupil. He was clearly nettled by Clough's praise of Burbidge, and felt that Clough had made an inadequate response to expressions of affection in his own letters. He particularly resented an allegation of Clough's that his emotional attitudes were conditioned by novel-reading (which Clough disapproved of: he confessed with some shame in his diary that he had wasted time during the previous term reading *Nicholas Nickleby* and two of Scott's novels) (C i. 74, 81).

The first entries in Clough's diaries for Michaelmas 1838 all concern the nature of his feelings for Ward. Does he have real affection for him? Should he call him 'dear'? Is not Ward imperceptive and indelicate? Is there not something unnatural in the expressions of emotion for which Ward clearly hungers? In the previous year, Clough had from time to time expressed his irritation with Ward's importunity, but had balanced this with several encomia on Ward's superior virtue, which he held up to himself as an example. Publicly jovial, indeed boisterous, Ward was in private frequently depressive; Clough recognized this as an illness, and regarded himself as having a duty to exhibit patience and understanding, however difficult it might be. Now, in his second year, he occasionally permits himself to reflect on Ward's defects. On 19 October he wrote, '[W]hat possible daily inter-course could I have with Ward: his want of perceptions leaving no chance of pleasant small talk: & any talk about high matters leading at once to formulism.' But on the following day he reminded himself that he was not taking sufficient account of Ward's illnesses. In any case, he said, on 21 October, 'in all the annoyances Ward causes me, I must remember that I deserve double'.

So preoccupied was Clough with Ward's needs that he forgot to note in his diary that he presented himself for, and passed, the first examination, Responsions, at the end of October. Apart from reflections on Ward the diary for this period is mainly concerned with transcribing, and commenting on, passages of St Paul's Epistles. This must have been for reasons of piety rather than for academic purposes, since the subject of his divinity studies this term, to judge by the Balliol examination book, was the Acts of the Apostles. He draws many arguments from the Epistles against what he calls the 'compulsory form' system of the Tractarians. He begins to denounce 'The Impolicy and Sin of Athanasianism'—by which he means the thesis that human beings are damned for ever for holding the wrong doctrines, as proclaimed in the Athanasian Creed in the Prayer Book.

On 11 November Clough attended an anti-Tractarian university sermon by Hawkins, the Provost of Oriel. Hawkins, he told Gell 'in a very good University Sermon last Sunday, on the *Duty* of private Judgment as opposed to the *Right* seemed to say that Undergraduates were to mind their Latin and Greek and nothing else or nearly so'. He kept drawing up work plans with a view to carrying out this advice; but the hours of work done never quite seemed to match the hours of work proposed. Each day he would note that number of hours' work done: rarely more than four. A typical entry is that of 15 November: 'Have read about 4 hrs lectures included but have had a hard day's work with Ward'.

The term seems to have been a lonely one. Uncle Alfred had now left his fellowship for a college living at Braunston. Stanley, worried that if he stood for a Balliol fellowship he might be rejected because of his liberal theological views, had accepted one at University college which he made no secret of regarding as a second best. In the November examinations Lake and Trower both won firsts in classics; Brodie obtained a second in mathematics and physics. There were no less than four vacancies for the Balliol fellowships at the end of the month. Three of them were filled by Balliol scholars: Lake, Lonsdale, and, astonishingly, Benjamin Jowett, who was still an undergraduate with a year to go before taking his final examinations—he was preferred before some fifteen candidates who had already taken firsts in Schools. These successes among the Balliol scholars moved some of Clough's friends into a less accessible sphere, so that he was thrown more and more into Ward's company.

During his first year at Balliol, Clough seems to have written no verse. At the beginning of the present term he wrote the poem 'Truth is a golden thread', one of the more mature of his youthful works, first published by his widow after his death. The diction of his own verse makes a contrast with the sometimes saccharine passages from Keble's *The Christian Year* and from the Tractarian anthology *Lyra Apostolica* which he occasionally copied into his diary. Burbidge, Clough told Gell, 'is very savage about the *Lyra Apostolica*, and is writing a review of it, the *Christian Year* and the *Cathedral* which he says he will send to every periodical in Europe in search of admission. I do not know what are the grounds of his wrath, but whether it be from their partisan character which superinduces slang and cant in various modifications or from the forced character of the church system generally they cannot produce good poetry.' Yet Clough recommended Gell to read some of Newman's contributions to the *Lyra* (C i. 85). And at Christmas, when he made a list of books to parcel up to take home for Christmas along with his set book of Sophocles, in addition to the Greek Testament, the Prayer Book, and three volumes of sermons, the only other books he took were *The Christian Year* and Isaac Williams's *The Cathedral*. He stayed the first five days of the vacation with Burbidge, so they must have had much time for critical discussion.

This vacation brought about a crisis in the relations between Clough and Ward. Ward had evidently tried to exact a promise from Clough not to see Burbidge. Clough wrote from Liverpool to tell Ward that he thought the two of them should see less of each other in the future, and that Ward should alter his manner to him. Ward replied in a long letter full of self-pity, saying that he had been 'cut up a good deal'. But he did offer to reform.

I think there will be no need of my making the attempt directly to like you less (in fact I do not see the possibility unless I leave Oxford) if I can succeed in shewing it less to you and getting by degrees to see less of you.

He went on to ask Clough to write a post-mortem about their relationship, and to give various undertakings about relationships to other people:

Further I *release* you from your promise about seeing Burbidge, wishing merely instead an assurance that I shall always know beforehand, and that for this year you will make no engagement inconsistent with your power of staying at Oxford till Eastern Friday and of seeing me as much as 3 or 4 weeks in the Long. Vac, should I so wish. (C i. 87)

It is clear that even at the moment of accepting that his emotions towards Clough needed to cool, Ward was still obsessed with possessive jealousy.

Years later, after Clough's death, Ward wrote to Clough's widow about their time together at Balliol. 'I hardly met anyone', Ward wrote, 'during my whole Oxford life to whom I was so strongly drawn. I saw clearly, indeed, from the first how far wider were his powers and perceptions than my own, and how large a portion of his character there was (including its whole poetical side) with which, from my narrowness, I did not come into contact. But I did perceive in him many qualities which greatly attracted me.' He went on to enumerate Clough's virtues—his conscientiousness, unselfishness, sweetness of disposition, piety, intellectual independence. Then he went on

What was before all things to have been desired for him was that during his undergraduate course, he should have given himself up thoroughly to his classical and mathematical studies; that he should have kept up . . . the habits of prayer and Scripture reading which he brought with him from Rugby, but should have kept himself aloof from plunging prematurely into the theological controversies then so rife at Oxford. . . . I fear that, from my point of view, I must account it the great calamity of his life that he was brought into contact with myself. My whole interest at that time (as now) was concentrated on questions which to me seem the most important and interesting that can occupy the mind. Nor was there any reason why they should not occupy my mind, considering my age and position. It was a very different thing to force them prematurely on the attention of a young man just coming up to college, and to drive him, as it were, peremptorily into a decision upon them; to aim at making him as hot a partisan as I was myself . . .

The result was not surprising. I had been prematurely forcing Clough's mind, and there came a reaction. His intellectual perplexity for some time preyed heavily upon his spirits; it grievously interfered with his studies; and I take for granted it must have very seriously disturbed his religious practices and habits. I cannot to this day think of all this without a bitter pang of self-reproach.

As regards his ordinary habits at the time, since I was a Fellow and he only an undergraduate I cannot speak with certainty; but my impression is that from the first he very much abstained from general society. This was undoubtedly the case at a later period, when his intellectual perplexity had laid hold of him; but I think it began earlier. I remember in particular that every day he used to return to his solitary room immediately after dinner, and when I asked him the reason for this he told me that his pecuniary circumstances incapacitated him from giving wine parties, and that therefore he did not like to wine with others. I think also there was a certain fastidiousness of taste and judgment about him which prevented him from enjoying general society. (Ward, 110)

The letter has been admired as a model of candour and generosity. But in fact it greatly understates both the degree and the nature of the intimacy between the two men. Clough spent more of his private time with Ward than he did with any undergraduate, and no one was better placed than Ward to judge 'his ordinary habits'. And the injury Ward did to Clough's studies and spirits was not due simply to theological perplexity. No doubt the comment recorded by Stanley gives a just account of the impression made in Oxford when Clough and Ward were seen walking together: 'There goes Ward mystifying poor Clough, and persuading him that he must either believe *nothing* or accept the whole of Church doctrine.' But in his years at Balliol Clough did not find it difficult to fend off the intellectual assaults of Ward's theological logic: as he used to say in later years, 'Ward was always trying to put me on the horns of a dilemma; but somehow I generally managed to get over the wall.' What wore Clough down was the constant emotional harassment from a close neighbour, a man in authority over him, seven years his senior. He sympathized with Ward's needs, and bore them with patience; he complained only rarely to his diary and almost never publicly.

Later, after he left Balliol, he managed to see less of Ward. 'When I am talking to Ward', he told a friend, 'I feel like a bit of paper blown up the chimney by a draught, and one doesn't always like being a bit of paper;—so I sometimes keep away from the draught' (Ward, 110). This was as far as he permitted himself to speak publicly against Ward. He probably had in mind not only theological blasts but also gales of emotion.

The Lent term of 1839 was comparatively free of emotional turmoil. Clough saw Ward less frequently, and indeed at one point reproached himself for leaving him too much on his own. He was able to work fairly regularly; the diary entries become shorter and more factual, the lines of self-reproach more curt.

Clough dined with Newman on 6 February, and met him again

at breakfast three days later. He was sufficiently excited by these meetings to send a description of them to Gell in Cambridge, with an account of Newman's church-doctrine straight from the horse's mouth.

Reason teaches, according to Newman

that Christian privileges and covenanted salvation have been attached to the use of certain forms and sacraments whose only qualified administrators are the Apostles' successors, the Clergy: that these gifts and graces cannot be obtained except through the medium of these divinely-appointed priests. All persons therefore who wilfully refuse to receive God's blessings through this channel are guilty of very great sin and put out of the covenanted privileges of Christians.

The answer to this, Clough wrote, must be in pointing to the lives of good men who lived out of the influence of such ordinances, 'though when anyone speaks of such they at once cry "Name", which it is perhaps difficult to do' (C i. 89).

In this second year Clough decided to enter for the university's English Verse prize. The topic for the year was Salsette and Elephanta: these are two islands off the Indian coast, famous for temple caves. Clough began work for the poem on 1 March. He identified the cave of Salsette with Buddhism, and that of Elephanta with Hinduism; the poem aims to show that both religions are corruptions of a single original knowledge of Truth. He drew much of the information on which the poem is based from *Essai sur la langue et la philosophie des Indiens*, a French translation, published in 1837, of a work of F. W. Schlegel. The poem was to be submitted at the end of the term, with a view to being recited, if it was the prizewinner, in the Sheldonian Theatre on the occasion of Commemoration in the summer. Among Clough's friends Stanley and Lake were also submitting prize compositions; altogether, Clough was told by Keble, one of the judges as Professor of Poetry, there were some fifty entries.

Easter was spent at Rugby, with Bonamy Price, one of the housemasters, and his wife, to whom Clough was very attached. He described this time as 'a great rest and renovation' and he used to look back on it as an ideal vacation. He was able to make a jaunt to Warwick and Kenilworth with Burbidge and Simpkinson. On his return to Oxford he reminded himself, 'My main duty what God wishes me most to do is my Work for my degree and preparation for active life afterwards. The more rigorously I devote myself to this the better—uniting it with devotional exercises, & cultivation of such feelings as Repentance for past neglect & hope of future activity.' And he added sternly, 'Be ready to be insulted, and thought badly off by any body'.

Once again he began to worry about excessive familiarity with Ward: and now a new relationship began to be troublesome, that with a rather shadowy figure named William Tylden. A typical entry is that for 18 April, 'A great deal too much talk &c with Ward—too little restraint and too much indulgence. Too much also with Tylden. also drunk rather too much wine which made me communicative.' Overindulgence in wine became a recurring theme; thus on 24 April, 'Took too much wine at Fanshawe's. Isn't 2 glasses enough?' And in the last entry before the Long Vacation he records that he dined with his uncle and 'drank & enjoyed myself a great deal too much'.

During the term Clough began to read Plato's *Republic*. This must have been on his own initiative, as his collections at the end of term were set on Aeschylus and Aristotle, and none of his essays was on a Platonic topic. But Clough became enthusiastic about Plato and wrote at some length about him to Gell, who having finished his Cambridge tripos was planning to emigrate to Tasmania. 'Do you think it would be advisable', he wrote, 'to turn Her Majesty's Colony of Van Diemen's Land into a Platonic Republic?' (C i. 91).

The College syllabus this term called for him to study the first thirteen of the Thirty-nine Articles. There is hardly any theological jotting in the diary, though on one occasion he notes that he was visited with 'dreadful feelings of unbelief and atheism'. To Gell he commended Germanized scholarship as a 'great Bulwark against Newmanism' (C i. 92).

Towards the end of the term Simpkinson came to stay in Oxford: he remained for the Commemoration, at which Wordsworth received a Doctorate of Civil Law. Clough did not win the verse prize: the successful candidate was John Ruskin. Stanley, however, was to recite his Latin essay on the duties of the university to the state, and Arnold came to Oxford for the festivities (Prothero, 217). Clough was unable to enjoy them to the full because of a hangover from a dinner with his uncle the night before.

Once liberated from Oxford Clough rushed, as ever, to Rugby where he and Burbidge stayed with Arnold. After a week or so in Liverpool he set off on a tour with Ward, with whom he spent the greater part of July. They went through Derbyshire and Yorkshire to the Lake District, where they stayed at Keswick. Ward used to recall this as a very happy time. His son tells us:

Clough, he used to say *interpreted* scenery for him. Ward loved natural scenery almost as he loved music, though his eye was not accurate and he could not explain the features which struck him. When first he and Clough came in sight of Grasmere, coming suddenly upon a view of the lake from behind the hills, Ward was fairly overcome and burst into tears. (Ward, 106)

Before returning to Liverpool Clough visited Durham and York and admired the cathedrals.

His time at Liverpool was spent largely reading Tacitus, who was one of the authors set for the Michaelmas term. He enjoyed this: 'I think Tacitus rather like Carlyle, whose Fr. Revoln. I have [been] reading for the first time through, and with increasing admiration' (C i. 93). He also read Goethe with his sister Annie, and did some Sunday school teaching. He found it difficult to keep order, and even when he did was dispirited by the answers he got to his questions. 'Who wrote the book of Genesis? 1—Simon Peter—2. Mary Magdalene' (C i. 93-4). He should have been working hard at mathematics, of which he told Gell he had a power to wade through before October. But though it stood before him 'like a great black cloud', other things commonly came before it, and he would reproach himself for working almost wholly on Thucydides instead. Altogether it was a fairly dull and home-bound vacation. As he put it, he was 'shut up to bake in Liverpool' while Simpkinson and Burbidge were both touring the Continent, and Gell was preparing for his voyage to the Antipodes in November.

For a few days in September, however, he took a holiday in Wales with his elder brother George who was over from America. 'We are going to walk, eat, and sleep exclusively for four or five days among the mountains, which is a sure means of gaining health and strength' (C i. 94). During the last week of the vacation Ward came to stay with the family in Liverpool. There were family worries: it was likely, Clough told Burbidge, that his father's business would break down before long (C i. 95).

On the way back to Oxford for the new academic year Clough stayed a couple of days at Rugby and a couple of days with his uncle at Braunston. He began the term in excellent health, but found himself with distaste once more within 'the vortex of Philosophism and Discussion (whereof Ward is the Centre)' and resolved to escape it as far as possible since it was the most exhausting exercise in the world. He told Burbidge, 'I go however pretty regularly to Parson's Pleasure to bathe before breakfast as last term I did; and boating is very pleasant, the trees just beginning to be bright for autumn.' The diary does indeed presume a daily bathe, and notes scrupulously the days when the bathe was missed. Among the reasons for missing, he notes that on two days at the end of October he was 'unwell . . . with Cholera'. On 18 November he records a 'skiffing accident'.

Among the new scholars who came into residence in Balliol in Michaelmas 1839 was John Duke Coleridge from Eton, the future Lord Chief Justice. Frederick Temple, the future archbishop of Canterbury, was in the same year, but had come into residence as a Blundell scholar during the spring. Both of these junior contemporaries became friends of Clough, and their names from this point onwards make frequent appearances in his journal. Temple and Coleridge were both soon elected to the Decade: they made two Tory members of that otherwise Whiggish body (Sandford, i. 40).

During this autumn Clough took an increasing interest in the writings of Carlyle. When four volumes of *Miscellaneous Essays* were published, he devoured them and admired them even more than *The French Revolution*. He thought of giving the volumes to Gell as a present for the Antipodes, though he said that it went to some extent against his conscience because Carlyle was 'somewhat heathenish' (C i. 96).

Mathematics became more and more of a problem. The topic set for examination in Michaelmas 1839 was mechanics. In spite of the resolutions of the early part of the vacation, as late as 19 October Clough was still resolving, 'Set to Mathematics Next Week.' And even after his collection in mechanics, during the Christmas vacation, he was still striving to understand the lever, the pulley, and the screw (C i. 98). Ward had a reputation as a good tutor in pure mathematics, but a hopeless teacher of applied mathematics (Sandford, 50). It was decided at the end of this term that Clough should go to an outside tutor, Lowe, for tuition in science during the coming Easter term.

The major excitement of the term was the marriage of Uncle Alfred at Braunston, which Clough attended as groomsman in the last week of November. He walked twenty miles of the way to Braunston, and almost all the way back—forty miles, twenty of which were in the dark—'a very rash experiment', as he wrote to Burbidge on 30 November, 'especially as the road is sufficiently ugly and the day was sufficiently rainy. The consequence is that I am tied to my room today by a strained ancle which I managed to get myself in feeling my way along the dark and dirty road. I believe part of my motive for attempting it was the desire to be as long out of Oxford as possible.' Despite the accident, he enjoyed the excursion, and wrote around enthusiastically to his family to describe the wedding, the first he had ever attended (C i. 97 and Mulhauser, 97).

Once again Clough decided to compete for the Newdigate prize in English verse. The subject this year was 'The Judgement of Brutus'—the stern Roman consul who passed sentence of death on his two sons for conspiring against the Roman Republic to restore the exiled tyrant Tarquin (see Greenberger, 211). This time, Clough began work on the poem earlier, and a draft of one passage appears in an entry for 5 December, though the deadline for submitting the poem to the Registrar was not until 10 April.

The end of term collections, on 9 December, were the most successful yet: his work was described as improved and very good. His morals, as ever, were 'uniformly good and exemplary'. According to his usual custom he stopped off with the Arnolds at Rugby on his way home for the vacation at Liverpool. The vacation was spent partly reading Goethe and Schiller, partly in attending balls at Chester and Denbigh, partly in 'dissipation' with his sister Annie, partly in entertaining Uncle Alfred and his bride on their honeymoon trip. Not much time was left for academic studies; at the year's end he accused himself of 'mulish idleness, indolence and easiness'. To Simpkinson, now a private tutor in Cambridge, he wrote on 31 December, 'I have but little appetite for work Mathematical or Classical, and there is as little compulsion to it and as much enticement from it as is possible in our ways of life in Oxford. I would give much for the pleasant treadmill routine of school' (C i. 98).

New Year's Day 1840 was Clough's twenty-first birthday. It was not until he returned to Oxford that he marked it, rather belatedly, by entering in his diary a dismal sonnet, 'Here have I been these one and twenty years . . .', which concludes:

> Here am I brotherless mid many brothers
> With faculties developed to no end
> Heart emptied & faint purpose to amend.

The sonnet was sent to Burbidge, who was spending the year on the Grand Tour with a pupil named Ramsey. Burbidge's praise of it was noted by Clough as an occasion of sinful vanity.

The term was indeed a depressing one. Among his old friends, Lake was becoming impossibly Newmanistic; for support against the Tractarian tide he had to depend on Rugby friends outside Balliol—Congreve at Wadham and Stanley at University, now newly in deacon's orders (C i. 97–8). Early in February one of his younger companions, Currer, a rowing man, was drowned near Sandford lock. His funeral coincided with the celebrations for the wedding of Queen Victoria to Prince Albert, and there was much discussion whether it was seemly for Balliol to join in the illuminations of the city with a student's body still unburied. Hardly had Lent begun when Clough was confined to his room for two miserable weeks with a gathering on his knee. 'From my foolishness & yieldingness at this time', he recorded, 'got infinite harm.'

For the first time, Clough began the serious study of logic. It was perhaps this which was the occasion for his poem 'written in a Balliol lecture room', which begins,

> Away, haunt not thou me
> Thou vain Philosophy.

This was the first of the poems entered in his diary which he thought worth including in the volume of collected verse which he was to publish with Burbidge in 1848.

His Cambridge friends were about to be launched on their careers. A curacy had been found at Hurstmonceux for Simpkinson, and there were plans to find one for Burbidge at Rugby when he returned from the Continent. Gell was established in

Tasmania, sending descriptions of colonial life which took half a year to reach their destination, and receiving from Clough long budgets of out-of-date Oxford gossip. To Simpkinson Clough wrote in March from his sickbed, or rather sofa, 'I, with the cloud of degree right before me, cannot realize except very dimly, the irreparable nature of the leap in taking orders and going to a Curacy' (C i. 101).

Term ended with the usual compliments at collections and he left swiftly as ever for Braunston and Rugby; he divided the vacation between the two places and enjoyed the company of Arnold, the Prices, and his old schoolfellows returned from Cambridge. He watched cricket and attended a mesmerizing session; at the end of the vacation he once more walked to Oxford because the coach was full.

In Easter term of 1840 the diary entries are sparse, and no letters from these months have survived. He was working on St Matthew and the Book of Common Prayer for divinity, on Horace's Odes for Latin, and on Herodotus and Aristotle in Greek. Once again he was unsuccessful in the English verse prize. Lake won the Latin essay prize, Tickell, a Balliol scholar a year his junior, won the Latin verse prize, and the veteran Stanley carried off yet another prize for an English essay on 'Do States, like Individuals, inevitably tend, after a certain period of maturity to decay?'

The long vacation of 1840, like that of 1839, began with a holiday with Ward in the Lake District, this time at Grasmere. The rest was spent at home in Liverpool: Clough wanted to devote himself to the final preparation for the examinations he was due to take in November, and he also wished to spend as long as possible with his two brothers, who were about to leave for America. His diary for most of the vacation is little more than a record of the number of hours reading done each day. He had to apologize, afterwards, for cold-shouldering his younger brother: 'I was anxious and not in very good health during the summer vacation and had a good many things on my mind' (C i. 105). Once or twice he slipped off to Wales for a break. Gradually, he became convinced that he was not yet sufficiently prepared to take his degree examinations. He wrote to Ward for advice on 26 September; a week after arriving back in Oxford he was convinced, 'Putting off seems absolutely necessary'.

Having resided in college for three years, Clough moved at the beginning of this term into lodgings in Holywell, a street five minutes walk from Balliol and near the baths where he would take his daily dip when river bathing was too cold. He took rooms in a house belonging to a college scout called Jones, whose wife was pregnant and was delivered of a daughter ('over my head' as Clough noted) half way through the term.

The time secured by the postponement of Schools was devoted to further study of Aeschylus and the painful working through the examples in Whateley's *Elements of Logic*. He continued to be active in the Union and in the Decade, attending a debate on Chartism in the former and proposing in the latter a motion condemning the reading of novels (of the value of which, unlike Ward, he held, in theory, a very low opinion). He began to write the poems which eventually formed the sequence 'Blank Misgivings of a Creature moving about in Worlds not realised', later published in *Ambarvalia*.

If, in his early days at Balliol, Clough was reluctant to give and take 'wines' (i.e. dessert parties) this was certainly no longer the case: and between October and Christmas of this year no less than twenty-three wines are recorded in his diary. An account of one of them was given, many years later, by G. G. Bradley, then dean of Westminster.

It was in November 1840, when, as a freshman from Rugby, I was asked to join, after dining in my own college hall, a party—'a wine' in Oxford language—at A. H. Clough's. Clough was then living in lodgings, on the ground floor of a small house, near Holywell Church, which I have often in later years pointed out to those who were interested in all connected with his memory. It was my first visit of the kind to one to whom I looked up even then with something more than ordinary schoolboy veneration; whose Rugby poems I knew largely by heart, and whose countenance, already familiar to me, though I had barely spoken to him, still shines to me out of the distance as one of the most impressive, and in a sense, of the most beautiful that I have ever seen.

Bradley could recall the names of the other guests: Congreve, Blackett, Coleridge. Conversation, he tells us, was about Wordsworth and about S. T. Coleridge's *Aids to Reflection*. Bradley was particularly struck by his neighbour, a strongly built man with a Scottish accent.

As the talk went on—not exactly in the direction to which I had thus far been accustomed at ordinary 'wines'—I remember my neighbour becoming extremely animated, and talking with such vehemence and gesticulation that my wine-glass was sent flying; and I still can see him pausing for the moment, with perfect and unexpected grace, to apologise to me, and then plunging headlong into the now long-forgotten argument which he was maintaining against all comers. (Knight, 49 f.)

The Scotsman was John Shairp, later principal of St Andrews, who had just joined Balliol from Glasgow university as an exhibitioner on the Snell foundation (which had in the past supported other Balliol Scotsmen such as Adam Smith and William Hamilton). Shairp, though three years junior to Clough, became one of his firmest friends in future years:

Later in the term the best known of all Clough's circle came up to try for the Balliol scholarship. On 16 November Clough wrote to his sister, 'Our Scholarship examinations are just beginning—who are to get them, no one can guess at all. There are 2 candidates from Rugby, one of them Dr Arnold's son and he of the two has the best chance.' On 27 November he was able to enter into his diary, 'Riddle & *Mat. Arnold Scholars*'—and he underlined jubilantly the name 'Mat. Arnold'.

Compared with the diaries of 1838 those of 1840 contain relatively little that throws light on Clough's religious frame of mind. But there is nothing to suggest any weakening of his faith. He notes as a fault the occasions when he misses daily chapel, and from time to time he worries about attending Communion. But this is from doubt about his own worthiness, not any lack of belief in the sacrament. Indeed he deplores, in an entry on Advent Sunday, the general carelessness of college Communions. He continues to attend Newman's services, and like Newman he thinks of the reception of Communion as a serious matter, not to be undertaken lightly.

Clough stayed in Oxford during the Christmas vacation, moving into college once rooms became vacant there (this led, inevitably, to further complications with Ward) and taking only four days' break over Christmas itself at Braunston and Rugby. The winter was so cold that he allowed himself the luxury of a fire in his Balliol rooms. A guilty entry for New Year's Day, his birthday, reads, 'Not up till past 9, after 10 hours in bed;—fire all day;—have seen no one at all; walked alone; 3–5 dined alone—& luxuriated with fire 5 to 8'.

When the men came up for the Lent term he returned to his lodgings in Holywell. His health began to give trouble again, and he was put on to one regimen after another, beginning with 'Drops and Rhubarb system'. The business troubles of his father lead to financial worries: he wrote to his brother Charles, 'I have cut my moorings and am living on my fortune, namely, my Rugby Exhibition and my Scholarship, amounting to about £100 per ann., and this I trust will keep me awhile without any further applications to Father's assistance' (C i. 104). This made it the more urgent that he should obtain a first-class degree, so that he would be able to attract pupils for the long vacation and earn money by tuition.

Another problem now came to a head. Clough's relationship with Tylden reached a point where it needed the same sort of careful definition which he had had to impose upon Ward's advances two years previously. On 25 January he sent the following carefully drafted letter, preserved only in his diary:

My dear Tylden

First of all let me say that I repeat again the expression of which you spoke and that there is no one here for whom I feel more kindly. At the same time you know this is nothing very exclusive—and I am afraid that my kind feelings are worth but very little—and are sure to be very often overcast with uncertain behaviour & made almost worse than nothing by my way of now saying overmuch & then withdrawing. Indeed I am so apt to promise what I cannot in the end perform that you run some considerable hazard in accepting any such promise from me.—However I do with these cautions offer you something beyond a mere acquaintance to be dropped, or casually renewed, as may happen, after we cease to be brought together as now: and shall be very glad to see you, as at present, on Sunday mornings: this I do deliberately & I hope not without due consideration. Meanwhile I caution you of what you may expect: and above all I beg you not to let yourself rest on me ever, so as to interfere with your sense of the need of something surer & stronger & more likely to endure without deceiving you.

Believe me therefore now and to remain

Yours sincerely

A. H. Clough

I must further say that I think at the present time it is likely enough that occasionally my manner may say more than it will be right for you to expect. & which after seeing my friends at home & elsewhere wd probably be withdrawn.—for I have been so long from home, & so much alone & besides weaker than usual from having been unwell & under medicine during pt of the Vacn that I feel myself apt to lean on every chance neighbour. I shall however try & exert myself as much as possible to render my behaviour more certain & conscious always.

Clough and Tylden breakfasted regularly together for most of the rest of the year; but from time to time there appear in the diary notes of unspecified 'trouble' between them.

In the larger world of Oxford the most important event of the Lent Term of 1841 was the publication of Tract XC, the last of the *Tracts for the Times*. In this—originally anonymous—tract Newman claimed that it was possible to subscribe the Thirty-nine Articles without rejecting anything of Catholic belief: the doctrines which are there condemned are not official Roman Catholic teaching, but only corrupt versions of it. The tract gave great offence to those who saw the Articles as a bulwark of a Protestant Church of England against Romish superstition. The tract was published on 27 February; on 8 March Tait, as Senior Tutor of Balliol, with three other tutors from other colleges, published an open letter of protest. 'The Tract', the four tutors said, 'appear[s] to us to have a tendency to mitigate beyond what charity requires, and to the prejudice of the pure truth of the Gospel, the very serious differences which separate the Church of Rome from our own, and to shake the confidence of the less learned members of the Church of England in the Scriptural character of her formularies and teaching.' They deplored the anonymity of the tract and called for the author to come forward.

Clough makes no mention of the tract's publication in his diary, though it must have been a topic of conversation during the two hours he spent with Ward on 28 February. Ward had been extremely excited by the tract and it was indeed he who had brought it to Tait's attention, bursting into his rooms on the Saturday morning, and throwing the pamphlet down on the table with the words, 'Here is something worth reading!' The topic of the tract, subscription to the Thirty-nine Articles, was to prove one of the gravest importance for the future careers of both Ward and Clough. But for the present, to judge by his diary, Clough was more concerned with following out yet another prescription from his physician Tuckwell (a new lot of drops, and great quantities of castor oil) and the early primroses which he found in the rain near Horspath.

Perhaps because of his poor health, he obtained leave to depart early at the end of term and spent ten days at Rugby. There he listened to Burbidge's first sermon, and discussed Tract XC with the Prices. As he wrote to Gell,

Price was busy writing a vehement article against Newman, who has just issued a Tract to show that with the exception of that on the Pope, a Roman Catholic may conscientiously sign the 39 Articles; at any rate that as to Purgatory, Pardons, Masses, Saint-Worship etc., the Articles condemn merely the existing unauthorised teaching of Rome, not even the Tridentine doctrines nor those held by the better and truer Romanists. (C i. 108)

By this time the Hebdomadal Board, the governing body of the university, had resolved that the principles of interpretation in the tract were inconsistent with the statutes of the university, and the bishop of Oxford had informed Newman that he regarded the tract as dangerous in its tendencies. Newman acquiesced, with various reservations, and the series of *Tracts for the Times* came to an end. But this was not the end of the controversy, and as Clough told Gell, 'pamphlets are appearing in shoals'.

Clough walked back to Oxford in good time to sit his last college collections on the first two days of April, being complimented once more on good work and uniformly exemplary morality. He spent two weeks of the vacation in lodgings in Cavendish Square in London, principally to take tuition from Lowe, his special science tutor. While there he wrote a disdainful sonnet, 'To the Great Metropolis', half in mockery of Wordsworth's 'Upon Westminster Bridge': to the new visitor London appeared a huge Bazaar, a railway terminus, a gay hotel—'Anything but a mighty Nation's heart.'

Back to Oxford on 21 April, with just four hot weeks left before the postponed examinations. He worked feverishly and slept badly. He tried his best to avoid Ward, who was now deeply involved in the pamphlet war over Tract XC, rushing to support Newman with a defence which was embarrassingly frank in its hostility to the Protestant Reformation. He spent a mysterious amount of time in the area of Elsfield and Woodeaton, a few miles away to the north-east of Oxford, walking out there even on examination days on which he had sat two written papers, and immediately after his viva voce examination on 18 May.

Despite all the years of preparation, Clough failed to do himself justice in the examination. He had left Oxford for a walking tour before the class lists were published; the news was brought to him at Bragborough that he had been awarded a second class. He at once went to Rugby to communicate to Arnold what he saw as his failure.

Clough's friends and tutors blamed the examiners for mistaking their man. Tait went about the university denouncing their incompetence. 'They had not only a first-rate scholar, but a man of original genius before them, and were too stupid to discover it' (Shairp, quoted in Davidson, i. 72). Clough himself did not question the fairness of the verdict. Before the result was known he wrote to his sister, 'I did the papers much worse than I expected'; and afterwards he told Simpkinson, 'My papers I am quite sure, deserved no more than a second'. He told Annie that the result 'has not lessened my own opinion of my ability—for I did my papers not a quarter as well as my reading would have naturally enabled me to do and if I got a 2nd with my little finger it would not have taken two hands to get a double first (there's for you).' A few days later he hastened to add that she was not to blab this bravado any further: 'I do not doubt that there are many men in every Examination who are capable of as much and fail much in the same way as I, only nobody knows anything about it' (C i. 110). Two or three other 'certain firsts' from Balliol had got seconds, and it was said that a pall hung over the Balliol high table which was not relieved until Constantine Prichard won a first in the following November.

After the post-schools break, there was still the fag end of term to stay out in Oxford, and Clough was there for almost the whole of June. Parliament was prorogued and an election called on the issue of Free Trade; the Decade discussed the Corn Laws in a debate on 8 June. Prince Albert and the duke of Wellington were to be given honorary degrees; for a moment the prorogation called this in question, but in the event Commemoration went off as planned on 15 June.

In the Balliol senior common room, the controversy over Tract XC raged with a remarkable combination of *odium theologicum* and personal affection. By this time Jenkyns was regarded as a constitutional monarch, with Tait as his prime minister, Scott having moved away to a college living in Cornwall; and it was

Tait who had led the opposition to the tract by the four Tutors. Ward, on the other hand, had written a couple of pamphlets in favour of Newman. Many stories are told of the arguments between the two in the common room. 'At any rate, Ward', said Tait, 'your views are not such as should be held by a Fellow of this College.' 'I wish to know', replied Ward, 'whose views are more in accord with those of the founders of the College, yours or mine?' At the end of May, just after Clough's examination, Ward had published the second of his two pamphlets, 'A few words more in defence of Tract 90'. This was written to defend the tract from an allegation of dishonesty; but it went much further than the tract. Ward did not deny that the natural sense of some of the Articles was Protestant. 'Our twelfth Article is as plain as words can make it on the evangelical side. Of course I think its natural meaning may be explained away, for I subscribe it myself in a non-natural sense.'

Tait and some of the other tutors represented to Jenkyns that the doctrine contained in the pamphlet made Ward unfit to hold his tutorship. As Ward's son tells the story:

The Master, who always had a personal liking for Ward, was not very eager in the matter at first; however he undertook to read the pamphlet. He was no great theologian, and his first attempt to make his way through the ninety pages of close logic and technical phraseology proved a failure. He was discovered by one of the undergraduates asleep in his arm chair, with a copy of *A few words more* in his hands. For a time it was thought that the matter had blown over, and that Ward's tutorship was safe. (Ward, 174)

But Tait drew Jenkyns's attention to specific passages referring to 'the present degradation' of the Church of England, and 'the darkness of Protestant error'. Jenkyns was much shocked. 'He is a most dangerous man: what *heresy* may he not insinuate under the form of a syllogism!' Ward's logic lecturership at least, therefore, must be removed. Jenkyns found it difficult to screw up courage to dismiss him, and was in any case unsure that a majority of the fellows would support such a step. Jowett told Ward's son the sequel.

Your father gave him an agreeable surprise by going to him one morning after chapel and saying, in his lively way, 'Master, I am come to resign into your hands my two lectureships'. Nothing more was said; a weight had been removed from the bosom of both of them, and they talked merrily together. (Ward, 175, 437)

Clough, writing to his sister, makes clear the undergraduate perception of the episode. 'Did I tell you that Ward, my friend and George's, has been turned out of his tutorship for ultra-Newmanism?' (C i. 110).

So Ward was no longer a tutor, and Clough was no longer an undergraduate. One complication in their relationship had been removed permanently. But Clough's other tortured friendship had reached another crisis. On 19 June he notes, 'Tylden's trouble' and then adds, in enormous letters, 'What am I to do?' Two days later the entry contains both 'wrote to Tylden' and 'answered Tylden's answer'. Then, on the following day, 'Answered Tylden again and ended it'. This was not the last time he saw Tylden; but entries in the diary about him are henceforth rare.

During Clough's undergraduate years one of his major problems had been dealing with the emotional demands of people, senior or contemporary, who were far more fond of him than he was of them. The tables were shortly to be turned.

For the long vacation of 1841 the immediate practical problem was to obtain some work as a tutor, without having obtained a first-class degree. This turned out to be less difficult than expected. Theodore Walrond, now head boy of Rugby, wished to enter for the Balliol scholarship in the following November; and through the good offices of Burbidge it was arranged that he should receive a month's coaching from Clough in the Lake District. Clough went to Westmoreland on 1 July, after a week in Liverpool, during which he had the opportunity to vote in the election which brought the Conservatives to power under Peel, and he was joined at Grasmere by Walrond on 8 July. They worked together and walked together until well into August. Clough described this time in a letter to Gell:

The first month of the vacation I spent at Grasmere with young Walrond, endeavouring to produce from our two past idlenesses one industry to bring him to Balliol as a Scholar or at any rate keep him from the office at Glasgow: to the latter degree I hope it is secured, but of the former there is of course all kind of doubt; and I fear he is not very decidedly reformed. We had however a pleasant month or rather six weeks at Grasmere. (C i. 112)

He described a typical day in a piece of doggerel sent to Burbidge:

> Until four in the day
> We are reading away
> And then after four
> It would be a bore
> For at mealtimes I'm talking
> As also when walking
> To myself or to Todo
> So that time will no do . . .
> Grasmere and Rydal
> We can walk too, though idle
> But for them I must trouble you
> To refer to W.W.
> Who you know very well
> Of your own pretty sell'
> Has wrot all can be wroot and said all can be said
> Of Grasmere lake foot, or of Grasmere lake-head
>
>   (M 158)

In his diary, along with itineraries of walks, Clough noted that he was 'resting idly on Walrond' and that Walrond was suffering from his tutor's lack of seriousness. A typical entry is that for 6 August, 'I am now all along resting on the fancy of affection in Walrond; whereas I have no reason to believe he cares for me, nor yet could be justified in expressing to him that I care for him.' From time to time they would visit the Arnold family at Fox How in nearby Rydal. While there Clough received news of the collapse of his father's business; it was just after he had left, in consequence, for Liverpool that Arnold learnt that he had been elected to the Regius Professorship of History in Oxford (C i. 112).

At this time of poverty an ill wind from Rugby gave Clough an unexpected chance to earn some money. There were fears of typhoid fever at Rugby, and a number of wealthy Liverpool families who had had sons at the school kept them at home and engaged Clough to tutor them until the scare was over. The journal for the end of August and the first weeks of September records the appointments with these pupils, from which, for a few weeks, Clough could boast that he was earning at a rate of £1000 a year (C i. 112). He found the work tiring—though once he got back to Oxford he was prepared to assert that boy-teaching was far preferable to man-teaching (C i. 114)—and as a relaxation permitted himself some novel reading, especially of Miss Martineau. There were no walks to be got at except, as he told Gell, 'by wading through a couple of miles of town', and there was time only for brief weekend breaks in Wales.

Poetically the summer was reasonably productive. Two or three poems were written in the Lake District, and even in the busy days of his Liverpool 'Academy' he found time to send a package of poems to Burbidge, some of which would find their way eventually into their joint anthology—including what is perhaps the first of his poems on love, 'Thought may well be ever ranging' (M 26). This poem seems to have grown out of the circumstances of a weekend visit to Mold where the diary tells us he was 'foolish', but we are told no more of the nature of the foolishness than we can guess from a cancelled name which may perhaps be 'Dora'.

Back in Oxford, after a briefer than usual stopover at Rugby, in mid-October Clough found Ward his first visitor: the deposed tutor had spent his summer writing a 65-page attack on the writings and theological character of Arnold for the Tractarian periodical *The British Critic*. Clough moved into new lodgings, still in Holywell (Ward had offered him the use of his dressing room in Balliol, but the offer was wisely refused). The major task which faced him, now that he was a Bachelor of Arts, was to prepare himself for the examinations for the Balliol fellowship in November. If he succeeded in this, he would redeem his comparative failure in Schools, and also solve the pressing financial problem.

Clough seems to have taken a fairly relaxed attitude to the preparation for the fellowship examination; indeed in his diary he was prepared to call his time as a bachelor an 'interval of leisure'. He had only a single pupil in Oxford, Heywood by name. Matthew Arnold had now come up to reside as a scholar at Balliol, and Clough reported to Gell that it was whispered that he had been going out with the Harriers. Clough joined in the festivities in early November to mark the birth of Queen Victoria's heir, the future Edward VII. On 19 November Walrond came up to sit the scholarship examination; Clough took him to Newman's evening service two days later. Two days after that, on 23 November, he began the five days of written papers for his own examination. On the Thursday, despite Greek prose and verse composition and a viva voce, he found time to go on the river with Matthew Arnold and Walrond. On Saturday, after the last paper, Ward told him that the leading candidates were Lingen of Trinity, Karslake of Christ Church, and himself.

Walrond won his scholarship, but once again Clough was disappointed. Lingen seems to have been first choice of all the fellows. For the second place, Clough believed that Tait, Ward, and Lake voted for him, and perhaps also Oakeley; but four fellows voted for Karslake and the matter was put beyond doubt by the Master's double vote. Among those who voted against Clough was Benjamin Jowett, who afterwards declared his vote had been a mistake. One of the examiners told Shairp that a character of Saul which Clough wrote, presumably in the divinity paper, was 'the best, the most interesting thing he had ever seen written in any examination' (PPR 22). Stanley wrote from University college to Simpkinson,

[I]t seemed so great a misfortune that I cannot help venting my lamentations over it. But there is this great comfort. Some of his papers were done so splendidly as fully to show that the spring of genius has not yet dried up within him, and therefore I hope he will get in at Oriel. (Prothero 1895: 65)

A fellowship at Oriel was, indeed, at least as good as a fellowship at Balliol, and at this date some even among Balliol men regarded it as the highest distinction in the university. The Oriel fellowship examinations were at Eastertide, so that Clough had yet another term of cramming ahead. The last part of Michaelmas term and much of Lent term was enlivened by the visits of Arnold to give his history lectures as Regius Professor. His inaugural lecture on 2 December drew an enormous audience unparalleled since the Middle Ages, and the Lent lectures continued to attract large crowds.

Clough's Christmas vacation was divided between Rugby, Oxford, and his relations in Wales. Some religious scruple troubled him concerning the taking of Communion; he wrote about it to Ward and to Arnold and on Christmas Day he noted in his diary, 'missed Communion openly'. During the early days of January he gave tutorials in Liverpool to some of his pupils of the summer. He read a great deal of Kant, an author whom he had first picked up the previous summer just a few days after his final examinations. Once returned to Oxford, he looked back on this vacation as a period of great dissipation.

If the preparation for the Balliol fellowship examinations had been relaxed, the diary for the term before the Oriel competition showed many signs of strain. Early in February he had written home complaining of poor health and his father wrote back, 'I do beg that you will not be injuring your health by over exertions and extra work [to assist with the family's financial problems] as nothing on earth can compensate for *loss of health*' (C i. 115).

Clough began to see night-time visions; to be possessed of a feeling of forgiveness of sin which he alternately greedily welcomed and disowned as a delusion. Once again he felt drawn to a younger man, whom he usually denotes in his diary by the symbol B. Most probably B. was a Balliol commoner contemporary of Matthew Arnold's called Thomas Battersby. This young man he described as 'refilling his empty heart'. The fancies of him which he kept trying to reject did not altogether blot out his fond remembrance of Walrond, and on one occasion in March he notes that he called up a hope or image of Walrond to help him get through a tutorial with a difficult pupil.

The 'forgiveness fancy' continued to possess him. But surely forgiveness was not to be had easily: at the very least confession was an essential prerequisite. So we find him entering in his diary notes such as 'Confession seems the only plan', 'to write & tell all my foolishnesses to Burbidge', or 'filled with a fancy of writing a confession to Arnold'. One would have thought that Arnold would have been the last man to encourage such a Puseyite practice, but on his next visit to Rugby Clough did try the experiment. More intelligible is the entry for 10 March when, after breakfasting with Battersby, Arnold, and Walrond, Clough paid a two-hour visit to Newman. The temper following that visit, he felt in the following week, was the truest he had had for some time. He rebuked himself for 'continual takings of help & love & then cutting them'. His diary for this period peters out into incoherent expressions of hopelessness.

As so often, a visit to Rugby at the end of term set him on his feet again, and he was able to return to Oxford to sit the Oriel examination in much better spirits. As he moved into the college for the papers he wrote in his diary, 'I have as yet, thank God, no connexions here at any rate.'

Four days of papers are noted for the last days of March; then on 1 April follows the laconic entry, 'Orielensis factus. breakfast with Shairp.' Shairp himself has left a fuller account of the occasion.

The examination was finished on the Thursday evening. I had asked Clough and another friend, who was a candidate at the same time, to breakfast with me on the Friday morning as their work was just over. Most of the scholars of the College were staying up and came to breakfast too. The party consisted of about a dozen. We had little notion that anything about the examination would be known so soon, and were all sitting quietly, having just finished breakfast, but not yet risen from the table. The door opened wide; entered a fellow of another college, and, drawing himself up to his full height, he addressed the other candidate: 'I am sorry to say you have *not* got it.' Then 'Clough, you have' and stepping forward into the middle of the room, held out his hand, with 'Allow me to congratulate you'. (PPR, 23)

Congratulations flowed in from relieved friends and family. Uncle Alfred congratulated not Clough, but Oriel. 'You could not have introduced into your Society', he wrote to Provost Hawkins, 'a more amiable young man. During his Father's absence in foreign countries I have watched over his earlier years and have never known him guilty even of a boyish fault' (C i. 116). To Gell Clough wrote to describe his new life:

I am now fairly domesticated, having undergone the pomps and vanities of High Table and Common Room almost daily without intermission since Term began. I am very sorry however to leave Balliol, which I confess to liking better I fear than Rugby itself, and never expect to find equalled by Oriel: nor do I altogether like the change from independent Bachelorship to High Table and Common-room-dom. (C i. 117)

He went on to list his new colleagues—Newman, now mostly absent at his parish of Littlemore, two miles off; the bashful and evangelical Lytton; Eden, a university pro, one of the examiners who had given him his second class; Marriott a silent, sleepy, and likeable Newmanist, and then the juniors:

Fraser a tutor, who is an Ireland Scholar, a Shrewsbury man, etc,; Church and Christie—Newmanists better and worse; Cornish, on a local foundation, who is nothing particular; and Daman, who is married and retains his fellowship therefore only for this his year of grace. Lastly, Chace, elected with me.

During the Easter term Clough was quite busy with pupils—

private pupils as he was not yet a tutor of Oriel. Their names—Robbins, Ivory, Carey, Tuckwell, Hayley, Addington, Alstone—fill the pages of his diary. His spirits were better than in the previous term, but he still reproached himself with setting up sham relationships. He experimented with new forms of verse: a poem in a medieval Latin style (a light-hearted reference to the nightly visions which had not altogether ceased) and a misanthropic piece in Swiftian vein ('Believe me lady . . .').

As a colleague of Newman, he naturally dined with him from time to time. But he also records a number of discussions with him which from their context were clearly not mere social exchanges. Newman had moved far in a Catholic direction since Clough had first fallen under his influence in 1838. Then Newman had regarded the Church of England as the *via media*, the happy mean between the opposite excesses of Romanism and Protestantism. Later he had come to think that the Roman Church had as good a claim as the Church of England to be best present-day representative of traditional Christianity. He was fast moving to a position in which he saw it as the one true Church. The Church of England stood to it, at best, in the relationship which schismatic Israel stood to chosen Judah in the days of the division of the Hebrew kingdom. Clough's diaries, while they continue to show concern with the state of his soul, show no sign of an interest in Newman's Romeward progress. On the other hand, his own movement in the opposite direction was not to begin for some time yet.

From time to time there are the familiar expressions of self-censure, but now in a somewhat cryptic form. 'I seem to know nothing except that I am wholly wrong within', he wrote, less than a week after his election to Oriel; and he exhorts himself to humility, self-mistrust, and above all avoidance of 'positiveness'—presumably dogmatism in the expression of his opinions.

If, in his first years at Oriel, Clough was suffering perplexity about Christian doctrines, the diaries give no indication of the nature of any such perplexity. At the end of his first term there he wrote:

My evident tendency just now is to set up some protection, to build up hurriedly a new self upon hypotheses. Indeed it seems to be already done—& if it were to be taken from under me I should be left with nothing—& so it is clear enough I shall stick to it.

There is no indication what is the nature of the 'hypotheses'. But he goes on to rebuke himself for acts and feelings 'against or without truth', in particular for 'the reading Poetry, especially Goethe', in whose *Faust* he had been immersed. He ended

Work—Work—Work—Not to be positive—Stat Veritas.

At the end of term he received one solid, if mundane, gratification. From the money which he had earned from his pupils he was able to send £66 home. It was his first contribution to the family finances. But no sooner was term over than he suffered a devastating blow. Arnold, in the prime of life, was struck down by heart disease and died within a few days. Clough, shattered, went on a long solitary walking tour, first in Derbyshire and then in Wales. His first encounter with any of his friends was when he met Shairp at Tan-y-bwlch on 23 June. Shairp records:

In the summer of 1842, while I was reading in a retired part of Wales with two or three others, Clough, then wandering through the Welsh mountains, one morning looked in on us. I took a walk with him, and he at once led me up Moel Wyn, the highest mountain within reach. Two things I remember that day—one, that he spoke a good deal (for him) of Dr Arnold, whose death had happened only a few weeks before; another, that a storm came down upon the mountain when we were half-way up. In the midst of it we lay for some time close above a small mountain tarn, and watched the storm wind working on the face of the lake, tearing and torturing the water into most fantastic, almost ghostly shapes, the like of which I never saw before or since. (PPR 23)

His solitary walking continued for a full month, until he returned to Liverpool on 14 July. But he kept in touch sufficiently with what was happening to write a testimonial, from Carnarvon, to the Rugby Trustees in support of Tait's application for the headmastership in place of Arnold.

Among Clough's pupils at Oriel in the previous term had been an Irish student, from Rugby, Octavius Carey, the son of General Sir Octavius Carey, the general in command of the Cork district. Carey engaged his tutor to coach him during the long vacation, and so Clough crossed to Ireland on 17 July and stayed there until early September, bringing over another pupil, How, to share tutorials. After the tour was over, Clough described it to Gell:

We saw all the world military there, captains and colonels and Knights in Arms, which last title might be given to some of the infant Careys (the family consisting of a dozen, besides one son in Affghanistan) for it seems they all go into the Army, excepting the genius under my tutorage, and even he says that if he does not get a good degree he shall give up all thoughts of the Church and get a commission.' (C i. 122)

In September, after a brief visit home and to Rugby (where Tait had now been elected) and to Leicester (for a christening in Burbidge's family), he went back to Wales—this time in company with Constantine Prichard and some of his pupils. In October in Liverpool he said goodbye to his father and brother on yet another crossing of the Atlantic.

The Oriel diary of 1842–3 is much more terse and factual than the diaries of the Balliol years, little more than a record of pupils, guests to breakfast, dinner, and wines, walks with their destinations and companions. This is probably a good sign: Clough's volubility in his diary seems to have been generally in inverse proportion to his general state of spirits. Tom Arnold came up to University college, and Walrond took up his scholarship at Balliol. Clough saw much of both of them: relationships with Walrond no longer seem to have been a source of inner tension. Though Clough did not altogether keep his resolution, noted on 11 February, 'not to talk to Ward', relations with his old tutor seem to have been much easier now that they were separated by the High. Carey obtained a fourth-class degree, applied for a commission, and set off for India. Prichard, Temple, and Shairp provided plenty of uncomplicated friendship.

The diary in the Easter term of 1843 shows Clough, Walrond, and the Arnolds fairly set on the round of easy-going companionship in Oxfordshire excursions which has been commemorated in *The Scholar Gipsy* and in *Thyrsis*. Thus, in the week beginning 14 May we are told on Monday, 'Mat & Tom up Charwel: at Walrond's to tea'; on Tuesday, 'Mat and Walrond up Charwel. here to tea'; on Friday, 'With Walrond to the Fox [on Boar's hill] & at tea. Tom & Mat. Visio beatifica'—though the nature of the beatifying vision is left to the imagination.

The last date recorded in the Oriel diary is Commemoration, 28 June 1843. This was the day (though the diary does not tell us) on which Matthew Arnold was due to recite to the assembled university the poem, *Cromwell*, with which he had won the Newdigate prize. He was unable to recite it because the theatre was in turmoil because Tractarian students were demonstrating against the award of an honorary degree to the American ambassador, who happened to be a Unitarian (Honan, 71).

It would be pleasant to see this, the last of the regular Oxford diaries, as providing a lighthearted happy ending to the series which began in such solemnity and proceeded through such misery and anguish. But that would be wrong. Internal struggles of a new kind were about to commence: Clough began to be worried, not about his own failure to measure up to the demands of various interpretations of Christianity, but about the intellectual basis of Christianity itself as represented by the Church of England.

After the last dated entry, the Oriel diaries peter out in a series of teasingly cryptic remarks.

Not being able to get on without a heart I have as it were chosen my Rugby heart—when I might have better fallen back on my home heart— or might I not have found some rest of the kind with a more round choosing faculty at Oxford? . . . That I have no knowledge of truth to guide my choices; and an excitation making it quite necessary for me to make some choice.

The most important choice facing Clough at this time was the choice of his future career. If he was to stay in Oxford and accept a tutorship, he must proceed to his MA; and to do so he must subscribe to the Thirty-nine Articles still imposed by the university as a test of Anglican orthodoxy. The first clear indication of discomfort with the limits imposed with the Church of England is contained in a letter to Gell at the end of the long vacation of this year. Gell had been hearing rumours that Clough at Oriel was becoming too sympathetic to Tractarian formalism. Clough replied:

I do not think I am particularly inclined to become a Puseyite, though it is very possible that my Puseyitic position may be preventing my becoming anything else; and I am ruminating, in the hope of avoiding these terrible alternatives, a precipitate flight from Oxford—that is, as soon as my Exhibition expires, for I cannot think of sacrificing £60 on any consideration. Also I have a very large amount of objection or rather repugnance to sign 'ex animo' the 39 articles, which it would be singular and unnatural not to do if I staid in Oxford, as without one's MA degree one of course stands quite still, and has no resource for employment except private pupils, and private reading. It is not so much from any definite objection to this or that point as general dislike to Subscription and strong feeling of its being . . . a bondage, and a very heavy one, and one that may cramp one and cripple one for life. (C i. 124)

Gell wrote back to encourage him to sign, conceding that the Articles were unnecessarily burdensome for the present age, but hoping that they might be revised so as to 'leave a bond, but one as worthy of free agents as the XXXIX Articles were when first produced'. Correspondence between England and the Antipodes was so slow that by the time Clough replied in turn, it was nine months later and his doubts had, for the time, receded.

I did . . . sign [the Articles], though reluctantly enough, and I am not quite sure whether or not in a justifiable sense. However I have for the present laid by that perplexity, though it may perhaps recur sometime or other. (C i. 128)

Early in the next academic year, 1844–5, the doubts did return.

If I begin to think about God, there [arise] a thousand questions, and whether the 39 Articles answer them at all or whether I should not answer them in the most diametrically opposite purport is a matter of great doubt. If I am to study the questions, I have no right to put my name to the answers beforehand, nor to join in the acts of a body and be to practical purpose one of a body who accept these answers of which I propose to examine the validity. I will *not* assert that one has no *right* to do this; but it seems to me to destroy one's sense of perfect freedom of inquiry in a great degree, and I further incline to hold that enquiries are best carried on by turning speculation into practice, and my speculations no doubt in their earlier stages would result in practice considerably at variance with 39 Article subscription. (C i. 140)

Clough was soon forced to think once more about the constraints exercised by the Thirty-nine Articles The precipitating cause was the controversy which brought to an end the Oxford career of W. G. Ward. Since the days in which the two men had been close friends at Balliol, Ward had continued to develop his thought in a Romeward direction. In June 1844 he had published a work entitled *The Ideal of a Christian Church considered in comparison with existing practice*. The argument of the book was that the Church of England, in moral discipline and saintliness, fell far short of the Christian ideal. The way to reform it was to bring it closer to the principles and doctrines of the Church of Rome and to renounce the schismatic errors of the sixteenth-century reformers.

The work caused an immediate scandal. In October Gladstone

attacked it in the *Quarterly Review*; in December the university authorities announced three propositions to be put to convocation in the following February: the first stating six passages from the book to be inconsistent with the Articles and with Ward's good faith in signing them; the second depriving him of his degrees; and the third proposing a general test by which the Articles for the future must be accepted in the sense in which they had been originally uttered, and in which the university imposed them.

When the propositions were announced, Clough wrote to a friend:

I shall vote against all three ... The matter is clearly judicial and ecclesiastical; the Convocation is not a court of justice, nor an ecclesiastical body. What right have our MA's to say whether statements x, y, z agree or not with the Articles, or say in what sense the University, which imposes the subscription simply as a Church of England body, understands the Articles? If the Church does not settle it, the University has no business to do so. (C i. 143)

The proposal for the new test had to be dropped. It was opposed not only by Tractarians but also by liberals who saw that they too would fall victims to any attempt to enforce the Articles in the sense of the sixteenth century. But the other two proposals were carried in convocation on 13 February 1845: the passages from the *Ideal* were condemned, and Ward was degraded from his degrees. A third proposal, to condemn Tract XC and thus associate Newman with the degradation of Ward, was vetoed by the Proctors.

Ward had already resigned his Balliol tutorship because of the outrage over his book; he now resigned his fellowship too, for a different and astonishing reason: he was engaged to be married. Clough defended Ward against the charge of hypocrisy which many levelled against such an action on the part of a priest who had extolled the value of clerical celibacy. But he may well have been relieved at this signal of the final end of the emotional threat presented by his old tutor. In the summer Ward and his new wife were received into the Roman Catholic Church, and in October Newman at last took the same step. The Tractarian movement, thoroughly demoralized, must have ceased to hold for Clough any attraction it may once have had. Moreover, the two colleagues who had been the most famous exponents of the permissibility of subscribing to the Articles in a loose sense had now left Oxford and the Church of England. This must have made Clough reflect once more on his own ambiguous position.

In November he learnt of a proposal to set up in Ireland a group of non-sectarian colleges. He asked to be considered for a professorship, naming Provost Hawkins among his referees. Hawkins summoned him and asked him what was his opinion of the Church of England, and whether he had any intention of taking orders. Clough responded

It is quite possible that I may feel it allowable and desirable for me to take them, 5 years hence. At present it is neither. I cannot profess to have wholly got rid of certain scruples and questions which I have had occasion to name to you before. And one inducement for seeking duty in Ireland is my conviction that Oxford is not the best place for clearing oneself from such troubles. (C i. 165)

Hawkins did not consider that 'the personal scruples about which we communicated' stood in the way of his writing a reference, but he said, 'I take it for granted that you are a serious member of the Church of England.' Clough did not demur, though two months earlier he had written to Gell that reading the life of Blanco White had momentarily almost persuaded him to turn Unitarian (C i. 155).

In his reference Hawkins wrote:

I appointed him one of the Tutors of this College about three years ago; which I should not have done if I had not believed him to be a well-principled man as well as a good scholar, and especially if I had not had reason to believe that he was untainted with the principles of the Tract party. (C i. 166)

Hawkins, as Provost of Oriel, had suffered much from the scruples and shifts of Newman and the other Tractarian tutors. Clough's support of Ward at the time of his degradation may have made him mistake the direction in which Clough was moving. If so, he would soon be disabused.

The scheme for setting up non-denominational colleges was delayed, and Clough's application came to nothing. He continued at Oriel for two further years; from a personal point of view the college was most congenial, since in 1845 the fellowship elections brought onto the governing body one of his best friends, Matthew Arnold, like himself redeeming a second in Schools with an Oriel triumph.

The seventh volume of Clough's diaries contains notes of travels in the long vacation of 1846 and 1847. From the last week of June to the end of July 1846 he travelled on the Continent, visiting Germany, Switzerland, and the Italian lakes. In August he took a reading party to Castleton, near Braemar, in Scotland; the pupils who accompanied him, H. W. Fisher and George Warde Hunt of Christ Church, John Deacon and J. S. Winder of Oriel, were all later canvassed as possible originals of the characters in *The Bothie of Tober-na-vuolich*, the long narrative poem about a Scottish reading party which Clough was to write in 1848. Certainly a number of the episodes in the poem seem to have been suggested by events on this party. From Castleton Clough wrote to Hawkins to say that he had given up any intention of taking orders, and suggesting that the tutorship which he held should become a half-time post. He quickly gave up the suggestion after a frosty response (C i. 173–4).

Little is known, whether from diaries or correspondence, of the external details of Clough's life in the academic year 1846–7: it is most memorable in his biography for the publication of the first of his prose works, the pamphlet on the Retrenchment Association written in haste in April 1847 to urge, in despite of *laissez-faire* economists, that conspicuous consumption in England, and especially in Oxford, should be curtailed in order to help the Irish poor now suffering a disastrous famine.

It is clear that Clough was fast reaching a position which made it impossible for him long to remain part of Oxford as Oxford then defined itself. A letter to his sister in May of that year contains a long postscript, which is the clearest statement we have of his religious position between 1845 and his resignation of his Oriel fellowship.

His continuance in Christian belief, he said, had been partly due to the influence of Coleridge. He went on:

My own feeling certainly does not go along with Coleridge's in attributing any special virtue to the facts of the Gospel History: they have happened and have produced what we know—have transformed the civilization of Greece and Rome, and the barbarism of Gaul and Germany into Christendom. But I cannot feel sure that a man may not have all that is important in Christianity even if he does not so much as know that Jesus of Nazareth existed. And I do not think that doubts respecting the facts related in the Gospels need give us much trouble.

Believing that in one way or other the thing is of God, we shall in the end know perhaps in what way and how far it was so. Trust in God's Justice and Love, and belief in his Commands as written in our Conscience stand unshaken, though Matthew, Mark, Luke and John or even St. Paul, were to fall. (C i. 182)

In the summer he took another reading party to Scotland, this time to Drumnadrochet on Loch Ness. Hunt accompanied him once again; so did John Blackett of Merton, George Scott, later archdeacon of Dublin, and the future novelist G. A. Lawrence from Rugby and Balliol. The party was joined, for a while, by another one, consisting of a number of Clough's old friends, including Walrond, Shairp, and Tom Arnold, plus Charles Lloyd, a Student of Christ Church, and Scott's brother Edward. The excursions of Clough's party are recorded in detail in his diary; the meeting between the two groups is described in the reminiscences of Edward Scott.

No precise appointment had been made as to the date of our arrival. We were to appear when we could. As it was, we turned up in the small hours of the morning, and did not even know which was the inn. I remember, in the twilight, Arnold climbed in by an open window, and returned with a book which proved to be [George Sand's] Consuelo. Assuredly a book from Oxford. Meanwhile Walrond, always practical, had gone upstairs and invaded a bedroom. The occupant started and remonstrated, but Walrond nevertheless had secured his prize, and returned triumphant with a sock on which was marked the name Scott. This was taken as an indication that my brother and Lloyd had arrived . . . Putting together these sufficient tokens, we felt justified in rousing the household, and accepting what beds we could get. We stayed three days. It was a visit not to be forgotten, because the poem of *The Bothie* may have been already in contemplation. It was written, if I am correct, in the following summer. Certainly Drumnadrochit formed the background in several marked particulars. 'The grave man nicknamed Adam'; 'the kilted Hobbes'; 'Arthur, the glory of headers'—all arise before my mind in the persons of Clough himself, Warde Hunt and Walrond; while 'Philip' recalls to me traits both of Shairp and Tom Arnold, while there are elements in him that belong to neither. (Knight, 110)

Philip, the hero the *The Bothie*, in the course of the reading party falls in love with a Highland girl called Elspie and migrates with her to New Zealand. Tom Arnold, in real life, set off thither, unaccompanied by any Elspie, on 22 November of the same year.

Clough's diary resumes briefly to note his visit to London to see the emigrant aboard in company with Walrond and Thomas's brother Matthew.

Shortly afterwards, Clough's position in Oriel was called in question by a remark of Hawkins in casual conversation. Clough drafted in his diary (in a passage here not reproduced) a serious inquiry: he thought the matter so sensitive that the draft was in a (rather transparent) code: 'You spoke of a 7 being a 7 of 421 . . .' In clear, the letter eventually sent to Hawkins read thus:

You spoke of a Tutor as a Teacher of the 39 Articles. For such an office I fear I can hardly consider myself qualified. I can only offer you the ordinary negative acquiescence of a layman. I do not think the non-natural acceptation consistent with honesty, but I do hold the doctrine, disputed I know, but not, so far as I know, authoritatively condemned, that the M.A. subscription is not perspective and continuous, but only implies your assent at that time, pledging you thenceforth to nothing. (C i. 191)

Hawkins must have felt that that explanation was as disingenuous as anything contained in Tract XC. But Clough, having explained that his current lectures were exclusively classical and mathematical, admitted that his position was perhaps not consistent with a tutorship, and placed his office in the Provost's hands.

Where Clough was concerned, Hawkins was always patient and considerate. In Oriel with four tutors it was not necessary that each should carry out the duty imposed by the university statute of teaching the Articles, and Clough might therefore be excused.

He conceded that no one pledged himself by subscription to hold the same opinions for ever. 'But if he seeks an office to which Subscription is the necessary passport, he is surely pledged to resign the office if at any time his opinions shall become changed.' In particular, in the case of a Master of Arts

so far as he knows that he could not have been admitted to the M.A. degree, had he held certain opinions, and so far as he has obtained privileges by a subscription implying his then assent to Articles which now he does not hold, I think a person bound not to exercise functions which in his present condition he could not obtain. (C i. 193)

Clough sought to avoid Hawkins's conclusion. Just as subscription does not commit a man never to change his mind, he wrote, so, I conceive, until he definitely takes a position opposed to the teaching of the English Church he is not bound to forego his privileges. How far this allowance should extend I do not clearly see, but I feel the less scruple in stretching it, inasmuch as I suppose the University to be protected by a power vested in the Vice Chancellor to claim at his discretion a renewal of subscription from anyone exercising an M.A.'s function. (C i. 194)

Hawkins was not surprisingly unconvinced.

I *should by no means wish to hurry anyone into Dissent*. But when his mind was decidedly made up, *upon the best evidence he could procure*, then I think he ought not to wait for the V.C's inquiry, but act upon his own convictions. (C i. 195)

Not just a tutorship, but a fellowship itself, Hawkins continued, implied a willingness to subscribe to the Articles: 'We only hold our places in the College as Graduates of the University.'

Under these circumstances, Clough felt that he had to resign his tutorship, as Ward had done long ago, but he did not feel called on to give up his MA. Hawkins encouraged him to retain his tutorship until the end of term, and take counsel before taking any further step: 'I am very sorry to see whereabouts you stand. I am afraid of unrestrained speculation leading to scepticism—a very unhappy state and one for which God did not design us. In truth, you were not born for *speculation*.' (C i. 198).

On the last day of January 1848 Clough wrote to give Tom Arnold news of his resignation of his tutorship.

I feel greatly rejoiced to think that this is my last term of bondage in Egypt, though I shall, I suppose, quit the fleshpots for a wilderness, with small hope of manna, quails, or water from the rock. The Fellowship however lasts for a year after next June: and I don't think the Provost will meddle with my tenure of it, though I have let him know that I have wholly put aside adherence to 39 articles. (C i. 199)

To be a hired labourer, he wrote, was more honest than being a teacher of the Articles.

After resigning his tutorship Clough went to Paris, where he was not only a witness of many of the dramatic events of the 1848 Revolution, but also—of more significance for his long term development—struck up a friendship with R. W. Emerson, dining with him almost daily. The day-to-day details of this visit to Paris form the next substantial entry in the seventh diary, and the final dated passages concern Emerson's course of lectures, which he attended on his return.

Emerson later used to tell the story of his farewell to Clough as he sailed back to America from Liverpool on 16 July 1848. Clough said, 'What shall we do without you? Think where we are: Carlyle has led us all out into the desert, and he has left us there.' Emerson replied by placing his hand on Clough's head, announcing that he was to be 'bishop of all England' and show the wanderers in the desert the way to the Promised Land.

Whatever—if anything—was meant by this gesture, Emerson's departure left Clough in an exalted state. On the pages of his diary following that on which he noted Emerson's departure on the *Europe* ('Explicit liber Emersonianus') Clough began a meditation on life, work, and death which suggests he believed himself to have had a mystical experience.

This is the last, and one of the most puzzling, of the substantial entries in this diary. Clough's pen sped over the paper, filling it with pseudo-biblical rhetoric, writing and crossing out, rewriting and interpolating. Pages upon pages pour out, bombastic and bathetic by turns. No exact date is attached to this effusion, and it is hard to know whether we are meant to take it seriously, or treat it as parody. On 15 August 1848 the diary resumes with sober entries about the rent of houses for reading parties, and misprints in an edition of Keats.

Yet these embarrassing passages were not to be the last word in the diaries. Just after the August entries there comes the following passage:

The Games & Dinner (& Dance?)
The Tour.
The bothie of Topernafuosich.
Oh if your high born girls only know the charm the attraction. . . .
Or high kilted perhaps—interposed the 　　　in anger
Or high kilted perhaps, as once at Dundee I saw them
Petticoats 　　　to the knee or indeed a trifle over
Shewing their thighs were more white than the clothes they trod in their washtub.

Any reader of *The Bothie* can recognize here a few lines which were taken into the finished poem with very little alteration. The fragments in the diary are the first indication that Clough's muse, liberated, had reached maturity. The 1700 hexameter lines of the poem were written with astonishing rapidity during the autumn of 1848: the finished work is the first of the poems for which Clough is admired today. So the diaries did, after all, have in a sense a happy ending.

What do we learn from the diaries of the genius and personality of Clough? Do they reveal anything which would be inaccessible without them? Or do they raise as many problems as they solve?

There is little difficulty, on the surface, in deciphering the diaries. Clough's handwriting, even when he is obviously under emotional stress, is commonly easily legible, and his contractions are not often difficult to expand. The initials which he uses to refer to his friends have as their purpose to abbreviate rather than to disguise. It is an annoyance to an editor that some of the people who were important in his life shared the same initial (Burbidge and Battersby, for instance) and some even shared the same first and last letter (so that 'Wd', out of context, can stand for Ward or Walrond). However, in almost all cases it is easy to disambiguate.

In describing his sins and emotional crises, Clough adopts some disguises, so that the meaning would not be obvious to, say, a prying Balliol scout; but it is commonly easy enough for a systematic reader of the text to understand what is meant. He uses Greek words to describe a number of his traits and defects: this may well be less for concealment than because he thought the Greek vocabulary better adapted for character description. Similarly when English words are written in Hellenized form in Greek characters this is often with facetious motive rather than for purposes of disguise; though undoubtedly he does sometimes use Greek to refer to episodes he found embarrassing.

One of the most transparent of Clough's symbols is the one which he uses in connection with what he calls 'the wretched habit' which he contracted when he was at Rugby and brought with him to Oxford. On 6 April, in the second diary, he notes, 'I was as nearly as possible committing my worst sin this Morning. I was not *quite* roused from sleep, but fully conscious.' Two weeks later he notes on one day, 'my wickedness & weakness have gone their full length' and on 3 May, 'I have gone my full length—precisely in the same way as twice before'. At the end of the diary he lists four times, including these three, on which 'I have committed my worst sin'.

In later diaries on particular days he marks a large star, sometimes encircled and sometimes hedged about with lines. From the prose which sometimes accompanies these stars we can see that they are meant to mark the occasions of commission of sin; and from the description of the context it seems certain that what is meant is solitary masturbation ('✻ after not getting up', '✻ almost wilful though asleep', '✻ after too much exercise and perhaps too much wine'). I have reproduced the stars in the text, because it is clear that the guilt and tension engendered played an important part in the depression which beset Clough at this time. At one point he went so far as to discuss the matter with his father, and to consult a Liverpool surgeon about it: he clearly was tempted to regard his self-abuse as something almost pathological.

At this level, even when Clough is using code, it is not difficult to understand what he wishes to record. What is much more difficult is to evaluate the real meaning of the less specific allegations of sin which he makes. The vanity, the untruthfulness, the insincerity, the idleness, the 'luxuriating'—were these serious defects, or are we simply reading the exaggerations of an over-sensitive conscience? There is something comic about the contrast between Clough's daily denunciations of his folly and wickedness, and the uniform praise for his diligence and exemplary character in his tutors' reports and his contemporaries' reminiscences. Clearly somebody had got matters badly wrong: was it the public Clough deceiving his peers, or the private Clough deceiving himself?

The poems which are scattered through the diaries form an interesting contrast with the prose in which they are imbedded. Most of them are of mediocre quality; few of them were thought worth publishing by Clough himself, and those that he did publish appeared in his early work *Ambarvalia*, which is not much read today. But even at their poorest they show a tautness and a discretion which contrasts with the repetitive self-indulgent self-reproach from which they are, as it were, secreted. Clough worked hard to produce verse which was an authentic expression of genuine feeling, without falling into the crude self-revelatory mode which he found distasteful in the poems of his friend Burbidge.

Some of the most difficult material to evaluate concerns the close emotional relationships between Ward and Tylden and Clough on the one hand, and Clough and Walrond and Battersby on the other. Some of the journal entries would suggest to the unwary reader that these relationships were explicitly homosexual, at least on one side: thus, for instance, the entry immediately succeeding the poem 'Truth is a golden thread', where Clough says 'Ward has asked me to make unnatural demonstrations'. These relationships were clearly highly intense, and had a strong erotic element. There is no other explanation for Ward's possessive jealousy of Burbidge; and the diary which records the height of Clough's affection for Walrond has his name written in Greek over and over again all over the cover of the book. But though in one sense Ward was clearly in love with Clough, and Clough with Walrond, it is unlikely that there was overtly sexual expression of affection between them. Anything of this kind would have been seen by any of them—however they might differ over the finer details of Christian morality—as a heinous crime. Clough, who agonized so much over masturbation, would have been tormented with guilt by sodomy. When he is trying to come to terms with Ward's demands, insincerity is the sin he always worries about, not unchastity. Every reader will no doubt make up his own mind about the 'unnatural demonstrations'; in my view they are likely to have been nothing more than verbal.

Even greater obscurity covers the question of what, if any, were Clough's erotic relations with women during this period. In 1841 a mysterious Susan makes an appearance; she appears to live in Woodeaton and Clough refers to his dealings with her on one occasion in the Greek which he used to cover his embarrassment over his relationship with Tylden. The parish records of Woodeaton contain mention only of one Susan who would have been of an age to have an assignment with Clough in this year: Susanna Neale, the daughter of Robert Neale, a shoemaker, and Mary his wife, who was christened in October 1826 and therefore would have been 15 or 16 at the time. The theme of love, and lust, between Oxford undergraduates and simple country girls is a common one in Clough's poetry, and many commentators have suggested that this may be based on a first-hand experience, though Scotland rather than Woodeaton is usually suggested as the venue.

Elsewhere in the diary we find records of series of successive visits to Shotover, quite unlike the usual variety of destinations for

Clough's daily constitutionals. Some of these, in their context, are clearly associated with something of high emotional importance, and again a possible explanation is that Clough was visiting a woman there. In one of the entries of his Oriel period the name Bessie Gray is mentioned in connection with one of these visits. Conjecture here can have very little solid basis. The only occurrence of the name Gray in the records of the parish in which Shotover was situated is that of Susan Gray, daughter of Charles Gray, who in 1841 was married to James Vallis, a High Street baker in Oxford.

The ambiguity which covers Clough's emotional life during this period attaches, to an even greater extent, to his religious life. It is difficult, even after a close reading of the diaries in conjunction with his correspondence, to discover how far he ever really entered into Newman's version of Tractarianism. It is difficult to work out the difference between the self-examination and emotional repudiation of sin at which he worked so hard in these diaries, and the exaggerated sentimental religiosity of the evangelical tradition which he so frequently denounces. At the moment when his own belief in Christianity begins to weaken and wither, the diaries leave off, forcing us back on conjecture for the immediate basis of his loss of faith.

To his contemporaries and even to his close friends, Clough was always something of an enigma. Even when we are allowed to come as close to him as these diaries permit, he remains an enigma. That is because he was an enigma to himself: in his own words, a *dipsychus* or double-minded man. No single, synoptic, vision of this divided mind was possible to him; nor is it to us while we read this tormented story of Dipsychus at Oxford.

Note on the Text and the Principles of Editing

THE journals of Clough which are here published are contained in a series of notebooks which were in his widow's possession after his death and remained with his heirs until Miss Katherine Duff generously transferred them to Balliol College in 1974. There are in all seven notebooks, which between them cover events from March 1835 to August 1848, but the coverage is very uneven and is not continuous, particularly during the years after 1843.

The first diary is marked on the front 'Journal March 1835–July 1836'. It was written at Rugby and is not here reproduced. The second diary has a label on the cover, 'Journal August to December 1836'. It does in fact contain entries which go up to late March in 1838. The second half of this diary, which concerns Clough's second term at Balliol, is the first portion of the journals to be reproduced here.

The third diary is continuous with the second, and takes the story up to the latter part of May 1838. The fourth diary, which is much the longest, is adequately described by the label on its cover, 'Journal Oxford March 1838–June 1840'. The fifth diary is inscribed in Clough's hand 'A. H. Clough Holywell 1840'; it contains entries from August 1840 to March 1842, just before Clough left Balliol for Oriel. The sixth diary deals with Clough's first four terms as a fellow of Oriel, with entries from March 1842 up to June 1843.

The seventh diary is not a continuous journal: it deals principally with events during the long vacations of 1846 and 1847 and the Easter vacation of 1848.

The diaries consist of very varied material; sometimes pages of consecutive prose, at other times the briefest notes of an itinerary. Poems and passages of discursive prose sometimes interrupt the narrative. There are frequent lists of names, indicating letters to be written, guests to be invited, calls to be made.

For many years the diaries were in the custody of the late F. Mulhauser. He carefully extracted from them the poetical material, which he included in his edition of Clough's poems in 1974, the notes to which are an enormous mine of information about the Clough manuscripts, including the journals. He also made transcripts from the diaries which are now in the Honnold library in Claremont College, Pomona.

In the judgement of the Oxford University Press, with which I concur, the diaries are too repetitive and unwieldy to deserve publication in facsimile or in full. I have therefore made a selection, preserving some 75 per cent of the text, and indicating with a series of asterisks the places where part of the original has been omitted. The passages omitted consist principally of quotations from other writers, repetitious passages of self-reproach in the earlier volumes, and memoranda whose purpose was unintelligible or could have been made intelligible to the reader only at the cost of disproportionate annotation. Where the text omitted consists of quotation from the Bible or from other writers, an indication of this has been given within [   ] brackets.

In the text which has been reproduced no attempt has been made to render the printed page a facsimile of the manuscript, a task which would have been virtually impossible. It cannot be assumed, therefore, that the breaks between one line and the next in this edition correspond to those in the diary. Where several entries are made for a single day they are here given in the order in which it appears they were written, rather than in the topographical relationship which they bear to each other in the manuscript.

Individual words are reproduced in a manner which enables the reader to see exactly what Clough wrote. Spelling has not been corrected or modernized. When, as very frequently, Clough contracted words, the contraction has been expanded, the expansion being placed within ⟨   ⟩ brackets; in cases where I was unable to conjecture the correct expansion of a contraction the contraction is indicated by the sign ⟨. . .⟩. It is in the case of proper names where the expansion is least likely to be something less than certain; I have expanded in the way which seemed most plausible in the context, but the presence of the angle brackets should be a constant reminder to the reader of the element of conjecture here. Contractions have not been expanded where they are still in common use—e.g. 'hrs' and '&c'.

Clough's punctuation has been preserved in the text. There is a symbol frequently used which can, with equal plausibility, be rendered as a dash or a period; I have followed the practice of previous editors of Clough's poetry and prose by rendering this by a full stop. Where Clough uses points of omission these have been standardized to three.

Clough was inconsistent in the method by which he indicated the day on which he made an entry in his journal, sometimes giving the day of the week, sometimes the day of the month, sometimes the ecclesiastical title of the day, and sometimes more than one of these. I have inserted, in square brackets, the date of every entry where it was missing.

I have tried to keep annotation to the minimum. Foreign words and phrases have been followed in the text by a translation in [   ] brackets, except in cases where the translation has already been given within the immediate context. The authors of classical works are likewise inserted, for identification, in the text. The notes do not contain comments on surnames occurring in the text. The basic biographical information about the persons mentioned by Clough will be found in the index of names at the end of the volume.

DIARIES

DIARY 2

LENT TERM—1838

First Week.

Worked fairly—at least kept the object in sight.
I–IV [Ovid's] Tristia. IV [Horace's] Carm⟨ina⟩ & a little Cicero.

Second Week.

Worked irregularly—by reason chiefly of having been cut short in my course by poorliness—but very much in fault—

Only   1 tr⟨anslation⟩ of Scotts
               4 tr⟨anslation⟩ of Massie
               1 Latin Theme
and a little Middleton's Cicero, & Döring de Metris.

Have been frequently up late at night, & three times I think, also in the Morning.

Tuesday
Jan⟨uary⟩ 30
Jan⟨uary⟩ 31st   Letter from Arnold
Thursday
February 1st   Admitted to the Union
                    Stanley's return
Walked with Tylden to Cumnor Hurst.

Friday night. February 2nd. I find from my exceeding irregularity and inconsistency, and hardness & I much fear profound self-deception, that I must take to this work once more. All the enjoyment, and attention, & be-praisement of this Place is too much as yet for me. Alas, alas, for those half years at Rugby! so graciously given, so gracelessly thrown away, so fitted to bring me forward, so perverted by my own wickedness so as almost I fear to make me more backward than before! May God give me grace now to look steadily before me to my prospects, & round me on my duties and to feel my own very great sinfulness. How many there are whom I may sorrowfully contrast with myself. Highton & Lake. Fox. Emeris. Stanley. Ward—and many, many others.

Uncle Alfred arrived.
                                            Stanley at breakfast—
                    [*   *   *   *   *]
                                            Letters from Home.
Saturday [February 3] Arnold arrived at ½ p. 4.
                                            Walked with Stanley.
                                            My first Wine Party.
                                            Breakfasted with Lewthwaite—[* * *]

I have only worked about 3 hours: & have not done my things for
Massy. And it is now past 11. All this is wrong. Thank God for
Arnold, and his kindness of which I am most unworthy indeed—
Alas, alas, for those half years! Stanley spoke of little ffolkes today
rather strikingly: and told me of his family, and how it was,
therefore, as I suppose, that he did not attend the Sacrament the
next time. May God bless him and forgive me, who have abused
the like privilege so utterly. This coming week may I be enabled to
rise early & go to bed early, two things in wh⟨ich⟩ I am seriously
tempted:—tho⟨ugh⟩ I know very well that my health—bodily,
mental, & spiritual, is much concerned. O Lord, forgive & help
me.

fo. 38 Sunday, Feb⟨ruary⟩ 4

Breakfasted with Lloyd. Church at St Peters. Arnold 'To as many
as received him he gave power to become the Sons of God'.
Walked with Lake. Had him, Stanley and Brodie to wine. Tead
1st with Arnold, 2nd here with Ward.

I have spent a very happy day, altho⟨ugh⟩ for the last half almost
exhausted with ὕπνου καὶ καμάτου [*sleep and fatigue*]. I am now so
tired as to be incapable of thinking over the day. I trust the early
part was an improvement, for wh⟨ich⟩ Christ be thanked. May
the new Week be so too! but I am very unstable. At 1st Chapel I
was very inattentive, at St Peters a good deal better.

Monday, Feb⟨ruary⟩ 5

Breakfast at H. Hill's with the Arnolds etc. Lunched at Balston's
with d⟨itt⟩o. Walked with Poole. Arnold in Balliol. Wined with
Lloyd.

I have been very tired and poorly all to day, I trust, without any self deceit; quite 'impotens' in company, wh⟨ich⟩ was very painful: more so than it sh⟨ould⟩ have been, from my mistrust of myself, wh⟨ich⟩ made me forget that it is God's dispensation, sent perhaps to teach me the value of Time: which I am constantly and totally forgetting. I am utterly without fore-thought. May God give me some for myself, and my father, & mother, & Annie too perhaps. I have read about 2½ hrs. having missed Massey.

Tuesday, Feb⟨ruary⟩ 6   fo. 39

Saw Arnold off at 10. Went to Tuckwell, walked with Uncle A⟨lfred⟩, dined with Ward. Arnold has seen Pusey.

[*   *   *   *   *]

Divinity Exercise
Rhetoric Analysis
Scholarship-work

A day of illness, but not unhappy. Tuckwell has greatly reassured me. It is all owing to my irregularity. May God forgive me, and help me henceforth! Have been able to read about 1 hour. 11 o'clock. Up till 11′20′

Wednesday. [February 7]

Wined with Waldegrave. Helen Wrench at Oxford.

A day of illness: and I fear ill-spent. I have neglected my dev⟨otions⟩ reading sadly these two or three days, and to-night in especial have carelessly let time slip away, till it is become too late for anything but bed. Lake and Stanley both very kind. I am afraid Ward is & will be a trial, though I hope it may be only passing irritability. I feel the effects of my neglect to be great, & growing evils. O Lord, forgive me, and give me help to avoid this wickedness to-morrow! ¼ p. 11 o'cl. Up till 11′30′.

Thursday. [February 8]

Dined & tead with Ward. Conversed [i] about the Strength of 'Tradition' viz the Unity of opinion as expressed at the Nicene Council: [* * *] [ii] The 'being alone' question [iii] the 'expression of affection' question. In both these I am in excess: & must try & mend. [* * *]

A variable day as to my mind—rather excitable, and forgetful. A   fo. 40
most pleasant & happy conversation, & opening with Ward, as to

my need of being left alone, bro⟨ught⟩ on unconsciously, and I
almost dare to think, by God's express providence. O Lord Jesus, I
thank thee: Help my unthankfulness. Give me grace to use these
new opportunities aright. I fear I am now sadly excited. 10′ b. 11′
o'cl. Up till 11′ 30′

Friday, Feb⟨ruary⟩ 9

The London University News. Wined with Stanley: Brodie &
Moncrieff call L⟨ord⟩ Brougham our greatest Man.

I passed a very excited night, wh⟨ich⟩ has thrown me back in my
health, I fear. Was able to read about 2 hrs; but in the evening
became very tired. I am now quite awakened. I have been reading
with great pleasure Galatians V & VI; how very beautiful it is! O
Lord Christ, cleanse, I pray thee, with thy Holy Spirit all thoughts
& feelings of self conceit, and presumption from my heart, and
grant that I may daily grow as in the earnestness, so like wise in
the purity of my desirings after holiness and the Love of thee, and
Union with thee. I fear there is great need for me to pray against
the infection of worldly & most hateful vanity with my pleasure in
reading the Scripture, and writing this. [* * * Philippians 3: 13,
Galatians 6: 5, Matthew 25: 15 *quoted*]

fo. 41 Saturday Feb⟨ruary⟩ 10.

Breakfasted with Lloyd, Tate, Hodson, Lonsdale, Hobhouse,
[* * *] Wined with Hobhouse 3 o⟨'clock⟩ A Large Party.

Health much as yesterday—read about 2½ hrs. I am not nearly
enough by myself: the effect of which is that I get quite excited
before the time and all my wholesome drowsiness gone, and the
excitement to be cured into the bargain. If I can leave all wine
parties by 7 and have Ward from 8½ to 9½ o'cl., or something of
that sort, it will be better. Have read Newman's Faith &
Obedience, and the very beautiful one on Excitements & their
Remedy. Vol. III. I have had pleasant thoughts of little ffolkes
tonight: and am only too complacently happy wh⟨ich⟩ I have no
right to be at all. O that I could but see Sin, and conceive some
little portion of God's hatred of it?—11° 45′.

Thank God for all this Week's Blessings.

End of Third Week

Sunday. [February 11]

Breakfasted with Brodie. Went to Hamilton's Prayers & Communion. Walked with Stanley. St⟨anley⟩ says that he thinks it possible that from the examination of the Fathers, a case may appear not to be explained otherwise than on the Newm⟨anist⟩ Principle of a Traditional Revelation providentially preserved to us in the Fathers. Dined with Ward, & went to Brodie for an hour. Ward tead here.

A very foolishly excited & bad night. Went to Communion at Hamiltons, 10 or 11 Balliol men being there: very pleasant: but much tired by the length of the Service. Ward very poorly in body & mind to day. Thank God for giving me something to do, that I am capable of. I hope I have not, & shall not yet lose the impression of the Communion: but I am turned by the least thing. 11° o'cl.

Monday [February 12]

Walked with Lake—called on Palmer. Wined with Prior. Stanley spoke to the Master, who eat dirt, and Chapman, who tried to convert him beforehand. Wrote to Conybeare, Walrond, Burbidge.

I have been writing to Rugby all my time to day—and I have been careless enough to let myself go on till 11 o'clock, so that I must now go to bed. I have also been foolishly & petulantly captious with regard to Lake, who is very good. Have not been to Massy, or Lecture. Part of the day very poorly. May God give me grace, that I may be more careful to-morrow. 11° 20′.

Tuesday, [February] 13th.

Breakfasted here with Lake at 8½ o'cl. Walked a solitary: Wined with Moncrieff. Hobhouse, Tylden, & Buck visits.

A tolerably pleasant & happy day. Read about 3 Hrs. Have been a little tried as to my non-S⟨elf⟩ Esteem; and occasionally felt quite weak & helpless. [* * *]

Wednesday [February] 14th

Breakfasted with Lake at 8½ o'cl. Walked with Congreve. A Wine Party. Lloyd, Crowder, Lewthwaite, Moberly.

A day of unwell-ness, and low spiritedness for the most part. A pleasant time with Congreve, in and out. I do not know what to think of my health & prospects for the present. Is it indeed a punishment for my folly, & wickedness? May God forgive and put away my Sin; but may I see it daily more & more! May he help to determine for myself without self deceit, what I ought to do!

[*   *   *   *   *]

fo. 44   Thursday, Feb⟨ruary⟩ 15th

Breakfast as before 8½ o'cl. [* * *]—Read about 3½ Hrs. Walked with Lake. Called on Palmer. Stayed 1½ hr. with Congreve. Wined with Buck Ward fr⟨om⟩ 7¼–9 o'cl. Tea with Brodie 9–10° 25′

Tait sent for me at 11 o'cl. Very kind: as also Scott. May I be grateful!—The Record rejected by 48 maj. Cotton spoke & well.

A day of high spirits, and hopefulness; but I do not know—How can I ever be in high spirits with all my wickedness to be looking at? I have let myself get quite 'up', and now I must try & cure it.

[*   *   *   *   *]

Friday, [February] 16

Br⟨eakfast⟩ as bef⟨ore⟩

Spent the morning with Massey. Congreve and Brodie. Walked with & bro⟨ught⟩ to dinner Hoskyns. Lake with me afterwards. I have only worked about 2½ Hrs, if so much.

A very bad and wicked night. How humiliated I sho⟨uld⟩ be, and how blind I am. 3 o'cl. p.m.

I feel tolerably sensible of sin, but I fear it is but a transient, earth-born feeling. It is most humiliating indeed to look back on all my follies & wickednesses. O Lord Christ, help me to be vividly impressed with their reality, which I do not truly believe in with my heart.

11° 5′

fo. 45   Saturday [February 17]

Breakfasted with Fox. Worked from 10½ to 2—only. 6 Al⟨caic⟩ St⟨anzas⟩. From 3 to 4½ with Ward. Wined with Collis. Wrote 2

letters home, from 9 to 9½ with Stanley & thence to 11 with Uncle
Alf⟨red⟩, before his starting for Chester.

[*   *   *   *   *]

To day Jowett made Powell Scholar.

Up to 11 o'clock a tolerably fair & quiet and equable day. I have
most wickedly (as I would fain try & feel it to be) let myself get
excited by talking to Tylden, and now it is too late to sit up & cure
it. I have lost the fruits of yesterday.

¼ to 12° o'cl.

How irregular I have been this week, with how little temptation,
and what great need of not being so! I think above all things in my
Dev⟨otio⟩ns; by neglect of which at their seasons I lose way
constantly, and make void all lessons of experience. [* * *]

End of 4th Week

It is now Sunday Morning

Sunday, Feb⟨ruary⟩ 18.   fo. 46

S. Wilberforce preached. A Protest against the notions of Pusey on
Sin after Baptism, founded on the Parable of the Prodigal Son,
who is evidently the type of a man fallen from grace. He makes the
only barrier against wilful sin, the human misery & the risk. Very
beautiful, heartfelt and eloquent.

Went to Ward—12 to 2—Talked about the Sermon, Stanley's
Essay & diverse things. Walked a little with Lake—wined also
with him.

I had a bad night, and am not very well to day. I ought to be a
good deal moved by Wilberforce's Sermon, but am not, and it
should sober me to think of what struck me, when I was with
Ward just now, that a sort of penance is a necessary accompani-
ment to a repentance intended to be the beginning of a lasting
change. ½ p. 2 o'cl.

There is a very striking passage in Pusey's baptism to this point,
and I fear, quite applicable to me. ib.

I have now got quite quiet: and hope to sleep well, & be up before
½ 7 to-morrow, and work well for the beginning of a new Week.
[Not up till 8¼] It will be advisable too, I think, to consider about
a system of dev⟨otio⟩ns on a better scale, but I must not try

overmuch. What a great blessing it is, that I am not excited to-night! May I be grateful for it, and all God's many mercies, not in word, but in deed.

10 o'cl.

fo. 47 **Monday [February] 19**

Breakfasted with Lake. Went to Massey & Scott, not Tait. Walked with Stanley. Wined with Hobhouse, a freshman's Party. Tead [i] with Brodie [ii] with Ward here. Have read incl⟨uding⟩ lect⟨ures⟩ about 4 Hrs, a bit of Latin & ½ [Sallust's] Bell⟨um⟩ Catil⟨inarium⟩. I hope much more to-morrow. I feel sure I might at least have read Middleton for 2 Hours.

Robinson & Bence rusticated this day. A very nice letter from Burbidge, may God bless him, and keep him; and with him all the companions of our pleasant walks in the old fields & lanes.

Read Newmans Sermon on Bodily Suffering.

20 p. 11°.

A day of unwellness though not quite of idleness, but it is absurd my not doing more. I am pretty well [perhaps over-well] satisfied. My sin is punishing me severely, (but not fully) and I do not think of it or feel sorry for it. Ward always bepraising me, & so many thinking well of me, and I myself, alas, alas, what am I? O that I could for one moment realize my wickedness! And all these comforts too!

20′ to 11° o'cl.

I trust however that I am in a better way than I was some little time back, and chiefly perhaps thro⟨ugh⟩ the instrumentality of this journal-writing. What a blessing that God put the thought into my heart! And how do I know how imminent was the danger & how narrowly I have escaped it by this little pathway between great chasms. [* * *]

fo. 48 **Tuesday, [February] 20th**

Up by 9. Breakfasted with Scott. Went to Tuckwell, read the Examiner. Dined with Ward, & he tead with me. Have read about 4½ Hrs. the 6th Aeneid with Warburton. Heard from H. Bunsen of that brutal outrage committed on Emeris.

I am not quite so well content with this day either as regards reading, or otherwise. I am not ready enough to do what God sets before me. I do hope that, thank God, I am getting on, or at any rate not dropping down the stream of this luxurious, & care-estranged life—but what I effect is very, very little, and I do not know whether it will not be necessary to do more, & try some stronger means, even to keep myself from that state of relapse and no more. Perhaps Froude will help me to see. [* * *]

20′ to 11° o'cl.

Wednesday [February] 21   fo. 49

Up at ¼ to 9

With Ward from 1¼ to 5. Dined with Davies. Uncle Alfred. Have only read the last half of the Bell⟨um⟩ Catil⟨inarium⟩ i.e. about 2 Hrs.

To morrow I have got to do

L⟨atin⟩ Lyrics	Catechetics	9 to 2
L⟨atin⟩ Prose	Essay	& 7–9
Ovid & c.		

I fear this has been a foolishly spent day—I have given way to the little indisposition caused by my medicine overmuch. I will try and conquer it however.

10′ to 11 o'cl.

Thursday [February] 22

Up at 10½ Did scarcely any Work. Went to Ward at ¼ to 2, stayed till 2¼. Went to Congreve till ¼ to 5. Dined with Ward. Ward here from ¼ to 8 to ¼ to 11. Very poorly & fanciful, poor man. What can I do?

I have worked about 2½ Hrs. and have only done my 12 Elegiacs & 2 or 3 Alcaic Stanzas. [* * *] I have felt very unwell part of the day & do not know whether I shall not have to see Greenhill, & tell him. This Evening I am much better, and think perhaps it is only a passing unwellness. To-Morrow is Friday. May God help me to make it something of a fast-day, to get up (if possible to Chapel if not at least) to breakfast with Lake. May I be as well to-morrow as now.

10′ p. 11° o'cl.

Friday, Feb⟨ruary⟩ 23   fo. 50

Eve of St Matthias

Not up till 9. Went to Scott & Massey, not Tait. Read in

Congreve's room from 1 to 3½ the 4th Aeneid. Walked with Uncle Alfred. Wined with Tylden. [∗ ∗ ∗] Stayed till 8: very agreable. From 8 to 10½ Essay. Thus I have worked 5 hrs besides 2 lectures to day, & do not feel tired.

I fear this has not been quite a careful, thoughtful day. Not at all a fast day certainly, which I had meant it to be. The fault of not getting up in proper time was the chief reason. I quite feel the Want of more devotion; which I neglect too much a great deal. I am forgetting my wickedness, altogether. This is a double fast, but I dare not sit up much later.

¼ to 11 o'cl.

Thank God, Sunday is coming: may this one be better spent! Alas, parts of this day I have felt quite independent of God. This is the way I abuse my health.

fo. 51 **Saturday [February] 24**

Up to Chapel. Breakfasted with Lake, Woolcombe, Southey, Lonsdale, Goulburn, Waldegrave, Moncrieff, Greenhill. Stayed discussing till 11. Went to Ward at 1, to 2. With him & Uncle Alfred & Congreve from 3 to 5. After dinner lay down till 7½. Ward here from 8° to 9° 20'. Have only read about 2½ hrs. & done 5 Stanzas of Alcaics.

My average reading inclusive of four Lectures has been nearly 4 hrs a day: exclusive, about 3.

> Virgil Aen⟨eid⟩ IV & VI
> Bellum Catilinarium
> 3 Translations . Pr⟨ose⟩ El⟨egiacs⟩ Alc⟨aics⟩
> 1 Essay

In consequence of going to bed too late had not enough sleep, which has rendered this day one uncomfortable tissue of dreamings.

[∗ ∗ ∗ ∗ ∗]

End of Fifth Week

fo. 52 **Feb⟨ruary⟩ 25 Quinquagesima Sunday   Sixth Week**

Up at ¼ to 10 o'cl.

Thro⟨ugh⟩ my own folly lost a good night's rest. Could not get up to Chapel. Went to Hamiltons, afterwards to Ward & Brodie &

out walking with Lake & wined with him & Stanley. After Chapel began Catechetics & talked to Ward till ¼ p. 10: read Sᵗ Peter's 1st Ep⟨istle⟩ till 11: I fear too critically, not enough otherwise. A very nice letter from Walrond.

This also has been but a careless day, I am afraid: What am I doing? How do I know what distance I may yet be from the uttermost peril? Occasionally I have those aweful feelings of practical ᾽Αθεϊσμος [*atheism*]. All because my careless & hurried & heartless dev⟨otion⟩s, I sho⟨ul⟩d suppose. Shall I never try & go forward? I hope Froude will do me good: but of course neither Froude, nor any one else will if I am so foolish. I must try also & make something of Ash Wednesday. I am marvellously well pleased with my wretched attainments and enjoy above all things playing with God's word to feed my vanity. May he forgive me, and show me my great wickedness, and give me the spirit of a true love for Truth & Holiness before him, & not men.

Monday, [February] 26th

fo. 53

Up after a fairly good night by ¼ to 9— but not even 8 hrs enough for me just now, as I had got up with & retained thro⟨ugh⟩ the day a headache at eyes & ears.

Went to breakfast to Stanley, to Lecture to Scott who spoke to me very kindly, and to Massey. After that not to Tait, but Congreve's rooms, where I did a few Elegiacs in about 1½ hr. Walked with Tylden to Sunningwell, & home thro⟨ugh⟩ Bagley W⟨oo⟩d. Wet thro⟨ugh⟩ & very dirty—wined with him.

Read a little Cicero. Ward came & had a very pleasant talk with him & readings of Froude's Remains. 8 to 10¼

I cannot have read about 2½ hours besides 2 lectures, which is quite wrong & so I hope I feel it to be. I long very much to be regular & diligent; without, if not ill-health, at least self-deceit. My present notion is ⟨very strongly⟩ that it will be my best plan for this end to stay the Easter Vacation.

I have done many wrong things this day, been vexed with Lake, undecided, & diffident, idle, & godless.

Is it true that my true time of ripening was October–35, & that all I can now do is sort of late gathering up the fragments? Is it not true that 'there is a tide in the affairs of men' spiritually? It is sad to think of, but only may I feel duly humiliated & at the same time resolved to 'gather up . . .' in earnest & at once. I have been reading Froude's Journal wh⟨ich⟩ is indeed most instructive.

[∗   ∗   ∗   ∗   ∗]

fo. 54 Tuesday [February 27]

In bed by 11¼

Asleep by 12¼ by my own fault.

Up after a good night by 9, breakfasted with Palmer, Faber & one or two others. Worked tolerably (at iners) [*but idly*] from 10½ to 2 Elegiacs & Mathematics. With Ward till ½ p. with Brodie, & Congreve till ¼ 5. [∗ ∗ ∗] With Ward till Chapel. Missed Goulburn's party, carelessly. Went to Jesus & Moncrieff &ᶜ till ¼ to 8, and what with H. Bunsen coming in & other things lost the time sadly & could only do about ½ hrs worth Mathematics with Ward, then read the Tempest with him. He went at 9° 25′. he has been much better wh⟨ich⟩ is a great & undeserved blessing.

Thus I cannot have read 4 hrs at best, which is much too little. The time was lost by my forgetting to go to Uncle Alfred & by reading Froude at wrong times, but for wh⟨ich⟩ I might have got a full hour more at least.

Began to read at ¼ to 10. Heard of poor Jowett's loss of his Sister.

Was cross with Lake—unsteady at work—inattentive at Chapel—read Froude when I ought to have been at work for full 20 minutes, and indulged, as I do constantly, vain thoughts & self-conceit when with Ward. [∗ ∗ ∗]

How heedless in watching my ways I am compared to him [Froude]! What clear broad faults these are compared with his thin, airy existence!

Resolve ⁱ to be up early & in bed early, both of them self denials at present. ⁱⁱ Never to indulge in ex-tempore second thoughts in my resolutions here registered, see Froude I p. 50. ⁱⁱⁱ to look after small self denials in eating [∗ ∗ ∗] ⁱᵛ to allow myself no ex-tempore indulgences in things yet unconsidered, at least tomorrow.

My Vanity is terrible, & my pettishness with Lake. [∗ ∗ ∗]

fo. 55 Ash Wednesday Feb⟨ruary⟩ 28

Not asleep till 12¼ not I think much thro⟨ugh⟩ my fault.

Up at ½ p. 7 to Chapel.

Lake breakfasted here. From 10 to 11 Alcaics.

11–12 Massie. 12 to 2½ Alcaics & Catachetics.

2½ to 4½ Walked with Stanley, and had a talk de rebus Neumaniticis, et de Constantino [*about Newmanist matters and about Constantine*]. Chapel. From ¼ to 6 to 7 lay down half asleep. 7 to 9 with about half an hour interval of reading Froude doing questions for Massie.

Thus I have read, l⟨ectures⟩ inc⟨luded⟩ 7 hours full to day; which I hope will not be too much for me.

I have not been to Uncle Alfred yet, which is wrong.

Poor Jowett not in at either Chapel. Lectures all excused.

To be considered—

Whether I am fit to attempt interpreting S⟨acred⟩ S⟨cripture⟩ till I become more honestly desirous of truth and more habituated to drawing lessons from it which I have lately not done much.

I am now in an excitement of vanity after my good 7 hrs & talk with Stanley, and I fear I have been thus much of the day: wh⟨ich⟩ too is a Fast-Day.

A little quarrelsome with Lake—[* * *] began to be vain with my Verses & quite upset by the walk. Quite inattentive at 2nd Chapel & I fear utterly given to vanity from that time to this.

How bad I am, and how good I think myself to say so. May God cleanse my heart of that evil thought, wh⟨ich⟩ is so constantly bubbling up in it.

25′ to 10

I have now got a little better, but am still much too self-complacent, tho⟨ugh⟩ in a way more like mending.

Memor⟨anda⟩

i. to take the earliest opportunity of thinking of a plan to cure my conceit & pettishness. I fear fasting wo⟨uld⟩ only make it worse as yet

[ii to read before long Pusey's Baptism] 20° 25′

[* * * * *]

In bed 20′ to 11° Asleep 11°20 a very good night

March 1st Thursday

Up res⟨olved⟩ 7 rea⟨lly⟩ 7½ wr⟨ong⟩ chiefly my fault. Have worked pretty fairly for 6 hours about 2 Mathematics 1½ Latin Prose 2½ Questions & Writing out Verses etc. Got very tired after Ward's Lecture & am so indeed now. With Ward almost all the day.

I felt when I awoke as if all my views & vows were mere dreams: excitem⟨ents⟩ being gone. But to day has been I trust on the whole an improvement. I got on much better with Lake, quite without pettishness, except during Prayers (alas). My work also was more steady. I do not know what might have come of my Vanity, but that God has mercifully taken away the weight of temptation by reason of my present rather exhausted State. But some part of the day it was sadly strong, especially when with Ward, to whom I talked far too much de re Christiana-Ecclesiastica [*on Christian church matters*]. And how disappointed I felt after the least word, which fell under my extravagant notions, from Ward's mouth. After all, it was no great things [*sic*]: yet I can now, I hope, dare to thank God, most humbly, that I have done Stanley this good. But tainted as it is with my folly, how can it be acceptable to Him?

I dare not yet count up my wicked thoughts, which come thick & often on me, unclean, & complacent especially. If I can controul my vanity a little, Ward's society will be of great benefit.

I think I may now make the Resolution for one week to avoid altogether any trying at interpreting Scripture without seeking an immediate practical lesson.

10 o'clock

In bed ½ p. 10
Asleep
Up, I hope, before 7.

Friday, March 2nd

Most wrongly I let myself keep awake so as not to be asleep till past 12. So I was not up till ¼ p. 8. I fear to day has been anything but an improvement. I have not been so well, wh⟨ich⟩ is something, but assuredly I have been much less single-minded to day: and not at all active; quite standing still.

Was at my 3 lectures & worked about 2½ besides: a little Lucretius, and I. Essay for Hall. 5½ hrs [* * *]

Saturday, March 3

Was in bed, 11 o'cl.

Asleep directly.

[* * *] ½ past 11 a.m. I have been rather in a bad temper all this Morning, and am thoroughly put out now and why?—because the Master, abused my poor 'Sermon' Essay 'de Jure Gentium'. Proh, Vanitas! [*Ah! Vanity!*]

This folly lay on me from 11 to 5 more or less, with the interval of about 1½ hr—from 11½ to 1¼. And then at last it was not quite conquered so much as diverted, by being with Ward: whom by the bye I tried to day terribly by keeping him waiting from 4 to ½p. which again I do not think tho' accidental w⟨ould⟩ have happened, had I been careful. Very inattentive in Chapel.

Lake at 8½: W⟨ar⟩d 1–¼2. Congreve walk till 4½. Dined with W⟨ar⟩d & at tea. I have worked not more than 4 hrs certainly, besides the unfortunate hour with the Master.

I have read this week about 5 hrs a day—l⟨ectures⟩ inc⟨luded⟩, & above 4 l⟨ectures⟩ ex⟨cluded⟩,

    5 Translations
    1 Essay
    3 or 4 Question Papers
    Catachetics
    A little Cicero, Virgil, & Lucretius

I am now very quiet & quite free from Van⟨ity⟩ troubles, of either Kind, only with a H⟨ea⟩dache. I only hope I am not solely recovered on grounds of human opinion of me, & recovered Self-Complacency on that foundation of sand. I fear much that I have not used the temptation as God would have had me do. It has, at any rate, been useful to me in a high degree.

I do not know what to think of my health. Ought I to tell my folly? Shall I have to do so, ere God will bless me with strength again?

¼ p. 10

*Mem[orandum].

To settle my times of dev⟨otio⟩n once for all & not to leave it to be

done ex tempore. Journal so much. Reading so much. Morning &
Evening. Time of getting up & bed, at least within some bounds.

I do not think I find it so easy to be good now as in Oct. 35. How
humbling this is!

Sunday, March 4. 1st in Lent. Seventh Week

Kept from 11 to $\frac{1}{2}$ p. 7 with a bad interval of terrible pain in the
head. Got up very unwell & am so certainly still, with this
headache wh⟨ich⟩ comes no doubt from the Stomach.

I do not know quorsum haec tendunt [*where these things are tending*]:
but if it is not a mere passing indisposition, & I have to tell
Greenhill I hope I shall not fail. And at any rate I must not forget
this warning of my guilt, as I did the former one. It has struck me
that I have three Strong Impulses. One of Voluptuousness, one of
Love of Praise, & one of Worship. The first seems pretty nearly
exhausted if not conquered, but I cannot now judge of it. The 2nd
is as strong as ever & has been well cultivated, the 3rd has been
much neglected, but is still alive, I am pretty confident, though I
have made but little use of it as a means of improving in other
respects.

fo. 60 And the graces, which I had not given me naturally, & which I
have been striving after, in this desultory manner, in reality,
hardly at all, in profession, this long time are i—Humility-with-
Self-Confidence in a word Independence, that is of man's opinion
as man's & Dependence on God's only.

ii. Abhorrence of all uncleanness, and lust &^{c} &^{c} This is to be
sought & cultivated always, tho⟨ugh⟩ the actual temptation does
not, I think, come on me except in case of my darling pleasure, the
good opinion of men being removed from me, at least of late it has
not.

And if with all my advantages & opportunities I have as yet done
so little, what sho⟨ul⟩d I have been without them?

My intellectual faults, wh⟨ich⟩, however I will not consider now,
are I think chiefly to be referred to a love of the Marvellous, acting
along with my Love of Praise.

$\frac{1}{2}$ p. 11

I am just returned from Newmans Communion, wh⟨ich⟩ was a
largely attended one. I was afraid when I went in that from having

been ½ an hr with W⟨ar⟩d all my humility wo⟨ul⟩d have evaporated: however I kept myself pretty well under; & managed to join pretty well in the Prayers, &ᶜ tho⟨ugh⟩ occasionally wandering. [* * *]

I am afraid I have never got to true humility—I have been fo. 61 sometimes prostrated by human derision—but without that I never can humble myself before God so as to be thoroughly free from some lurking root of 'conceived superiority' & fancied goodness, which soon grows up again in the sun-shine of Men's good words: I hope it may not be so now.

2 o'clock

Staid with Ward till 4 o'clock. Did a beginning of the Divinity Exercise, Joshua I–VI. Newman dined with me. Whether from being tired or from carrying out my humility in such a way as to make an excuse for, or rather to turn it into indolence & self-indulgence, I felt a wish that he sho⟨ul⟩d not come, & did not exert myself when he was so to entertain him. He staid till Ward came, viz. ¼ to 9 and *he* till ¼ to 10. I was sadly inattentive in Chapel: but have roused myself a little since then, but I fear I am not quite right yet. [* * *]

Newman preached on Fasting. What is to be thought of it?

*Mem[orandum]

I have great difficulties in re humilitatis [*in the matter of humility*] when with Ward. Shall I say anything to him, or try and remain unmoved by it? [* * *]

Monday March 5   fo. 62

Slept from 11′ to 7½ most comfortably—still not attentive at Chapel. I am now quite out of humour, because Lake does not breakfast with me; tho⟨ugh⟩ he told me he sho⟨uld⟩ not last night, & I misunderstood him. Perhaps it comes partly from his saying to me—'How stupid you are, always misunderstanding people', tho⟨ugh⟩ only in jest. I could not join in the prayers with him the least for it.

9 o'clock

I am now quite out of sorts again at not having prospered in my Wine Party altogether, having got nervous & afraid of things not being right, & not contented with having done my best, & afraid that it was observed, or some thing of this sort, foolish & absurd enough whatever it may have been. I think Lake observed it & Waldegrave & Brodie; who were all very kind.

$\frac{1}{2}$ p. 8 o'cl.

[*   *   *   *   *]

All that I can by any means call reading, including 3 Lectures does not come up to more than 5 hours. $\frac{1}{2}$ p. 9 to $\frac{1}{2}$ p. 2 a little Cicero & Virgil being the best part. 2$\frac{1}{2}$ hrs Walking, 3$\frac{1}{2}$ Dinner & Party, 1$\frac{1}{2}$ letter to Arnold, $\frac{1}{2}$ to Ward; wh⟨ich⟩ brings me to $\frac{1}{4}$ to 11 o'cl. This is not well.

*I think the cure of my unreadiness will be in getting up before Chapel to d⟨evotio⟩ns. This will give me preparation, fore thought, & fore resolution, I hope, and provide for the balancing of my two objects—Independence of Man—& Dependence on God & Humility, which I hope will soon coalesce into one.

I have also got my Walk with Stanley to look to.

Tait & Anderton elected to the University Scholarships, this day.

5′ to 11 o'cl.

Tuesday, March 6th

Slept from 12 to $\frac{1}{4}$8, was in bed by 11$\frac{1}{2}$.

Breakfasted with Lake.

I do not know how it is, but all this morning I have been in the worst possible humour, for no reason at all that I can see. I have been trying to work but have done nothing but a Satire & a half of Persius & a few Words: though I got myself excused Ward's Algebra on purpose to cure it. This is all I can say for—actually 4$\frac{1}{2}$ hrs.

2 o'clock

Was with Ward $\frac{1}{2}$ an hour—walked with Stanley till 5. Wined with Trower. Ward from 7 to 9$\frac{1}{2}$.

Have worked perhaps = 8 hrs

I have been much in the same way as in the Morning, and feel pretty sure of its being an illness, perhaps from want of sleep. I have not treated rightly, nor acted as I ought: [* * *] This will never do for the Hartford: but if it only does for God's service, I have no place for complaining, & much to be thankful for—

without looking to gaining money, or credit for myself, or Rugby.
I only fear I am getting sadly ἄθεος [*atheist*] I was rather
'dependent' at Trower's; inattentive in Chapel; and thoroughly
pettish the most part of the day.

¼ to 10 o'cl.   fo. 64

Lloyd elected to Jesus Coll. Scholarship.

Wednesday, [March] 7th

Slept from 11 to 8½: but after all might as well have got up at 7, for
I think was not much rested.

Have read about 5½ hrs including 2 lectures—a little Pliny (3
epistles) a piece of Latin Prose, and Catachetics.

I got on pretty well in the Morning, but I am in a very bad way
this Evening, and do not know what to do. A little illness puts me
quite out. And I have all sort of wicked fancies and feelings of
carelessness. My corruption is indeed terrible. What shall I do?

So far as I can see at present I have lost more in the last two or
three days, than I gained all the four before it.

10 o'clock

Thursday, [March] 8th

Slept from 11 to 7½

The Morning was not over well spent, I fear—sat in the Schools—
where I joined in laughing immoderately—and did other foolish
things.

But after dining with Ward, and talking him out of one of his
troubles I feel much better. And in health I am very much better.
I do not know just now how far this is only an earthly change of
spirits; but I will at any rate try & make good use of the
'Unrighteous Mammon'.

I have 200 lines of Lucretius, about ¾ hr's work, and skimmed
thro⟨ugh⟩ Aen⟨eid⟩ VII in the Schools. I suppose these wo⟨ul⟩d
come to a full 2½ hrs work, altogether. I must try and be very
active to-morrow, not forgetting that it is Friday.

5′ p. 10 o'clock

The Ministry in by 29.

Friday, [March] 9th

fo. 65

Slept from 11¼ to 7½, breakfasted with Goulburn. Worked about

$4\frac{1}{2}$ besides 2 lectures, but did not do much besides the Essay, & that not well.

Had a very pleasant walk with Tylden from $\frac{1}{4}$ 2 to 5, to the top of Wytham Hill. In the evening about 9 Ward came in & stayed till 11 in a very bad way. I went to bed directly, but did not get up this morning till past 8.

Saturday morning

Saturday, [March] 10th

I have read to-day about 5 Hrs—a book about = 1000 l⟨ines⟩ of Lucretius—and [Cicero's] Or⟨atio⟩ in Catil⟨inam⟩ ⟨Pri⟩ma but might & ought I think have got 2 hr^s more.

This Weeks Average is l⟨ectures⟩ inc⟨luded⟩ $4\frac{1}{2}$ l⟨ectures⟩ ex⟨cluded⟩ not quite $3\frac{1}{2}$: the falling off is chiefly owing to my having lost Thursday in the Schools, but not entirely I am sure. I have done a little Cicero & Pliny, Virgil, Lucretius, and Persius, and Niebuhr. 2 Translations, 1 Essay, Catachetics.

Altogether the Week has been one of relapsing. My resolutions are so vague that I can do what I please with them & I let any little unwellness serve my purpose. If I do not back them up, I shall inevitably fall back utterly & perhaps for ever. It is quite possible that a man should be punished by continual inadequate and δυψυχος [*double-minded*] efforts to be good. [* * *]

I must indeed try and do better next week, or it will go very ill with me for a long time. The main thing is, I think without doubt, getting up early.

10 o'clock

fo. 66   Eighth Week 2nd Sunday after Lent March 11

Resolutions

    i   To be up at 7 o'cl. exactly, for 3 days
    ii   S⟨acred⟩ S⟨cripture⟩ as before
    iii   ext⟨ra⟩ res⟨olutions⟩ [as before]

I was up 7′ p. 7 but not dressed till 10′ to 8. I have been in too great spirits all day, & inattentive mostly at both Chapels. I have let myself make a regular Pleasure day of this Sunday: wh⟨ich⟩ to say the least was a doubtful course after such a week as my last. In short I have abused my recovered health & strength & confidence.

I have however done my little work—14 ch.' of Joshua. Catechetics except 1 q⟨uestio⟩n and a letter to Walrond. This however was no conquest: but quite a pleasure.

Mem[orandum]

Quaere. Should I ever let myself into high spirits just yet? I think not.

I think all my spirits wo⟨ul⟩d depart at the least human rebuff.

I was also very pretending, & broke res⟨olution⟩ ii in spirit, when with Lake.

$\frac{1}{2}$ p. 10

Monday, [March] 12th

I was up not till 25′ p. 7 having overslept myself after rather a bad night: and have not been quite right all to-day. I have worked 4 hrs full besides 2 lectures: perhaps I might have got another if I had not wasted my strength at the first. I have done about 1$\frac{1}{2}$ hr. 200 l⟨ines⟩ of Persius, and 1$\frac{1}{2}$ 550 of Lucretius, and a little Niebuhr.

In the Morning I was too high, in the evening too low in spirits: at best, but unthoughtful.

Young Walrond I hear has got the Scholarship.

Stanley went to Rugby.

My indisposition has bro⟨ugh⟩t me to a better temperament: may I only make good use of it.

$\frac{1}{2}$ p. 10

Tuesday, March 13   fo. 67

Was not up till $\frac{1}{4}$ to 8: I do not seem to mind breaking my resolutions the least. I will try & be more careful to-morrow and get up exactly. [* * *]

Was quite upset because I behaved awkwardly on meeting D⟨...⟩ T⟨...⟩ in J⟨esus⟩ C⟨ollege⟩ quad⟨rangle⟩: & this folly staid on till after Chapel, more or less, i.e. full to 3$\frac{1}{2}$ hrs: & was then recovered only by behaving well by mere chance to Jowett. I am quite a slave of this foolish fear of ill-manners, and now 2 or 3 hours with Ward has quite righted me, humane. I have neglected several errands I had to do: I have read very little, having only got thro⟨ugh⟩ a dozen Elegiacs, and about 250 l⟨ines⟩ of [Ovid's] Fasti & Ep⟨istles⟩ & Pont⟨ica⟩; and 400 of [Horace's] 1 sat⟨ires⟩

(viz. I. III–IV;)—besides a little Mathematics altogether not 6 hours.

I must really continue to go to bed earlier.

Res⟨olution⟩. To be in bed to-morrow night by ½ p. 10 & leave off work at 9.

I shall, I hope, have from 9½ to 12, & 7 to 9 for work.

½ p. 10

Wednesday, [March] 14th   3rd in Lent.

Was not up till ½ p. 7, after a worse night than I have had of late.

I have worked rather better than 4 hrs, besides 2 lectures, to which however I did not much attend. Have done about 20 Elegiacs, & 320 l⟨ines⟩ of 1 Sat⟨ires⟩ (V.VI.VII.VIII) and read part of Buttmann, de Personis Horat⟨ii⟩ & a few etc.

I fear I have not got on rightly: certainly I have been in a very godless frame of mind all day: I have felt tolerably active & almost eager to keep at some work that I might not be pestered with uneasy fancies &ᶜ. [* * *]

¼ p. 10

fo. 68 Thursday, [March] 15th

Was not up till ½ p. 7 out of pure luxury, tho⟨ugh⟩ I was in bed by ¼ to 11. I have worked to day nearly 6 hours having read [Virgil's] Georg⟨ic⟩s II, [Cicero's] in Catil⟨inam⟩ II; 400 l⟨ines⟩ of [Ovid]'s Fasti I & [Cicero's] pro Sextio fr⟨om⟩ 1 to lx, besides a few questions; but I fear rather carelessly read.

Ward owing to my note not been bro⟨ught⟩ him in time has been in a bad way all to day, & is so now in especial. He could not go till 20 to 11.

I have been in a careless frame of mind, tho⟨ugh⟩ better world-wards than usual. Had a very nice letter from Burbidge.

11 o'cl.

Friday, [March] 16th

Not up till ½ p. 7. To day I have worked besides 3 lectures rather better than 4 hours. Have done the rest of Pro Sextio, & of Fasti I; also 300 l⟨ines⟩ of Georgic IV, and my Essay. I hope this will not knock me up. I do not seem to take much thought of other & more necessary matters, and I am getting rather vain, & occasionally have sanguine fancies about the Latin.

$\frac{1}{2}$ p. 10

Lingan Ireland Scholar

Saturday [March] 17th

This has been on the whole a good day: though after a quite bad   fo. 69
night I have read full 5 hours, & done in them a piece of Latin, and 1200 l⟨ines⟩ of Virgil pretty carefully. My work this week has averaged full 6 hrs l⟨ectures⟩ incl⟨uded⟩ above 4$\frac{1}{2}$ l⟨ectures⟩ ex⟨cluded⟩

> 550 l. Lucretius
> I Fasti & 250 l⟨ines⟩ besides, Ovid
> 200 Persius
> 720 Horace I Satires
> In Catilinam II^{da}
> Pro Sextio 50 to end   Cicero
> & one or two things more
> [Second] Georgic
> Aeneid IX & p⟨ar⟩t of X
>   Virgil
> a Latin Essay
> 32 Elegiacs
> I L⟨atin⟩ Pr⟨ose⟩ Translation

& a little Niebuhr & Buttmann.

Altogether it has been a week of great blessings: but I have not been innocent of carelessness, & godlessness. Frequently cast down from fancied contempt & dislike of people about; occasionally foolishly excited: sometimes vexed with Lake, not seldom impatient of Ward's troubles: and as for my resolutions & memoranda I have been quite thoughtless. I feel confident of the usefulness of the one, & I constantly am reminded of the need of considering the others. I have been very heedless of the fast, & of the Preparation for to-morrow, and I have done nothing towards curing my inattention in Chapel. All this I will diligently consider to-morrow.

11 o'clock

fo. 70   Ninth Week 3rd Sunday after Lent March 18th

Was not up till 8 o'cl.; after a good sleep of 8 hrs, but even then with a headache. I have neglected to prepare for Communion. I have quite forgotten my yesterday's resolution. I have let myself be vexed when with Lake, & conceited when with Ward. I have been acting the interpreter, was inattentive at Evening Chapel, & have let myself now get into a conceited & rather feverish frame of mind: it is true I have been unwell & very weak, but these things need not have happened.

[*   *   *   *   *]

Monday, [March] 19th

Most wrongly I let myself be kept awake till past 12: tho⟨ugh⟩ I was in bed before 11.

I have worked to day only 2½ hrs, besides 3 lectures, at most. [* * *] 700 l⟨ines⟩ Aen⟨eid⟩ X.

I got on fairly well till dinner, then I got very tired & 'dependent'.

½ p. 9

[*   *   *   *   *]

fo. 71   Res⟨olutions⟩

    i   To be up by 7, & in bed by ¼ to 11
   ii   To avoid extempore alterations
  iii   [To avoid] interpretation of S.S.
  iv   to have 20′ dev⟨otio⟩n before 8

Tuesday [March 20]

I overslept myself & was only up by ¼ to 8. Even then tired & poorly. I have however worked rather more than about 5 hrs incl⟨uding⟩ 1½ with Massie: have read about 300 l⟨ines⟩ of Virgil, done a piece of Latin, twice over: & read some Copleston's Praelectiones.

I have got on tolerably on the whole: but was inattentive in Chapel, & occasionally vain with Ward. [* * *]

Wednesday [March 21]

Up at ¼ p. 7 after a good night.

Have worked inc⟨luding⟩ 1½ with M⟨assie⟩ about 7 hrs, but

lightly: done 36 elegiacs; read Moretum & a little Cic⟨ero's⟩
Ep⟨istle⟩s & Aen⟨eid⟩ VII, & learnt several passages out of
Copleston & finished my Catechetics.

Got on tolerably till Noon. But when out with Lloyd at the
Beegarden & river found myself rather absurd & dependent &
praise-desiring. I conquered in some degree at dinner, but not so   fo. 72
as to regain my ground wholly. I fear missing the two lectures was
rather a doubtful step: [* * *]

Thursday [March 22]

Up by 20′ p. 7: in a terrible bad temper, which kept on me all
morning, and quite worried me & has made me sadly tired. I
have, I fear, got on but badly. However I am not quite so much
vexed as usual, at having been stupid at Lowe's.

I have only read 4½ hrs incl⟨uding⟩ 1 with M⟨assie⟩ a few
Hexameters, and Juvenal X.

To night again I am late & cannot be up before ¼ p. 7.

20′ to 11°

Friday [March 23]

I was not up till ¼ p. 8; tho⟨ugh⟩ knowing all the time that it was
not right. And I have gone on all the Morning with scarcely one
thought of the matter, going fast down the hill. I must stop at
once, or else may be I never shall.

2 o'clock

I have worked to day n⟨early⟩ 8 hours, full 3½ at my Essay to   fo. 73
night & n⟨early⟩ 4½ at Latin, inc⟨luding⟩ 1 hr with Massie; only
did a dozen Hexameters, and a piece of Prose: & two or three of
[Cicero's] Ep⟨istles⟩ XIII.

I have been very well, but I fear abused my strength, tho⟨ugh⟩ I
did not at all mean my Essay to keep me so long. I did not get on
quite well even after 2 o'cl.

11 o'cl.

Saturday [March 24]

Up to Chapel. I had a very poor & bad night: and am sadly tired
this Morning, though I think my health is not hurt at all. [* * *]

I have spent, I much fear, an idle day: having read not nearly all I
sho⟨ul⟩d have: only a few letters & 4 Ch. of [Cicero's] De Oratore

III, and about 300 l⟨ines⟩ of Lucretius & a little Martial: altogether not so much as 5 hrs good work.

My average is not quite 6 hrs l⟨ectures⟩ incl⟨uded⟩ & 4½ l⟨ectures⟩ ex⟨cluded⟩: a little less than last week & certainly less satisfactory

> 300 l. Lucretius
> 1000 Virgil Aen⟨eid⟩ & Moretum &ᶜ
> About 1 book of Epistles, Cicero, &ᶜ
> Juvenal X & a little Martial
> Copleston's Praelectiones about 3 lectures & several passages by heart.
> English Essay
> about 40 Elegiacs & 20 longs
> 3 Latin Pr⟨ose⟩ Translations

Altogether this week is one not at all satisfactory: only too fit an ending for this book. Time wasted and resolutions broken—inattention in Chapel, mean dependence in company, Vanity, & many other sinfulnesses & follies. Presumption in holding forth my speculatiunculae [*little speculations*] to Ward, ill-humour, neglect of dev⟨otio⟩ns, and with all this weight of sins & of corruption scarce enough good left in me to feel that there is something.

¼ p. 10 o'clock

Resolutions

1 To be in bed and up again both early.
2 Not to make extempore alterations
3 To look for small self denials in eating.
4 Not to try & interpret S⟨acred⟩ S⟨cripture⟩ except for d⟨evou⟩t l⟨esso⟩ns
5 To be up every morning at 7 exactly

DIARY 3

Last Week but one.

4th Sunday after in Lent, Festival of the Annunciation.
March 25th

[also Froude's birthday]

Was only up to Chapel:— Went to Sermon at New College. with
Ward till 2. Walked with Lake. Wrote to Simpkinson. Ward 8½
to 9½ p.m.

I have not nearly recovered my folly of Friday last even now, and I
fear I have not done all I might to day, or nearly. I have felt
occasionally so dreadfully double-minded that I do not know how
I shall ever get on.

I have been inattentive too at Chapel, presumptuous about
S⟨acred⟩ S⟨cripture⟩ &c with Ward, and indeed got on quite
miserably till 4 o'cl.; when I set to work at S⟨impkinson⟩'s letter,
which did me a great deal of good, from its being at any rate an
occupation: & a duty. This is clearly the right remedy, & if I can
but get a good day's work to-morrow it will go, I hope, a good way
to restore me.

i

I mean to try this week to get up regularly at ½ p. 6 and for that
purpose must be in bed regularly before ½ p. 10; and must
therefore also get Ward to go before ½ p. 9 at latest.

ii

I must too, I am sure, avoid discussing τα βιβλικα και ἐκκλησιαστικα
[*Bible and church matters*], with Ward at any rate:—as also
int⟨erpretation⟩ of S⟨acred⟩ S⟨cripture⟩ as before

iii

I must too remember my self-denials: which are quite of high
importance.

And I must never pass a day without trying to realize all my exceeding wickedness and abuse of God's grace from my very childhood. More especially during the last 2 Years & all the incalculable harm thereby done to myself & to God's Kingdom.

fo. 2ʳ ## Monday [March 26]

Was in bed by 25′ to 11 & asleep soon after 11. Up in time.

Have not left off not in time:—it being now just ¼ to 10.

Have worked today n⟨ear⟩ 5½ hrs, besides 2 lectures. But have only done about 900 l⟨ines⟩ of Terence & a copy of Hexameters.

I have got on pretty well, excepting about 1½ hr fr. 6½ to 8 when I was foolishly excited—very inattentive at Chapel. [* * *]

fo. 2ᵛ ## Tuesday [March 27]

In bed not before 20′ to 11′: up after not very good rest [* * *]

I have been not very well & have not worked more than 4 hrs at most besides one with Massie:—have done 10 Hexameters and some of Cicero's Prefaces.

I have had a good deal of trial today in various ways: have got on middling: but have been very forgetful & aimless.

Ward did not go till 25′ to 10: it is now ¼ to 10.

My d⟨evotio⟩ns have been better (how they sh⟨ou⟩ld be so, I do not see, as I can hardly be improved to day), but not any thing like satisfactory.

Wednesday [March 28]

Was not up till 8 after a bad night. Have been unwell, & taken a holiday, I think, wisely.

fo. 3ʳ I hardly know how I have got on: not altogether well, certainly: especially when with Congreve.

Greenhill was very kind.

                                             10′ to 10.

Thursday [March 29]

To day also has been one of unwellness & I have done no work at all to speak of: though I went to Massie, did a copy of Terentians, and read a little Horace. Altogether perhaps 3 hrs. How I have got on, or whether I have got on, or not, I do not know, & do not see how I can discover.

$\frac{1}{4}$ to 10

I have been careless over my dev⟨otio⟩ns and altogether I fear I am not quite right.

[*   *   *   *   *]

I must remember also that I purposed receiving the   fo. 3ᵛ
Comm⟨unio⟩n on Sunday.

I will try then to morrow to be dressed by $\frac{1}{2}$ p. 7, and consider these matters a little more,—to go to Chapel and after breakfast set to my work, which till then I will endeavour to forget altogether.

I wonder when a week will come in which I shall be able to keep my Sunday resolutions. [* * *]

Friday [March 30]   fo. 4ᵛ

Was not up by reason of oversleeping myself till Chapel-time. Am rather tired and not quite well, but a good deal improved, I hope, in all ways.

$\frac{1}{2}$ p. 10 a.m.

Even to day I have done poorly. Constantly forgetting and getting into the wrong way: first of all I did not at once occupy my mind with good thoughts: so that I became wandering and rather inattentive in Chapel. This produced inattention at dev⟨otio⟩ns afterwards & increased itself thereby. Then after being with Massie I took to my Terence instead of Horace, as I sho⟨ul⟩d have done. And got into my old foolish way with Congreve. The last thing that tried me has been Ward's saying that Massie expected Arnold to beat me, which has, I am much ashamed to say, bothered me a good deal.

Altogether I have done most meagrely considering how much I   fo. 5ʳ
purposed last night. I have worked, I suppose, 5 hrs incl⟨uding⟩ Massie:—the rest of [Terence's] Heautont⟨imoroumenos⟩ & 380 l. of Hor⟨ace's⟩ Ep⟨istles⟩ I. [* * *]

To morrow again I must try & be dressed by $\frac{1}{2}$ p. 7 & go to   fo. 5ᵛ

Chapel:— till then I must try to forget these troublesome reading matters altogether.

25′ to 11

fo. 6ʳ **Saturday [March 31]**

Was not up till Chapel time. Had a very strange night: how far guilty I cannot possibly know.

10 a.m.

I think I have done to day quite as much, not as I can perhaps, for that I never do, but surely as I have ever done lately, yet I do not seem to have got on at all well.

I have read perhaps 3 hrs worth and have been in a most uneasy state all day.

My reading average this week has been only 4 hrs l⟨ectures⟩ in⟨cluded⟩ 3 hrs l⟨ectures⟩ ex⟨cluded⟩ about

> 400 l. of Horace
> a Play & a half of Terence
> 3 Translations
> a little Cicero & Tacitus—

fo. 6ᵛ Whence the uneasy & restless frame I have been plagued with proceeds I can't quite make out. I do not think it is entirely from mere mortification at my chance being looked upon as so slight for this Scholarship: Nor yet perhaps is it entirely from the impatience of not getting forward as I hoped, and from the constant obtrusion of my own corruption on my sight.

[*   *   *   *   *]

fo. 7ʳ I remember not long ago saying in myself that persons with a good many natural virtues were badly off in this way, as they got be-praised, & became complacent on less than their neighbours— from a confusion of principal & interest, which things we cannot separate for our neighbour, only each for himself. [* * *]

fo. 8ʳ **Last Week**

April

PASSION SUNDAY
or 5th Sunday in Lent

April 1st.

Was only up to Chapel, after a good night, but rather too short. I have got on pretty tolerably to day on the whole. Was rather faulty in conversation with Ward after 12 o'cl. which nearly upset my humility before Newman's Communion and altogether restored me my Self-Complacency, which is no great blessing really, though it is rather more comfortable. I wish I was rid of it again. Also I was in fault a little as regards Lake, and inattentive at Chapel.

I am afraid I have done foolishly in letting myself talk περι των βιβλικων [*on Bible matters*] with Ward. [∗ ∗ ∗] It seems to me just fo. 8ᵛ at present, that from what Ward reports of Newman's sermon about the kinds of venial sins, & of his opinion about sins that put us out of a state of grace, that for the 2 first years after my fo. 9ʳ Confirmation the struggle was with & the victory over such things as keeping on in sin once begun & other foolishnesses chiefly Evangelical. Then from that time—the Autumn of 35 began the contest with the mere sins themselves [∗ ∗ ∗] when I might have done so much good of all kinds to others and perhaps more than I can have a notion of, for many opportunities which have now perished unimagined and unknown except to God, might have probably arisen, and when I might have improved so very rapidly myself, so as to be able to do much at this present time fo. 9ᵛ which now I cannot,—in which with all these opportunities I did such mere nothing, nay worse than nothing,—so as perhaps to cripple myself for my whole life long. And now after all that I should be blest with so much aid in all these things around us at Oxford. New wisdom and new exercises of devotion, and that I with all this profusion of God's gifts and all this overwhelming weight of ingratitude should go on as I do, careless at public and private devotions—ever feeding a foolish vanity on praise or mortification, ever presuming to be the Interpreter of the Word of fo. 10ʳ Him I have despised & rejected and crucified afresh & afresh— murmuring too forsooth at little pains & troubles, & ever forgetful of my own Sin, and God's hatred of it, and goodness nevertheless to me, who am so laden with it.

I think probably the great thing that upset me in my second 2 years—or rather up to this time, has been the want of Newman's strong doctrine about Sins after Baptism—or rather I sh⟨ou⟩ld say of what is the substitute suggested by that doctrine of his, and Froude's noble example. How strange that I should owe so much to Arnold & so much to him! How have I deserved this second enlightenment? It almost seems as if my weak was destined to be a kind of βασανος [*touchstone*] of doctrines—so weak—with such utter want of moral strength joined with much moral perception, as that nothing but the real & whole truth should be strong enough to cure it and not only set but keep it right. I fear this is, as it now is, a vain & foolish conceit: at least it is one which it will not do to dwell upon, at least in this light, which is the most presumptuous I could put it in. *Very* likely there is no truth in it at all: nor in all this paragraph: but *most* likely, I think, there is some.

[* * * Rom. 2: 4 *quoted*]

Monday, [April] 2nd

I was not up even in time for anything but very short devotions, and altogether this day have been a great deal too much taken up with the Scholarship Examination: this added to bodily weakness & ill health has put me in an ill-regulated and un-self-controuled condition today. However the sense of both bodily and intellectual want of strength has prevented my going very far astray. But this does not lessen my sinfulness in leaving myself no time for them this morning. I fear I have gone back, rather than forward to day: & simply & solely because of that neglect. As if this Examination was of any importance! I must try and put away all other things, and look solely and stedfastly to that one object, which with I know not how little carelessness more may be lost to my sight for ever:—from which great peril Good Lord, deliver me! & teach me too to feel how near & how terrible it is. [* * *] No one has the slightest idea of my exceeding wickedness, but my own wretched self, who am so ever ready to forget and believe it was more good than harm. What an awful being-alone! With all one's unknown sins around one! For the present and for as long a time as I should look forward to I think I must cast utterly away all my grand thoughts of being a great Theologian—or Politician—or Poet—of our grand Rugby Set, of doing good with a high hand of Scripture interpretation & solution of Church doctrine-difficulties—even of hopes of honours for Rugby—in fact of every thing except this one that I want so much—the seeing my own wickedness. [* * *]

Would Sunday-Schooling be a good exercise?—There will doubt- less be a good many incitements to Vanity in all these things, perhaps I shall never have a field so exactly fitted for my benefit as

that of Oct. 35—but that very name Oct. 35 should be a most
ample spell for driving everything of that sort away.

[*   *   *   *   *]

Tuesday [April] 3rd   fo. 13^r

Again I am later by ¼ hr than should be.

½ p. 8 A.M.

I hope I have got on rather better to day than yesterday. I have
certainly had more self-controul about me: though I have
certainly given way occasionally to foolish feelings. And perhaps I
am a little too cheerful. [* * *] I ventured this evening to talk   fo. 13^v
βιβλικα [*Bible matters*] with Ward, thinking to avoid all harm by
not giving any opinion or starting anything new myself, & this
did, I think, answer for the time. But it is still very doubtful how
far such conversation is justifiable, as the thoughts & habits of
looking at Scripture speculatively remain with me quite strong
afterwards, and it is probably unwise to get into the way of talking
so exclusively on those subjects, even without any reference to my
own especial case. So I will certainly try and avoid it.

I am afraid I let a ριζα πικριας [*root of bitterness*] spring up to day by
suffering myself to be encouraged by the 2nd Latin Prose Paper; it
was very subtle at first, as it seemed to be only getting a proper
appetite for my work, but my mind has since then being   fo. 14^r
constantly running on Prizes. E⟨nglish⟩ V⟨erse⟩ Latin Verse etc.
Bentley's Horace to be read—and how I shall get on as soon as this
is over . . . etc. etc. As for the Prizes etc. I am quite sure I cannot
think of them purely, at present. My way must be to habituate
myself to look to them i as increasing my chance of an income to
help my Father & Mother & Annie with & ii as doing honour to
Arnold. However for the present I had better not think of them
more than I can possibly help.

[*   *   *   *   *]

Wednesday [April] 4th.—[* * *]   fo. 15^r

My conceitedness & folly & rottenness of heart is very great: if I
could but get to feel it so. I have contrived by going to sit with
Tylden to get rid of the very powerful effect my bumptious
manner to Ward had left working on me with increasing strength:
and now feel my weariness, which is a little step. [* * *]

fo. 15ᵛ Thank heaven, this weary bondage is over at last; and I may now do according to my 'own sweet will' for some little time pretty completely. I ought to make a great deal of it; especially as Fox stays up; but I must above all things get two or three hours a day to myself, & consider my way very closely especially just at first, or I may be quite sure of doing myself much more harm than good.

At present my tendency to luxuriating in some imagined good opinion of men, or consciousness of recovered strength is quite terrible. But it is perhaps an advance on my former trials, as certainly it is far more difficult to manage.

11 o'cl.

fo. 16ʳ Thursday, [April] 5th

Being very much tired I have to day relaxed a good deal: I believe with no further harm than the lulling myself a little to sleep as to the call on me for self-denials etc., which I hope I see again very strongly to night. A very pleasant nine hrs with Ward: I however talked again about τα ὑψηλα [*high matters*], wh⟨ich⟩ I am afraid will do me no good, tho⟨ugh⟩ it was in better style than usual, as not referring to Scripture much, but rather things Ward knows best, τα ἠθικα κ.τ.λ. [*ethics etc.*]

I propose at present to rest pretty wholly till Monday Morning— when Ward also begins his privations. I must try & do something then I am quite sure. [* * *]

[1 John 5: 3–5 *and* 18 *quoted*]

fo. 17ʳ Friday, [April] 6th

I was as nearly as possible committing my worst sin this Morning. I was not *quite* roused fr⟨om⟩ sleep, but fully conscious.

And now I have heard that I am in the Seven for this unhappy Hertford and not yet knowing further particulars my vanity-beridden imagination is running off with me in the most terrible fashion.

I should have very probably got it if I had been in good health— this is as much as I can dare to conceive true. And what has prevented me from being in good health? *My own wretched folly & wickedness*, and that not of some time ago, but chiefly of last ⟨Christ⟩mas Holydays, as I sho⟨ul⟩d think very likely the case is;

fo. 17ᵛ certainly of no more distant period than my 1st Term, perhaps even so late a one as this last Term. Yet this is a thing wh⟨ich⟩ would have greatly pleased both my relations, especially uncle Alfred whom I owe so much, & Arnold. would have 2dly done Rugby great credit—and 3dly increased my chance of doing good in College & Oxford, as well as 4^{thly} of obtaining a fellowship. I do not know what amount of blessings I have turned from me in my wickedness at Rugby, but this I think can be put to the account of the last 6 Months by themselves.

And yet I can be glad at hearing this? Because forsooth men will think higher of my abilities for it—or at best because it relieves me from the distress of thinking my powers at all lessened & restores my self complacency more fully. But as I had not lost this much fo. 18^{r} before, this can have but little share in it.

However it is quite right to be glad (i) so far as it conduces at all to the pleasure of my relations, or friends—as it prevents disgrace on Rugby—and my own character as a reading steady person in the College. (ii) so far as it gives me hope of effecting something towards these objects hereafter & convinces me that I have still ability to go forward to these objects—without much prejudice to my Class. [* * *]

$\frac{1}{2}$ p. 11 a.m.

After all it appears that I did but very poorly—so that all my fo. 18^{v} reasoning has but little further purpose than to overcome a passing attack of vanity. [* * *]

It is mere madness to go on without taking a sober couple of hours to consider matters. As I have been fool enough to let to-day pass uselessly, I must have them to-morrow—from 11 to 1. [* * *]

Dined at Dr. Foulkes'

Saturday [April 7] fo. 19^{r}

My wickedness & neglect has at last reached its heighth. It is beyond all I can say—but the worst of all is that I am almost wholly blind to it.

Again, after this, when I had such imperative need of my long purposed 2 hrs—the neglect of which has bro⟨ught⟩ all this sin & misery on me—even now this day I have been so wretchedly foolish & wicked as to let myself stay *a whole hr* with Massie (which I need not the least have done) though I thereby must lose one of fo. 19ᵛ these never-forthcoming two hrs. For I must go to Ward or else I don't know what will come to him.

It is quite clear that is impossible to force oneself into a right state of repentant & humbled feelings—and that this one must wait for. But we can & must do something, & what is it? Repeating the Lord's Prayer...? 1 o'cl.

I had begun to see what I ought to do, and now I have done myself grievous & (to night) (I fear) irreparable harm by neglecting to
fo. 20ʳ manage my conversation with Ward so as to tend to humility. I have been with him from 1½ to 10 o'cl., and during that time have often quite gone wrong [* * *]

fo. 20ᵛ On this day that I have spent so ill, on this day, as it were,—1800 Years ago,—our Lord was in Bethany, just arrived;—this His last sabbath day. His last day of rest before the aweful week, with all its changes, & all its exertions, & all its wondrous sufferings—

[* * * John 12: 7–8 *quoted*]
[* * * John 19: 41 *quoted*]

fo. 21ʳ This is the first day of the Nine successive ones we can distinguish. Found historically only in

Sᵗ JOHN's GOSPEL
ch. XI 55 to XII 11
Comp⟨are⟩Sᵗ MARK ch. XIV 7 to 11
Sᵗ MATTH. ch. XXVI 1 to 16
answering chronologically to
Sᵗ MARK between ch. X & XI,—to
Sᵗ MATTH. between ch. XX & XXII,—& to
Sᵗ LUKE at v. 29 of ch. XIX.
And the Eve too of Palm Sunday.

It is now just 12. That is a new Week just begun, namely Passion
fo. 21ᵛ Week. How many good men here, (& else where too some) are fasting & praying, I dare say, at the entrance of the Holy Week.

I am a little improved in my immediate state of feelings, but the real thing to be kept in mind is,—that I am bound

To keep ever before my eyes as my aim, & to seize every opportunity of encouraging & cultivating the better perception of my sinfulness, & the growth of true repentant feelings, that may never obstruct the entrance of the Holy Spirit into my heart.

PASSION WEEK
PALM SUNDAY

April
8th

[*   *   *   *   *]

[2 Cor. 7: 10–11 *and* Eph. 4: 30 *quoted*]

Missed Morning Chapel by accident fr⟨om⟩ weariness.
With Ward from 9 to 11¼
At Newman's fr⟨om⟩ 11½ to 1
Writing to Gell fr⟨om⟩ 1 to 2
With Ward fr⟨om⟩ 2 to 4
Writing to Gell & Lake to 5¼
With Ward to dinner at ¼ to 6 & fr⟨om⟩ 7¼ to 9.

I have got on pretty tolerably I hope, have been tired all the latter
half of the day and very weak, & open to fancies etc.—but I think
I have not been much given up to them except during Service.
Was very much struck with Newman, reading the Gospel in
especial: so completely taken up with the Service, & the Time. I
hope I shall be able to do something for myself during the Week.
There are patterns enough here.

Sᵗ JOHN'S GOSPEL   ch. XII 12 to 19
Sᵗ MATTH.   XXI 1 to 17
Sᵗ MARK   XI 1 to 11
Sᵗ LUKE   XIX 29 to 44

Our Lord's triumphant entrance into the City and Temple, his
lament over the City. He returns for the Night to Bethany.—

Newman Vol. III, sermon X.
Chr⟨istian⟩ Year Advent Sunday

[*   *   *   *   *]

MONDAY IN PASSION WEEK

April 9th.

[*   *   *   *   *]

Our Lord leaves Bethany (for the last time apparently), the
Miracle of the Fig-tree [* * * Mark 11: 15–19 *quoted*]

In St. Matthew from this Morning in Sᵗ. Luke & John from the
previous day, and his first Entrance into the City there is no note

of time in St Matthew till Tuesday Evening XXVI. 1, in St Luke
& more decidedly John till Thursday Evening and the Last
Supper.

fo. 24^r I must keep in mind

i   That I am going to attend the Communion twice this week—
and must do all that I have to do to day, to-morrow,
Wednesday, & Thursday.

ii   That this Week is my last clear one of Preparation and of
Disciplining myself properly for a very long time, the best
opportunity so far as I can see that I shall have till Passion
Week comes round again.

And that if I neglect it, I may not improbably thereby disorder
altogether & most certainly do serious injury to all prospect for
keeping down το της καλοκαγαθιας ἤδη αυξανομενον κακον [*the
already growing evil of gentlemanliness*] in as much as the annihilation
& extirpation of all my false shame & miserable approbativeness
& degraded dependency in rebus gentlemanlicis [*in gentlemanly
matters*] is absolutely ἀναγκαιον [*necessary*] to this object; without
which no other sorts of ὑλη [*matter*], supposing them obtained
without it, (as my B⟨alliol⟩ Scholarship etc. at Rugby) can be of
service.

And that if I fail in this second great trial, as I did in the first, I
dare not look or hope for another, that in all probability it must fix
my character for life & probably my happiness or misery for ever:
[* * *]

fo. 25^v In addition to this

iii   That next Week I shall have a great many excitements, and
temptations very probably.

iv   That many persons of the most advanced piety and goodness
are this week engaged in all sorts of self-denial, & mortification, fasting from food & sleep, amusement & society—
Newman for instance, whose errors as we believe them to be

fo. 26^r must not make me ever forget how far he is above me in
goodness and piety, and wisdom too, tho⟨ugh⟩ in certain
points we with less power may by our advantages be nearer
the real truth, and though less wise have more wisdom.
Rather for the present should I endeavour to forget all such
matters, and to try and look only at my own terrible sins and

wickednesses past, & miserable corruption now, and seek not
to find out the true sense of disputed Scripture or evolve
doubtful doctrines, but to obtain more and more of that Spirit
of God which hateth all sin & brings us to love Holiness and
Christ and makes us able to overcome the one for the sake of   fo. 26ᵛ
the other: which will help me

—to be attentive in Chapel
—to make good use of my d⟨evotion⟩ time
—to be independent of man's ill opinion in society etc.
—to make God's will my motive in all I do
—not to be excited by praise from Ward or any one else
—nor by thinking I have got on well, & left a favourable
   impression on anyone
—nor by thinking that I have made much progress in reading
—nor by believing myself clever interp⟨retation⟩ etc. if ever   fo. 27ʳ
   I am forced to talk about them with Ward or any one else
—nor to be depressed by the reverse of these four
—not to let any vague feeling of despondency or mistrust come
   so much over me as to prevent my working
—nor any feeling of idle humility—a sort of presumptuous self-
   complacent laziness
—to conquer laziness & greediness

I think most of my misdoings & misgivings will come under these
causes, or heads.

                          1 o'clock

[∗ ∗ ∗ 1 John 5: 4 *quoted*]

I have spent nearly an hour in making out the arrangement &   fo. 27ᵛ
division of the four accounts of this Week. Certainly I have acted
wrong in letting so much time be taken up by it, and I almost
think even in touching such a matter at all in my present weak
state. It would at any rate, have been a piece of self-denial, and as
such I must practise it henceforth.

I do certainly find it difficult to find myself proper self-denials so as
not to weaken myself too much: but I have taken but little thought
about it as yet. And there are certainly a good many things—
reading subjects one does not fancy—putting aside those one   fo. 28ʳ
does, e.g. Horace & Bentley, and such luxuries as walking round
the Parks wh⟨ich⟩ I have taken twice to day, & going to Tylden
wh⟨ich⟩ I have just done.

In short now I come to look more closely I seem to have passed a most unthinking time on these points: without doubt it has been a most luxurious day on the whole, more especially after 1, and worse again after Chapel, i.e. so soon as ever I began to get tired. Indeed, my eating has been quite luxurious, and less fasting than most days hitherto.

To morrow morning I must find time to consider this subject & see what I can furnish myself with.

$\frac{1}{4}$ to 11

fo. 28ᵛ **Tuesday in PASSION WEEK [April 10]**

I have done most foolishly and left myself scarcely a good $\frac{1}{4}$ hr to consider all I have to consider. I am greatly fear I have been resting on my oars & going down the stream fast.

$\frac{1}{4}$ to 3

Again I have been unwise, and not be [*sic*] at all watchful to keep things so as to be able to gather up humility & consciousness of Sin, so that my 5 o'cl. skiffing has but made me worse.

I feel in good health & improving. Surely it ought to make me humble to think that I, so far as I can see, deserve nothing but fo. 29ʳ weakness & ill-health for a long time to come. So, also ought the example of Ward, & the thought of Newman this week. But I cannot get them to do so now.

Up to 1 o'clock I got on pretty well, excepting that I was careless in Chapel, and not very watchful. But having chiefly by miscalculation left myself barely $\frac{3}{4}$ hr for being by myself, and having from a mistaken fancy & I am afraid a dislike to other things in comparison taken up the Gospels to finish for Ward I went on so as to leave myself scarce $\frac{1}{4}$ hr over. I could have hardly calculated on an active day, with having to spend 2 hrs with Ward fo. 29ᵛ and to read Stanley's Essay, for my Morning's work . . . But I think if I had had time to look forward I sho⟨uld⟩ have given up reading Stanley's E⟨nglish⟩ E⟨ssay⟩ altogether, which wo⟨uld⟩ have given me a good 2 hrs for being by myself. Yet I think I was not wrong in lying in bed till Ch⟨apel⟩ time. However it is clear that it wo⟨uld⟩ have been the wisest plan, & indeed quite necessary,—now. And I ought to have thought of it last night.

I have been careless at both Chapels, much wanting in my d⟨evotion⟩ time—and in fact at one time or other guilty in all the points specified [* * *], except those of depression—I have also done most sinfully, in eating, quite greedily, at dessert.

[* * * * *]

WEDNESDAY IN PASSION WEEK [April 11]

fo. 30ᵛ

[* * * * *]

There is no especial mention of what our Lord did on this day, nor the following till the Evening.

—Two silent nights and days
In calmness for his far seen hour he stays

I feel pretty certain that I have given myself already quite enough enjoyment for my health, and I may & therefore must now take to completer fasting and self-denial.

fo. 31ʳ

[* * * * *]

Perhaps the most beneficial thing I can do will be to read the N⟨ew⟩ T⟨estament⟩—solely with a view to God's hatred of sin. If more especially the Gospels as they show our Lord's character in this light.

fo. 31ᵛ

St. Matth. XVI. 13 to 28 is instructive in this way, as showing the immediate change of our Lord's language to Peter. Surely one may attach an idea of exceeding sternness, and, what in man, would be anger, and a hatred of Sin such as none but God could have or could dare to express to the awful rebuke

fo. 32ʳ

[* * * Mt 16, 13–28 quoted]

This will bear a very close examination.

fo. 32ᵛ

Anything that shews God's hatred of sin, the sinfulness regardless of & godlessness of ὁ κοσμος [*the world*] the absolute necessity of giving up the things ἐν τῳ κοσμῳ [*in the world*], & seeking God only, i.e. the utter uselessness & absurdity of διψυχια [*double-mindedness*] is most useful to me: and there is, I am sure, a very great deal.

I must take care not to seek to be brilliant in conversation, nor yet again to be lazy & indolently self-indulgent to my own dulness.

1 o'cl.

I do not seem to have got on very well to day—[* * *]—but I have not been well, having had indigestion, simply I believe by my

fo. 33ʳ

own greediness yesterday at Moncrieff's, and headache. So perhaps it is better than I think for I seem to have been more active a great deal for my strength than yesterday, and my illness will be beneficial as humbling me. [* * *]

fo. 33ᵛ I am not an innocent sufferer, but am rather a sinful & silly δυψυχος [*double-minded person*]. For if I had not been so, I should never have cared for the ill impression I might happen to leave on the gentlemenλικωτατοι [*the most gentlemanly people*]

[*   *   *   *   *]]

I incline to think that I give too much time to my j⟨ourna⟩l & too little to other things; which are the more important, that I have only to-morrow's interval before Newman's Good Friday Communion.

fo. 34ʳ THURSDAY in PASSION WEEK

Ap⟨ril⟩ 12th.

[* * * Jas 1: 7–8 *quoted*]

I think I had no business after my walk with Moncrieff to go & spend a whole hr in reading the Pilot. I believe it partly upset me, & turned me out of my road, otherwise I should have been more cautious at Waldegrave's to avoid brilliancy etc. in conversation, which as it was I gave way to most foolishly. And this again perhaps has been the cause of my not getting Ward on so well tonight as this Morning, which may be to him the cause of great trouble. [* * *]

fo. 34ᵛ [Friday April 13]

[*   *   *   *   *]]

fo. 35ʳ I have had a long talk with Waldegrave & Brodie from 9 to near 12—chiefly about high Matters—Froude—Immediate Conversion—The Apostacy [* * *] & conseq⟨uent⟩ inapplicability of Scripture Promises & Threats to us in their whole sense. I am afraid it was all folly to try and enter into it—a few decided expressions were quite enough for Froude's benefit— and my thoughts about other things are so exceeding crude, that

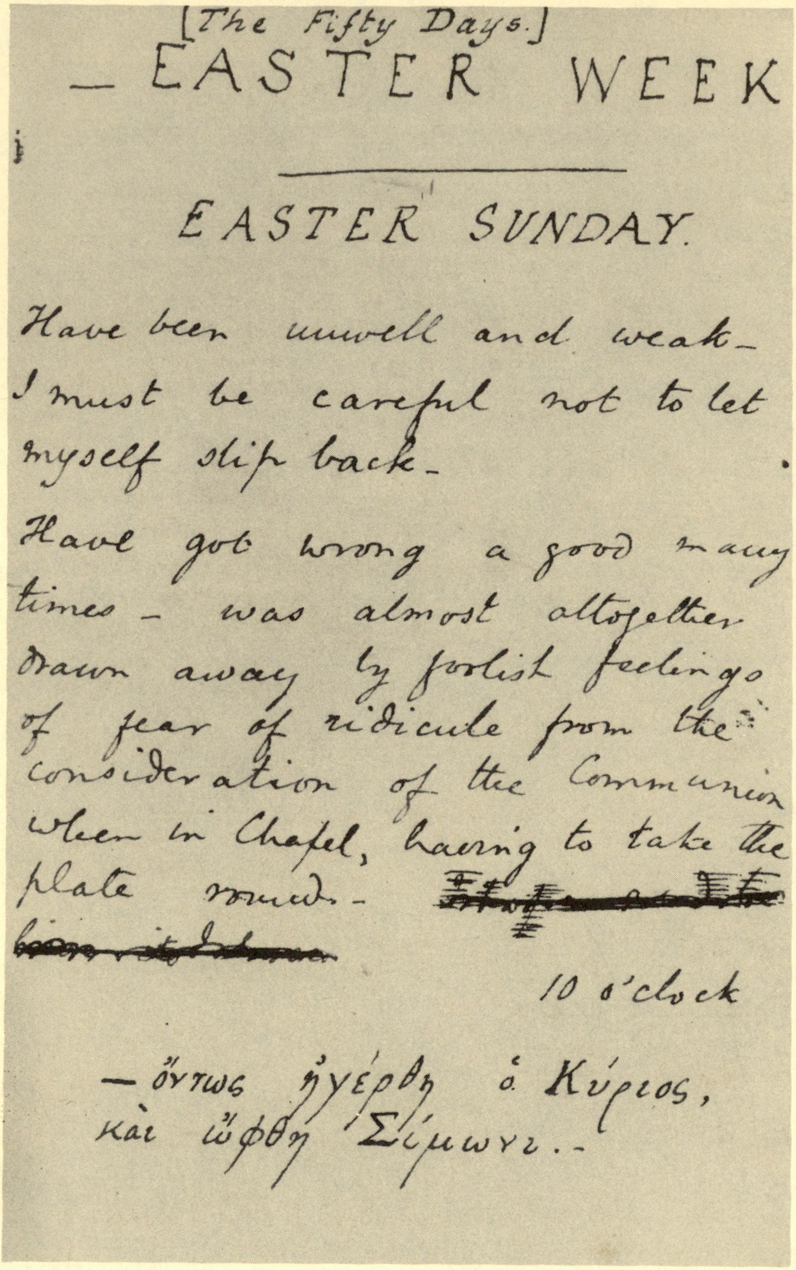

— EASTER WEEK

EASTER SUNDAY.

Have been unwell and weak —
I must be careful not to let
myself slip back —

Have got wrong a good many
times — was almost altogether
drawn away by foolish feelings
of fear of ridicule from the
consideration of the Communion
when in Chapel, having to take the
plate round —

10 o'clock

— ὄντως ἠγέρθη ὁ Κύριος,
καὶ ὤφθη Σίμωνι. —

Fig. 2 Clough's first Easter at Balliol

to argue about them with two persons is mere folly. More fo. 35ᵛ
especially when I have so little power over myself as to day I have.

12 o'cl.

I have been very tired & done up all to-day: but have been careless more than in proportion, I fear by a good deal. Have let myself read the Pilot, from 12 to near 2, and then in walking with Tylden wh⟨ich⟩ was fr⟨om⟩ 2 to 4 was not very well under orders, and had to spend fr⟨om⟩ 6 to near 8 at Round's—and then after that had Tylden here till 9. So that I greatly fear I have passed an utterly unprofitable day: to what degree sinful I cannot tell, but certainly so to a very considerable one.

I gave up last night all thought of going to communion, on Ward's fo. 36ʳ notion: but I believe it would have been best, as things were. [* * * Gal. 6: 9 *quoted*]

Saturday EASTER EVE April 14

At length the worst is o'er, & Thou art laid fo. 36ᵛ
  Deep in thy darksome bed—

[*　*　*　*　*]

This day also I fear I have wasted a great deal of. From about 2½ fo. 37ʳ to 4 was most unprofitably spent in a sort of idle hesitation like yesterdays, not knowing whether I ought to let myself relax yet unwilling to try any exertion. Again after dinner I let myself get careless, so that in the moment of trial about Scott's Catechetic I was degradingly mean & dependent, insomuch as to spoil my Chapel time & some more after—But I have been greatly helped by many happy occurrences.

It has been indeed a poor week compared with my hopes.

¼ p. 10

The Fifty Days
EASTER WEEK

fo. 37ᵛ

[April 15]

EASTER SUNDAY

Have been unwell and weak—I must be careful not to let myself slip back.

Have got wrong a good many times—was almost altogether

drawn away by foolish feelings of fear of ridicule from the consideration of the Communion when in Chapel, having to take the plate round.

10 o'clock

[* * * Luke 24: 34 *quoted*]

fo. 38ʳ **EASTER MONDAY** April 16th

I have been careless & I fear hardly even δίψυχος [*double-minded*], but wholly given up to τα ἐν τῳ κοσμῳ [*wordly matters*], which is so much the more hateful as I seem to have had but little to struggle against, and most, nay all my yesterday σκανδαλα [*stumbling-blocks*] removed. It has sprung from my old fault of neglecting morning dev⟨otio⟩ns altogether precisely as last Tuesday.

[* * * * *] ½ p. 3 o'cl.

fo. 38ᵛ Whatever be the amount of my guilt to day it is clear that I have, as so often before, abused God's great goodness to me this day.

Most truly indeed I, who have kept no fast, must not now dare to keep feast. I *will* be up tomorrow, hap what will, by ¼ p. 7, and will also have from 20′ to 10° to 20′ to 11 by myself before I go to Ward. [* * * Luke 13: 24 *quoted*]

Let me not trust therefore to my long series of resolutions—as I am

fo. 39ʳ I fear but too apt to do. [* * * Luke 13: 27 *quoted*]

11 o'c

EASTER TUESDAY April 17th

I have been very foolish again at Tylden's breakfast.

10 o'cl. a.m.

Again very foolish in losing a most precious ¼ hr at Fox's.

2 o'cl.

I have been exceedingly wandering and unfixed—but that I am very weak bodily it wo⟨ul⟩d be exceeding bad. It is not right at all as it is.

fo. 39ᵛ Sᵗ Luke from XII–XIV is very useful in many parts to people like me with good resolutions & an inconsistent course of halting, double-minded conduct.

[* * * Luke 14: 35 *quoted*.]

½ p. 2.

Again I have let myself get into presumptuous feelings from my way at Uncle Alf⟨red⟩'s & more still, the consideration of poor Tylden. And then again I ought to be strengthened by Ward's noble example. But I do not know whether I ought to try & force my feelings round, more for my own comfort than anything else it seems to be.

11 o'cl.

Wednesday in EASTER week   Apr⟨il⟩ 18th   fo. 40ʳ

I have let my foolish presumptuous feelings go on without any regular fight, and now I have pretty well got rid of them. [* * *] But I do not quite see just now what line we ought to take, and how far they should be regarded as quite extraneous things not to be meddled with—quite separate from our 'Reflection' or Reason which one must evidently strive to keep up in his sovereign power over all these feelings—so far as they come forth in real actual manifestations. It is a very difficult subject—& I dare not now fo. 40ᵛ think of it—or it will make me quite vain & puffed up—but I do not wish to lose wholly these facts & feelings I have now, as they may be useful in my induction.

With dining at Uncle A⟨lfred⟩'s, Ward & Brodie I am kept up fo. 41ʳ later than I have been a long time. [* * *]

12 o'cl.

[April 19]   Thursday in EASTER Week   fo. 41ᵛ

I have got letters to write to

Vaughan—to day. V
Burbidge ⎫
Conybeare ⎬ per Fox, Monday
Walrond ⎭
C. B. C⟨lough⟩
my Father

Horace
Algebra . . .
Homer Il⟨iad⟩ I–XII—
Euclid I–VI—

[*   *   *   *   *]

I am exceedingly tired & done up ὕπνου και καματου [*with sleep and* fo. 42ʳ

fatigue]—have been at work all day with Ward—letter-writing, &
Tylden—one continued series of exertions, almost: this is rather
fortunate: I only hope I have done no harm; for, alas, this work is
not so clearly God's work as my old task at Rugby: there is not
more opportunity, I think, for δυψυχια [*double-mindedness*] insinuat-
ing itself—much; but far more for mis-trust.

10 p.m.

fo. 42ᵛ [April 20]   Friday in EASTER week

I have got up. I do not know how or why, with a very bad temper,
to be fought with.

9 o'cl.

I have now come into a state of over-confidence which may united
as it is with great want of self control may bring me I know not
into what misery.

2 o'cl.

Be not high-minded; but fear.

I have been foolish this Evening at Uncle A's; chiefly from wishing
to pull up my spirits for the occasion lest they sh⟨oul⟩d think ill of
me: but after all it matters very little, as I cannot help it. I have
been in a weak poorly State, which I hope is one great Cause of it.

fo. 43ʳ [April 21]   [*   *   *   *   *]
Saturday in EASTER week

My wickedness & weakness have gone their full length.

I think I must have gone wrong in giving up so little time
yesterday to dev⟨otio⟩n. My fears at 2 o'cl. were quite just, but
my strength was so small from bodily fatigue, that it required a
much greater time of d⟨evotio⟩n to produce sufficient support.
And the indulging for so many hrs the foolish feelings of last night
fo. 43ᵛ was enough to upset all moral strength altogether. My only way
was to Sit up & try to regain something & this I will do, and must
do, in any like emergency henceforth.

[*   *   *   *   *]

fo. 44ᵛ With regard to the matter which put me out last night; it is
certainly a difficult question. I cannot trust myself at all, to there

being no mixture of foolish over-desire of leaving a good impression on them: & to indulge such is most hurtful, as I have seen: yet again it is clearly my duty to be cheerful & not spoil their pleasure by more bad spirits than I cannot prevent.

It comes again to the old difficulty of cases where Sanctification & 'Duty-proper' clash. Is it possible that it may be one of the punishments all Sin must involve on even repentant sinners, that fo. 45ʳ the very things they are bound to do will hurt them—that the very things that are best for their spiritual improvement are such as they may not use. It comes in the end, like the questions of Exception, to the Grand Question of the Nature of Good and Evil; I rather think, at least, it does. How far is a man bound to sacrifice his own highest interests, to those of Society in general? seems to be a still further question upon that grand one; however, all I can do fo. 45ᵛ is to pray for the removal of my δυψυχια [*double mindedness*] and to let myself be stupid wherever my particular duty does not require the reverse. [* * *]

1 o'cl.

The point to be struggled for is to conquer my great sense of pain fo. 46ʳ & embarrassing distress at not 'showing well' and if this trial will help me towards this object, it will be no loss.

How little however should any of these feelings be able to touch me, when I ought to be wholly given up to the remembrance of my sinfulness before God.

So ends my Easter Week—not one of the best order, most certainly.

½ p. 11

[April 22] fo. 46ᵛ

viii. Low SUNDAY, or 1st after EASTER

It seems quite clear that for the present occasion I cannot overcome my foolish compound of μικροψυχια μετ' ἀρεσκειας [*small-mindedness and complaisance*]—which has been tormenting me so grievously these two days & this morning also a little. All I can do therefore is to try and be patient under it & seek not to mind appearing such a poor contemptible selfish being, as I must do. And most assuredly a very great part of which I feel on the subject is very much of a contemptibly selfish nature; wounded self-conceit and mortified vanity & disappointed desire of pleasing fo. 47ʳ

continually brought about by its being my duty to seek to please
and my being unable from μικροψυχια [*small-mindedness*] to bear up
when I fail at all in so doing.

Altogether it is just like my state when Arnold was here: only I
seem worse. This however, I must remember, by no means
implies a worse state generally. It almost seems as if as one goes on,
all one's former earthly supports drop off, & so leave one
seemingly & in our apparent actions & untoward tokens of
strength in a worse, whereas really when we are weak, then are we
strong.

fo. 47ᵛ   11 o'cl.

I have been nearly upset again at Ward's—how or why I hardly
know.

[* * * Gal. 6: 9 quoted]

And how long or how steadily & diligently have I been at work,
that I sho⟨ul⟩d dare to complain in my heart? Have I not been
frequently letting my wrong feelings so grow on me as to carry me
into actual wickedness? Have I not been continually careless
about my health & neglectful of my dev⟨otio⟩ns? How long ago is
it that I was a wilful rebel & outcast? is it two days or three?

fo. 48ʳ Then let me be contented under whatever afflictions (I am
ashamed of so grand a word) may come on me: for I am sure I
deserve much worse pain: and let me be careful and not neglectful
in my dev⟨otio⟩ns that I may not be really, or not be harassed
with the thought that I am cast out & deprived of all assistance
from God.

[*   *   *   *   *]

fo. 49ʳ   —Newman on the Gainsaying of Korah
            —April 22 My Father's Birthday also Uncle Charles'.

fo. 49ᵛ ix. Monday [April] 23rd.

Besides letters to Rugby and home & to C. B. C⟨lough⟩, I have
Mathematics to do all this week. I have to give a Wine Party &
Breakfast.

[* * * Gal. 6: 9 *quoted*]

                                                        11 o'cl. a.m.

A very happy time. δεκωραιος χρονος [*ten hours*] with Ward: and on the whole, I hope, well spent though not without many little foolish vanities & indolences.

I have found out from Ward the chief source of my difficulties & perplexities [above]. viz. a false idea, presumptuous & rationalistic, that what we are to do here is to make ourselves holy, supposing that we can acquire qualities making us fit for Heaven, & that to acquire such is our grand object. Whereas it is really to do God's will to love i[a] him & ii [b] our neighbour. fo. 50ᵛ

It may however be annexed as a punishment to a past course of sin, that the Performance of God's will sho⟨ul⟩d interfere with our own spiritual advancement.

[* * * * *]

Easter Univ⟨ersity⟩ Term fo. 51ʳ
Tuesday, April 24th

It is indeed advisable that I sho⟨ul⟩d set to my work as soon as possible, but I believe honestly that I am so weak & fatigued that I had better give up my Proposed Wine Party for to-day.

½ p. 10 A.M.

I have been with Ward from 10½ to 4½ & again from 7 to 11, with Rogers also. I am in consequence of this latter stay sadly—wickedly I ought to say, puffed up with vain & complacent feelings—from which Good Lord, deliver me.

I must try and realize all the trials that are coming on me, and all that I much brace myself up to. Again all that I have failed in

[* * * * *]

Lastly I may call to mind all the love & kindness which I so unworthily have met with—more especially Home—Burbidge—Charles—Uncle Charles—& Alfred. fo. 51ᵛ

All this to aid me in coming to a proper sense of my Sinfulness, or rather to avoid the increase of my wicked Self-Complacency.

½ p. 11 P.M.   fo. 52ʳ

xi) Wednesday, April 25th
—St. Mark's day—
(also Sᵗ Polycarp's day [Evans])

Psalms *XV, XVI, XIX*

I am quite μεστος της κακιστης νοσου [*full of the foul disease*] of Self-Complacency.

[*   *   *   *   *]

fo. 53ᵛ I have been to Binsey Chapel, which has quite taken my fancy at present. So much so that I have been wasting a full half hour in letting myself run on about it. It is quite clear, I have done very wrong: ½ hr, it is nearer a whole one I believe, is not easily regained. Let me call to mind again that Term with all its trials of
fo. 54ʳ my ἀρεσκεια, μικροψυχια, διψυχια κ.τ.λ. [*complaisance, small-mindedness, double-mindedness* etc.] will be full on me at any rate next week—and that I purpose being at Newman's Communion on Sunday next. With all this before me & with health but just restored here I am I wasting it as soon as given.

I must be up to-morrow so as to have 10 min. at any rate for pr⟨ayer⟩ which I neglect most wantonly.

[*   *   * Eph. 4: 30, Luke 13: 24 *quoted*]

fo. 54ᵛ   xii) Thursday, April 26th

I feel in good health & full command of all my faculties—God preserve me from presumptuous use of them—I must try and bring myself down to-morrow. Perhaps however I am hardly broad awake: as I do *not* feel quite full *command* of my faculties, though I do feel full *presence* of them: my 'reflection' seems, as it were, to have left the chair for an interval: i.e. tho⟨ugh⟩ present, mingled with the herd of impulses & feelings. So I must try and find a Vice-President to keep order. Or rather put the rule into the hands of a Committee of Safety, where President Reason shall
fo. 55ʳ only be a sort of Centre, and not αὐτοκρατωρ [*dictator*]: Fear, Shame, Reverence, and Love shall be its principal Members.

I believe this is true: but it seems & is really great trifling, when I remember my wickedness and danger.

O Lord God, who seest that I am, as it were, in sleep, open to all impressions good or evil, and greatly liable to be given up thereto without power to controul myself: govern thou my heart & guard the entrances thereto, give me good thoughts, and keep me from
fo. 55ᵛ evil ones: or so aid & support me that I may be enabled to keep my words & deeds above their power.

I feel certain now this is wrong—I lose my time of dev⟨otio⟩n utterly.

½ p. 11

I have lost I do not know how much way simply through my foolishness and wickedness last night. And moreover it may conduce not improbably a good deal to Ward's low spirits this Morning. [* * *]

xiii, Friday—April 27th   fo. 56ʳ
Last day of College Vacation

I have been not very strong to-day, and have done very little written 2 letters and had a Wine-pty. I did not behave altogether as I ought; [* * *] but better perhaps than I might have hoped. I fear there was great allay of fear of ridicule in my motives & supports. However I must rub it off by a constant succession of parties. [* * *]

All annoyance, and vexation, and weariness, and sinking of heart, and painful apathy & weakness is far less, I should ever fo. 56ᵛ remember, than I deserve: and if, after all my wickedness & obstinate resistance of God's holy Spirit, I get safe at the price of the greatest pain & misery, it will be, so far as I can see, an undeserved & exceeding blessing. So I must not mind tho⟨ugh⟩ Ward, & Lake externally, and all my μικροψυχια & ἄρεσκεια [*small-mindedness and complaisance*] internally vex me daily & hourly, though with these trials & with illness all plan & regularity & pleasant industrious habits be cut up, and hopes of the future constantly darkened by a cloud of present fears. I must try and make up my mind to all this, and that without pride, simply as my fo. 57ʳ punishment justly due.

Trials of Temper (a) with Lake & Ward
   (b) with having my plans & regularities knocked on the head (i)
   by them or (ii) by illness or (iii) by having too much to do.

Trials of μικροψυχια [*small-mindedness*] (a) with the Master
  with my Wine Parties
  at the decade
  at parties at Jes⟨us⟩ Coll⟨ege⟩ or calls on Lowe etc.

Then I shall be sure to have also Temptations to Excitement &
Presumption, or Ease & Indolence

> at Parties
> at the Decade

fo. 57ᵛ   In case of uncertain health
and constantly enticing desires
> to put off disagreable duties
> to indulge in pleasures too long
> to neglect dev⟨otio⟩ns

I will try and hope as little as possible of this Term: if I only look to
have what I deserve, it will be little enough of pleasure. [* * *
Galatians 6: 9 *quoted*]

fo. 58ʳ   xiv)—Saturday, April 28th—
First day of College Term-time

My temptation to day has been to indolence & ease, not being
quite well: And I have, I see clearly, given way to it: so as to
indulge myself too long in pleasures; & to neglect dev⟨otio⟩ns.

Owing to Lake's return with the account of the way Arnold speaks
of Froude, and the news of S⟨impkinso⟩n's misfortune I have got
into a sort of feeling, which I am strongly tempted to plume myself
upon as religious: but it is not so: and I must not mistake it: and if
fo. 58ᵛ it was, what then? the object I should strive after is Self-Controul,
not Feelings for wh⟨ich⟩ however I may & sho⟨uld⟩ be grateful.

[*   *   *   *   *]

fo. 59ᵛ   xv) 2nd SUNDAY after EASTER, April 29th

My temptation to-day has been a presumptuous, unparticularis-
ing frame of mind: which strengthened itself on some hastiness of
manner with Highton & Jowett after Comm⟨union⟩ this morning, & I have been unable to shake off ever since.

5 o'cl.

This has coloured all I have done, and had an effect I do not know
how great on my actions. This evening in especial it brought on
me a spirit of peevishness with Ward, wh⟨ich⟩ I fear has given
fo. 60ʳ him great pain. My self-complacency however I am glad to feel
rather lessened to night: tho⟨ugh⟩ I dare not believe that I have
had any hand in reducing it. [* * *]

xvi) Monday, 30th of April

> Seek we no more, content with these
> Let present Rapture, Comfort, Ease
> As heaven shall bid them come and go.

My temptation to day seems to have been, I think, from having no very decided faulty feelings & tendencies to strive against, & yet not enough health to make me very zealous & much encourage, to lapse into a sort of aimless, indolent State, of practical *Αθεισμος* [*atheism*] nearly; to which also my unwellness tended.

On this before dinner a sort of *μικροψυχια* [*small-mindedness*] began to spring up, followed at Chapel by Presumptuous & when with Ward of Peevish feelings, & now by Complacency at having cast   out this last.

Before this I wasted much time from my sluggishness & have rather neglected again my dev⟨otio⟩ns: and I was very inattentive in Chapel. Besides awaking in an over-indulgent State wh⟨ich⟩ made me lie in bed till ½ p. 8 & led to evil dreams. [* * *]

xvii) Tuesday, MAY-DAY
Sᵗ. Philip's & Sᵗ James' Day

Owing to a very bad night, & continual feverishness bodily, my great trial has been to keep down flighty, presumptuous thoughts.

I did very, very wrong this morning in letting myself leave the slightest root behind: whereas I rather encouraged it.

I was not careful either afterw⟨ar⟩ds in several cases.

And now it is so strong upon me that I cannot do anything.

God only knows what degree of trial my illness by itself has been: it is however certain that I have done unwisely, & not unavoidably so.

May he forgive me, & either remove these feelings or if not give me patience & strength to controul myself under them. [* * *]

Wednesday, May the 2nd.

I have been careless all to-day: & not tried at all to overcome my temptation. It arises chiefly from bodily feverishness and weakness. I must arouse myself and be active, ready & vigorous: not looking for pleasure, nor avoiding things unpleasant. The reason of it all is that I neglected my morning dev⟨otions⟩: as usual.

Thursday, May the 3rd

fo. 63^r I have gone my full length—precisely in the same way as twice before, Friday before Palm Sunday, & Friday in Easter Week.

Friday, May the 4th

I did not get on properly even yesterday. My plan must be to day to do at any rate something which is against my natural tendencies.

I find myself terribly sluggish & unwilling to exert myself for myself. Even to day I have not given at all due time to considering my ways. I must strive to-morrow & Sunday to regain my active & ready views, & cast out this wretched διψυχια [*double-mindedness*]. How conceited & wicked I have been!

½ p. 10 p.m.

fo. 63^v   xxi) May the 5th—, Saturday

I have got letters to write to J⟨ohn⟩ P. G⟨ell⟩ C⟨harles⟩ B. C⟨lough⟩ [* * *]

I have to prepare every week

 3 lectures in Rhetoric,
 2 in Terence
 1 in History
and 1 Essay to do

Also answers to Catech⟨etics⟩ Lect⟨ure⟩ and a Divinity Exercise for the Term.

fo. 64^r Next I have

 2 lectures in Algebra &
 1 in Trigonometry—weekly
and to prepare for the schools
 12 Books of Homer—
 3 of Euclid—
 6 Plays of Terence—

[*   *   *   *   *]

fo. 64^v How I have got on to day I hardly know: I have certainly been more what I was 3 days back—more active & hopeful—but I have been self-indulgent in several things, self denying in scarce any.

I must set myself rules, or all will go wrong.

I have gone wrong from my very childhood, I have abused God's mercy continually, at this day my motives are such as I dare not examine, I have lost much time & opportunity, I have been unclean, selfish, cowardly, conceited, and still am so, I have done much harm & committed great & crying sins. Yet I am still undecided, & withal self complacent.

xxii) Third SUNDAY AFTER EASTER, May 6th

I am still in a very inactive & I fear δυψυχ⟨ος⟩ [*double-minded*] state: I get but little time to myself, and what I get I use but little.

Monday, May the 7th

To day has I hope been better on the whole, but I have had no trials at all to speak of. For my general tone of mind & purpose I can say little good—active but not more.

Tuesday, May the 8th

Again—careless & pleasure-seeking—wandering at m⟨orni⟩ng dev⟨otio⟩ns—& filled with complacent & presumptuous thoughts now. I fear I have abused great opportunities.

Wednesday, May 9th

I hope to get l⟨ectures⟩ incl⟨uded⟩ at any rate 5 hrs. beside a letter written.

9–11 Tylden lost me ½ hr & I was not steady at all, but worked at what I settled
12–1 Writing Catechetics, unsteady—
2¼–3 Writing to Gell
3–4 With a few interruptions from Ward, read Odyssey

I have got 5 hrs, but only poor ones.

I must learn more & more to give myself heartily up to whatever may befall me, however distasteful or disappointing.

Edm. Foulkes & J. Farrar put my idle ways terribly to shame.

Thursday, May the 10th

Either bef⟨ore⟩ 8 or after 9. 1 hr dev⟨otio⟩ns but unsteady

Between 9 & 12 2½ hrs. Scott's L⟨atin⟩ Pr⟨ose⟩—Terence—Algebra. 2 hrs only & not very steady.

Between 2 & 4 1½ hr. Odyssey, or, if tired, letter to H. W. W⟨alrond⟩—barely 1 hour.

4–9¼ Ward. ex⟨cept⟩ Chap⟨el⟩

My total of work has been barely 5 hrs, l⟨ectures⟩ incl⟨usive⟩: the cause of my not getting another was chiefly an accidental σκανδαλον [*scandal*] given to Ward.

[*   *   *   *   *]

Friday, May the 11th
        7½–9
    10–10½ Very negligent & scanty
    10½–11 Rhetoric
    12–4 essay   Lost nearly 2 hrs

I think I have been in worse health to-day than usual. I have certainly got on worse. I cannot have lost less than 2 hrs between 12 & 4, which assuredly sho⟨uld⟩ not be given up without consideration when I have so much to do. So that 4½ l⟨ectures⟩ in⟨cluded⟩ is the most I can say. I do not feel & have not this long time felt my due strength. Assuredly I do not deserve it.

Saturday, May the 12th
    9–10 Dev⟨otio⟩ns 9¼ to ¼11 wrote only
    10–11 Whately—or the M⟨aster⟩—
    11–12½ Ward lecture
                12–2
    12½–2 Terence or Wha⟨tely⟩
    6½.–8 Terence   Lost

I have done hardly anything of what I intended.

I have not got on rightly with Ward, nor are my feelings quite what they sho⟨uld⟩ be towards him. I must be ware of ever putting on the least show of feeling I am not sure of. I have striven, but not rightly. I sho⟨uld⟩ have roused myself first. I have in consequence got into a sort of conceited insincere frame of feeling. It is without doubt very hard to get on right with him—but I ought to be very glad to have opportunity of doing any good.

Fourth SUNDAY after EASTER
        10–½
    12¾–4½ was with Ward all except ¼ hr.
        6½–9½ do

I see many things to be done, little time, little strength, & many σκανδαλα [*scandals*]—Talking with Ward, when I am not strong, leaves me in a sort of φαντασια ὑποκρισεως [*fancy of hypocrisy*] state. I suppose it must be disregarded: But it is the worse as it affects my devotions. I feel sure it is a mere φαντασια [*fancy*], but that does not cure me.

I was very indolent & let myself go quite wrong at Chapel, was very inattentive & foolish. this I think must have been the Pr⟨incipium⟩ Morbi [*origin of the disease*].

I see more & more the strong need I have of being constant, & regular, steady & earnest in my dev⟨otio⟩ns. All the day dep⟨en⟩ds on my Morning one in Especial.

Monday—May the 14th— fo. 68ʳ

7–¾   was not up till 20′ to 8. d⟨evotio⟩ns
¼8–9   B⟨rea⟩kf⟨a⟩st—Lake—   very ill-tempered
9–10   Lecture
10–11
12½–2½ Terence
2½–4½ Slept
4½–8½ Ward's   Staid till near 9—
8½–9½
9½–10 Ward

My day has been very out of rule, but I believe was fairly too tired & done up

[*   *   *   *   *]

[1 Peter 1: 13–16 *quoted*]

Tuesday—May 15th fo. 69ʳ

7½ to 8
9 to 12 Dev⟨otio⟩ns/Math. I have worked besides 2 lectures about 2 hrs
2 to 4
6 to 6½ Catechet⟨ics⟩ Went to Newman's lecture
7½ to 9

My temptation this Morning seems to be t⟨o⟩w⟨ar⟩ds vanity & being elated.

I have been in a very dreamy, imagination-berid state all today— and I do not know the best thing for this.

But I am sure that I have done wrong in not working more than I
have.

Wednesday—May 16th

I have done little or nothing during the day, & am now come back
hot & excited from the Decade. This is I am sure wrong.

12 o'clock night

fo. 69ᵛ   <center>Thursday—May 17</center>

My Vanity is boiling up fearfully—this Decade work must be
looked to—

I had a terrible night with it

Friday—May 18.

    $8\frac{1}{2}$ to 9 D⟨evotio⟩ns—
    10–$10\frac{1}{2}$ D⟨evotio⟩ns
    $10\frac{1}{2}$–11 Loitered sadly
       12–4 Essay 3 hours—Calls
       4–$7\frac{1}{2}$ Wine-Party—Goulburn
    $8\frac{1}{2}$–$9\frac{1}{2}$ I have been loitering & taking my ease again:—am

now rather conceited: tho⟨ugh⟩ I was μικροψυχος [*mean-spirited*]
at the Wine Party, to a sad extent.

I have not been tempted so much to be idle to day—& have not
been—Have worked $3\frac{1}{2}$ hrs only, besides 2l⟨ectures⟩; but have
done well in them.

Altogether an easy kept poorly spent day.

fo. 70ʳ My Vanity is strong to night, & seems to have gathered strength of
late, thro⟨ugh⟩ Decade φαντασιαι κ.τ.λ. [*fancies etc.*]

Altogether I am sure I am going on very idly & badly: as I always
seem to do when I am not under regular rule as Massie's
Tutorage, e.g.—I have neglected to cultivate my Forethought:
and am I fear also relaxing from my Economical feelings and
generally from all sort of Self-Controul, beginning to be contented
with having turned the right way, & seemingly wishing to keep in
it with as little loss of worldly enjoyments as may be.—

I must indeed work.—

If I do my work decently to-morrow I may perhaps make a plan
for my remaining 3 Weeks.

I have perhaps read 2½ hours worth; not more certainly.   fo. 71ʳ

I have this w⟨ee⟩k read a little Terence, Aristotle, & Mathematics, & have written 4 letters.

My Average being c.l⟨ectures⟩ excl⟨uded⟩ not more than 3 hrs a day I sho⟨ul⟩d think.

XXXIV ROGATION—SUNDAY—or   fo. 71ᵛ
5th AFTER EASTER—
May—the 20th

```
  9–10   with Ward
10–10½  [with Ward]
11½–4                11½–12½  For the most p⟨ar⟩t loitered
                              away by myself
                     12½–2½  with Ward
                     2½–4    [with Ward] here, abstracted
                              XII Ch⟨apter⟩ 1 Sam⟨uel⟩
6½–9½  6½–8 Walking   with Ward
        8–9½      at tea with Ward
9½–10¾
```

I think & trust I have been tolerably active—but everything has been in a very small way.

Rogation Monday
May—the 21st

```
Up by 10 to 7
     8–9   Br⟨eakfast⟩ Party
9–10–11   Dev⟨otio⟩ns chiefly wasted
   11–1¼  Terence
   1¼–4   Walk
   4′–′7  Dinner & Party
   7–7½   With Lake
   8–8½   Terence
   8½–10  Lake—talk⟨in⟩g
```

Thus I have only had 2¾ W⟨or⟩k to day—I have let my bad   fo. 72ʳ
feelings get the rule even over my actions to a great degree: the best I can say is that I began well & have been 'doing' all day—tho⟨ugh⟩ not against altogether but more in obedience to wrong feelings. I have been very wrong in many things. I got out first between 1 & 11 thro⟨ugh⟩ carelessness.

Rogation Tuesday
May the 22^d

$7\frac{1}{2}$–8 Not up till 8   Thus I have only got about 2 hrs reading.
8–$\frac{4}{9}$9 Breakfast $8\frac{1}{4}$–9
$\frac{4}{9}$9–$9\frac{1}{2}$ Dev⟨otio⟩ns 8–$8\frac{1}{4}$
9–10 Ward & Algebra

Society—Lake & Ward. Br⟨ea⟩kf⟨as⟩t.

10–$10\frac{1}{4}$ Devotions to 11
$10\frac{1}{4}$–12 Fr⟨om⟩ 11–12 Algebra   Dinner about $4\frac{1}{2}$ hrs
2–3 Ward Algebra   Devotions $1\frac{1}{4}$
3–4 Skiffing   Skiffing $1\frac{1}{4}$
4–6 Dinner & Chapel   Newman
6–$\frac{1}{2}$ &c   Chapel $1\frac{1}{2}$
$6\frac{1}{2}$–$7\frac{1}{2}$ Newman Lectures 2
$7\frac{1}{2}$–8 Ward & Lake

fo. 72^v This is very bad & will never do for Little Go or anything else. I do not flourish in health either, but that I could not hope.

Rogation Wednesday [May 23]

Up to 8 only
7–9 Chapel   Thus I have read $3\frac{1}{2}$
9–11 Dev⟨otio⟩ns & Catechetics
12–1 History   Lecture 2
2–$3\frac{1}{2}$ Terence   Walk 3
$3\frac{1}{2}$–$4\frac{1}{4}$ Talboys etc   v.e.n. 1
$4\frac{1}{4}$–$5\frac{1}{2}$ Dinner etc   Chapel $1\frac{1}{2}$
$5\frac{1}{2}$–$6\frac{1}{4}$ Chapel—Terence   Meals $2\frac{1}{4}$
$6\frac{1}{4}$–$8\frac{1}{2}$ Walk
$8\frac{1}{2}$–$9\frac{1}{4}$ [Walk]

$13\frac{1}{4}$

fo. 73^r I am in a very bad way—utterly wanting in Earnestness for Goodness or for Truth, & influenced in all I do simply by a desire for Praise.

How to escape this evil in a place where all that is praised much is good is a very difficult problem.

I have, I hope, got on better to day, but I am very behind-hand indeed, & have I fear lost a good deal in real activity since this Book began. Were it not that I am unwell, there is much that wo⟨ul⟩d be wilful sin to-day.

I have been having a long talk with Congreve de rebus Newmaniticis [*on Newmanist matters*] supporting the ground Ward took that the Evidence of the existence of the Church System under Apostolical guidance is the sole ground disputable.   fo. 73ᵛ

But it seems to me now that the Ch⟨urch⟩ Syst⟨em⟩ doctrines are irreconcileable with Scripture, the Sacramental View e.g. spoken of very differently from the Doctrine of our Lord's Divinity. Which last is expressly stated in Sᵗ John, in a manner so far as I see not to be explained away on any apparent Mode of Expression or Conveying of Truth, such as does explain the use of the Sacr⟨amental⟩ Figures; nay further would on the Ch⟨urch⟩ Syst⟨em⟩ Literal Interpretation Principle make us believe things they did not in old times believe—e.g. Concerning Baptism.

Also I think the types 'Hebrews'—etc.—etc. are different subjects of rejection quia contra rationem sunt [*because they are against reason*] from the Incarnation, Atonement etc. etc., as these Violate the Principles of Reasoning, which the Atonement, nay even the Trinity, does not.

HOLY THURSDAY
or ASCENSION DAY—May 24th
fo. 74ʳ

I have been, I see, very careless with regard to this Communion— I have thought too little a great deal about my sins & corruption—and a great too much about τα ὑψηλα [*high matters*]— as great a σκανδαλον positively as the other negatively—Four times in this Book I have committed my worst sin—

Friday bef⟨ore⟩ Palm Sunday Ap⟨ril⟩ 6
Friday in Easter Week Ap⟨ril⟩ 20
Thursday after last Comm⟨union⟩ May 3
& Friday after Decade May 18

9–10½ Chapel. Ward   fo. 74ᵛ
10½–1 Pr⟨ayer⟩ Dev⟨otio⟩ns & Comm⟨union⟩
  1–2 Ward—Tylden
  2–2½ Terence
2½–4¼ Ward. Dinner
4¼–6 Terence
  6–8 Walk
  8–9 Ward [* * *]
Mem. to Make Some Rules—

DIARY 4

[Thursday, May 24]

I have to read 2½ Plays of Terence ⎫
        12 Books of Odyssey ⎬ by Tuesday fortnight
         3   ,,   ,, Euclid ⎭

I have an Analysis of ½ Aristotle's Rhetoric ⎫
       to do   ⎬ by Monday 4 weeks
     Abstract of 1 & 2 Samuel ⎭

I have 2 lectures in Algebra ⎫
     3   in Rhetoric ⎬ to prepare weekly
     1   in History ⎭

  Catechetical Answers ⎫
  2 Pieces of Latin or 1 & an Essay ⎬ to write

  2 lectures in Terence ⎫ to attend
  2 lectures in St John ⎭

fo. 1   Friday [after Ascension-day] May 25 ⟨1838⟩

Up by /8 only
  8–¾ Breakf⟨ast⟩ &c.
  ¾–9 Dev⟨otio⟩ns . . .
 9–10 Lecture
 10–½ Dev⟨otio⟩ns . . .
 ½–11 Aristotle . . .
11–12 Lecture
12–3 Terence . . .
 3–4½ Skiffing
4½–5½ Dinner
5½–6 Chapel
 6–7 V.E.N.
 7–9 Tea. W⟨ar⟩d—
 9–¾ Spec⟨ial⟩ Lat⟨in⟩—

Thus I have had about 3½ full reading, l⟨ectures⟩ excl⟨uded⟩.
              2 lectures
              6¼ Meals—Ex⟨ercise⟩—W⟨ar⟩d.
              1¼ Chapel & dev⟨otio⟩ns

$\frac{3}{4}$ Waste of Reading

———

$13\frac{3}{4}$

Active, but without much exercise of self-control: only a little at first. Latterly, tired: otherwise I sh⟨oul⟩d have been very wrong, as I am quite foolish & heedless, in not looking a head so as to prevent my being so late as I am. I have spoken uncharitably & presumptuously about Lake &c to Ward, and am rather full of self-complacency &c. and I am so tired that I cannot shake the bad feelings that pester me off, nor have the least feeling of their wickedness, so that vanity taints the least things I do.

Saturday. May 26

Up after a bad night by 8. Only had $4\frac{1}{2}$ hrs good sleep.

$8\frac{3}{4}$ Breakfast . . .

$8\frac{3}{4}$–10 D⟨evotio⟩ns. . . .

11–$\frac{1}{4}4$ Terence . . .

$\frac{1}{4}4$–$9\frac{1}{4}$ Dinner. Chapel Walk. Tea. W⟨ar⟩d.

Thus I have had $3\frac{1}{2}$ full, reading

    1 with the Master

    $6\frac{1}{2}$ M⟨ea⟩ls: Ex⟨ercise⟩: W⟨ar⟩d: &c

    $\frac{1}{2}$ Waste of R⟨eadin⟩g

    $1\frac{3}{4}$ Chapel &c

    ———

$13\frac{1}{4}$

Both last-night & tonight I have been very wasteful of the time after the Ac⟨coun⟩t.

I certainly did wrong in composing my disturbed self-conceit by Ward's r⟨ea⟩d⟨in⟩g my Essays. Also I was too wasteful of time. And I let in several bad feelings about Lake. I have not been at all steadfast & single minded; and have kept none of my hrs cleanly.   fo. 1ᵛ

Sunday after Ascension-day—May 27th

✳

I seem to have lost all notion of sin. I must keep fast every day to the end of term except Sundays & Holydays or else I shall never keep right.

$11\frac{1}{2}$–1 Ward

1–3 1 hr with W⟨ar⟩d 1 here but not doing much
6½–9 to 8¾ with W⟨ar⟩d here.

Thus my folly has already lost me a good deal of way in what I have on hand; as I sh⟨ou⟩ld have written to Burbidge, done my Catechetics, & also some of the Abstract had I been well.

fo. 2ʳ Monday. May 28

(up by) 7½–¾ D⟨evotio⟩ns . . .
              7¾–9 Br⟨eakfast⟩ with Brodie
          10–11 ½ hr D⟨evotio⟩ns . . .
                    Aristotle
          12–1½ Ward
          1½–2½ Union &c V.E.N.
          2½–3½ Ward . . .

Up to this hour I have, as I richly deserve, spent a very disagreable time—latterly full of tormenting thoughts about Ward taking up so much time, & my having so many things to do. Whereas I am sure that it is my own wickedness that loses me the time first of all, & then blames Ward for it.

¼4 to 10¼ with Ward.

I have got on rather better, but am in a miserable sort of state. It is all my own fault for having abused this Term so disgracefully: so I must be quite patient & thankful it is no worse. What do I not deserve?—

I have put off my Little-Go.— ½ p. 10

fo. 2ᵛ In another half-year I shall be 20. And with good impulses very early aroused I have been loitering & losing time & ground all the time. I have never yet gone forward for anything like a single year, steadily and consistently at all. My last one at Rugby was worse perhaps than any. My first at Oxford now nearly completed has been very like it.

It is five Years since My Confirmation:—five & a half since I contracted that wretched habit which still clings to me: by this I may measure how little I have really done: I have externally improved much no doubt, but that is a very uncertain rule.

In two years & a half I shall be going up for my degree: on which will depend not only my own but my father & mother's & sister's situation perhaps,—to a very great degree.

Tuesday, May 29

Up by ½ past 8

8½–9½ Breakfast
 9½–¾ D⟨evotio⟩ns
 ¾–10 Ward
10–¾   D⟨evotio⟩ns . . .
 ¾–12½ Catechetics L⟨ati⟩n Prose
12½–1 Ward
  2–6 Ex⟨ercise⟩ Dinn⟨er⟩ Chap⟨el⟩.
  6–½ Letter to Stanley
  ½–7½ Newman
 7½–9½ Ward

Thus my reading to day has been only 2 hrs:—chiefly so little, because I have been unwell certainly,—& it is a very just punishment. [* * *]

Wednesday. May 30th.

 8–9   Not up till ¼ p. D⟨evotio⟩ns . . .
 9–10 Breakfast—
10–11 Dev⟨otio⟩ns . . . Aristotle ½ hr
12–¼4 Missed my lecture at 1—talking to Ward περι ὑψηλων [*about high matters*] the whole time till 3: then business in the town.
 ¼4–9 Excepting ½hr at Chapel with Ward
 9–11½ Decade

I have clearly acted very sinfully today. Up to 12 all was right;—& promised very fairly then I acted wrong & almost wilfully so in beginning the talk with Ward, who himself quite abstained: then came the questionable point of missing lectures: then I got excited in my talk; & came under a state of feeling which has kept its hold on me throughout this time influencing all my actions: last of all I staid too long at the Decade, & from pure vanity, I believe.—I think I have been saying to myself such things as 'Oh, its no great harm'—'just for once' &c &c; forgetting that these things that are 'no great harm' are hateful to God & that they may be the means of ruining me everlastingly.—

Thursday, May 31st.—

I was not up till 9 which I think now was wrong:—

9–10 Breakfast, & ½ hr lost between Tylden & A Hobhouse.
10–11 D⟨evotio⟩ns.

My state today seems to be one of great excitability & no self-control.

11–6 11–3½ a letter & a half.—a lecture ½ hr talk with Ward.
   Terence 1 hr
3½–6 Ex⟨ercise⟩—Dressing—Chapel.
6–10 Dinner with Uncle Alfred, at which I got on very fairly,
   though not in a right state of feeling. I sh⟨oul⟩d rather say,
   under wrong feelings which were in part my motives.

fo. 4ʳ Friday,—the first of June.—

Was not up till ½ p. 9

9½–10½ Breakfast. Lake—
10½–11 Aristotle
11–12½ Dev⟨otio⟩ns . . .

I am full this Morning of vain Castle-buildings,—concerning the
Union,—for instance, that I sh⟨ou⟩ld come forward in it, & be a
great personage, & develope my views & be the leader of a great
party of disciples;—and concerning such things as writing comments on the Psalms—dividing them so as to be useful in the
different stages of ⟨Christ⟩ian life—rise & progress,—& selecting
Scriptures for the same Purpose;—and the like. And all this from
pure self-conceit & love of my own exaltation—

[*   *   *   *   *]

I am evidently much stronger & in more hopeful state this
fo. 4ᵛ morning: for wh⟨ich⟩ I sh⟨oul⟩d be most humbly thankful:—&
how wicked it will be, if I abuse these beginnings of returning
health.

12½–4¼ { ¾ hr—Brodie—Tylden &c
        { 3 hrs—Essay
 4¼–6 Dinner—Chapel
 6–10¾ Brodie
 ¾–11¼ &c &c

Thus I have had 3½ good work: & a 4 hrs walk. I got on mostly till
after dinner very tolerably: but talking with Lake about
Burbidge's book seems to have upset me. I did not wilfully stay so
late certainly: but if I had been thoughtful & really anxious about

it I should have thought of refusing to go with Brodie to tea. I did not get on quite rightly with him; not from any particular faultinesses, but rather from having got into a wrong frame of mind. I seem to have got into a conceited habit of talking περι μεγαλων μαλα σεμνως και δογματικως [*about great things very pompously and dogmatically*] of late.

[* * * Matthew 16: 26 *quoted*]

What I must try & do this Term will be   fo. 5ʳ

   Scripture Abstract
   Aristotle's Rhetoric III with Analysis
   Terence—the Six Plays perfect—
   Algebra & Trigonometry so far as to begin Con⟨ic⟩ Sect⟨ions⟩.

Ward. Brodie. Lake. etc.—
The Decade—
My Accounts—

Saturday June 2d   fo. 5ᵛ

9½–10½ Dev⟨otio⟩ns . . .
       ⎧ 10¼–11 Br⟨ea⟩kf⟨as⟩t
10¼–4 ⎨ 11–3½ Ward
       ⎩ 3¼–4   Edm⟨und⟩ Foulkes
  4–6 Dinner &c with Newman. too late for chapel
  6–8½ Walk. Congreve
8½–10¾ Scott—Ward—Brodie . . .

I took up Nich⟨olas⟩ Nickl⟨eby⟩ & so wasted a full 20 minutes at breakf⟨ast⟩, though my dev⟨otio⟩ns were not finished;—& have not been to this time, half feeling it to be wrong.

I indulged for 3 whole hours reading B⟨urbidge⟩'s book & talking to Ward unnecessarily: which was quite and thoroughly wrong, & I half suspected it to be so.—

[* * * * *]

I have kept no fast, but rather feast, what with B⟨urbidge⟩'s book &c &c.

WHITSUNDAY   (Ember Week fo. 6ʳ

I also did most wrongly last night in letting Brodie stay so long, & in wasting thus & in other ways the very short time I had left myself for sleep & dev⟨otio⟩ns. And the consequence was that I had a fair quantity, though not enough, of sleep; and very scanty dev⟨otio⟩ns.—Also Ward might well feel (as he did in some degree) that all the time I could spare from these two necessaries was due to him being so unwell as he was.—

> 9–11 Chapel & d⟨evotio⟩ns
> 11–2¼ Breakf⟨ast⟩ & Ward
> 2¼–⅓3 D⟨evotion⟩ns &c
> ⅓3–4½ Walk with Tylden
> 4½–5½ Dinner & Lake
> 5½–6¾ Chapel
> 6¾–9 Ward—Analysis
> 9–10½ etc & D⟨evotio⟩ns.

During my first stay with Ward I got full of φαντ⟨ασιαι⟩ ευδ⟨οξιας⟩ [*fancies of good repute*] which have been on me ever since. I nearly got rid of them by dinner time; but I became less careful & Ward's hour upset me finally.

fo. 6ᵛ I caught myself doing, what I am afraid must be often the case, while with him, cultivating αρεσκεια [*complaisance*] as a ready substitute for the φιλια [*friendship*] he taxes so hard. Hence my φαντ⟨ασιαι⟩ υποκρ⟨ισεως⟩ [*fancies of hypocrisy*] & his own fears lest it should be merely 'good Nature'—It is very bad not having seen this before: I only hope that I have not said anything. It is clearly the evil that I have long felt myself to derive from being with him—but for my folly at Rugby the tendency would have been well rooted out now.—This is a grand discovery.—

Again from my exceeding shudderingness at the thought of certain things I had committed (against good taste etc.) I found out the sense of floggings &c which is bringing home to one's prudential part the real wrongness of things & depends on the theory of forms. I am sure that is just what I want very much—for I have not the least real sense of the wickedness of uncleanness or of vanity &c. Can not I therefore devise something or other to serve the purpose of these bodily punishments to my ακολαστ⟨ος⟩ [*intemperate*] state of mind? But I do not know at all what.

fo. 7ʳ Monday in Whitsuntide. June 4th.

> 9¼–10 D⟨evotio⟩ns
> 10–¾ Breakf⟨ast⟩ A⟨lfred⟩ B. C⟨lough⟩. &c.
> 10¾–1¾ Aristotle . . . Ward . . .

$1\frac{3}{4}$–$2\frac{3}{4}$ E⟨dmund⟩ F⟨oulkes⟩ & talk with W⟨ard⟩.
$2\frac{3}{4}$–4 $\frac{1}{2}$ hrs Mathem⟨atics⟩ & Waste
4–$10\frac{1}{2}$ Except Chapel, with W⟨ar⟩d.

2 hrs Work
$1\frac{1}{4}$ Chapel etc.

The rest, i.e. 10 hrs given up to talking, walking & meals.

My first great false step was going on my own episodes out of the Rhetoric, which was quite wrong, & I was not quite sure it was not. Then it was still worse talking to Ward about it: in fact of real reading I could only have got about 2 hrs altogether.

More from the lack of temptation I think than any self control I have got on better since 4 o clock; though I am not satisfied that I set Ward (with whom I had a long talk in our walk) quite right. Poor poor Ward.

Tuesday in Whitsuntide—June 5th.   fo. 7ᵛ

9–$10\frac{1}{2}$ Br⟨eakfast⟩ & D⟨evotio⟩ns
$10\frac{1}{2}$–12 Mathem⟨atics⟩
  12–2 Lectures
  2–6 Ward—Talb⟨oys⟩—Skiff⟨in⟩g
  6–$\frac{1}{2}$ Catech⟨etics⟩
  $7\frac{1}{2}$–9 Catech⟨etics⟩ & Ward

Not up till $\frac{1}{4}$10:—$\frac{1}{4}$10–$\frac{1}{4}$11 D⟨evotio⟩ns except $\frac{1}{4}$ lost in b⟨rea⟩kf⟨ast⟩ making, with W⟨ar⟩d, & with some foolish fancies.

12–1 Lat⟨in⟩ Pr⟨ose⟩ Terence . . .
2–$2\frac{1}{2}$ Catechetics . . .
6–$6\frac{1}{2}$ ib
7–$8\frac{3}{4}$ ib
9–10 Brodie & Catech⟨etics⟩

About $2\frac{1}{2}$ hrs Reading.

10–$\frac{1}{4}$11

Have been at d⟨evotio⟩ns, but have been run away with foolish digressions

[*   *   *   *   *]

Wednesday—June 6th.

Not up till 10

10 to 20' Br⟨ea⟩kf⟨as⟩t & Tylden
20' to 45' Aristotle
45" to 11 D⟨evotio⟩ns
 11 to ¾ Lecture
 ¾ to 12½ D⟨evotio⟩ns.

I am still in a terrible way with my Vanity—it seems to poison every thing I do & (except just learning a Psalm) most of all my d⟨evotio⟩ns. It kept me awake last night till past 1 o'cl.

fo. 8ʳ 12½ to 4½ With the exception of ½hr with Ward—was employed in Acc⟨oun⟩ts, and in writing to my father. Except perhaps ½ hr which Edwyn Vaughan took from me. This was my best time of the day, my φαντ⟨ασιαι⟩ ευδ⟨οξιας⟩ [*fancies of good repute*] being fairly got down p⟨ar⟩tly by my not talking very well to E⟨dwyn⟩ V⟨augha⟩n. By some means or other it was aroused again.

4½–6 during Dinner and Chapel, probably the latter, from my making a response or two from αρεσκεια [*complaisance*] not the proper πιστεως εφεσει [*desire of faith*]. This was rather cultivated by my

6–8½ walk with Jowett, but so as to make me fairly sick of all αρεσκεια, [*complaisance*] & see it in its true light as a mere selfish desire of fascinating. I am sure it is this hot-house atmosphere which destroys all strength and healthiness of genuine feelings in me. It is a most terrible thing for me in this way having W⟨ar⟩d to take care, but I hope it is compatible with overcoming it:—by looking on it, in

½–9 with W⟨ar⟩d) the disagreeable duty line. I must try, & if not I believe I must tell him.

Deliver me, O Lord, from lying lips and a deceitful tongue. [Ps. 120: 2]

O for those blessed Half Years at Rugby, so graciously given, so gracelessly wasted—capable of so much good & productive of so much evil to myself & to others—then, now & forever, perhaps.

fo. 8ᵛ Thursday. June 7th

Not up till 9
9¼ to 10 ¼
Read about 3½ hrs. Mathematics & Terence.
Was kept up by Ward till near 12, being very ill in mind.

Friday—June 8th.

Was not up till ¼ past 10

10¼–11 Breakfast etc
  12–1½ Ward & D⟨evotion⟩s.

I am quite sure that I am in a much worse state than I usually
imagine. The thought of my exceeding wickedness that I fell into
during the ⟨Christ⟩mas Holidays five years ago Jan⟨uar⟩y 1833
has come upon me this morning: but I can hardly for a moment
realise in the very least degree that I really am the same person,
that my identical self did these things. I believe that something of a
consciousness that it was so was growing up in my last term but my
Vacation follies and luxuriousness quenched it altogether. I think
therefore I may reasonably believe that the present is quite the   fo. 9ʳ
first real time that I have begun to try to live by Faith. God alone
knows the Real History of my past life, how much real conviction I
have sinned against, & with how great temptation. I am quite
sure my education was a bad one for me—I think I could have had
scarcely any proper faith in me when I went to School. I am sure I
have very little now. I sh⟨oul⟩d suppose however that something
of the sort was mixed up a good deal with my October 35 feelings.
But I may safely say this that before coming to Oxford I never saw
that the right way was to get to hate Evil by a faith in Punishment,
& not to try & keep oneself by a love of good.

1½–⅓3 I have been writing the above & thinking up the events of
my time in England 1828–1838.

⅓3 to ¼4 Theme   fo. 9ᵛ
¼4 to 8½ Dinner with Bunsen—Chapel—Skiffing.
8½ to 9½ Theme
9½ to 10 Tea & Ward

I am doubtful whether I did not go wrong in my occupation from
1½ to ⅓3:—I certainly should not have taken so much wine at
Bunsens—& was altogether too indulgent,—& at Chapel I was
not very attentive . . .

I am a good deal tired and lowered in spirits to night, I suppose
thro⟨ugh⟩ my last night's sitting up till 12: for I have made no fast
of it today, though I have made more use of it than I have of any
day yet this term perhaps.

I incline to think that I ought to give up seeking much about the great Newm⟨anism⟩ Question: for I have little or no real earnestness.

Would it not be best to make something of the Fridays to come as Fasts and to follow them by Communion on the Sundays? There are but two more, alas, & I have wasted a long list of such opportunities.

fo. 10ʳ Saturday, June 9th.

Mathematics is to be my work this day:—unless my bad night prevents it: I was not asleep till past 3, nor up till 8.

8–9¼ Breakfast with Tait. A letter from Gell took me fr⟨om⟩
¼–½ but I wasted it rather too:. The letter has filled me with all sort of Newm⟨an⟩ & Burb⟨idge⟩ fancies
½–10¼ so that I could hardly get at all into my dev⟨otio⟩ns.
10¼–12 With about ½ hr's Waste worked at Algebra
12–2 Talking with Ward almost solely which was certainly unadvisable: tho⟨ugh⟩ partly I c⟨oul⟩d not avoid it.
2–⅓3 Letter to Burbidge
⅓3–¼4 Trigonometry
¼4–¼9 Except ½ hr—with E⟨dmund⟩ F⟨oulkes⟩ at dinner & walking.
¼9–10½ Letter to B⟨urbidge⟩ & Ward.

I have been very careless—& so very wicked since Chapel. I thoughtlessly went on in my walk as if I did not know that Stanley w⟨ou⟩ld pretty certainly not be come, & when I came back pretended that I supposed he w⟨oul⟩d have been here.—I also behaved ill to Tylden & to Lake.—And am clearly in a praise-desiring, selfindulgent state of mind.

fo. 10ᵛ I think the evil must for the most part have grown while I was with E⟨dmund⟩ S. F⟨oulkes⟩: for I took to the ἀρεσκεια [*complaisance*] line as usual without any care lest I should be yielding to μικροψυχια [*mean-spiritedness*]—and this I evidently indulged sadly & most degradingly, indeed:—so it was no wonder that I told Ward those lies I did, I think they deserved to be so called, about Stanley & the River, & treated Lake & Tylden ill out of ἀρεσκεια [*complaisance*] to Brodie & Ward.

[*   *   *   *   *]

TRINITY SUNDAY [June 10]

Was only just up to Chapel: & from that time to this 12 o'cl have been with Brodie & Ward & had no time at all to myself.—

12–1 Comm⟨union⟩.

1–4½ Ward—Lake—Walk.

4½–7 Dinner—Trower's—Chapel.

7–9 Ward.

I have been very tired & done up ὕπνῳ και καματῳ [*with sleep and fatigue*] to day which I think is sufficient to excuse my doing nothing in it.   fo. 11ʳ

Only I must not let it run on into tomorrow.

I must be up to Chapel certainly.

St Barnabas' Day
Monday June 11th

8–10 Ch⟨apel⟩—Br⟨eakfast⟩—D⟨evotion⟩s

10–¼4

¼4–

Was not up till ½p 9:—br⟨eakfast⟩ & d⟨evotio⟩ns rather scanty till 11. from that to ¼4 about 3 hrs work. 2 hrs waste & talk with Ward, & consideration of my letter from Annie.

¼4–¼10 Dinner, Ward. Chapel. Vaughan. Walk, Congreve. Tea, Ward. Decade Notes.

In the morning I thought I must be very poorly—but it got much better very soon. I fear I am very selfish and praise seeking in all I do. If I was not, I sh⟨oul⟩d feel Ward's goodness much more than I did or do. What I seem to have settled now is that I should go if my father can manage the time accordingly—put off their going, namely, to the end of July. But I had rather not write to B⟨urbidge⟩ till I hear from him first. I must write home tomorrow without doubt: 6 to 6½, 7½ to 8 will perhaps do for it.

[*   *   *   *   *]

        fo. 11ᵛ

Tuesday, June 12th.

Was not asleep till past 1 nor up till ¼ to 9: nor away from breakfast till ¼ to 10

10 to 11 After scant d⟨evotion⟩s wrote out heads of my last 10

y⟨ea⟩rs. I suppose this is not unadvisable for I am sure I want very much a feeling of identification with my conduct in them and if I can but avoid complacent recollections of good feelings &c it will surely much increase my prudential sense.

11 to 4 I think with about an hr's waste, reading. Terence. L⟨atin⟩ Prose. Trigonometry. Eq⟨uatio⟩ns. was certainly very tired at the end.

4 to 7½ Dinner. Stanley. Chapel. Stanley, Newman's lect⟨ure⟩

7½ to 10½ Boat-race with V⟨augha⟩n mi⟨nor⟩ & tea. Farrar & Buck.

10½ to ¼11 Ward who is terribly distressed, & complaining but certainly most courageous & determined.

fo. 12ʳ I do hope & trust it may go on right. I must do what is right & leave the rest to God—but it is very terrible if a false step I may take in some hour perhaps of carelessness ruin his peace for life:—I only trust it is not thus at all as yet.—If I was but well rid of my ἀρεσκεια [*complaisance*] all would be well, I am sure:—

Wednesday [June 13]

I have most foolishly & carelessly sat up till ½ p. 11 doing Verses, & I must be up by ¼ to 8 tomorrow. Have had 2 lectures & 2½ reading:—and have otherwise got on pretty fairly.

Thursday, June 14th

Not up till ¼ to 9:

¼ to 10 to ¼11 D⟨evotio⟩ns . . .
¼ to 11 to 2 about 1 hr work 1 hr lectures 1¼ talking with W⟨ar⟩d &c.
2 to 4 Stanley—Brodie—Ward
4 to 10¾ Dinner,—Ward, Walk;—tea &c.

I have been idle and careless in many ways to day. I must therefore be very cautious tomorrow or I shall be upset. Ward has kept me so late that I cannot spare more than a few minutes for dev⟨otio⟩ns, as I must be up to Chapel.

[*   *   *   *   *]

fo. 12ᵛ ### Friday. June 15th

I did not get up till ½ p 8. after 8 hrs sleep: I am sure that I should have done so.

8½ to 9 D⟨evotio⟩ns

  9–12½ Lectures. B⟨rea⟩kf⟨ast⟩. Rhetoric. Ward.

12¼–7½ With about ¼ hr waste, d⟨evotio⟩ns.

  1½–3 Letter to B⟨urbidge⟩ & Ward

  3–6½ Except ½ hr Chapel, Essay.

6½–10½ R⟨eadin⟩g R⟨oo⟩m—Brodie,—Walk,—Ward

About 3½ hrs reading—have been ἀρεσκος [*complaisant*] occasionally & foolishly worried with W⟨ar⟩d but on the whole have got on fairly well & am greatly inclined in favour of fasting.

Saturday—June 16

Was not up, after all, till 7½;—I think too so far wrongly that if I had been determined from beforehand I shd not have done so.

  8–½ Message to the Pig ½–9 Dev⟨otio⟩ns.

  9–10 Br⟨ea⟩kf⟨ast⟩ with Prior—Lingen.

10–11 D⟨evotio⟩ns 11–12¼ Lake & Ward & ab⟨ou⟩t ½ hr reading

12¼–1 Trigon⟨ometry⟩. 1–4 About 1½ reading & 1½ Ward

  4–9½ Dinner, W⟨ar⟩d, Chapel, Walk, tea &c.   fo. 13ʳ

    altogether pretty nearly 3 hrs reading.—

I have had a good deal of ἀρεσκεια [*complaisance*] upon me;—& ought I think to have made it more of an abstinence day than I have: Was foolishly inattentive at chapel.

—1st Sunday after Trinity—
June 17th

At Communion, tho⟨ugh⟩ with too slight preparation.—

  7–9 Com⟨union⟩ & Chapel. 9–10½ Breakfast 10½–12 Sermon 12–1½ Ward 1½–2¾ Walk 2¾–4½ . . . Abstract 4½–5½ Dinner, Brodie 5½–6½ Chapel 6½–9 Abstract & Ward.

Altogether I have indulged myself very much beyond my proper maximum I am sure: especially during Univ⟨ersity⟩ Sermon let myself run into all sorts of foolish & conceited fancies.

[*   *   *   *   *]

I must evidently be up to Chapel & work very hard tomorrow: only be prepared for interruptions.—

I must be awake also to the great need of keeping down my   fo. 13ᵛ
ἀρεσκεια [*complaisance*] at all times so as to be ready for Wards

χρειαι [*necessities*] which are likely to be pretty numerous henceforth.—

Monday. June 18

Up to chapel. Worked about 4 hrs besides 2 lectures
Walked with Tylden 5½–9¼ Decade till 12.

Tuesday. June 19

Up & breakf⟨as⟩ted by 9½: I am in a terrible state of vanity I fear with the Decade: I have thought it best to write it out and so have done with it till next October: after all my speech was but poor as a speech & nothing to be at all conceited with.—

I let myself be satisfied with very scanty devotions this morning: and have altogether I think let myself waste more time than my headache or fatigue required.

I believe I was right in missing Scott's lecture & Davies' dinner: and in not going out a walk, most likely I did not do wrong. And I have after all been at work full 3 hours.

But I was quite wrong in not setting as hard as I c⟨oul⟩d to work while I was so strongly under the power of my vanity this morning. I evidently was very much elated by it, & ashamed to show the least that I was so. But I do not understand my
fo. 14ʳ condition. How is it that while I have been doing 'Samuel' this evening I have been haunted by all sorts of wicked & unbelieving fancies.

[*   *   *   *   *]

Wednesday [June 20]

Was up to Chapel. breakfast with Stanley—let him stay too long. Enquiries about Coach &c. Ward

It is now near ½ p. 12.—I do not quite know what is the matter with me: but I am in a very strange way. I was made almost furious just now by a little want of delicacy (I suppose this was what it was).

[*   *   *   *   *]

¼ 2 o'cl.

fo. 14ᵛ I have spoken to Ward—I hope not wrongly, and yet not rightly in some smaller points.

I have since the morning most wickedly given way to ἀρεσκεια [*complaisance*] first at my Party, 2ndly with Congreve. What do I not deserve to suffer for it.

Thursday June 21st

Again I have given way to αρεσκεια [*complaisance*]—at breakfast with Stanley

Friday June 22nd

Up to Chapel. Short dev⟨otio⟩ns. Br⟨ea⟩kf⟨ast⟩ with Lake, St⟨anley⟩ & Vaughan.

Collections—to about 1

From 1 to 3½ lay on the Sofa reading Leg⟨end⟩ of Montrose &c. sleeping.

3½ to 5½ Young Conybeare & Theme
    5½–7 Dinner. Lake. Chapel
    7–⅛ A⟨lfred⟩ B. C⟨lough⟩'s rooms. reading M⟨aid⟩ of Perth. &c&c
    ⅛–9½ Walk solit⟨ary⟩
    9½–

Saturday June 23rd   fo. 15ʳ

Was not up to Chapel & have consequently been to neither. I think weakly & foolishly.

  8–9 Dev⟨otio⟩ns. 9–10½ Ward 10¼–11 &c
11–1 with ½ hr's exception, when Stanley came, Trigonometry
  1–2 At Jesus Coll⟨ege⟩ Parkers &c &c.
2–¼4 (except ¼ hr Stanley) Conic Sections.
¼4–9 Ward

Had a slight fit of ἀρεσκεια [*complaisance*] at 12 o'cl.

2nd Sunday after Trinity. St John Baptist's Day. [June 24]

      7–9 Ch. Ch.
    9–11¼ B⟨rea⟩kf⟨ast⟩ Blunt & Conyb⟨eare⟩ mi⟨nor⟩.
11¼–1½–2¼ Ward—Lake—A⟨lfred⟩ B. C⟨lough⟩
    2¼–3½ Letter Home & acc⟨oun⟩ts.
    3½–⅘5 With Lake [* * *]
    ⅘5–5 Farrer mi⟨nor⟩.
    5–5½ D⟨evotio⟩ns.

Did wrong in not getting up at once. Should have been more thoughtful & ἐγκρατης [*self-controlled*] at breakfast or else I sh⟨oul⟩d not have kept W⟨ar⟩d waiting. Have been of late very much puffed up with φ⟨ανтασιαι⟩ δ⟨οξης⟩ [*fancies of reputation*] having been as I fancy rather witty.

fo. 15ᵛ Thought of asking for ½ com⟨mons⟩ and yielded to my impulse not to do so without sifting it—till I remembered that probably they might think I only meant to have ½ of one ½ of a 2nd dish & then consented to so doing, though I feel hardly inclined to do so even then.

Monday June 25th.

I have already lost a full hour. ¾ in bed, & ¼ with Stanley, both rather of doubtful justifiability. And this will leave me only a ¾ hr for my business surplus—for I must not & will not take it out of my d⟨evotio⟩ns and if possible not out of Ward either. Possibly I may get 9 hrs if I am dil⟨igent⟩ tomorrow.

fo. 16ʳ   ### Wednesday July 4th
Patterdale.

I am sure that for the last week I must have been going steadily backward. I do not think I have had one suff⟨icient⟩ day's d⟨evotio⟩ns since the last Sunday at Oxford.

I must try and rouse myself to be active, earnest, thoughtful & vigorous, at once and henceforth. [* * *]

Thursday, July 5

*

Friday [July 6]

fo. 16ᵛ Monday, July 9th

At 4 p.m. Burbidge went to Penrith.

4–5½ Lay half-reading, half asleep on the Sofa.
5½–6½ Washing bill &c
6½–7½ Walk
7½–9½ Read a little Rome, but mostly map-making.

For the most part I have been clearly wasting time, which I

sh⟨oul⟩d have made a good deal of.—Tomorrow without fail I must begin to work vigorously.

Liverpool, Sept⟨ember⟩ 15   fo. 18ʳ

[* * * Ephesians 1: 18–19 *quoted*]

[*   *   *   *   *]   fo. 18ᵛ

If any man be afflicted, let him pray, &c. [James 5: 13] means 'the uses to be made of Changes of Spirits'.

Years must pass of hard striving-upward before I shall be at all able to do anything in the way of judging.—

'Trust thou in the Lord, & be doing good, dwell in the land, & verily thou shalt be fed.' [Ps. 37: 3]

The only thing that makes a Diary offensive is affectation, and if fo. 19ʳ there be a real desiring for good under the surface of many evident tokens of unconquered faults, these will not matter nor prevent the benefit of the book—(?)

I am afraid I shall be continually running into formula-following—perhaps the remedy is being by myself: devotions more after the old Rugby fashion.

Would it be advisable to count the Changes as they occur?

Diarium to keep up the memory of one's Past States of Mind; lest one sh⟨oul⟩d drop any of the good parts.

[fo. 19ᵛ *blank*]

Rugby. Saturday September 29th.   fo. 20ʳ

Talk about Montaigne & Pascal with B⟨urbidge⟩

Stoics (pride) / Pyrrhonians (lacheté) = Revelation. Our human weakness & divine strength.

Is renewal by the Holy Ghost the great abiding ⟨Chris⟩t⟨ian⟩ truth.

Sunday [September 30]

a little talk *de re Sacr⟨amentaria⟩* [*about the Sacraments*]

I spoke of a bodily effect.

Any moral effect of the physical agent *he* says is so wholly denied by the Spirit of ⟨Chris⟩t⟨iani⟩ty.

Monday [October 1]

Made a great stumble thro⟨ugh⟩ want of readiness for all things brought on by not setting to work in the Morning.

[*   *   *   *   *]

fo. 20ᵛ ## Tuesday [October 2]

A long talk with B⟨urbidge⟩.

Prize Poem
Scholarship.

Christ Goodness & Wisdom, with the Power resigned.

We must pray to love God, not to escape particular temptations. these we must avoid looking at.

Does not approve the good-overcome-by-mans-evil notion. e.g. loss of miracles &c.

Does not see the Diff⟨iculty⟩ of Ex⟨istence⟩ of Evil. Free-will the great Difficulty. v. Coleridge.

Inspiration. They had something to deliver;—but the manner & circumstances of delivery are quite their own. Very certain.

fo. 21ʳ ## Wednesday [October 3]

Too idle, [therefore] foolish.

Is it not one reason of the corruption of religious teaching that weak people find it safest to satisfy their weaknesses at the first & so never really eradicate them: whence in giving directions μαθηταις [*to disciples*] they lay stress on P⟨oin⟩ts which to their cases were expedient perhaps, but are not universal?—cf Compulsory Confession, a corruption of the Services of the R⟨oman⟩ C⟨atholic⟩ Ch⟨urch⟩.

Need of Fasts— / pinching /

Saturday [October 6]

Have acted in several ways & on several occasions weakly & foolishly since W⟨ednes⟩day.

Coleridge's Notion concerning the Will as the Originating Power—struck me a good deal tonight. Is the (Holy Spirit) (Redemption) Inspired Volition, renewal of the Will. It comes into my Notion of Faith.

Monday [October 8] After a miserable period of Questioning,
Doubt &c again the feeling has come very strongly on me that we
must walk here in a state of unconsciousness to most of the terrible
realities existing about us: only trusting in God.—

[* * * * *]

Think of saying at once to Ward that I have no settled, habitual
affection for him.

Thought last night that the necessity-of-form-&-fast notion was
objected to by St Paul in the ἐθελοθρησκεια [*will-worship*] passage
of Colossians. [2: 23]

Feel confirmed by my much healthier feelings to-night of the
rightness of this line

In reading Wordsworth tonight have been struck again with the
interference of the vague excitement of my Marvellousness-bump
with better Poetic enjoyment.

Wednesday. [October 10]

At the Prices to-day Mrs P⟨rice⟩ spoke highly of Ward—his great
acuteness & clearness of head. I think all this from my being then
in an excited state has had a consid⟨erable⟩ eff⟨ec⟩t on me.
[* * *] forms useful but better without [* * * Col 2: 22 *quoted*].

Thursday [October 11]

It seems as if Mrs Price's line of talk & other vanity exciting things
had had a very evil effect.

Long talk with Ward. in which many such occurred.

I seem to have slipped at once into a sort of Pseudo. Affection
requiring vigorous & rigorous Examination. & extirpation, if so
be. My feelings with Ward were certainly so far as I c⟨oul⟩d see
unmixed with Van⟨ity⟩ exc⟨ept⟩ up to a certain point in the
conv⟨ersatio⟩n & quite healthy.

These Vivacities certainly do not well suit me.

Friday morning. [October 12]

It seems to me that talking concerning these matters is not at all
beneficial to me: as I lose my ways—(not to say with the
excitement) even with simply hearing other views &c.

I wish very much I had had a long talk with B⟨urbidge⟩ before I came away.

Must not indulge W⟨ard⟩ in re 'dear' etc.

Even now I seem to perceive distinctly a difference between my feelings for Ward and real affection. They seem a sort of mixture of pleasure in his conversation, and general kindness which I feel equally to almost any one else.

Have spoken about a certain peculiarity of manner.

Ward says my own manner is much kinder today than yesterday.

fo. 23ʳ —— evening

Felt while with W⟨ard⟩ this evening something more like affection:—but I think there is some reason to suspect this state of feeling—for I am conscious of some other kind of excitement. Something of fireside complacency seemed to me to fit it to night.— I think there is no vanity or aff⟨ectio⟩n further than in occasional exaggeration of manner on my part, or toleration of it in him: which is suff⟨icien⟩t I suppose to acc⟨oun⟩t for such feelings prevailing after being with him.

[* * * Matt. 7: 13 *quoted*]

Saturday [October 13]

My feelings seem to partake in some degree of the same sort of excitement that I felt on coming here last October.

Sunday night [October 14]

I am afraid it is quite clear that I must say a good deal to Ward. At any rate that my words & manner of last term are not to be regarded as the true index of my feelings to him.

fo. 23ᵛ In thinking about it before dinner felt great disgust at his indelicacies—but assuredly it is much better now:—When in Magd⟨alen⟩ Walk seemed to feel not a single beginning of affection. Is there nothing between o & what Ward w⟨oul⟩d wish? e.g. Burbidge: Gell or Mayor or others

> Truth is a golden thread seen here & there
> In small bright specks upon the visible side
> Of our strange Being's party coloured web
> How rich the converse. Tis a vein of ore

Emerging now & then on earths rude breast
But flowing full below. Like Islands set
At distant intervals on Ocean's face
We see it on our course; but in the depths
The mystic colonnade unbroken keeps
Its faithful way invisible but sure.
O if it be so, wherefore do we men
Pass by so many marks, so little heeding?

Monday [October 15]   fo. 24ʳ

Ward has asked me to make unnatural demonstrations.

I have I believe told him all. It seems to me that part of my grief took an affected line. I seem even now to feel more the relief to myself than the misery to him. May I only be honest for the future & never forget the evil ensuing from even the least false step. I fear I feel his misery scarcely at all. tho⟨ugh⟩ it is indeed monstrous that I sh⟨oul⟩d not.—

[∗ ∗ ∗ Gal. 6: 3 *quoted*]

Tuesday [October 16]   fo. 24ᵛ

It certainly does look to me as if I had said more than was needful to W⟨ard⟩—that his ways do not well suit me, that I am often worried, often disgusted is quite true, & that his lack of Poetical Perception & of quietness destroy much of the sympathies of daily intercourse.—Just at present I feel quite as I used to do in Lent Term only more healthily. O that I may be able ere long to say so—but I must test myself in all possible ways.

I think I had exaggerated the probable diff⟨erence⟩ of opinion. Possibly however this may only come from the somewhat exaggerated manner he has required of me today. His progressiveness struck me to night as being something better even than Burbidge's frame of mind.

All this evil is but the fruit of the evil tendencies I let grow up in strength during my last 2 yrs at Rugby—as the state of things there now is the fruit of the weaknesses which let these tendencies grow.

Wednesday [October 17]   fo. 25ʳ

Self Chastisement is certainly one way of getting out of a worldly or wrong frame into a heavenly one.—

$\frac{1}{4}$11 Conversation with W⟨ard⟩ about Bunsen. Their notions of the Comm⟨unio⟩n & Fasting quite separable, as also τα πρακτικα [*behaviour*]—Real Presence.

Party of Rugby Men on Saturday.

[*Here follows a list with some crossings, ticks, and various symbols, including the following names*:] Congreve, Fox, Lloyd, Arnold, H. Bunsen, Lake, Balston, Blunt, Lewthwaite, Rawstorne

I have, I fear, been very careless and idle to.day—letting myself lose opportunities of subduing wrong feelings desire for praise &c.—and not reading at all diligently.

fo. 25ᵛ My manner to day to Ward has been false and foolish—I cannot, after my affectations and my foolish neglect and want of vigilance regain the feeling of anything higher than mere love of pleasing— nor, therefore can look on the misery I have caused either as misery or as my fault.—

But I must struggle and recover myself, or all this term will be a series of evil effects to myself & all I associate with. And I feel confident I shall get better if I do but do my part.

[✳ ✳·✳ Eph. 1: 18 *quoted*]

To see what prospects are set before us.—

(1) what a glorious state we are to strive to obtain
(2) & how great the assistance God will give us in so striving.

fo. 26ʳ   witness first Christ's resurrection bodily
        second your own change morally—for think what a wretched state of sin you were in—& thence conclude how great his Power must have been to renew you, for his Power, his gift it was—even your own belief & trust in him—you cannot boast, for of your own endeavours you c⟨ou⟩ld have done nothing—(compared with what has been done for you, & what he does for you, all your strivings are as nothing) yea rather we are his own making, creatures created in Christ Jesus to show his glory in the performance of good actions which he himself gives us the faculty of performing.

Discipline is perhaps the thing to cure me. if not must try fasting?

Might not my old system of being ready for the worst come in?

fo. 26ᵛ Thursday morning [October 18]

It seems to me that the 2 causes which have chiefly operated to make this a case of so much self deceit are 1st that from Wards deficiencies it would only be in higher points that I c⟨ou⟩ld have sympathy with him. & in these one is liable to great changes & improvements & I especially to *temporary* excitements of strong sympathy from my exaggerative tendencies of Marvellousness and Approbativeness.

2nd His being ill when our intimacy commenced so that I bore many σκανδαλα [*stumbling blocks*] as natural in that state & merely temporary, so that I did not see the deficiency of minor sympathies;—just as from the first cause I did seem to see the existence of more higher sympathies than really did exist. Yet even granting the operation of these 2 causes I must have discovered it long ago but for my follies especially at Easter when the tide began to turn.—at Patterdale in the first few days,—and at Beaumaris.—

[Thursday] Evening.

I have this evening experienced more healthy feeling t⟨o⟩w⟨ar⟩ds W⟨ard⟩—not indeed so as to well to realize the separation; but more like my feelings of Friday, Saturday & Sunday.

I look to being of the same opinion much more probably & see many σκανδαλα [*stumbling-blocks*] in this respect cleared off or nearly.

His manner still is indelicate etc. and I feel the lack of quiet common-conversation as after dinner very much.

Many of the unhealthy symptoms of last Term came from my own conceited theorising.

The same sort of undefined feeling was with me latterly tonight— (not fireside complacency, certainly). Something of a religious συμπαθεια [*fellow feeling*] it seemed: tho⟨ugh⟩ not very individual to him—it runs into approb⟨ativeness⟩: but perhaps from exagg⟨eration⟩ of manner. Is there anything of the complacency of Patience in it? I think I detect in these feelings, something of the same sort, as marked those of Lent Term wh⟨ich⟩ led me so far wrong.

I have f⟨oun⟩d this exagg⟨eration⟩ on his part, very terrible to bear,—but I do not at all realize the cause of it. I am sure it is not right for me to endure it, under my present feelings. something

like a complacency produced by conscious kindness & attention to
a sick person. If so had I better say anything tomorrow? W⟨oul⟩d
it not be dangerous?—

I must at any rate keep to the Cold Manner of tonight: as it is my
only chance of not going wrong: tho⟨ugh⟩ itself very bad unless it
lead to something higher.

If I am enabled to renew a⟨cquai⟩nt⟨ance?⟩ with W⟨ard⟩ at any
rate I must make conditions—not to talk about theological
matters &c so continually—nor to have any manner on his part
beyond wh⟨at⟩ my own justifies. It must of necessity be very slow
as resting on such gradual matters.

If I can only avoid affectation & approbativenesses, my time by
myself will keep me steady & correct all that is wrong.—

I have been more careful & diligent & generally better today, but
have left many opp⟨ortuni⟩ties unused, & often been negligent.
E.g. I have only read about $3\frac{1}{2}$ hrs.

Whether or not we best communicate truth acquired by Poetry or
Systematic Philosophy, assuredly we acquire it only by τῳ
δοκιμαζειν τι ἐστιν εὐαρεστον τῳ θεῳ [*proving what is acceptable to the
Lord*, Ephesians 5: 10] by the teaching of the Spirit. The great
danger for me is to get glimpses of the truth & theorize; & so follow
formulas. Hence much of the exceeding unsatisfactory nature of
my Dev⟨otio⟩ns of Easter Term. I got hold of a theory of forms: &
παθητικα [*passivities*] & left my own impulses to follow this.

fo. 29ᵛ Friday [October 19]

It is Newman's idea that ἐργα [*works*] in St Paul means 'works of
the law' ('performance of the commandments' or 'acting up to the
law within'

[* * * Eph. 2: 11–22 *paraphrased; this continues through fos. 28ᵛ and
29ʳ*]

fo. 29ᵛ It has just occured to me what possible daily intercourse c⟨oul⟩d I
have with W⟨ar⟩d: his want of perceptions leaving no chance of
pleasant small talk: & any talk about high matters leading at once
to formulism.

Ward has just reminded me (with reg⟨ar⟩d to my note) of the way
I used to feel towards him, in the ⟨Christ⟩mas vacation: also one
evening after a walk with Congreve: as also of the fact of his having

been so ill & still being: so as to make his manners & ways (in small matters) 'worse than they naturally are[']—The Point for Consideration now is how far his Perceptive deficiencies render daily intercourse impossible, or rather make me feel disgust or annoyance.

Today I am afraid I have been less vigilant than yesterday:—I have however read, I suppose, $4\frac{1}{2}$ hrs.

$8\frac{1}{2}$–$9\frac{1}{2}$ Br⟨eakfast⟩. $9\frac{1}{2}$–10 R⟨ea⟩d⟨in⟩g $10\frac{1}{4}$–$\frac{1}{4}$12 Dev⟨otio⟩ns etc. about $1\frac{1}{4}$

$\frac{1}{4}$12 to $\frac{1}{4}$3 reading with about an hours interval.
$\frac{1}{4}$3 to $7\frac{1}{4}$ Exercise etc. $7\frac{1}{4}$–$9\frac{1}{2}$ with $\frac{1}{4}$hr lost reading.

If I kept the proper degree of vigilance & activity & single- fo. 30^r mindedness thro⟨ugh⟩ the day, I sh⟨oul⟩d be better fit for devotions at night, & able to enter into them without a struggle.

One of the Practical ways of realising W⟨ard⟩'s business to myself will be calling on myself at all times to be ready to give up anything.

So also perhaps to be ready for the worst . . .

Saturday. [October 20]

Eph⟨esians⟩ 2. 18 The Trinity. Christ who has obtained us forgiveness & access through the Spirit. The Spirit the means of access thereby obtained. The Father thereby approached.

[* * * *Comments on Eph.* 2: 11–22, *continuing onto fo. 30^v*]

I feel that I am frequently deceiving myself about Ward: & being fo. 31^r teased into the notion that he is less deficient in Perceptions & delicacies than he is. Yet I do not take into account as reg⟨ar⟩ds the latter his illnesses.

My dependence & desire for praise has got very bad.

I have only read 3 hours today: which is very bad: but my calls, & Party have come a good deal in the Way.

I think I am getting somehow into a less lifely kind of state than that of wh⟨ich⟩ I felt the beginnings at Rugby. Certainly somehow or other B⟨urbidge⟩ does and W⟨ard⟩ does not very well suit me in these respects.

Settle about Manner.

fo. 31ᵛ Sunday Morning. [October 21]

Perhaps if I had improved my feelings of last night I sh⟨oul⟩d have got nearer right: as it is I have been obliged to give up the beginnings of a consciousness of W⟨ard⟩'s deficiencies & to take more to the same way I was in before. I believe there is not a little approb⟨ative⟩ness in it:—Perhaps the only way to cure it is by at any rate keeping a rein on myself when with him; & attacking it with all my might with others.

ου μη ποτε συλλεγοντες τα ζιζανια εκριζωσητε αμα αυτοις τον σιτον. [*Nay; lest while ye gather up the tares ye root up also the wheat with them*, Matt. 13: 28] may serve as caution ag⟨ain⟩st theorising.

It struck me today that perhaps the worst this may come to will be that for some years W⟨ard⟩ & I shall not be able to see much of ea⟨ch⟩ other: but then a good deal.

W⟨ard⟩ did no doubt supply many of my wants: but when the Vacation came I f⟨oun⟩d that (as I might have guessed, had I been honest) I had higher, or at least, other ones unsupplied.

fo. 32ʳ In all the annoyances W⟨ard⟩ causes me, I must remember that I deserve double:—if I can only do this, & yet avoid any αρεσκεια [*complaisance*] keeping up my coldness, I shall do best.

I am quite deceiving myself as to my own goodness. ει τις δοκει ειναι τι μηδεν ων εαυτον φρεναπατα. [*If a man think himself to be something, when he is nothing, he deceiveth himself.* Gal. 6: 3] I do not call to mind my offences nearly enough. Getting up & setting to at once—

It is very well for B⟨urbidge⟩ perhaps & others to think comparatively little of repentance for the Past: but for me it is very different—wilful sinning fr⟨om⟩ the first.—

Brodie. my Uncle.

fo. 32ᵛ Monday [October 22]

It seems uncertain to me how far it is the highest way to be ready for the worst: but I incline to think that it is my only way for escaping in temptation.—

Tuesday morning [October 23]

[* * * *Comments on* Eph. 1: 23 and 3: 2–4]

—evening

Conv⟨ersatio⟩n with W⟨ard⟩ in the morning about Bunsen's
Real Presence—belief &c: & tonight with [Ward] & St⟨anley⟩
about Robertson, Whately & a variety of gossip: I am afraid it will
not have past without some effect on me.

Worked well from 10 to $1\frac{1}{2}$ in the morning, but only about $\frac{3}{4}$ hr
since. $4\frac{1}{2}$ is the very utmost.

Dinner. Excitement seems to upset me.

[* * * *Comments on* Eph. 4]

Wednesday [October 25]

A long day with W⟨ard⟩—My feeling just now is to be
exceedingly vexed with his indelicacies—but I do not realise the
circumstances. I think I must be justified in denying it as yet to
him. Yet I do not think I ought to endure the degradation of
allowing such things as he forces upon me—I do not think that I
ought ever to indulge anything like anger towards him.

I have not read more than $3\frac{1}{2}$ hrs.

I trust I have felt today the beginnings of more independence both
in manner to W⟨ar⟩d & in discussions. not going so readily as I
used into formulisms—as also an increase tow⟨ar⟩ds realizing the
separation.—

Thursday [October 26]

[* * * *Comments on* Eph. 4: 29]

[* * * *Comments on* Col. 1]

Walk in Magd⟨alen⟩ Meadow

Saturday [October 27]

It is observable that B⟨urbidge⟩'s temper &c are much the best
suited to repressing my faults &c—so also it is when I am in the
healthiest state that I feel myself least awkw⟨ar⟩d with W⟨ard⟩—

I have, I think, been getting of late into a sort of fatalism.

Sunday [October 28]

[*   *   *   *   *]

W⟨ar⟩d's—
    avoid love of pleasing &c

cultivate realizing & general improvement.

Ward's Notion about Heresy.

a lack of πιστις αὐξανομενη [*growing faith*]

These doctrines & these forms are those which h⟨ave⟩ satisfied the highest ⟨Christ⟩ians. ὁσοι οὖν τελειοι τουτο φρονωμεν [*Let us therefore as many as be perfect, be thus minded.* Phil. 3: 15] For the ἀτελοι [*imperfect*] to say that they are idle & foolish of course is absurd.

fo. 35ʳ But is the Athanasian Creed & the compulsory-form system in accordance with the Spirit of ει τι ετερως φρονειτε και τουτο ὑμιν ὁ Θεος αποκαλυψει? [*and if in anything ye be otherwise minded, God shall reveal even this unto you,* Phil. 3: 15]

+ +
+ +

It is quite clear to me that in no case of W⟨ard⟩'s misbehaving have I any right to think myself wronged as I do:—but much rather to feel myself quite wrong in not having realised his trial sufficiently to prevent any temptation to such feeling. On the other hand I may perhaps tell him that his demonstrations tend to deceive me, if not him. I am sure that I am constantly cheated into a belief of liking him better than after seeing other people I sh⟨oul⟩d do, from this behaviour: & that I do act on this & am more kind (& more than kind) in manner than I am justified in being. [* * *]

The Will—Energy
Activity—Benefit of.

fo. 35ᵛ [* * * *Many crossed out names*]

Monday [29 October]

I have found out that my exceeding distress & bother today comes from being too bent on going forward. which W⟨ard⟩'s little necessities always come in to prevent.—this tempts me to being over-kind in manner & this often annoys me

fo. 36ʳ [* * * *Quotation and translation of* Col. 1]

fo. 36ᵛ [* * * *Quotations and notes on Ephesians*]

Wednesday [October 31]

[* * * *quotations and translations from* 1 Thess.]

Divinity Exercise
Ethics with Analysis
Trigonometry & conic sections
Catechetics
Latin Prose for Scott.
Agamemnon
Vulguses
Essay

Monday	9–10	Vulg⟨us⟩
	10–12	D⟨ivinity⟩ & Eth⟨ics⟩ Lecture
	12–2	Agam⟨emnon⟩ & Lect⟨ure⟩
	7–9	Cat⟨echetics⟩ Math⟨ematics⟩
Tuesday	10–1	Ethics—Math⟨ematics⟩
	1–2	M⟨athematics⟩ L⟨ecture⟩
	7–9	Hist⟨ory⟩ Math⟨ematics⟩
Wednesday	9–10	Vulgus
	10–12	D⟨ivinity⟩ & Eth⟨ics⟩ L⟨ecture⟩
	12–2	
	7–9	L⟨atin⟩ Ex⟨ercise⟩ & Math⟨ematics⟩
Thursday	10–1	Essay
	1–2	M⟨athematics⟩ L⟨ecture⟩
	7–9	Math⟨ematics⟩
Friday	9¼–10	Vulgus
	10–12	D⟨ivinity⟩ & Eth⟨ics⟩ L⟨ecture⟩
	7–9	
Saturday	10–1	
	1–2	M⟨athematics⟩ L⟨ecture⟩
	7–9	Math⟨ematics⟩

fo. 37ᵛ

To morrow [* * * *erasure*] 7–9 Math⟨ematics⟩ (or nothing?) with   fo. 38ʳ
Ward.

Friday	9–10	Vulgus or breakfast?
	7–9	Essay

Thursday [November 1]   fo. 38ᵛ

I last night felt quite strong feelings of my not having any
development of highest feelings with W⟨ard⟩—was very foolish &
careless about making the most of them.

[* * * *Notes on* 2 Thess.]

fo. 39ʳ Friday [November 2]

3 lectures & about 2½ or 3
Tomorrow.
    A vulgus. some Aristotle. Mathematics.
    A letter to Gell or Burbidge.

[* * * *List of names, erased.* 2 Cor. 5: 14 *quoted*]

Saturday [November 3]

Woodgate says: Christ⟨iani⟩ty is exactly paralleled by Tastes.
    But de gustibus non est disputandum
    Ergo.

It proves perhaps the Evil & Sin of Heresy—but it tends also to
Prove the Impolicy & Sin of Athanasianism.

fo. 39ᵛ [* * * *Translation and note on* 2 Cor. 1: 6 ff.]

Sunday [November 4]

fo. 40ʳ [* * * *Greek text of* Rev. 3: 17–18]

I feel convinced that there are many secret things to which I
sh⟨oul⟩d apply this in myself—and that unless from time to time
at any rate such a feeling of it returns to me, I shall not be going on
right.

fo. 40ᵛ Monday [November 5]

fo. 41ʳ [*translation and notes of* 2 Cor. i: 15 ff.]

general laxity of discipline—irregular hrs &c.

I seem to have been going on ever since this day 3 weeks on the
lower line—which it is clear I must do no more, so, at least, as I
have done—I must be always ready to regard his advances as to
night i.e. to say 'You must not'—I am sure I had not the least
sense of disgust—nor w⟨oul⟩d it be right—only 'Such things
cannot be except reciprocally' (whether to say it out or not?—) I
must try in all my converse with him to keep mindful of the
possible call for this sort of thing.

'The gate of Heaven, and yet we know it not' [* * *]

I did not know (nor indeed perhaps now except a little) the
importance of my 2 last years at Rugby (to eradicate my 2
particular impulses & create my higher one [e/g/]) So also

doubtless now—tho⟨ugh⟩ how much is gone for ever & how much still attainable I cannot know—

Read today perhaps 3 hrs besides 1 hr lecture. Ought to have had fo. 41ᵛ 2 more

Tomorrow.
8½–9 10 to 1 Catechetics. Ethics, Mathematics
2½ to 5 Walk. Bunsen. Bills (Wises?)
5–5½ Letter or Vulgus
I may work pretty hard in the morning bec⟨ause⟩ of dining out.

It is quite evident that in giving him vain assertions &c mine was the whole fault. His indelicacies now seem nothing to me.

12 o'clock

Hobbes & Conscientiousness
A lady's conduct

Tuesday [November 6] fo. 42ʳ
Breakfasted with Stanley—dined at Jesus Coll⟨ege⟩. Walked by myself. Worked not more than 3½ l⟨ectures⟩ incl⟨uded⟩.

Must try & get at least 4 hours beside lectures tomorrow.
10–12 12 to 2 7¼–9¼

Wednesday [November 7]
I have only read 2½ instead of 4
Tomorrow
¼ to 10 to 1. Mathematics for Lecture. Ethics and
7 to 9 Essay. Trigonometry.

Thursday [November 8]
My whole conduct to W⟨ard⟩ has been a series of Vaughanian affectation of affection—and I am afraid I let much of it still be so.

[* * * * *] fo. 42ᵛ

I have read today 4½ hours at Mathematics and about ½ or ¾ hr at Aristotle. This I find with a walk with Greenhill & Ward's business to be too much for me.

[* * * * *]

Friday [November 9]

[* * * 2 Cor. 5: 15 *quoted*]

I have been evidently trifling with wrong & right—& it is no wonder such evil ensues.

It is most certain that in any case almost, my manner will be too kind: so that to let it be so consciously is mischievous to an indefinite extent.

fo. 43ʳ Saturday [November 10]

It seems evident to me that concerning the degree of my liking for W⟨ar⟩d I cannot possibly dare to judge till next Term.

I, too, which I seem to have quite forgotten, have but one thing left, & that is to give myself solely up to God's service—in society generally to try to be kind & agreeable without ἀρεσκεια [*complaisance*] with Ward to avoid every sort of affectation & with him & away from him to bear continually in mind the wrong I have done him—and to work for my degree as hard as I can, constantly. [* * * 2 Cor. 4: 10 *quoted*]

fo. 43ᵛ I see clearly that there is an infinity of dangers before me & I dare not hope to escape all—I am pretty certain to be self-deceived again: & I fear I shall be continually getting into affectations with Ward.

Reading B⟨urbidge⟩'s poems & Wordsworth
Devotions with more regularity & attention
Solitary walks
resolutely grappling with any feeling of affectation.

Again I feel convinced that we are in darkness—thro⟨ugh⟩ which we see strange shapes, partial revelations of truth. at one time these, at another those, but the whole at once never. We must not stop to strive & use our eyesight in this darkness, but let it come as we journey on: nor must we deceive ourselves with filling up from the fancy outlines of the fragments we see around.

fo. 44ʳ At least if we do amuse ourselves in this way, we must not act upon the imagined results.

Sunday—Nov⟨ember⟩ 11

Hawkins παντα δοκιμαζετε . το καλον κατεχετε [*Prove all things; hold fast that which is good.* 1 Thess. 5: 21]

The Duty of Private Judgment.

Tomorrow

9 to 10 ⎫ 4 Hrs & 3 Lectures
12 to 1 ⎬ Catechetics. Ethics
7–9 ⎭ Trigonometry

Monday [November 12]   fo. 44ᵛ

Only about 2 hrs work beyond my lectures: wh⟨ich⟩ is nothing.

Tomorrow   ¼10 to ¼1   7–9
    Vulgus to 11 Mathematics   Ethics [L⟨atin⟩ Pr⟨ose⟩ for Scott?]

Must get thro⟨ugh⟩ the Abstract to the end of Book I Ethics. and the Essay—(allowing Thursday night for M⟨a⟩th⟨ematic⟩s?) and then the Trigonometry & Conic S⟨ectio⟩ns musť be looked over. On Saturday may I hope to start fair on the Hierosolyma.

[* * * 2 Cor. 5: 15 *quoted*]

Tuesday [November 13]   fo. 45ʳ

Read from 10½ to 1 & 7½ to 9 4 hrs + 1 lecture—still but little.

Tomorrow

9 to 10 Ethics 12 to 1. . . . 4 to 5½ Ethics—L⟨atin⟩ Prose for Scott

1 to 2 L⟨ecture⟩ 2 to 3 W⟨ar⟩d. 3 to 4 Walk &c

Wednesday [November 14]

Lea Rawstone Ingram Bunsen Breakfast Friday

Ewart Hutchins Fox & Fox mi⟨nor⟩ Congreve Arnold Lewthwaite Poole Wine

[* * * *List of names, deleted*]   fo. 45ᵛ

Thursday Have read about 4 hrs L⟨ectures⟩ incl⟨uded⟩ but have had a hard day's work with Ward

Tomorrow: 12 to 1 Essay (2½ to 5) 5 to 5½ Essay 9½ to 10

[* * * Phil. 3: 10 *quoted*]

Saturday [November 17]

[* * * *Four stanzas of* Lyra Apostolica Lxxii *quoted*. Rev. 3: 17 *quoted*]

fo. 46ᵛ Sunday [November 18]

[* * * *List of names including:*] Doxat, Congreve, Fox, Lewthwaite, Rawstorne.

Tomorrow 7′20 to 8
  9–10 Conic Sections
  11–1 Catechetics . . . Davison or Vulgus
8½–9½ Davison.

Have read a good deal of Milnes' first vol⟨ume⟩.

I think Society will be an excellent thing for me.

Monday [November 19]

Wine Party—Doxat etc.

Tuesday [November 20]

[*Translation and annotation of* Jas 1: 3 ff.]

Have wasted my dev⟨otion⟩ time as usual.

fo. 47ᵛ Thursday [November 22]

I feel greatly perplexed about trying to realise to myself Ward's unhappiness. it seems so completely unnatural to me. But I think it is quite certain I must, as it is quite impossible to avoid falling into great errors without it.—

I may feel confident than when I do not realise it more or less I am going wrong.

Friday–Saturday [November 23–4]

This evening (Fr⟨iday⟩) I let myself drink too much & enjoy myself too much at Congreve's—and in consequence I have lost a great deal that I might have done both yesterday & today.

I am very wandering at my d⟨evotio⟩ns. which it is very important I should not be.

[*   *   *   *   *]

fo. 48ʳ Sunday [November 25]

Laziness at 7. Inattention in Chapel
Loitering &c at 1. Indolence &c at Dinner.

Monday morning. [November 26]

Zacchaeus stood forth & said to the Lord,

Laziness at 7 & 8 too. Inattention at chapel & a n⟨umber⟩ of negligences.

Tuesday [November 26]
I fear a general carelessness.

[*   *   *   *   *]

Sunday [December 2]   fo. 48ᵛ
[*The following words deleted*]: Catechetics. Divinity Analysis. Look over Liv⟨y⟩ lib⟨er⟩ III. Agamemnon Lecture. Ethical Lecture. Divinity Lecture. History

    Mathematics
Letters to Simpkinson. Gell. Burbidge [*deleted*] Mrs Price. Home. Calls on Massie Mrs Foulkes Mrs Wynter
Breakfast: Fox Rawstorne [* * *]

Saturday [December 8]   fo. 49ʳ
These two things should ever in my mind. A Sense of the evil I have done at Rugby—the characters I have ruined—the Pain I have caused Arnold.

A sense of the Folly of my conduct to Ward and the Pain I have so caused him.

I am in a continual state of self deceit on these 2 things (in especial) and if I cannot otherwise bring them into my mind I must by mortification.

Think not of rest: though dreams be sweet   fo. 49ᵛ
Start up, & ply your heavenward feet:
Is not Christ's oath upon your head
Ne'er to sink back on slothful bed,
Never again your loins untie,
Nor let your torches waste and die,
Till when the shadows thickest fall
You hear Your Master's midnight call.

Sunday [December 9]
I fear there is much to be very anxious about in the next 5 weeks.

    Discipline—getting up—and reading regularly.
    Quiet & sober & deliberate behaviour.

As much as possible like my old Vacation at F⟨inch⟩ House.

fo. 50ʳ W⟨illia⟩ms. ⟨Christia⟩n Y⟨ea⟩r P⟨rayer⟩ B⟨ook⟩ Bible G⟨reek⟩ T⟨estament⟩ Hare's S⟨ermo⟩ns Arnold's ⟨Sermons⟩. [Newman's IV] Sophocles

fo. 50ᵛ Liverpool. Sunday Dec⟨embe⟩r 30

Staid from Tuesday 17 to Saturday with Burb⟨idge⟩

Have been very dep⟨endent⟩ & negligent.
Getting up early & discipline.
Chapels.

[1839]

Liverpool Friday Jan⟨uar⟩y 11

Have been at Chester & Mold for a week (2–9)

Saturday [January 12]—¼ to 10 to ¼ p. 2 Reading C.S. 2 hrs upst⟨air⟩s

Monday [January 14]

Tuesday [January 15]

Wednesday [January 16]
My reading has been sadly neglected & it is *the* thing.

fo. 51ʳ ## LENT TERM 1839

[*A list of names, some cancelled, including:*] Mrs Wynter, Massie, Tait, Oakley, Master, Palmer

Monday [January 21]—

Profound Self-deceit and Fancifulness.

Hard and constant Working, and readiness to meet very great troubles and difficulties—

Low line of liking, and so forth in society—just as in Oct⟨ober⟩ 37.

fo. 51ᵛ [* * * *list of times followed by blanks*]

Have read 5 hours of which nearly 3 were at mathematics. Was rather slovenly from 12 to 1½.

Letters to Gell—Home—Conybeare—Walrond.

Tuesday. [January 22]

Up at ½p: br⟨eakfast⟩ Lake

9¾ to 10¾ *Wasted my time very foolishly*

10¾ to 12¾ Mathematics.

1 to 2 Sophocles: rather slovenly.

2–5–7 Walk with Lake: dinn⟨er⟩: W⟨ard⟩ G⟨ou⟩lb⟨ur⟩n Ch⟨urton⟩

7–7¾ Tea &c.

7¾–9¾ Mathematics

I must work my very hardest for I do not know how much I　fo. 52ʳ
have lost by this idle Vac⟨atio⟩n.

W⟨or⟩ked 5 hrs. 4 at Mathematics.

[*　　*　　*　　*　　*]

Wednesday [January 23]

Have worked 5 hrs or nearly: besides 2 lectures.

[*　　*　　*　　*　　*]

Have worked good 4 hours at Mathematics.

But have been foolish and indolent latterly.

Friday Jan⟨uar⟩y 25.　　　fo. 52ᵛ

Sophocles—Have read about 3½ besides 1 lecture: which is but very little.

9–10 B⟨rea⟩kf⟨as⟩t

10½–1, 5½–5¾ Walked with Tylden

Dined with Uncle Alfred which has done me no good.

I am afraid a day of great idleness

Can I not manage 6 hrs on no-lecture days.

Saturday [January 26]

　Not dressed till ¼8

　Breakfast 9–10

　Work Sophocles 11 to 12¾ 7½–¾ = 2

　　Mathematics 12¾ to 1½ 8–9 = 2¼

rather more than 4 hrs. [* * *]
Nearly 4½ without lectures.

fo. 53ʳ I must bear in mind that to acquire strength to hope to be able to go on, is but a first thing. I do not know how many years it may take to 'work out' salvation and those years of continuous labour. [* * *]

The only reason for a hope is the ἀρραβων [*earnest-money*] of the Spirit—but it is uncertain whether at any time any sense of assurance may be trusted, much less looked for.

Work for Tuesday Analysis Eth⟨ics⟩ Catachetics.
12 to 1 Aesch⟨ylus⟩ 2½ to 3 Aesch⟨ylus⟩. 8 to 10 Math 3½ + 3
Notes for Friday

[* * * *List of names, some cancelled, including*] Mrs F⟨oulkes⟩ Massie, Churton, Palmer, Bunsen, Tylden, Prichard, Moberley, Fanshawe

fo. 53ᵛ Monday [January 28]

Have read 2½ hrs besides 3 lectures.
I have let Ward do everything: & have done nothing myself.
I am also getting idle. p. 59

Tuesday [January 29]

Not up till ½ p. 7
11–2½, 7½–9½ Reading:—5½ hrs; but I am in a slovenly way.
More especially careless or rather indolent when with Tylden after dinner.

Tomorrow. Catechetics. Diligence Humility.

fo. 54ʳ Wednesday [January 30]

Lazy about getting up.

Wandering in devotions.

Began pretty well but have ended ill.

Read not above 5 hrs & that slovenly for the most Part.

Industry Economy. *Work hard & be ready for any annoyance*

Thursday. [January 31]

Still indolent. [*list of times, blank*]

Read 6 hrs without difficulty, 3 at Mathematics.

Read Roman History when I sh[oul]d not.

Did not exert myself when with Ward.

Friday [February 1]

9¼–2¼—5 incl⟨uding⟩ 3 lectures. Walk with Congreve. Decade here.

Want of independence.

Was desultory in my work after 12.   fo. 54ᵛ

Was indolent with W⟨ar⟩d & Congr⟨eve⟩
and to night very careless.

Saturday [February 2]

[*   *   *   *   *]

Have only read 4 hrs or little more. Have let myself be idle & interrupted by Ward, with whom I have been too familiar.

Time is my fair seed-field.

Average reading 5 + with lect⟨ures⟩
                4 + without.

Sunday [February 3]   fo. 55ʳ

I have been haunted continually by the memory of Stanley's approving my Speech, & now again by W⟨ar⟩d's remark about self-reproach.

Monday [February 4]

My errors today have been carelessness at 1st Chapel & just after—& again & worse just after luncheon: & at my Party very bad.

I have read 3½ hrs besides 3 lectures.

General indolence & indisposition to exerting reason.

To remember that much depends on one's behaviour to others.

Tuesday [February 5]

Have read about 5 hrs:—and found this almost too much.

Ward here till 11

Wednesday [February 6]

$2\frac{1}{2}$ + 2 l⟨ectures⟩

fo. 55ᵛ Thursday [February 6]

Letters—Scotts Greek [& Latin]—12 to 1

Aristotle—Articles—Essay [*drawing of bow and Queen*]

$7\frac{1}{2}$ to 8

Dined at Oakley's—Newman, Rogers, W⟨illia⟩ms, Morris, Browell, Church, Tickell, Ward.

Activity. Regularity. Solitary Walks &c.
Self-deceit. great danger of:

[*   *   *   *   *]

fo. 56ʳ [*drawing of 3 heads, 2 bearded*]

Friday [February 8]

Have read about 3 hrs besides 3 lectures

Saturday [February 9]

Have read about $2\frac{1}{2}$ hrs.

Breakf⟨as⟩t at Rogers'. Newman, Oakley, Tickell.
A little about 3 hrs, l⟨ectures⟩ ex⟨cepted⟩. Have been clearly unwell most of the week.

Monday [February 11]

2 hrs + 3 Lectures. Br⟨eakfast⟩ with Tickell. Oakley, Churton mi⟨nor⟩, Lake, [* * *]

Tuesday [February 12]

Only 3 Hrs or so.

[Ash-] Wednesday [February 13] $6\frac{1}{2}$ hrs

Thursday [February 14] $5\frac{1}{4}$

Friday [February 15] 4 + 3 lect⟨ures⟩ but rather slovenly.

Saturday [February 16] 5

A little above 4 l⟨ectures⟩ ex⟨cluded⟩ & a little above 5 l⟨ectures⟩ incl⟨uded⟩

Sunday [February 17]   fo. 56ᵛ

I believe I have reason to hope:—but I must remember that it is a venture to believe this: and that assuredly the language of St Paul about the then Christians [* * *] are not to be at all assumed applicable.

I have been much struck with the necessity of an *evident* repentance like that of Zacchaeus

My average Reading hitherto is about 4 hrs l⟨ectures⟩ ex⟨cluded⟩ 5 incl⟨uded⟩

Monday [February 18]

3 lectures & only 2¼ besides, wh⟨ich⟩ is exceedingly small. It sh⟨oul⟩d have been at least 3 hrs.

*   *

This week about 3 hrs excl⟨usive⟩ 4 incl⟨usive⟩

Monday [February] 25th

4 hrs + 3 lectures, but chiefly at easy Work. I am not at all tired.

Tuesday [February 26]—About 3 hrs only bec⟨ause⟩ of Decade.   fo. 57ʳ

Wednesday. [February 27] Nearly 4 Hrs besides 2 lectures, but easy Work

Thursday [February 28] [Nearly] 5 [Hrs]

Friday [March 1] Only 3½ + 1 lecture. Was far too forward & familiar at my W⟨ine⟩ Party. Wasted a whole Hr at least. (8–9 with Tylden). Began my E⟨nglish⟩ V⟨erse⟩ & sat up doing it till ¼ pt 11 by which I procured myself a bad night.

Saturday. [March 2]

I am afraid only 2½: I might at least have got 5

Average 3½ excl⟨usive⟩ 4½ incl⟨usive⟩
Very idle & irregular,
Very much too familiar,
One fortnight remaining.

A good deal of exercise & rather severe has suited me very well yesterday & today.

fo. 57ᵛ I am to try at any rate for 5¾ incl⟨usive⟩

Monday [March 4] 5hrs & 1 lecture: but not very close work.

Tuesday [March 5] 5½ hrs but with difficulty & not very diligently.

*   *

An average of about 3½ excl⟨usive⟩ 4½ inc⟨lusive⟩

The first thing is my own very great sinfulness, which I must try & not let myself be persuaded into losing sight of—I should deem myself in a sort of disgrace. [* * *]

Monday [March 11] about 3 + 3 l⟨ectures⟩

Tuesday [March 12] about 4½ + 1 l⟨ecture⟩

Wednesday [March 13] about 3½ + 2

Thursday [March 14] about 4 + 0

Friday [March 15] 3 + 3

Saturday [March 16] 3½ + 1

Av⟨erage⟩ 5½ incl⟨usive⟩ 3½ ex⟨clusive⟩

I continually let myself forget that every thing I do wrong is sinful and grievous to Christ—tho⟨ugh⟩ of course if we forgive others their trespasses &c so that one must not be driven into wilful transgression by this sense of one's guilt by any means.

fo. 58ʳ Sunday [March 17] Did not go to Comm⟨unio⟩n wh⟨ich⟩ I am now sorry for.

My exceeding wickedness and Waste of Time Past My daily trespasses and double mindedness.

These must be kept in sight and gradually seen more clearly, or I shall never get on at all.

Perfect Humility & readiness to suffer wrong & insults and to be thought as badly and meanly of as possible.

Set to work early in the Morning. To try when at Rugby to be up & get my Dev⟨otio⟩ns done before Breakf⟨as⟩t and if possible, some verses.

Rugby

Saturday night [March] 23rd. Rugby at the Prices.

Have been very negl⟨igen⟩t both before I left Oxf⟨ord⟩ & here. Not observed even the commonest dev⟨otio⟩ns strictly.

John Napier Simpkinson

Sunday [March 24]

[*   *   *   *   *]

Did not do my reading 10–$\frac{1}{2}$ diligently.

Inattentive at both chapels.

This Evening a long talk—first with Pr⟨ice⟩ Mrs P⟨rice⟩ Cott⟨on⟩ & Meriv⟨ale⟩, then with P⟨rice⟩ & Mrs P⟨rice⟩ i de rebus Newm⟨aniticis⟩ [*about Newmanism*] ii Justification in which I was imprudent.

Easter Even. [March 30]

Jaunt to Leamington, Warwick & Kenilworth with B⟨urbidge⟩ & S⟨impkinson⟩

The grievousness of sin past & of our daily trespasses to God—the strictness & holiness of God—are things wh⟨ich⟩ I think I must try & bear in mind while at Rugby continually.

Oxford.

Thursday April 4th

Easter Term

Just returned from Rugby . . .

Active frame of Mind. Fridays & Communions.
Reserve, & Solitude,

As little talking about ἀρχαι [*principles*] as possible. at most, only ἀπο των ἀρχων [*arguing from principles*].

Verses . . . Burb⟨idge⟩ & Wordsw⟨orth⟩
Above all things to remember what B⟨urbidge⟩ said . . .
Work my way into a consciousness of sin.

Sunday. [April 7]

My main duty what God wishes me most to do is my Work for my degree and preparation for active life afterwards. The more rigorously I devote myself to this the better—uniting it with devotional exercises, & cultivation of such feelings as Repentance for past neglect & hope of future activity in the Oct⟨ober⟩ 35 line—humble and kindly feelings of all kinds.

fo. 59ᵛ Be ready to be insulted, and thought badly off by any body.

Monday [April 8]

Thursday ⎫
Friday   ⎬ 5 hrs full ea⟨ch⟩ but not fully at work
Saturday ⎭
Monday, hardly 5 hrs & not well at work

Dined in Common R⟨oo⟩m today & yesterday with Ward's father

Talking about one's Principles is a piece of confidential communication I feel surer and surer is to be avoided with Ward:—the Gellian concrete, if I c⟨oul⟩d acquire it, is the right thing.

Tuesday   ⎫
          ⎬ about 5 hrs
Wednesday ⎭
Thursday   only 3½ or 4

Friday [April 12] Did not get up till 20′ to 8
                  Read from 10 to 1¾ & 8 to 10¼
                  but only slovenly at times
                  Walked from 1¾ to 7 with Tylden
                  Not very pleasant. Northmore.

fo. 60ʳ Humility—Activity—& Self-content

Endeavour to realise by sober & rational self denial the truth of my sinfulness—the blessing of forgivenness. &c.

Saturday [April 13]

Up not till 20′ to 8: nor well at work before 11.

Read from 11 to 2 & 7½ to ⅛8: i.e. 4 hrs & worth any 5 before

Average up to this day—9 days—nearly 5 each.

Both in walking with Fox, wining with Congreve, where also I

drank too much, again with Ward & lastly with E⟨dmund⟩ S.
F⟨oulkes⟩ & my Uncle have given way to the boisterous
substitute for proper behaviour and altogether been foolish.

[*   *   *   *   *]]

Without Christ's death there would be no hope of forgiveness for fo. 60ᵛ
the past, nor help for the future.

Monday [April 15]—6 or nearly. Tuesday 4½ but not very close
work except about 1 hour at Mathematics.

Wednesday [April 17]
It is only by the exceeding mercy of Christ's death, & by giving
myself up heartily to the performance of God's will however
painful, that I can hope to be forgiven; and that this much I
should be granted, is a mercy beyond conception.

One thing I constantly forget now is the great value of every hour.

Wednesday [April 17] 4½ + 1 lecture. Not well ⟨because⟩ of bad
night.

Thursday [April 18]
  9–10 Breakfast with Ward
  10–11 About 20′ [Aeschylus'] Choephori lost about 15′
  11–12 Scott's lecture
  12–1¼ History & Scott
  1¼–2 Gell's letter
  2–½ Lunch &c
  2½–4½ Ward & Tallboys
  5–7 Dinner & Tremaine
  7–⅛8 Tea
  ⅛8–9 Mathem⟨atics⟩.
  9–9½ Foolish
  9½–10 [Sophocles'] Ajax

Altogether an ill-spent day   3 + 1 [+a letter]

A great deal too much talk &c with Ward—too little restraint and
too much indulgence. Too much also with Tylden. also drunk
rather too much wine which made me communicative.

[* * * *List of names, mostly cancelled; including:*] Mrs Wynter, fo. 61ʳ
Massie, Mrs Foulkes, Conybeare,

I must beware of familiarity with Ward & Tylden which I find daily increasing.

Friday [April 19] 4 + 2 lecture

Saturday [April 20] 4 or 4½ + 1 with Master.

Average

Between 4 & 4½ l⟨ectures⟩ excl⟨uded⟩ about 5 or little more incl⟨usive⟩

[*Drawing of a church gable*]

fo. 61ᵛ Sunday April 21st

[*   *   *   *   *]

10 Articles 11 Ethics

I ought to be glad of any insult or ill impression as conducing to remove my self deceit & put me on my right footing. And still more of anything troublesome or painful as being certain to make my faith securer & conviction more rational.

Monday [April 22] Only 3½ + 2 l⟨ectures⟩

Tuesday [April 23] 5½ + 1 but not very close work for the last 3½

Wednesday [April 24] 5½ but not very close work.

Took too much wine at Fanshawe's. Isn't 2 glasses enough? Have been indolent.

About 480 days of Work before degree.

Thursday [April 25] Not up till 20′ to 8. Wasted a vast deal of time & read very slovenly &c. Only 3 hrs good reading. 10–2

This is not serving God: the only way I have now to serve him is regularity & steadfastness at my work.

5½ not very close work.

fo. 62ʳ Friday [April 26]

[*   *   *   *   *]

Have read only 3 hrs & 2 l⟨ectures⟩ & 3 Decade. With unwellness.

Was visited with dreadful feelings of unbelief & ἀθεισμος [atheism] after Tylden's Party—I believe because of my being unable to Work.

—Regularity is my only line for the present.—

Resolutions to be up to Morning Chapel regularly.

Read about 5 & easy.

Average 4½ l⟨ectures⟩ excl⟨uded⟩ nearly 6 incl⟨usive⟩

Sunday Apr⟨il⟩ 28th.

Had a long conversation with Ward: the wisdom of which I doubt. Resolved: not to speak on such subjects till Wednesday 12 o'clock at any rate.

Had to be up till 1 A.M. ✻

Monday [April 29] about 3 + 2 Br⟨eakfast⟩ C. T. A⟨rnold⟩,   fo. 62ᵛ
Ll⟨oyd⟩

Tuesday [April 30] about 5 + 1 but not close or steady. Walk C. T. A⟨rnold⟩

[✻   ✻   ✻   ✻   ✻]

Wednesday [May 1]—5 Br⟨eakfast⟩ A. P. St⟨anley⟩ Walk with Lake

Thursday [May 2] 4 + 2 (+ Union)

Friday [May 3] 3 + 2 (+ Decade) Fox

Saturday [May 4] 5 + 1 Master. Greenhill ✻

τα τυλδηνικα [Tylden's matter]

Average 4 l⟨ectures⟩ ex⟨cluded⟩ 5 l⟨ectures⟩ inc⟨luded⟩

About the realisation of Ward's business, as this new one of Tylden's I am convinced again of the necessity of such a state of mind.

✻

Sunday [May 5]   fo. 63ʳ

Monday [May] 6th 5 + 2   ✻

Tuesday [May 7] 5½ + 1

Necessity of working my way into Conviction of Sin.

Wednesday [May 8] $5\frac{1}{2} + 1$

Thursday [May 9]—Ascension day—4.
  $8\frac{1}{2}$–$9\frac{1}{2}$ Math.
  $9\frac{1}{4}$–$10\frac{1}{4}$ Br⟨eakfast⟩ $10\frac{1}{4}$–11 Waste
    11–$\frac{1}{4}$ Math. $11\frac{1}{4}$–1 Newm⟨an⟩.
    1–$1\frac{1}{2}$ Waste $1\frac{1}{2}$–2 Plato
      2–5 Dinner etc.

Very irregular & inclined to take my own way & ease.

Value of time to come. Loss of time Past.

✳

fo. 63ᵛ Never to touch tea again for 3 weeks:—except out at breakf⟨ast⟩.
& then no sugar.

Friday [May 10]

Quite forgot the above at tea tonight

$5\frac{1}{2} + 2$ but am rather late tonight

$\frac{1}{4}$8–$8\frac{1}{4}$ D⟨evotio⟩ns $8\frac{1}{4}$–9 Fox's 9–11 [✳ ✳ ✳] Took too much
wine at Moberley's & read Ivanhoe.

Wasted nearly $\frac{3}{4}$ hr talking foolishly to Ward.

✳

fo. 64ʳ Saturday [May 11] $5 + 1$

Average 5 l⟨ectures⟩ excl⟨uded⟩ 6 l⟨ectures⟩ incl⟨uded⟩.

Sunday May 12

Monday [May 13] $4 + 2$
  $7\frac{1}{2}$–9 at Lakes
    9–$11\frac{1}{2}$ Lectures
  $11\frac{1}{4}$–12 D⟨evotio⟩ns
    12–$2\frac{1}{2}$ Plato 2 hrs
      $2\frac{1}{2}$–8 Bathe, Walk, Chapel, Dinner.
      8–10 Plato

Rather a poor & lonely day.

Tuesday [May 14] $4\frac{1}{2} + 2$ Not very well & did my work poorly.

Wednesday [May 15] 5½ + 1

Thursday [May 16] 4 + 1. Not very well . . .
       8–9 Breakf⟨ast⟩ at Queens
       9–10 Sowell
     10–11 D⟨evotio⟩ns
     11–2½ Reading.
2½–3 & 8–9 Magazine business.
       3–8 Walk dinner & chapel.
       9–½ Reading.

Did not exert myself properly after dinner—drank rather too much.

Friday [May 17]
   7½–8½ Doxat to Breakf⟨ast⟩
   8½–9 D⟨evotio⟩ns
   9–11 Lect⟨ure⟩
11½–2½ R⟨ea⟩d⟨in⟩g
   2½–4 Bathe & Row
    4–6 Dinner & Ch⟨apel⟩
    6–8 Walk
    8–10 R⟨ea⟩d⟨in⟩g
    5 + 2 ✳

Saturday [May 18] 5½
7½–9 Hall. D⟨evotio⟩ns. Br⟨ea⟩kf⟨as⟩t
9½–3 Work 3–10 Walk. ch⟨apel⟩ dinn⟨er⟩ Wa⟨rd⟩.

drank too much & was luxurious exceedingly
Aver⟨age⟩ l⟨ectures⟩ excl⟨uded⟩ 4¾ l⟨ectures⟩ incl⟨uded⟩ 5¾

Saturday night I think it will be best in consideration of my   fo. 64ᵛ
indulgences to night to add two days to my tea-abstinence & if
possible skip these 2 holidays Mon. & Tuesday.

WHITSUNDAY May 19th.
Oh I have done those things that my soul fears
And my whole heart is sick. My youth hath flown
The talents thou hast given me are gone
And I have nought to pay thee but my tears &c &c.

Monday [May 20] I fear only 4 [*blank times*]
Lost about ½ hr thro⟨ugh⟩ Ward & 1 thro⟨ugh⟩ the E⟨nglish⟩
verse & letter home.

Tuesday [May 21] I hope 6 but not hard work.
7¾–8¾ Lake breakf⟨as⟩t
8¾–9¾ D⟨evotio⟩ns
9¾–2¾ R⟨ea⟩ding
  2¾–9
  9–10 R⟨ea⟩ding.

Wednesday [May 22]

6 again, or nearly, but easy work.

    7–8 Chapel for the 1st time for 10 days or more
    8–9 Lake.
    9–½ D⟨evotio⟩ns
  9½–2½ Reading.
2½–4–8½ various things, dinner, ch⟨apel⟩ & Walks.
  8½–10 Reading.

fo. 65ʳ Temperance in food. Occupying my whole time. το ἐπιεικες
[*moderation*]

Thursday [May 23]
        [*   *   *   *   *]
3 + 3 I fear and I have done several unwise things—too indulgent
at dinner & too unrestrained at Lowes. ✻

Friday [May 24] 4½ + 2
8–9 Pritch⟨ar⟩d. 9–11 Lecture
11–½ D⟨evotio⟩ns 11½–2 R⟨ea⟩d⟨in⟩g.
2–6 Walk E. S. F⟨oulkes⟩ & dinner ch⟨apel⟩.
6–7½ walk 7½–9 R⟨ea⟩d⟨in⟩g 9–10 d⟨evotio⟩ns 10–½
r⟨ea⟩d⟨in⟩g

Saturday [May 25] 5 + 2

9–11 Lect⟨ures⟩ 11½ Letter from my father &c 11½–3 R⟨ea⟩ding
3–6 W⟨a⟩lk D⟨evotio⟩ns Ch⟨apel⟩ 6–¼7 R⟨ea⟩d⟨in⟩g ¼–9
Race 9¼–11 R⟨ea⟩d⟨in⟩g ✻

        [*   *   *   *   *]

Average 6 incl⟨usive⟩. 4¾ excl⟨usive⟩

I clearly do not work up to my strength—nor opportunities—far   fo. 65ᵛ
less.

Trinity Sunday [May 26]

Monday [May 27] Did not get up till past 8   4½ + 1

I think I am much too lax: & let my conscience get callous by little
indulgences &c.

Tuesday [May 28] 4 + 2 A bad & luxurious day—

Wednesday [May 29] 6 Busy and familiar

Thursday [May 30] 4 + 3 Foolish this evening & familiar with
Ward—

Friday [May 31] 4 + 2 Too familiar.

Saturday [June 1] 4½ + 1 My morning cut up in various ways &
generally a broken day.—Ate & drank overmuch at dinner
w⟨ith⟩ W⟨ard⟩.

4½ l⟨ectures⟩ excl⟨uded⟩. 6 incl⟨uded⟩

Rather under my strength, today at any rate;—& generally rather
lax, & free.

[Sunday June 2] 1st after Trinity

I find myself forgetting my continual failings & letting myself do so
from fear of discouragement: but this is clearly quite bad & must
be avoided.

Monday [June 3] 4 + 2½ Tuesday [June 4] 3½ + 3 dined with A.
B. C⟨lough⟩, not very right-behaved.

Wednesday [June 4]—Collections. 4½ hrs + 1.

   Friday. Tylden w⟨a⟩lk
   Saturday—How⟨ar⟩d dine & walk
   Monday Fox

[* * * List of memoranda, some cancelled, including:]
Rugby Mag. *Price's Commission* Calls on Dr Foulkes
Wynter. Exhibition. Tuckwell.

Thursday [June 6] Friday [June 7] about 4 hrs each. Simpkinson here

Saturday [June 8] Only about 3.

Still my old faults of waste of time and forgetfulness of its importance &c.

Have not read Script⟨ure⟩ enough this Term.

A wasteful gossiping & slovenly day.

Average not above 4½ including all.

Dined & walked with R.M.H⟨. . .⟩ wh⟨ich⟩ did me no good.

fo. 66ᵛ   [Sunday June 9] 2nd after Trinity

I do not at all realize the truths, I know, in my daily practice.—it is much more giving up just enough to stop my conscience. [* * * Phil. 2: 12 *quoted*]

It is very hard to make one's daily work here at all edifying but it must be done.—

Monday [June 10]
[* * * Wordsworth's *Excursion*, iv. 214–27 *quoted*]

fo. 67ʳ Tuesday [June 11]
Have been dining out with A. B. C⟨lough⟩ where the Howards were—drank & enjoyed myself a great deal too much:—was sick in consequence on Wednesday.

Long Vacation

*   *   *   *   *   *

Rugby

Per Chaise with Greenhill & Ewart to Arnold's, *Ǝ*, Gell, T⟨homas⟩ B⟨urbidge⟩

Saturday [June 15]
Have been as usual very careless since leaving Oxford.
    Temperance in food

I seem for this Week to have utterly lost my independence.

[*This folio covered with ornamental stars: those which seem more than* fo. 67ᵛ
ornamental are indicated below.]

3rd after Trinity [June 16]

On Tuesday left for Rothley, where I staid W⟨ednesday⟩
Th⟨ursday⟩ & Fr⟨iday⟩ leaving on Sat⟨urday⟩ morning at 6½
A.M.

✲ Thursday

LIVERPOOL

4th after Trinity. [June 23]

✲ Saturday

Monday [June 24]

I fear that owing to my negligence that evening with R.M.H. I
have lost a great deal of opportunity with B⟨urbidge⟩ & Gell.

Friday [June 28]

I find very great difficulty in taking any rest without letting myself
go a long way downhill. Must one make one's rest chiefly one of
Prayer. I lose all realisation completely—

✲

5th after Trinity [June 30]   fo. 68ʳ

   July—With Ward

✲

Saturday. [July 6] Bolton Bridge.

Left L⟨iver⟩p⟨oo⟩l Monday 10½ A.M.—to Birmingham, &
Derby with Ward—Tuesd⟨ay⟩. A. W. Pugin—Mattock to
Edensor

Wedn⟨esday⟩. Baslow—Sheffield—Leeds to Otley.

Thurs⟨day⟩ to Bolton Bridge. Friday Walk to P. Strid [?] with
guide.

6th after Trinity [July 7]

✲

Wednesday, [July 10] Keswick—

Must set to work again: so only I have strength, last East⟨er⟩ Vac⟨ation⟩ seems the only time I have been able to get proper rest—without some grievous stumble.

7th [Sunday after Trinity July 14] Keswick

8th [Sunday after Trinity July 21] York Minster

fo. 68ᵛ   LIVERPOOL

For books on Provincial Dialects—Smith, 4 Old Compton St. Soho.

Thursday July 25th ✳ and up to that time frequent

Wednesday July 31st ✳

Thursday August 1st

Letters to Ward Gell Simpkinson Mrs N⟨ewman⟩ Conybeare Ward Mrs A⟨rnold⟩ Mrs P⟨rice⟩ Burbidge Walrond [*Some of those listed have been cancelled*]

Herodotus Thucydides Virgil Horace Tacitus—V

I feel now in very good health & must not waste the blessing as I am but too much inclined to do. I have done nothing for 8 weeks or near it.

Saturday [August] 3rd 5 hrs Tacitus

10th after Trinity—[August] 4th

Monday [August 5]—5½ Tacitus. light W⟨or⟩k & rather slovenly.

fo. 69ʳ Tuesday [August 6] 5 hrs Tacitus but as yesterday. Eliza Broughton here.

✳

Wednesday [August 7] Not much above 4 today

I am exceeding ἀκρατης [*lacking in self-control*] & indulgent.—

Thursday [August 8] 4½ & a letter to Gell. Chas's return fr⟨om⟩ Br⟨aunston⟩ ✳

Friday [August 9] Hardly 3 Heard from T. B⟨urbidge⟩

Saturday [August 10] About 3½   2 Notes to Rugby
    Average 4 hrs only.

11th after Trinity [August 11]

    A very pleasant Sunday.—
  and a very miserable end *—

Monday, Tuesday, [August 12–13] average 4½—
Wednesday [August 14] 5, Thursday [August 15] 5½, Friday,
[August 16] 5½, Saturday [August 17] 5
Heard fr⟨om⟩ Mrs Price:—

Average 5 hours, Herodotus, & Tacitus, & a little Virgil
very easy Work.

12th after Trinity [August 18] Went to the School.   fo. 69ᵛ

*

Monday [August 19] 4   Fitzgerald & W⟨illia⟩m Crowder
dined with us.

Tuesday [August 20] 5½ Walked with Father—
—My contemptibility is most striking—

Wedneday [August 21] 5½ but poor work. Jaunt to Seaforth *

Thursday [August 22] 5¾ besides a letter to T⟨homas⟩
B⟨urbidge⟩ only walked 1½ & I fear I have gone too far.
I think I find here at home the lack of something to help me
actively in exertion very prejudicial.

Friday [August 23] 6 hrs I think.

Saturday [August 24] 6¼ but lighter W⟨or⟩k chiefly.
    Averaged 5½ hrs—a good deal tired.

13th after Trinity [August] 25th. *

Monday [August 26] 5 hrs: but the first 3½ not to much
Purpose.—

Whenever I come to enjoy anything like health or to be at all regular,—I always deceive myself & forget my wickedness & danger.—

fo. 70ʳ Tuesday & Wednesday [August 27–8] ✳ 6 each, but only Herodotus. Went to the Dingle.

Thursday [August 29] 5½ Went to see Mrs Cumming & H. Wrench. Wrote to H. W. W⟨alrond⟩

Friday [August 30]—6 Sent my letters to W⟨alrond⟩ & B⟨urbidge⟩.

Saturday [August 31] 6 ✳ Mrs N⟨ewman⟩—Conybeare— Gell—Tylden—Ward

Average above 5¾:—but not such hard & thoro⟨ugh⟩ working perhaps as the end of last Week.—

My great waste of time & wickedness & contemptibility.

14th after Trinity September 1st.

Communion at St David's—Mr Barber called.—

Monday [September 2] 5. As last t⟨er⟩m, I feel myself working but not up to my strength or opportunities. Dr Foulkes called.

Tuesday [September 3] 4½ Not very well.—Father left for Mold.

My working duties I perform pretty fairly: but my socialities require a great deal of amendment.

Wednesday [September 4] 4½ Have to dine out at Seaforth.—

fo. 70ᵛ Thursday. [September 5] Not above 3½: Went to Sefton &c & walked home by Walton. Not here till late; but lost about ½ hr or more after I came in. Father ret⟨ur⟩ned. ✳

Friday. [September 6] Good 6½:—Saturday [September 7] 7

Average this Week—5 & a little more [Mathematics & Thucydides]

✳

Whenever there is the least approach to wilfulness this Catastrophe occurs.

15th after Trinity [September] 8th

The cause of this was my yesterday's neglect of dev⟨otio⟩ns: My wickedness & wastefulness are what I am always forgetting.—

Monday [September 9] 5½ but almost wholly Thucydides.

The Source of this Mischief is clearly my neglect of dev⟨otio⟩ns *specially Penitential.*

Tuesday [September 10] 3. Still more unwell. Wednesday [September 11] 5 Thucydides

Average perhaps 4½ but easy & slovenly.

Saturday [September 14]   ✳

16th after Trinity [September] 15th   fo. 71ʳ

Got on badly with my class. Wrote to Mrs N⟨ewman⟩ & J⟨emima⟩ C. C⟨lough⟩.

Left L⟨iver⟩p⟨oo⟩l on Monday [September 16]

17th after Trinity at C⟨. . .⟩ H⟨. . .⟩.

✳ Wednesday [September] 25th after Caern⟨arvon⟩ Ball & otherwise scarcely once.

Returned Saturday [September 28] 10 p.m.

18th after Trinity [September] 29th

Did not go to School. Letters fr⟨om⟩ J. P. G⟨ell⟩ H. W. W⟨alrond⟩ & Mrs A⟨rnold⟩.

During this journey have been constantly giving way to ἀρεσκεια [*complaisance*] whereby I have lost a good deal I had gained during previous stay at home.

Monday [September 30] Ward here

Tuesday [October 1]

Wednesday [October 2] My father spoke about ✳. Aunt Martha here.

(October)   fo. 71ᵛ

What I am sure I am now most wanting in is penitential feelings &

sense of necessity of work. I am full of levity. Ward is quite a pattern to me[?]

Thursday [October 3]
Have been to Bickersteth about ✳—Chas returned.

Friday [October 4]
With Ward almost all the day—Aunt Jemima & Millicent

Saturday [October 5]
My father's note. Read Mrs Hemans.

19th after Trinity. 5th [October 6]
Monday [October 7] ✳ after φ⟨αντασίαι⟩ εὐδ⟨οξίας⟩ [*fancies of good repute*]

Tuesday [October 8] Rugby. the Arnolds—& Miss Arnold.

Wednesday, Thursday [October 9–10] Braunston—the Lambs

Friday [October 11] via Banbury to Oxf⟨or⟩d——

Saturday [October 12] ✳ after rowing.

fo. 72ʳ   OXFORD MICHAELMAS TERM. 20TH AFTER
                              TRINITY

[October 13]
A return to repentant feelings such as I felt last December is manifestly most necessary.

Society seems at present an evil as I cannot avoid levity in it. Such has been the case both at Rugby & Braunston, & before in Walks & with very evil consequences as I experience.

Had a long & I am afraid imprudent & familiarizing conversat⟨io⟩n with Ward.

fo. 72ᵛ   [*List of names some cancelled & some illegible, including:*] Greenhill, Dr Foulkes, Mrs Winter, Mrs Lower, Palmer, Magazine, Monument.

Monday [October 14] Must have read n⟨ea⟩r 6 hrs: but not to any great purpose. Thuc⟨ydides⟩ Math⟨ematics⟩ Soph⟨ocles⟩.

Tuesday [October 15] Missed Baths

10–1, 8–9, 10–$\frac{1}{2}$ 4$\frac{1}{2}$ only. Very great levity.

Walked to Littlemore.

I find the difference between home & this miscellanous society very great & of very bad effect.

Solitude & exertion & regularity in work.

So only I can work regularly & steadily & hard, and keep to quiet habits, avoiding much society either with W⟨ar⟩d, Tylden, Lake or any one, all will be pretty well.

Wednesday [October 16] 5 & 3 pages to B⟨urbidge⟩ & Wed⟨nesday⟩ bathing.

Thursday [October 17] 4 + 1 l⟨ecture⟩

Still very great levity—a row with Ward—

Friday [October 18]—St Lukes day—Missed Bathing   fo. 73^r

[*   *   *   *   *]

4$\frac{1}{2}$ + 1 Dined with Ward: Wined with Congreve. I have seen a good deal of society. Must have certainly eat & drunk too much & also talked.—

Saturday [October 19]. Statutes-morning.

Had a breakf⟨ast⟩. Bright, Battersby, Currer, Fanshaw, Doxat, I Farrer: did not get on properly at all. [* * *]

My behaviour to others is certainly quite on a wrong footing—I   fo. 73^v see too much society. It is pure vanity of one kind or another that gives me pleasure in it & desire for it. I must be more alone to rid myself of this.—

A conversation (from $\frac{1}{4}$9 to 9$\frac{1}{2}$) of $\frac{3}{4}$ hr with Ward: which was much too great letting out.—

About 5$\frac{1}{4}$
     Average incl⟨usive⟩ 5$\frac{1}{4}$: excl⟨usive⟩ nearly 5

Hard Work and no talking is my remedy.—

Set to Mathematics Next Week.

[Sunday October 20]   (21st after Trinity) Laurence   fo. 74^r
Sheriffe's Day.

I have seen Society all day long: and have been very free & talkative: chiefly with Ward.

Monday [October 21] $4\frac{1}{2}$ + 1

Tuesday [October 22] ib.

I missed this Morning a very good opportunity of getting rid of my conceit at Hobhouse's breakfast: where on the contrary I did but feed it.

Wednesday [October 23] $5\frac{1}{2}$ Missed bathing.

My duties here are very light: & scarcely ever disagreable:—they should therefore be done most completely.—

Found the benefit of hard exercise before dinner as reducing me.

✻

fo. 74ᵛ [✻   ✻   ✻   ✻   ✻]

Thursday [October 24] Missed bathing rain.—7
Breakfast with Prior: Wine with Northcote: Still the same faults.
✻

Friday [October 25] 5 Last Bathe in the river. 25th Charles sailed
Have just heard of Rob⟨er⟩t Howard's sudden death.
Drunk a great deal too much at Ward's. Decade

Saturday [October 26] 6. Missed bathing. Average $5\frac{3}{4}$ incl⟨usive⟩
Nr 5 excl⟨usive⟩.

[Sunday October 27] 2nd after Trinity
Heard from my Father. A disturbance with Ward.

Monday [October 28] 5 + 1 but slow   St Simon & St Jude's Day
Bathed at Holywell

Tuesday [October 29] 4 + 1 Missed Bathing

Wednesday [October 30] $4\frac{1}{2}$ Missed Bathing.
Unwell both days, specially Tuesday, with Cholera.

Thursday [October 31] 5 + 1 Breakf⟨ast⟩ with Churton—Wined with Coleridge—Walked with Ward—heard Congreve speak

Friday. All Saints 7 Nov⟨ember⟩ 1st. Br⟨ea⟩kf⟨as⟩ted with Tylden. W⟨a⟩lked with Congr⟨eve⟩. Dined with W⟨ar⟩d.—I fear Imprudent at all places—and this foolish laudation from Ward is exceedingly bad.

Saturday [November 2] 5½
Average 5 excl⟨usive⟩ 5½ incl⟨usive⟩

[Sunday November 3] 23rd after Trinity
✳ owing to not getting up.

Monday—[November 4] Did not get up till ½ p. 7
Also lost ½hr or near it with W⟨ar⟩d & Stanley.

Tuesday 5th Nov⟨ember⟩ Almost as late this morning.
Not very well, perhaps fr⟨om⟩ lack of meat at breakfast. Dined with W⟨ar⟩d, Rogers, Johnson, Stanley [✳ ✳ ✳]
A. B. C⟨lough⟩ arrived
1 hr short; and but little effected.

Wednesday. [November 6] 2½ short:—Dined with Dr. F⟨oulkes⟩.   fo. 75ᵛ
Eat & drank to much:—as usual.
✳

Thursday [November 7]—1½ sh⟨or⟩t.

Friday [November 8] 2 sh⟨ort⟩ in conseq⟨uence⟩ of Decade.
✳
Never to touch tea at the Decade again—
Lost a very great opportunity of steadying myself.
An idle unrestrained kind of day—
My behaviour tonight is clearly quite wrong.

Saturday [November 9]
Only ½ sh⟨or⟩t: but chiefly Plato.

Lost about 8 hrs this week: but have on the whole done pretty well.

[Sunday November 10] (24th after Trinity)

November 10th. A day of very considerable laxity in Society. NB. Read Poetry. Write Letters & stay at home.

fo. 76ʳ Monday & Tuesday [November 11–12] 3 lectures ea⟨ch⟩ day. Lost ab⟨ou⟩t ½hr in ea⟨ch⟩. H⟨ear⟩d fr⟨om⟩ T. B⟨urbidge⟩.

[* * * Phil. 2: 12 *quoted*]

Wednesday [November 13] Lost 1½: Staid at Goulb⟨ur⟩ns till ¼ to 7; and had a foolish business of familiarity & laudation with Ward. All owing to want of strictness & vigour & being on the watch this evening.

*

Thursday [November 14] Lost 2. Drank too much & staid too long & talked very foolishly at Congreve's.

Friday [November 15] Lost 1½: Walked with Tait & indulged myself with tea & familiarity with Ward—various other follies & neglects—lost my vantage point with Ward at 12: 2nd with Tait: 3rd with W⟨ar⟩d at 9.

*

Saturday [November 16] Lost 2½: A good many follies—especially in breakfasting with Tylden.

Lost 8½ this Week. Not in very good health & have done little.

fo. 76ᵛ [Sunday November 17] 25th after Trinity

Pusey's Sermon on Ecclesiastes at Ch⟨rist⟩ Ch⟨urch⟩ this Morning. Had a party to wine.

Monday [November 18] Missed Bathing. My skiffing accident. Wined with Tylden.

Tuesday [November 19] lost 2 hrs—dined at Lowe's & drank a great deal.

Wednesday. [November 20] Lost 3 hrs (& 1 wantonly)—Went

with Tylden to Bladon & drank too much again at Ward's. Very luxurious—also took tea—
Surely Temperance sh⟨oul⟩d be tried.

Thursday, Friday ✳, Saturday. [November 21–3]
Have seen a great deal of Society—and acted but very foolishly.

[Sunday November 24]   26th after Trinity.
Brodie visited me. Hampden on 'the Lord our Righteousness'.

Monday [November 25] the Scholarship & Decade.

Wednesd⟨ay⟩ Thursd⟨ay⟩ [November 27–8] My excursion to Braunston.

Friday [November 29]

December [1] Advent Sunday Comm⟨unio⟩n in Chapel.   fo. 77ʳ

Tuesd⟨ay⟩ [December 3] ✳

Thursday [December 5] dined; & drank & talked intemperately at the Principal's
So Brutus prayed. In Heaven the Prayer was heard
And heaven's high doors were opened at the Word.
As on parched earth, crisp leaf, and drooping flower
In summer falls the small and silent shower
So calm descended on the Sleeper's breast
And Resignation's fixed unvarying rest.
As sudden benighted men behold
The cloudy sky a starry space unfold
So in his heart he saw a wondrous light
Of peace, if not of Hope, illume his travels bright.

[Sunday December 8]   2d in Advent
Did not go to Newman. Walked with E. S. F⟨oulkes⟩ Writing Analysis. Shuttleworth on Justific⟨ation⟩.

Sophocles Terence Tacitus   fo. 77ᵛ
Thucydides (Livy)
Aristoph⟨anes⟩ Aeschylus Herodotus Lent Term
Horace

Sciences with Lowe Easter Term.

My last Week at Oxford—especially after Thursday—very idle & dissipated.—

Collections—walk & dinner with Ward, on Monday [December 9]

Tuesday [December 10] Went to Rugby & Wednesday with the Arnolds as far as Warrington & so to L⟨iver⟩pool.

fo. 78ʳ Saturday [December 11] I am exceedingly lazy but must try to work.

Thursday, Fr⟨iday⟩ & Saturday—about 3hrs each reading.

[Sunday] 3rd in Advent Dec⟨ember⟩ 15th.
Denbigh. Ball. Dolhyfryd. Aunt Martha & Annie—Mold.

[Sunday December 22] 4th in Advent.
Came home on Monday—did scarcely any thing this week.

[Wednesday December 25] ⟨Christ⟩mas Day

S⟨unday⟩ after ⟨Christ⟩mas—Dec⟨ember⟩ 29th

Monday [December 30] dined with the Swainsons. [. . .] Music

Tuesday [December 31] George at Chester Infirmary Ball
Heard fr⟨om⟩ Simpkinson.

My faults this Vacation were first not seizing the opportunity of steadying & supporting myself by beginning at once to go to School: and generally after this mulish idleness, indolence & easinesss.

fo. 78ᵛ   1840

January 1st—21 years old
Heard fr⟨om⟩ Mrs Newman.

                    [*   *   *   *   *]
Dissipation at Chester—with Annie—
                Thursday to Monday [January 2–6]
                        *   *

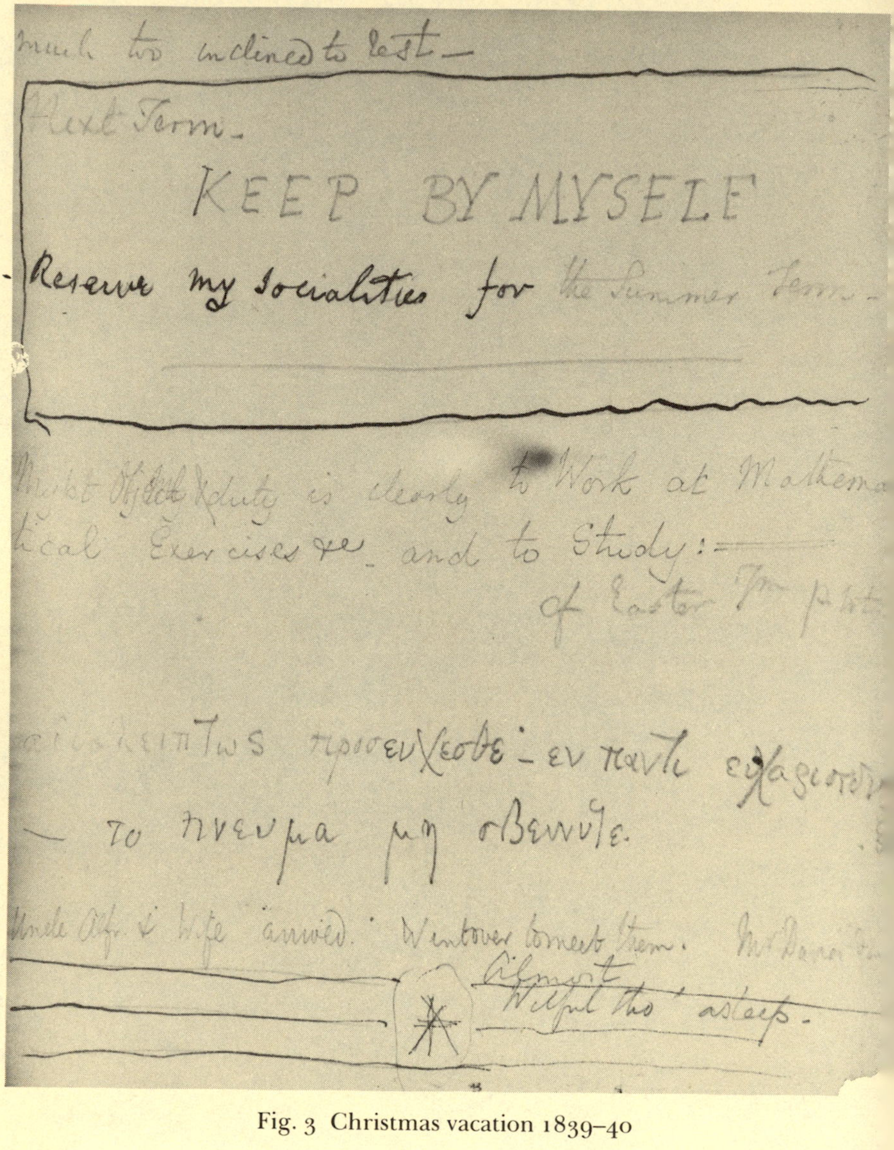

much too inclined to rest —

Next Term —

KEEP BY MYSELF

Reserve my socialities for the Summer Term —

My best Object & duty is clearly to Work at Mathematical Exercises &c — and to Study :—
of Easter Tm p...

...αδιαλειπτως προσευχεσθε — εν παντι ευχαριστειτ...
— το πνευμα μη σβεννυτε.

Uncle Alf & Wife 'arrived.' Wentover connect them. Mr Davidson...
Almost
Helpful tho' asleep —

Fig. 3 Christmas vacation 1839–40

[Sunday January 5] 2nd after ⟨Christ⟩mas
at the Cathedral—Communion

Monday [January 6] at the Cathedral—Came home

Tuesday [January 7] 4 hrs   George went to Min y don

Wednesday [January 8] 4 hrs   Went out to Seaforth

Thursday [January 9] 0   Walked to Sefton—fine day

Friday [January 10] 4 hrs   Came home—

Saturday [January 11] 5 hrs   L⟨iver⟩p⟨oo⟩l arrived with letter

[*   *   *   *   *]

*

fo. 79ʳ

[Sunday] 1st after Epiphany—January 12th
[*List of names, some cancelled, including:*] Gell Ward Swainsons
Buchanan Calders Barbers

Monday [January 13] 5 *

Saturday [January 18] 0. Read W⟨alter⟩ Scott's life
Not more than 4 on an average.

[Sunday] 2nd after Epiphany [January] 19th

Monday [January 20] I ought to have got up this Morning: but
was on the contrary later than ever.

Read a book of Aunt Harriets—Ch. in Army & Navy.

Walking Excursions—Regular & easy duties if I could get them
anywhere—Reading easy books straight on end—and being by
myself, with Prayer—are the only methods of Rest. Society is
mostly dangerous (especially Welsh) for it generally brings me
down. But I am probably much too inclined to rest.

Next term

fo. 79ᵛ

KEEP BY MYSELF

Reserve my socialities for the Summer Term.

My first Object & duty is clearly to Work at Mathematical Exercises &c and to Study. cf Easter Term Past

[* * * 1 Thess. 5: 19 *quoted*]

Uncle Alfr⟨ed⟩ & Wife arrived. Went over to meet them. Mr Davies dined. ✳ Almost Wilful tho⟨ugh⟩ asleep.

fo. 80ʳ Tuesday [January 21] Dined at Mr Barbers.

✳

My prevailing fault just now is indolence & easiness & levity.

Wednesday [January 22]
Mr & Mrs B⟨arber⟩ & Uncle C⟨harles⟩ dined. Went to Seaforth. ✳ Drank too much all these days.

Thursday [January 23]
Journey to Bragborough & Night there

Friday [January 24]
Journey to Oxford by Carriage Walking & Coach fr⟨om⟩ n⟨ea⟩r Adderbury. No dinner.

Lᴇɴᴛ Tᴇʀᴍ—Oxғᴏʀᴅ—Jᴀɴᴜᴀʀʏ 24ᴛʜ

Saturday [January 25]
Have, I fear been unwise & feel myself much more dependent than last Term I was.

Gell: Home: A. B. C⟨lough⟩ T. B⟨urbidge⟩

fo. 80ᵛ [Sunday January 26] 3rd after Epiphany
My Sins & Neglect Past—
The Necessity of Work now.

Saw a good deal of Ward to day also:—from whom I had a severe rebuking this night—not undeservedly as I ought to feel & know more than I do.

[*List of names, some cancelled, including*:] Dr F⟨oulkes⟩ W⟨ard⟩ Palmer, Churton.

Monday [January 27] 6

Tuesday [January 28] 6 but all merely Thucydides

Wednesday [January 29] $5\frac{1}{2}$ + 1

Thursday [January 30] 6

Friday [January 31] $5\frac{1}{2}$

Saturday [February 1] 5 dined with Tait. drank too much & was foolish & have behaved ill afterwards to Ward.

Felt a perfect Change this Morning—at Tylden's breakfast—much stronger & better in health: but much more social & inclined to levity.

Here have I been these one and twenty years   fo. 81^r
Since first to Being's breeze my Sail unfurled
A mariner upon the wavy World
Half idling, half in toil:—mid empty fears
And emptier hopes, light mirth & fleeting tears
Tacking & tossed forever yet in vain
Timidly now retiring, now again
Carelessly, idly, mingling with my Peers
Here having done, meanwhile, as little good
And as much evil to myself and other
As misused strength and guideless frailty could
Here am I brotherless mid many brothers
With faculties developed to no end
Heart emptied & faint purpose to amend.
Tuesday Night, January 28th

[Sunday] February 2nd 4th after Epiphany   fo. 81^v
Breakf⟨ast⟩ with Moberly—Tylden & Vaux. light & foolish
Went to Newmans Communion.

Fast & Penitential d⟨evotio⟩ns or else not go to C⟨ommunio⟩n.
Wined with Ward and after Chapel with Arnold to see the Grenfells

Monday [February 3] $4\frac{1}{2}$
Br⟨eakfast⟩ with Lake & Grenfell. Sent my letter to B⟨urbidge⟩
Lost $1\frac{1}{2}$ after lecture . . . Wined with Farrer. Very foolish, & idle, & social.

Tuesday. [February 4] Did not bathe. Not up till near 9: having been awake till about 1. partly through the fire:

3 lectures: Wined with Conybeare

5½ I am working but much below my strength.

Wednesday [February 5]

Not up exc⟨ept⟩ to Chapel
6½ Rowed:—Wined with Fox, familiar as usual.
—Keep to myself, if not for my own sake for others'

Thursday February 6 still late. 5½ but poor Work. Wined with Bunsen.

Currer drowned in Sandford lasher.

fo. 82ʳ Friday [February 7] 5½ Supped with Moorsom to meet Mat. Arnold 9–10½

The Inquest held at Sandford:—the body brought up & placed in the Treasury about 8 o'clock—the bell tolling &c till 9.

I drank more than I should at Moorsom's

[*   *   *   *   *]

Saturday [February 8]

6 but was not close at work. Also over social. Currer's Uncle and brother are here—the latter said to be very like him. Average 5½

Wined & Walked with Tylden & have also seen Ward 2 or 3 times: also drank rather too much at Tyldens, which has excited me a good deal.

[* * * *Latin inscription in memory of Currer*]

fo. 82ᵛ [Sunday] 9th Feb⟨ruary⟩—5th after Epiphany—

fo. 83ʳ My day has been spent as most of my Sundays idly & ill seeing a great deal of Tylden, Ward & others.

Comm⟨unio⟩n: br⟨ea⟩kf⟨as⟩t with T⟨ylden⟩—W⟨ar⟩d—letter to B⟨urbidge⟩—Lake—Arnold's Prophecy—W⟨ar⟩d & Stanley —Hall Tyld⟨en⟩ Moberly Temple—Chapel W⟨ar⟩d.

A very beautiful conclusion to his lecture from Tait on the subject of Currer—which affected the Master & many of us exceedingly.

Monday [February 10]

The Queen's Wedding Day

Illuminations; town & gown &c &c.

6 but Thucydides. Walked with Arnold. Sat after dinner with T⟨ylden⟩ and had Ward fr⟨om⟩ 8–11½ because of the Illuminations. Letter from Burbidge, announcing his coming.

It will be most especially necessary for me to keep by myself and $\quad$ fo. 83ᵛ work hard.

I clearly am as yet unable to behave rightly in Society.

✳ Tuesday [February 11]—5

Walked with E. S. F⟨oulkes⟩ & dined with Ward & Stanley. behaved imperfectly with both.

The Funeral Announced. Saw the body at ¼ to 8 this Morning.

Wednesday Feb⟨ruary⟩ 12th

The Funeral.

Met in Hall at ½ p. 1: the Mutes followed by all the College in Order before the Body. Blackett & others joining us fr⟨om⟩ Tait's room following next to the Mutes—the Six Mourners, W & R Palmer 2 Uncles & the Father & Brother joining from the Common R⟨oo⟩m after the Body—it borne by 8 [✳ ✳ ✳] He was buried on the East Side of St M⟨ary⟩ M⟨agdalen⟩ Burial Ground half way between the Church Hall & the Gate.

4 at most. Immediately after the funeral, Had to walk, dine & give tea to Ward also to be severely rebuked. He is certainly unfeeling.—Met Currer's brother in the Shop this morning.

[✳ ✳ ✳ *Latin prayer for Currer and his friends*]

Thursday [February 13] 5½ but only Thucyd⟨ides⟩. $\quad$ fo. 84ʳ

A good deal of idleness—had to walk with Ward 2 hrs & to wine with Mildmay where I was foolish.

Friday [February 14] 4½ Thucyd⟨ides⟩ & 2½ Essay

Foolish. letter to S⟨impkinson⟩ & to Stanley, perhaps; also in Essay

Saturday [February 15] 2½ After a very disturbed night, got up about 7.

Very tired & read but 2½

Walked with Fox

Had him, Cong⟨reve⟩ & Bunsen to Wine where I drank overmuch & was weak

I fear that for the present Society is of no good either to me or to others through me.

Average 5

[* * * *Variant of Latin prayer for Currer*]

Feb⟨ruary⟩ 16th Septuagesima Sunday.

Pusey's Sermon at Ch⟨rist⟩ Ch⟨urch⟩ on Romans V, 10

[* * * Rom. 5: 10 *quoted*]

fo. 84ᵛ   As usual too social [with Tylden at br⟨eakfast⟩]& with Ward after sermon but worse with Lake, & Tylden after dinner. Was laid up partly with headache.

Monday [February 17] 5

On the River. Wined with Rawstorne. Doubtful Behaviour.

Tuesday [February 18] 4 only

Walked with Ward—wined solus with Tylden *where I was exceedingly foolish.*

Rather luxurious both days, but apparently in need of it.

Wednesday [February 19] 4

Bathed & Walked with Tylden.

Wined with Moberley, staid late & drank much. ✻

Thursday [February 20] 4 Bathed with T⟨ylden⟩ On the River Wined with Tylden.

Both days exceedingly foolish Wednesday especially.

Friday Saturday [February 21–2] not much wiser.

Average perhaps 4½

Certainly not quite in health—very tired fr⟨om⟩ last Week's

excitement & not knowing how to rest. Hard frost all this week &
latterly had fires continually all day long.

> Away, haunt not thou me   fo. 85ʳ
> Thou, Vain Philosophy.
> Little hast thou bestead
> Save to perplex the head
> And leave the Spirit dead:—
> Unto thy broken cisterns wherefore go
> While from the secret treasures deep below
> Fed by the skiey shower
> And clouds that sink & rest on hill-tops high
> Guidance at once and Power
> Are welling, bubbling up unseen incessantly.
> Why labour at the dull mechanic oar
> When the fresh breeze is blowing
> And the strong current flowing
> Right onward to the eternal shore.

one great sort of weakness is dependence on y⟨ou⟩r own actions; fo. 85ᵛ
looking on possible motives as the real ones. giving yourself a bad
name & hanging yourself for it.

*

[February 23] Sexagesima Sunday
Temple & Tylden to breakfast. Several to Wine. Still weak &
yielding

Monday [February 24] 4½ Walked with Stanley. Wined at Jesus.
Decade at G⟨oul⟩⟨b⟨ur⟩n's

Tuesday [February 25] 4½ Heard from T B⟨urbidge⟩ Rather a
better day.
Very much vanity stricken from B⟨urbidge⟩'s praise of my sonnet.

Wednesday [February 26] 6 but only Thucydides & a little Butler
[* * * Rom. 12: 9 *quoted*]

Thursday [February 27] 3½   Dined with Lake.

Friday [February 28] 5½   Tylden's matter. Went on the River.

Saturday [February 29] 5½   Not quite 5. Still luxurious & not in strength.

fo. 86ʳ March the 1st Quinquagesima Sunday

Breakfast with Tylden—Ward—Comm⟨union⟩ Lake—Ch⟨rist⟩ Ch⟨urch⟩ Walk. Wine with Tylden. Tea with Ward. ✳

Monday ⟨March 2⟩ 6 or n⟨ea⟩rly but easy & slovenly

Tuesday ⟨March 3⟩ 6 but easy

[March 4] Ash Wednesday

5—In the morning not very well; By myself after Dinner—drank too much. Henry Foulkes here. Walked to Horspath & Garsington.

Thursday [March 5] 3 Dined at Jesus College—drank over-much. . . .
✳

Friday [March 6] 6

Saturday 5 Wined with Algar where was Congreve—and was foolish about no fires &c.

Average rather above 5

[Sunday] 1st in Lent March 8th Went to Communion.

Another sad stumble at breakfast; with Jocelyn, Henry, & Edmund; which I might have made very beneficial—& did make just the reverse.

fo. 86ᵛ On Monday [March 9] another piece of laziness with Stanley—8—10

From Tuesday 10th [March] to Tuesday 24th [March] Confined to my Room by a gathering on the Knee. From my foolishness & yieldingness at this time got infinite harm. ✳✳✳✳

Wednesday Lady day. March 25th 5½ Plato ✳

Thursday [March 26] 4½ Plato & Herod⟨otus⟩

Friday [March 27] 6 Plato & Essay.

Saturday [March 28] 5

[March 29] Midlent Sunday Communion in Chapel.

Monday [March 30]—5 ✳

Tuesday [March 31] 6 Butler & E⟨nglish⟩ V⟨erse⟩

Wednesday April 1st 5 with difficulty.

Thursday [April 2] 3½ only 1½ on the River. W⟨a⟩lked with W⟨ard⟩ & dined [chapel]   Walked r⟨oun⟩d the P⟨ar⟩ks 8. Friday 5

[April 5]   Passion Sunday

Monday [April 6] in at Collections.

Easter Vacation.

Tuesday [April 7]—to Deddington.

Wedn⟨esday⟩ [April 8] to D⟨aven⟩try.

Th⟨ursday⟩ [April 9] Braunston.

Fr⟨iday⟩ [April 10] Rugby & Burbidge.

[April 12] Palm Sunday

Tuesd⟨ay⟩ [April 14] to Br⟨aunston⟩ with Simpk⟨inson⟩.

Wedn⟨esday⟩ [April 15] the Cleves

Th⟨ursday⟩ [April 16] Mrs Harris

[April 17] Good Friday

Saturday [April 18]
Have been very foolish. W⟨al⟩r⟨ond⟩ at Br⟨aunston⟩

[April 19]   Easter Sunday

Went over for 1st Chapel to Rugby. Walked with Arnold & Simpk⟨inson⟩ & half way back with B⟨urbidge⟩

Tuesday [April 20]—Cricket—Rugby   the Prices—[* * *]

Wednesday [April 22]—Walked to Leicester

Thursday—[April 23] the Temple & the Bonfire

Friday [April 24]—B⟨urbidge⟩ ill. Burton Wood by myself.

Saturday [April 25] ibid. Old John. the Mesmerising.

Sunday [April 26]   1st after Easter—at Southland

Monday [April 27] to Rugby.

Tuesday [April 28] to Braunston by the Cleves—walked with them to Ashby—the Nightingale.

Wednesday [April 29] to Rugby & Crick. Bragborough.

Thursday [April 30] the Hurdles & Cricket etc.

*

after too much exercise & perhaps too much wine.

fo. 87ᵛ And ✱ during the last week quite frequent, occasionally before.

May 1st Friday—walked to Oxford;—the Coach being full.

EASTER TERM—OXFORD

Saturday [May 2] Walked with Ward.

Sunday May 3rd 2d after Easter
Br⟨ea⟩kfasted with Tylden. Walked with Lake.

Monday [May 4] Walked to Bagley Wood solus.
Have been exceedingly foolish during the Vacation.—a continual letting of myself down. I have lost probably an immense deal. At

present I am rather unwell (though only superficially, I believe)—
Ward & Tylden leave me very much to myself, or else I should be
in a bad way.

Tuesday [May 5] the River.

Wedn⟨esday⟩ [May 6] with Tylden to Bagley Wood. I hope
nearly 4½

Thursday [May 7] Medicine.

Friday [May 8] 5½

Saturday [May 9] very little. ✳.
[✳   ✳   ✳   ✳   ✳]

[Sunday] May 10th. 3rd after Easter.   fo. 88ʳ
Went to Comm⟨union⟩ though but little prepared for it.

Friday [May 15] 6

Saturday [May 16] not above 4
Average since Tuesday excl⟨uding lectures⟩ 4½

[Sunday] May 17th 4th after Easter.
A still idler week.

Sat⟨urday⟩ [May 23] ✳ owing to lying in bed.

[Sunday] May 24th. 5th after Easter.

Wednesday [May 27] 4½. . . .

Thursday [May 28] Ascension Day—about 4½ including
Thirlwall.
Heard of my Grandmother's death, which happened last Satur-
day 23rd.

Friday [May 29] 5½ ✳ lying in bed.

Saturday [May 30] 3—dined with Woolcombe.
✳

fo. 88ᵛ [May 31]   Ascension Sunday [*drawing of a leaf*]

Monday [June 1] ✳

Saturday [June 6] quite idle

[June 7] Whitsunday
Communion in Chapel—✳

Monday [June 8] 3½

Tu⟨esday⟩ [June 9] 3½

Wed⟨nesday⟩ [June 10] 4½ Brodie arr⟨ived⟩

Th⟨ursday⟩ [June 11] 3 St Barnabas. (2. l⟨ectures⟩ & dined with
Davies where I fear I have overdrunk). Heard from B⟨urbidge⟩

Friday [June 12] 4½ wrote to Ξ

Saturday [June 13] 3 at most
The Prizes announced—Lake—Stanley—Tickell—Av⟨erage⟩ 3½

[June 14] Trinity Sunday
Rather rowing & dissipated. Wrote to my father & to B⟨urbidge⟩

Mond⟨ay⟩ [June 15] 4½ Walk w⟨ith⟩ Brodie.

Tuesday [June 16] 2½ Arn⟨old⟩'s Picture.

Wed⟨nesday⟩ [June 17] o, Heard fr⟨om⟩ B⟨urbidge⟩ wrote

Th⟨ursday⟩ [June 18]. Decade.

[Sunday June 21]   1st after Trin⟨ity⟩

Monday [June 22] 3½:—

Tuesday [June 23] 3
Foolish at Tickell's   Decade from 8½ to 12. Coleridge &
Congreve.

fo. 89ʳ [Sunday June 28] 2nd after Trinity
Communion.

Monday. [June 29] Newman's Sermon. Walked with Ward.

[Sunday July 5] 3rd after Trinity. Went to Communion

Monday [July 6]✳.

Tuesday [July 7] dined with Brodie.

Wednesday [July 8] Commemoration. My breakfast.

fo. 89ᵛ

The shield and all thy holy armour on,
And on thy head salvation's helmet shone
Planted on earth in humble suppliant's guise
One knee—one arm uplifted to the skies.

But who of mortal race
Shall speak the steady lustre of thine eyes.
Where Patience shone from haughty pride
By pain & grief refined & purified.

As a glass of rich wine in the hand of a careless child, so are God's gifts to a vain man. The hand is unsteady, the step is uneven; the liquor is spilled on playthings & the floor.

DIARY 5

BOUGHT AT OXFORD—JULY 1840

LIVERPOOL—LONG VACATION 1840

Returned from Grasmere Thursday Aug⟨ust⟩ 6th

Tuesday & Wednesday [August 4–5]✻

[Sunday August 9] 8th after Trinity

Monday [August 10] 5½ but easy

T⟨uesday⟩ [August 11] ibid

Wedn⟨esday⟩ [August 12] 3½ Cha⟨rle⟩s r⟨e⟩t⟨urn⟩ed

Thursday [August 13] 5

Friday [August 14] [5]

Saturday [August 15] 4
Av⟨erage⟩ Above 4½

[Sunday August 16] 9th [after Trinity]

Monday [August 17] 5

Tuesday [August 18] 6

Wednesday [August 19] 5½

Thursday [August 20] 4

Friday [August 21] 4½

Saturday [August 22] 4½

Av⟨erage⟩ Alm⟨ost⟩ 5   Mrs Burley & Blacklock dined here.
Went to Bidstone with Father. Charles & George went to their
y⟨ar⟩ds

[Sunday August 23] 10th after Trinity
A Stranger preach'd at St David's

Monday [August 24] 6

Tuesday [August 25] 4½ ✱

Wednesday [August 26] 6 ✱

Thursday [August 27] 5½

Friday [August 28] 5½ ✱
Father and Cha⟨rle⟩s went to Sc⟨o⟩tl⟨an⟩d
Average 5½   Have written to T B⟨urbidge⟩ & J N S⟨impkinson⟩

[Sunday August 30]   11th after Tr⟨inity⟩

On Monday [August 30] and Tuesday [September 1] 0 being
unwell
Average perhaps 5 for the rest.

Wednesday [September 2] . . . Mother ill—Bank affair—

Friday [September 4] Father returned

Saturday [September 5] ✱

[Sunday] Sep⟨tembe⟩r 6th 12th after Trinity Communion

Monday [September 7] rather overworked

Tuesday [September 8] Uncle Cha⟨rle⟩s   Ought not to have
gone—Weakness

Friday [September 11] ✱

Journey into Wales Friday [September] 18th to Friday [September] 25th

Monday [September] 21st at Denbigh   ✱

Saturday [September] 26th ✱
Wrote to W⟨ar⟩d about degree

Left Liverpool October 3rd Saturday.

Rugby till Tuesday—Braunston. Oxf⟨or⟩d Wedn⟨esday⟩ night with B⟨urbidge⟩.

—OXFORD—

Am exceedingly wild and irrational.

Tylden Moberly Tyler also Tate—& now Barlow & Hobhouse.

Thursday [October 8] ✳

[Sunday October 11] 17th after Trinity

Monday 12th October—wrote the above.
7 hrs good, Thucydides
Average nearly 7 hrs.

fo. 2ᵛ [Sunday October 18] 18th after Tr⟨inity⟩ a rowing foolish day.
Try and assist W⟨ar⟩d, Tylden, & society in general.
lost much today with both

Monday [October 19]—6½ perhaps—but not much progress made. Putting off seems absolutely necessary.

Tuesday [October 20] ✳
Have put off

Thursday [October 22] 6 full

Friday [October 23] 5 only

Saturday [October 24] ✳

fo. 3ʳ [Sunday October 25] 19th after Tr⟨inity⟩
Tylden to br⟨eakfast⟩—Walk with Lake—Wine with Moberly—Ward to tea
Have been certainly contented with Society, & esp⟨ecially⟩ familiar with W⟨ar⟩d.

My own sins.—

T. B⟨urbidge⟩. Home. Relations. Simpkinson etc. J. P. G⟨ell⟩

Saturday [October 31]

Average this week not much generally perhaps 6 per diem, but the Decade & 2 Unions have interfered—today did nothing in the Morning & only 2 hrs at the very most tonight.

Monday [October 26]

Tuesday [October 27] Decade $8\frac{1}{2}$–$11\frac{1}{4}$

Wedn⟨esday⟩ [October 28] br⟨eakfast⟩ with W⟨ar⟩d. Walked with E. S. F⟨oulkes⟩. Wined with Prior.

Thursday [October 29] Union 9–$11\frac{1}{2}$ the President.

Frid⟨ay⟩ [October 30] br⟨ea⟩kfasted solo with Bunsen.

Sat⟨urday⟩ [October 31] Br⟨ea⟩kf⟨as⟩t with Coleridge. Karslake. Walked with C. T. A⟨rnold⟩   Had Coleridge to wine & Union $8\frac{1}{2}$–$\frac{1}{4}$10 & Bell

A most foolish wasted week.   fo. 3ᵛ

I must remember that all my actions are in a measure false. ✳

All S⟨ain⟩ts Day—20th after Trinity—November 1st

Pusey preached on Good Works. Wrote to B⟨urbidge⟩ & my Father—By Myself except with Mob⟨erley⟩ after Hall.

Monday [November 2] ✳

$5\frac{1}{2}$ or 6 but of the easiest kind of Work possible—A visit from Ward—bathed for the 1st time.

Tuesday [November 3]

6 but easy—walked with Ward & talked much

I am certainly resting on society & indiscriminately.

Wednesday [November 4]

6 full but easy—Wined tete a tete with Tylden

The Necessity of being alone and the unavoidable evil of all my dealings with others at present.

Thursday [November] the 5th ✳

5½ Aristophanes—bathed—br⟨ea⟩kf⟨as⟩t with Tylden 9–10½—
Walked with Arnold & called on Mr Combe—Wined with
Moberley—Had no reading till 12. A very foolish day indeed.
✳ Was certainly

fo. 4ʳ Friday [November 6] 6½ though still but easy.

Heard from B⟨urbidge⟩ & my Mother.

Saturday [November 7] 8 Whateley's Examples, which I do
slowly however having been W⟨orking⟩ all the Morning, I
suppose, over one breakfasted with Scott. My Work today again
was easy & hardly done as work—wh⟨ich⟩ I want it to be.

Average above 6 this week   ✳

[Sunday November 8] 21st after Trinity

Tylden to breakfast. Ward 12–1 Lake Walk Prichard Wine
Ward tea.

Had a bother with Ward about Novels.

A foolish, unprofitable or rather losing day.

Wrote to Burbidge & A. B. C⟨lough⟩   ✳

Monday [November 9]

7 or nearly—but still as before. Writing out Lowe in the morning.
Whateley's examples at night, no 47–70 in 3½ hrs wh⟨ich⟩ I
suppose is slow.

Only walked in Ch⟨rist⟩ Ch⟨urch⟩ 4–5 having things to do in
town.

fo. 4ᵛ Tuesday [November 10]

2½ a breakfast Party in the Morning and the Decade at night.
Moved ag⟨ainst⟩ Novels a failure.

Wednesday [November 11] 5½ Lowe's departure. Walked with
Ward Wined with Ivory. Mrs Jones delivered of a daughter about
10 p.m. over my head. up till 12½

Thursday [November 12] 6. Walked & dined with Edmund
[Foulkes] The Schools opened. Not quite well.

Friday [November 13] Read [Aeschylus'] Choephoroe in the Morning & did Essay at night. Was not quite well in the Morning—but I suppose 6.

Saturday [November 14] 6 [Aeschylus'] Eumenides & Prometheus. still not quite well. Alone except 2 short calls from Ward & visit to Congreve after dinner.

Average 5½, the Work latterly even easier ἁπλῶς [*in itself*] than before but ἐμοί [*to me*] I think, harder.

[Sunday]   22nd after Trinity   November 15th fo. 5ʳ

Began better than Usual, but ended badly: at tea with Ward. Feel utterly exposed to the influences of those about me.

Monday [November 16] Not out of bed till 9, nor at work till 11, but have read full 6 hrs. Walked with Congreve 4 to 5 only. σκοτος ἐμον φαος [*darkness is my light*]

Tuesday [November 17]

> O kind protecting Darkness, as a child
> Flies back to bury in his mother's lap
> His shame & his Confusion, so to thee
> O Mother Night come I,—within the folds
> Of thy dark robe hide thou me close, for I
> Have played the liar with external things
> So long so heedlessly—that all I see
> Even these white glimmering curtains, those bright stars
> Which to the rest shine comfort down, for me
> Smiling those smiles which I may not reply
> Or frowning frowns of fierce triumphant malice
> As angry claimants or assured expectants
> Of that I promised & I must not pay
> Look me in the face—Oh hide me Mother Night.

Have read full 5½ but chiefly Mueller's Eumenides—breakfasted fo. 5ᵛ
with Temple—went on the river—luxuriated at night— ✻

Wednesday [November 18] full 7 Aeschylus, Eumen⟨ides⟩ & Agamemnon—easy
Wined with Tickell: went on the river. 2nd time since term began. Snow.

Thursday [November 19] 6 [Aeschylus'] Agamemnon & [Sophocles'] Oed⟨ipus⟩ Rex. Again not up till 9:—had a walk with Tylden—Wined with Congreve—1st day of Viva Voce [Union de Chartismo] ✳

Friday [November 20] 6½ [Sophocles'] Oed⟨ipus⟩ Rex. Electra. Essay—Vox Populi. Not up till ¼ to 9:—wined with Ivory where I met Shairp.—this I ought not to have done. ✳

Saturday [November 21] 5 & very easy:—br⟨eakfast⟩ with Tylden, heard part of Congreve's viva voce—walked with Ward—altogether a very rowing and exceedingly foolish day. Congreve has got his first.

Average 6 but easy work, very,—I have lost in other ways a great deal since Sunday last.

fo. 6ʳ [Sunday] Last [23rd] after Trinity—November 22nd

Tylden & Temple to breakfast. Ann⟨ouncement⟩ of Communion. ✳

Monday [November 23] 4½ dined with Lake—the Greenhills. Not up till ¼ to 9

Tuesday [November 24] 6½ br⟨ea⟩kf⟨ast⟩ with Greenhill. Went to hear Lingan's v⟨iva⟩ v⟨oce⟩ 2½ to 4½ Wined with Doxat. ✳

Wednesday [November 25] 7½ but a good deal Mueller's disquisitions. Wined with Tickell—Staid till past 7—this also was foolish.

Thursday [November 26] 7½ not up till just 9: a quiet day by good luck. Chiefly Aristotle Eth⟨ics⟩ lib⟨er⟩ 3 & a little Mueller.

Friday [November 27] 6½ Had Fox to breakfast. lost n⟨ea⟩r an hour afterwards. Not at work till 11—dined at home. Wrote to Mrs Arnold. Aristotle I & Essay. Another quiet day.

[Riddle &] *Mat. Arnold, Scholar*[s]

fo. 6ᵛ Saturday [November 28] 3½ 1 hr with the Master 1 with

Woolcombe & 1 more in Hall & with Tait. And from 7½ to 11 in my bed-room. *Foolishly* went to Pritchard after dinner. The Class list.

Average 6 or very nearly—Chiefly philosophising on the Ethics, concerning which?

Have been out a great deal, & chiefly in unavoidable ways this week.

Advent Sunday   November 29th.

Communion in Chapel. Have been hesitating all week—& satisfying my reluctance with fancies of not going—in Chapel this morning could at one time hardly restrain from going out—but suppressed it as a mere passing fancy. I doubt however still, whether I am right in submitting to what except for submission's sake I should not have thought of, & would not venture to do. fo. 7ʳ Again the general carelessness of such Coll⟨ege⟩ Comm⟨unions⟩.

Walked with Lake. Ward to tea. Also was ¾ hr with Tylden

Monday [November 30] Breakfast with Ward—Walk with ditto. All these have been much against me—& I have behaved wrongly. Not above 5 I think—not a day of Work

Wine Party—Monday. [*List of names with ticks, stars, questions, and cancellations; includes*] Tickell, Coleridge, Temple, Prichard, Seymour, Ivory, Shairp, Farrer, Hobhouse, Fox, Tylden, Doxat, Foulkes, Jackson, Blackett, Crowder, Prior, Congreve, Watkins, Hobhouse, Arnold, Moberley.

Tuesday [December 1] 3½ only. Wasted fr⟨om⟩ 12 to 2 at least in writing some foolish verses. And had to attend the Decade where I was not Wise. Nor was I quite well. I had far better have skipped.
✳

Wednesday [December 2] 6 Aristotle lib⟨er⟩ V. Walked with fo. 7ᵛ Edm⟨un⟩d [Foulkes]. Letters from Simpkinson & Burbidge just before dinner.

Thursday [December 3] 6½ Aristotle lib⟨er⟩ V & VI & [Sophocles'] Philoctetes. Went my calls & invitations, & S⟨impkinson⟩'s commissions, & on the river. Wined with Moberly. A rowing kind of day.

Friday [December 4] 7 [Aristotle's] Organon & Essay. Walked with Congreve; talked perhaps too much a good deal. Both chapels.

Saturday [December 5] 6½ easy work. Walked & wined with Tylden—was rowing & noisy.

Average 5½ Decade, walks, breakfasts &c and on Tuesday my own foolishness.

[Sunday December 6] 2d in Advent.

Missed Chapel. Went to Newm⟨an⟩'s Service. Walked with Lake. Wined with Coleridge. Ward to tea.

fo. 8ʳ Monday [December 7] 4½ [Sophocles'] Trachiniae, almost:—Not up till ½ p. 9 by some mistake—missed both Chapels. Went on the River. My Wine Party wh⟨ich⟩ went off very fairly. 16 guests:— Fox, Hobhouse, Watkins defaulters.

Tuesday [December 8]

3½ Ethics V:—Missed Chapels again—breakfasted with Doxat & dined with T. Davies.—Walked (accidentally) with E. S. F⟨oulkes⟩ wh⟨ich⟩ did me some harm.

Wednesday [December 9]

6½ Walked with E. S. F⟨oulkes⟩ & Woollcombe's lecture, otherwise quiet:—argued foolishly with E. S. F⟨oulkes⟩ about Tutors. Ritter de Pythagora, & [Sophocles] Ajax.

Thursday [December 10]—4½ ib & p⟨ar⟩t of [Sophocles'] Antigone Breakf⟨ast⟩ with Tylden—Sharp;—staid over long: walked with Ward: dined & wined with Prior, & went to the Union to vote for Moorsom where I was foolish with Congreve. Visit from Farrer. Coleridge's Row.

[*List of names, some cancelled, including:*] Congreve Tylden Temple Tickell Doxat Sharp Johnson cum fratre [*with his brother*] Ivory Moberly

fo. 8ᵛ Friday [December 11] 7 Sophocles with Ellendt. Both Chapels. River. Wined with Moberly & made one or two invitations. otherwise quiet.

Saturday [December 12] 6 Sophocles ibid. Missed Chapels. Sent down for to Collections for an useless row. River Wine Party where I think I must have been familiar & foolish.

Average—rather under 5½: considering my interruptions not very bad: but this does not suit me.— ✳

[Sunday December 13]   3rd in Advent

br⟨eakfast⟩ with T⟨ylden⟩ & T⟨emple⟩. Walk with L⟨ake⟩. W⟨ard⟩ tea 10 to 11. read Moultrie.

Monday [December 14]

Collections & 3 Sophocles. I may call it I suppose 6. Walked alone. Wined with Ivory. Temple departing. Very hard frost & East Wind. ✳ both times thro⟨ugh⟩ laziness.

⟨Christ⟩mas Vac⟨atio⟩n Oxford.   fo. 9ʳ

Tuesday [December 15] Not up till ¼ to 9. A quiet day—though not very industrious. 5½ Sophocles. Sent letter to B⟨urbidge⟩ to Worcester. Hard frost as before.

Wednesday [December 16] Up at ¼ to 8 Went to Newmans. A quiet day though not more industrious & more luxurious than yesterday. p⟨art⟩s of [Sophocles'] Electra & Trachiniae. 6½ Heavy fall of Snow. Fires all day Tue⟨sday⟩ & Wed⟨nesday⟩.

(Balliol)

Thursday [December 17] Not up till past 9. Not a quiet day by any means, & only 3 at most, Trachiniae. Walked with E. S. F⟨oulkes⟩ Removed to College and dined at Jes⟨us⟩ Coll⟨ege⟩ lodgings.

Friday [December 18] 5 at most. Ward came in for 1½ hr in the Morning. I was foolish then in accepting p⟨ar⟩tly fr⟨om⟩ a sense of my duty to him, his approaches, wh⟨ich⟩ neither of us meant to be lasting. Walked with him 2–5 & wined with him.—An idle kind of day; but I am not quite well perhaps because of yesterday's dinner. Frost very cold.

Saturday [December 19] 6 A quieter day. Missed bathing. Not up till ¼ to 9 Dinner with Ivory solus. Ward for ½ hr at night.— (Skating on the River)

Average—not quite 5½ & very light work.

[Sunday] 20th December   4th in Advent

B⟨rea⟩kf⟨as⟩t w⟨a⟩lk & tea with W⟨ar⟩d. The Master Preached. Notice of Comm⟨unio⟩n.

Not up till ¼ to 9   9–10 br⟨eakfast⟩   10½–11½ Un⟨iversity⟩ Serm⟨on⟩. 12–1½ Coll⟨ege⟩ Chap⟨el⟩   1½–¼4 Walk   4–7 St Mary's. Hall & at Valpy's—8–10 tea with Ward.

Monday [December 21] Up at 20′ to 8. br⟨eakfast⟩ with E. S. F⟨oulkes⟩ 9 to ¼ to 11 (Lonsdale)

Wined with Tickell. Heard fr⟨om⟩ T: B⟨urbidge⟩

'C. T. Arnold app⟨oint⟩ed Master'. 4½ only

Tuesday [December 22] Up 10 after 8. Walked 2 to 4 Dinner in Common Room 5–8½ wh⟨ich⟩ it w⟨oul⟩d have been better to cut. Again 4½ only. ✻ laziness again or something like it.

Wednesday [December 23] Not up till ½ p. 8. Walked &c 2–3 & wasted on to ¼ to 4. Tea with Ward 8½ to 10. [Sophocles'] Philoctetes. Not much under 7 I suppose.

Thursday [December 24] 11½ am to Monday [December 28] 4½ pm away at Braunston & Rugby.

(Th⟨ursday⟩ to Chipping Warden by 6½ pm. ⟨Christ⟩mas day to Charwelton [Badby] Ch⟨urch⟩ at Daventry, Braunston 2½, Bragboro' to dine.

Sat⟨urday⟩ to Rugby. the Prices 6–11 p.m.

Sun⟨day⟩ Daventry Ch⟨urch⟩, Chipping Warden

Mon⟨day⟩ Ch⟨ipping⟩Warden to Oxford, br⟨eakfast⟩ at Adderbury.)

Monday [December] 28th. 2½ in the evening. letters fr⟨om⟩ T. B⟨urbidge⟩ & Annie

Tuesday [December 29] 6½ had to dine with Jowett vice Ward. Heard of Balston's death.

Wednesday. [December 30]

The Exam⟨inatio⟩n. & the necessity of hard work for it.

The impossibility of society in my present state.
6   Walked 3–5 had to dine with Ward doubtful behaviour. ✳

Thursday [December 31] 6 but with difficulty. Ethics.—tea with
Ward 8–9 Not up till past 8 nor at work till 11. Letter fr⟨om⟩
Simpk⟨inson⟩ incl⟨uding⟩ 2 from Gell. Thaw—after 3 weeks
frost.

JANUARY 1ST—1841   fo. 10ᵛ

Friday—5   A letter fr⟨om⟩ Mrs Newman. Not up till past 9,
after 10 hours in bed;—fire all day;—have seen no one at all;
walked alone; 3–5 dined alone—& luxuriated with fire 5 to 8

Saturday [January 2] 5   late again—had to walk with W⟨ar⟩d
& to take in Moberly for dinner.

[Sunday January 3] 2nd in ⟨Christ⟩mas
Coleridge came up. Renewal of frost.

Monday [January 4] After several puttings off at last went to
Tuckwell

Tuesday [January 5] br⟨eakfast⟩ with Woollcombe—dinners in
Hall recommenced

Wednesday [January 6] 12th Day   ✳

Thursday [January 7] Wined with Coleridge   ✳

Friday [January 8] Wined with Ivory. George Ferris' Row   ✳
Livy & Niebuhr this week. [Coleridge's] The Friend &
W⟨or⟩dsw⟨or⟩th. Medicine.
Walks in Ch⟨rist⟩ Ch⟨urch⟩ Meadow. Sore heel.

Saturday [January 9]   fo. 11ʳ

Sunday [January 10] 1st in Epiphany. Newman de levitate [*on
levity*] Ward—but not at tea propter [*because of*] Tig⟨...⟩ &
Oakl⟨ey⟩.

Monday [January 11] returned to lodgings. Wined with Moberly.

Tuesday [January 12] br⟨eakfast⟩ with Lake   Livy & Niebuhr
but very tired by end of the Week.

Wednesday [January 13] fires

Thursday [January 14] Deep Snow. Walked Ab⟨in⟩gdon
Road—Wined with Coleridge—large party Powles &c where I
was foolish.

Friday [January 15]

✳Saturday [January 16]. Went to Tuckwell. Drops & Rhubarb
system.

[Sunday January 17] 2nd in Epiphany
Short walk with Lake. Newman de Epiphania. Ward in
L⟨on⟩don   Wined in Common Room   Meyrick

Mond⟨ay⟩ [January 18]

Tuesd⟨ay [January 19] Wined with Tickell. Horace—

Wedn⟨esday⟩ [January 20] Prichard arrived   Bagley Wood

Thursday [January 21] Wined with Ivory

Friday [January 22] dined at home. Tylden's visit. Walked alone
but Ab⟨in⟩gdon Rd.

Saturday [January 23] br⟨eakfast⟩ with Temple. Tylden's Note.
At m⟨or⟩n⟨in⟩g Ch⟨apel⟩ Walked with Congreve.

fo. 11ᵛ   LENT TERM

[Sunday January 24] 3rd in Epiphany

Monday [January] 25th Have sent my letter to Tylden. quod felix
faustumque sit [*may it turn out happily*] to us both.

Tuesday [January 26] br⟨ea⟩kf⟨as⟩ted with Tylden. In
M⟨ornin⟩g Chapel

Wednesday & Thursday [January 27–8]✻ Walked with Prichard. Burb⟨idge⟩ plucked

Friday [January 29] went to Woolton bathed before dinner.

Saturday [January 30] Decade—dinner
Horace & Virgil & a little Aristoph⟨anes⟩ this week—usually after 9.

[Sunday January 31] 4th in Epiphany
B⟨rea⟩kf⟨as⟩t with Tylden A Company Day. Hampden ✻

Monday February the 1st. up ½ p. 9 Aristoph⟨anes⟩. ✻

Tuesday [February 2] Up, 10. Aristoph⟨anes⟩ Av⟨es⟩. 5¼ wined with Vaux to meet Goulburn.

Wednesday [February 3]—awake till 3 a.m. I suppose—up by 9 to breakf⟨ast⟩ with Jenkins.

My present State I fear must be very bad—I feel myself to be feeding on all sort of garbage in the way of sympathy and losing all recollection of the past and thought of the future & with little sorrow or uneasiness because of it.   fo. 12ʳ

22   Most true & yet—like those strange smiles
     (By present hope or tender thought
     From distant happy regions brought)
     Which upon some sick bed are seen
     To glorify a pale worn face
     With sudden beauty—so at while
     Lights have descended, hues have been
     To fill with half-celestial grace
30   The bareness of the desert place
               Tuesday—out walking.

Walked dined & wined with E. S. F⟨oulkes⟩ Went with Congreve to see the Arnolds ½ p. 4—letter from Mother—death of W. M. Perfect's Wife. Aristophanes Aves 5—but expended full an hour on doing Engl⟨ish⟩ verses.

Thursday [February 4] br⟨eakfas⟩t with Ivory—lect⟨ure⟩ with   fo. 12ᵛ
Woolecombe. called on Arnolds & walked 2–5. After Chapel went

to Common Room with Arnold to Oriel in wh⟨ich⟩ I was over free with him—hair cut & Union & then to Ward—till just 11. Read 2½ Arist⟨ophanes⟩ Aves.

Friday [February 5] Read 5 translations & Aristoph⟨anes⟩ Ach⟨arnians⟩ The Wine-business—Walked to Sunningwell 3–5 & made Verses—not up till 10 for no good reason.

31   Since so it is, so be it still
      Couldst only thou my heart be taught
      To treasure and in act fulfil
      The lesson which the sight has brought
      In this thy dull and dreary state
      To Work and patiently to wait
      Little thou thinkst in thy despair
      How soon the hidden sun may shine
      And e'en the dulling clouds combine
      To bless with lights and hues divine
      The region desolate and bare
      That weak unfaithful heart of thine.

fo. 13ʳ   Yet Marks where human hand hath been
      Bare house, unsheltered village, space
      Of ploughed but hedgeless land between
      From Nature vindicate the Place
      Such aspect as methinks may be
      In some half settled Colony
20   A wide & yet disheartening View
      A cold repulsive world—Tis true
      Most true—and yet &c.

Finished on Sunday Morning Febr⟨uary⟩ 7th.

Saturday [February 6] br⟨eakfast⟩ with Churton. Master—Essay 'The French'—Walked with Ward. Wine with Lake. & after Chapel fell into reading of 'Fairy Bower' in which I wasted 1½ at least. 3 Aristotle.

fo. 13ᵛ Feb⟨ruary⟩ 7th Septuagesima Sunday.

Feel strong & Well. May I make some use of it.

+ To write to Burbidge.

+ The Comm⟨unio⟩n.

Degree.

My obligations to all from whom I have accepted benefits during my bad health or whatever else it has been.

The great Cowardice of my conduct in it.

Lent.

Need of Penance & danger of Complacency.

Even in this recovery, if such indeed it be, how much rests on false f⟨oun⟩d⟨a⟩tions—how much is owing to aid I had no right to accept—how much have I lost that I had before.

Walked with Lake. Round the Parks 6 to 7. Ward to tea 8½ to 10½

The 'Recovery' I fear is not much of one.

Monday [February 8] Ch⟨apel⟩—6 hrs r⟨ea⟩ding. Wrote to   fo. 14ʳ
C. B. C⟨lough⟩ & G. A. C⟨lough⟩ Spoke to Susan but weakly & to no purpose. Discovered that Saturday last was the Anniversary —which I had fancied much later

(Feb⟨ruar⟩y 6th to 12th & Septuag⟨esima⟩ Sunday) br⟨eakfast⟩ & w⟨a⟩lk. ✳

Tuesday [February 9] 4—Arist⟨ophanes⟩ Ranae. Aristotle— Translations.

Up:—went to Tuckwell. Woolcombe—Tylden 2¼–⅘5—

Dinner at Jes⟨us⟩ Coll⟨ege⟩. A B C⟨lough⟩ & Aunt L⟨. . .⟩. 6– 10.

Familiar both with T⟨ylden⟩ & at J⟨esus⟩ Coll⟨ege⟩

Wednesday [February 10] 5 Not up till ½ p. 9—Walked & with A B C⟨lough⟩ 2–⅘5 Ranae Wined with Nevill &c. talked both there & at dinner much & loud. 5½–7½:—8½ to 10½ dressing & tea at Jes⟨us⟩ Coll⟨ege⟩

Thursday [February 11]—6 Transl⟨ation⟩ Arist⟨ophanes⟩ Ranae—easy.

Up:—2–5 at Jes⟨us⟩ Coll⟨ege⟩ & lionizing with C. Lamb & E S F⟨oulkes⟩

    The Thaw

Friday [February 12] Up:—did not eat till 2 Walked 2½–4½

6 Ethics & Essay. Heard fr⟨om⟩ Simpkinson. Ward 10¼–½

The Way I am resting in Society in a completely yielding improvident Spirit.

fo. 14ᵛ To be alone again seems to me the right thing.

Saturday [February 13] Up. 5½–6 incl⟨uding⟩ 1½ with Wool-combe. Ethics. Aristoph⟨anes⟩ Virgil. Jes⟨us⟩ Coll⟨ege⟩ & Walk with E S F⟨oulkes⟩ Hall. Wine with Moberly & Ch⟨urton⟩ 2½–7½ Rather tired fr⟨om⟩ yesterday. ✳

Average near 5½ this week.

[February 14] Sexagesima Sunday.

Br⟨eakfast⟩ with Tylden & Prichard. Hampden: letters to J N S⟨impkinson⟩ & T B⟨urbidge⟩ &c to ¼ to 4. Jes⟨us⟩ Coll⟨ege⟩ dinner there &c to ½ p. 6. Walk Chapel & Ward to tea to ½ p. 10. Heard of George's Arrival.

Monday [February 15] 4½ Up:—Sent Simpk⟨inson⟩'s books. Short Walk again today & dinner at Jes⟨us⟩ Coll⟨ege⟩ Edm. F⟨oulkes⟩. 9 Wine.

These Parties I fear are of great evil to me.

Tuesday [February 16] 3 Bathed. Late for Chapel: letter to Simpk⟨inso⟩n lost: walk; dinner with Vice Chancellor,—Decade 2½–10½ Poor law debate in which I have spoken & very decently to my great surprize had a good deal of the talk.

Wednesday [February 17] 2 only

It struck me this morning that in real truth the belief that I am acting on is a belief in Mrs Jones & Mrs Wynters. The Question is fo. 15ʳ then—is it right to act at all when acting is such stuff as this? or is it not folly to stop the Machine from such considerations? are we not fit to be above such things? &c.

[✳   ✳   ✳   ✳   ✳]

Walked alone Bagley Wood—but had to wine with E. S F⟨oulkes⟩ & to tea with the Master where I was as of old at the Mercy of any one.

Mrs & Miss Gaisford. Music &c.

✳ thro laziness

Thursday [February 18] 2½

Up at 8½

Wrote yesterday as above to T. B⟨urbidge⟩ & shall send it today. fo. 15ᵛ
My next step should perhaps be to refuse writing until I amend.
Lionized 3 to 4. Walked al⟨one⟩ 4 to 6½ Bathed & skiffed to 6

Dinner again at Jesus Coll⟨ege⟩ where I found myself recovered
to my old independence such as it was & is. Was foolish as usual in
the philosophic line with Mrs. F⟨oulkes⟩

Mrs Jenkyns Miss [Jenkyns], Mr & Mrs Wright—Pres⟨ident⟩ of
Trinity—Ed. Reynolds.

drank I dare say ½ doz glasses sherry french & claret, besides ½
glass of porter.

Friday [February 19]—4½ translations & L[atin] Essay
Walked alone to Kennington & saw nothing of the Lions. both
Chapels. Wrote ½ a letter to Gell.

Saturday [February 20] 4½ Aristotle 7 (chiefly) Virgil. departure
of A B C⟨lough⟩ & Co. Walked with Ward to Littlemore—both
Chapels. Tait & Essay.

Indigestion.

Average this week 3½ Have been in all sorts of tempers—& partly
from bodily causes I think.

Quinquagesima Sunday. Febr⟨uary⟩ 21st. fo. 16ʳ
Br⟨eakfast⟩ with Ward. Heard from Gell. Walked alone. Read
Virgil. Wined with Tylden. Ward 10½–½11

Monday [February 22] Walked alone—Wined with Bradley. Still
indigestive.

7 I think, but only Virgil.

Tuesday [February 23] ibid. breakf⟨ast⟩ with Tylden. Wine
Party. Cong⟨reve⟩ Tem⟨ple⟩ Tyl⟨den⟩ Sh⟨eppard⟩ Seym⟨our⟩
Jones Goulburn, Bradley.

4½ only Livy & Virgil. Quite Unwell in the Morning.

Wednesday (Ash) [Feburary 24] 6 I believe. Walk &c
alone   [Misop⟨ot⟩

Thursday [February 25] Wined with Prichard. The Bagley Wood Apples. 6 I dare say but easy [Misop⟨ot⟩ except the dep⟨osi⟩t

Friday [February 26] fasted till 1, but not to much purpose. Walked to Shotover. 7 I sh⟨oul⟩d think Aristotle, Livy, Essay. [Misop⟨ot⟩

Read my letter from Burbidge received yesterday ½ p. 9 tonight.

Saturday [February 27]—Up but did not go to Chapel. Hall. Read 9½ to 2 Went on the River & bathed to 5—dinner & Fanshawe's to wine & Chapel &c to near 8. Another letter from B⟨urbidge⟩ 7½ but not close work. My health improving fast.

Average 6   [Misop⟨ot⟩ exc⟨ept⟩ dep⟨osit⟩

fo. 16ᵛ **[Sunday]**   1st in Lent   Feb⟨ruar⟩y 28th

Up ½ p. 7 bathed after ch⟨apel⟩. T⟨ylden⟩ & T⟨emple⟩ letter fr⟨om⟩ Annie incl⟨uding⟩ one from Geo⟨rge⟩ with account of his voyage. Walked alone to Headington & Shotover & by Bullingdon home 12–3 then with Lake to 5 & again after dinner. Spoke with Tylden after chapel Ward 8½–10¼

Over familiar perhaps with Lake, at dinner, & with Ward.

My health much better & feel inclined either to play with any one or to cut every one just as I used. drank 2¼ cups of choc⟨olate⟩

Monday March 1st

6 but easy. Livy:—2½ called on Mrs Greenhill 3—5½

Walked to Horspath & explored the springs (rainy) Found Primroses. Not very well. drank nothing except my drops.

Tuesday [March 2] ⅛8–12¼ Wrote to Tylden. Read 1. Went to Tuckwell & had to surrender the Misopot system. breakfasted about 11¼ Wrote to Mrs Price.

Walked alone, only 1½ Wined with Congreve, Lingan, Vipont, Barker, Nicholls, Blackett—felt in a famished state did not go to Decad. 4 only.

fo. 17ʳ Wednesday [March 3] 5½ chiefly in the Morning. Translations. Up ¼ to 9. Had to walk with Ward unexpectedly 3–5½ very luxurious in the Evening.

Thursday [March 4] 4½ but mere writing out, a good deal of it. walked with E. S. F⟨oulkes⟩ & Congreve 2¾ to 5. Very luxurious after dinner & foolish also with Congr⟨eve⟩ Went to Tuckwell in the morning. His orders make me very luxurious & I go beyond them. Seemed last night exactly as I used to feel when staying out, early in my time at Rugby.

Friday [March 5] 5½ easy work.

A very wet afternoon, but walked nearly to Horspath & got wet through. Went to Tickells to wine.

Saturday [March 6] up to Hall only. 5 perhaps, Livy & Niebuhr only. Master. Walked alone to Horspath springs 3–5½. Wine with Prichard.

Average this Week 5.

The last 3 or 4 days have gone into Company more than I wanted—& being unable to get out walking &c through the rain & my medicine in the way I did early in the Week so as to defend myself. I seem to have giving in & suffering the same harm wh⟨ich⟩ I did this time last year from my ailments then.

[Sunday March] 7th 2d in Lent   fo. 17ᵛ

✳ Have been taking medicine all this week. Castor oil &c &c &c. Friday night was seized with temptation to my old offence, just such as at times I used to feel at Rugby & in the Holidays.

Saturday [March 13] Walked with Congreve—Magd⟨alen⟩ Br⟨idge⟩ ✳ Have been in all sorts of tempers—& do not know at all where I am.

[Sunday March] 14 3d in Lent

More troubles with Tylden.

Monday [March 15] Walked alone Wined with Doxat. Very weakly.

Tuesday [March 16] [Walked] with E. S. F⟨oulkes⟩ & wined with Jones. Ward. The Decade. A foolish & wicked day, specially at night.

Wednesday [March 17]—Walked alone. Wine with Shairp. Ward at night. Have got leave to go.

fo. 18ʳ Thursday [March 18] Went per Pig to Deddington—thence on foot to Ch⟨ipping⟩ Warden.

Friday [March 19] by Nuneham & Daventry & Barby to Rugby found B⟨urbidge⟩ & Mrs Rose at the Prices & myself expected there. ✳

Saturday [March 20] Calls &c.

Sunday [March] 21st B⟨urbidge⟩ morning Service—tea with B⟨urbidge⟩ & Todo & then again with C. T. A⟨rnold⟩

Monday [March 22] Walked with Arnold. a long talk with B⟨urbidge⟩ at night.

Tuesday [March 23] With B⟨urbidge⟩ to Braunston to breakfast—dined there & came on $(4-7\frac{1}{2})$ to Chipping Warden. ✳ laziness

Wednesday [March 24] Walked to Oxford—dining at the Fox. 11–9 ✳ laziness.

If I had not gone hence under the influence of the Decade-folly it would have been pleasant & very beneficial—but as it is I have got as much harm as good by it, indeed more harm.

fo. 18ᵛ Saturday [March 27] to Woodeaton.

[Sunday March 28] 5th in Lent.
Tylden to Br⟨eakfast⟩ Ward to tea.

Monday [March 29] Elsfield & Marston. Not up till 9 . . . $4\frac{1}{2}$ Thuc⟨ydides⟩

Tuesday [March 30]

Wedn⟨esday⟩ [March 31]

Thurs⟨day⟩ [April 1] Coll⟨ection⟩ Med⟨icine⟩ Brodie & Essay

Friday [April 2] Coll⟨ection⟩ Med⟨icine⟩ Lake's do. H⟨ear⟩d fr⟨om⟩ Lowe.

Saturday [April 3] Woodeaton   This w⟨ee⟩k read nothing &
Late continually. ✳

Palm Sunday April the 4th.
Br⟨eakfast⟩ with Tylden in Temple's rooms—accepted his kindness, yet I do not know how far I seemed to commit myself.

Monday [April 5] Woodeaton & τα συσανικα [*Susan's matter*]

Tuesday [April 6] Came off to London at ½ p. 9 in a weak   fo. 19ʳ
undecided foolish state fit to prevent my doing any good there.
Price of Jesus. Euston Hotel. St Paul's—Lowe—& at tea.

Wednesday [April 7] Walked & wasted the Morning. Mr Lowe in
the afternoon. Came into lodgings 11 M⟨argare⟩t S⟨tree⟩t
C⟨avendish⟩ Sq⟨uare⟩.
Returned Wednesday [April] 21st—f⟨oun⟩d Tylden away.   fo. 19ᵛ

Thursday [April 22] Went to Woodeaton.

Friday [April 23]

Saturday [April 24] Heard fr⟨om⟩ Father & George

Sunday [April 25] An unwise & idle day br⟨eakfast⟩ w⟨ith⟩
T⟨ylden⟩ & W⟨ard⟩ to t⟨ea⟩ w⟨a⟩lk solus [*alone*]

Monday [April 26] Had to walk with Ward ✳

Tuesday [April 27] do & wine with Goulborn—6 but easy
✳

Wednesday [April 28] to Elsfield—6 I suppose but Livy

Thursday [April 29] Charles' letter. Marston fields in Evening.

Friday [April 30]

Saturday [May 1] bathed with Goulburn in the Morning
wh⟨ich⟩ did me much harm I think. Very hot indeed—walked to
Elsfield 2–4

Sunday May 2d

Idly & foolishly gave way to 'passion for passion's sake'. Tylden to br⟨eakfast⟩ W⟨a⟩lk w⟨ith⟩ Lake & read Fairy Bower, also skipping Ev⟨ening⟩ Ch⟨apel⟩ In a feverish state, & did not sleep above 3 or 4 hrs, awake fr⟨om⟩ 1 to 5½

Monday [May 3] to Woodeaton nearly

Tuesday [May 4] black dose. Evening Walk in the fields. Awake most of the night.

Wednesday. [May 5] Bl⟨ack⟩ doze passing off [*sic*] Only walk in the fields.
Do duty feeling nought & truth believe
Love without feeling give not nor receive
Have been I fear very foolish since Saturday. ✳

Thursday [May 6] ✳

Friday [May 7] ✳

Saturday [May 8] Logic & Latin Prose.

Sunday May 9

Br⟨eakfast⟩ with Tylden & read Tennyson with him: walked alone to Tempe etc.
I fear foolish—it reminds me of this time /38

Monday [May 10] Ethics & G⟨ree⟩k Prose. Elsfield

Tuesday [May 11] E⟨nglish⟩ Ess⟨a⟩y & L⟨atin⟩ B⟨oo⟩ks—Walked Bagley-wards

Wednesday [May 12] History & G⟨ree⟩k Books. Elsfield ✳

Thursday [May 13] Cram & L⟨atin⟩ Oration. Tempe.
   Like one that in a dream would fain arise
    Toiling & striving—vainly striving still
   A strange & baffling torpor still replies
    To every pulsing of the restless will.
So think I, so I write—And so alas

Friday [May 14]

✱

or rather Sat⟨urday⟩ [May 15] M⟨or⟩n⟨in⟩g 5 o'clock

[May 16]   5th S⟨unday⟩ after Easter.   fo. 21ʳ

> I have seen higher heavenlier things than these
>   Therefore to these I may not give my heart
> Yet am I fainting for a little ease
>   I'll take & so depart.
>
> Ah hold: the heart is prone to fall away
>   Her high & cherished memories to forget
> And if thou takest how wilt thou repay
>   So vast, so dread, a debt.
>
> How should the heart which now thou trustest, then
>   Corrupt, yet in corruption mindful yet
> Turn with sharp stings upon itself? Again
>   Bethink thee of the debt

Wined with Seymour. Walked with Lake & W⟨ard⟩ to tea. but cut Tylden.

Monday [May 17] Tried fairly hard to work but effected but fo. 22ʳ little. Elsfield. ✱ I fear again. I am quite dispossessed of myself at night.

Tuesday [May 18] Walked Elsfield. 3½–5 Wined with G⟨oul⟩b⟨ur⟩n—E. S. F⟨oulkes⟩ & W⟨ar⟩d visited me.

Wednesday [May 19] Viva Voce—Mitchell, Dayman, & Eden W⟨a⟩lked to Elsfield.

Thursday May 20 Tylden to br⟨eakfast⟩ bathed   heard E. S. F⟨oulkes⟩   Elsfield & by Woodeaton field. Arnold's vol⟨ume⟩ of S⟨er⟩m⟨on⟩s. (Ascension day)

Friday [May 21] Chapel—bathe br⟨eakfast⟩ with T⟨ylden⟩ & Ward.

Degree, Wards Pamphlet &c to dinner. Ward to Walk. Queen's & Magd⟨alen⟩   I fear I have been very silly.

Saturday [May 22] not up till p. 8 Worked at Kant, chiefly

translating & again in the Evening, but was interrupted by
E. S. F⟨oulkes⟩ & had to walk with Tait in the evening. Iffley
path. Karslake's v⟨iva⟩ v⟨oce⟩ ✳

[May 23]   S⟨unday⟩ of Ascension

Notice of Comm⟨unio⟩n: br⟨eakfast⟩ with Tylden. Lowe Tylden.

Collegii de Balliolo sub R.I. summa laude florentis Bibliothecae
quod potuit contulit A.H.C. schol. dom. [*A. H. Clough, Scholar of
the House, gave according to his means to the library of Balliol College
flourishing in excellent repute under Richard Jenkyns*]

Walked along fr⟨om⟩ 1½ to 4 Tempe & Bagley Wood—dinner
Prich⟨ar⟩d Chapel. W⟨a⟩lk w⟨ith⟩ Lake & W⟨ar⟩d to tea. I fear
another silly day.

fo. 22ᵛ Monday [May 24] ? to see as little as I can of other people, &
Tylden in a limited quantity.

Walked for 1½–4 Bagley & B⟨urnt⟩ Gate. Hobhouse's for Wine.
Acland & Kaye. Moberly's v⟨iva⟩ v⟨oce⟩

Awake (bec⟨ause⟩ of ice) till 3 a.m.

Tuesday [May 25] Have written & received answer from
Greenhill & am to call at 11

Call'd, & wrote again with old Prescriptions, finishing the
Matter—another note from him. ✳

Wednesday [May 26]

Started at 9 the Fox. Deddington: Banbury. Mansfield-woman

Th⟨ursday⟩ [May 27] Ch⟨ipping⟩ Warden by dinner. bathed by
Edgcot by Trafford bridge. Lydon & Woodford to Charwell for
bed

Friday [May 28] to Braunston by 12. to Bragborough in the
evening.

fo. 23ʳ Saturday [May 29] '*Second Class*' by letter from Cha⟨rle⟩s
W⟨illia⟩ms at breakfast. Went to Rugby by ½ p. 1—bathed; tea
with A⟨rnold⟩ & supper with C. T. A⟨rnold⟩

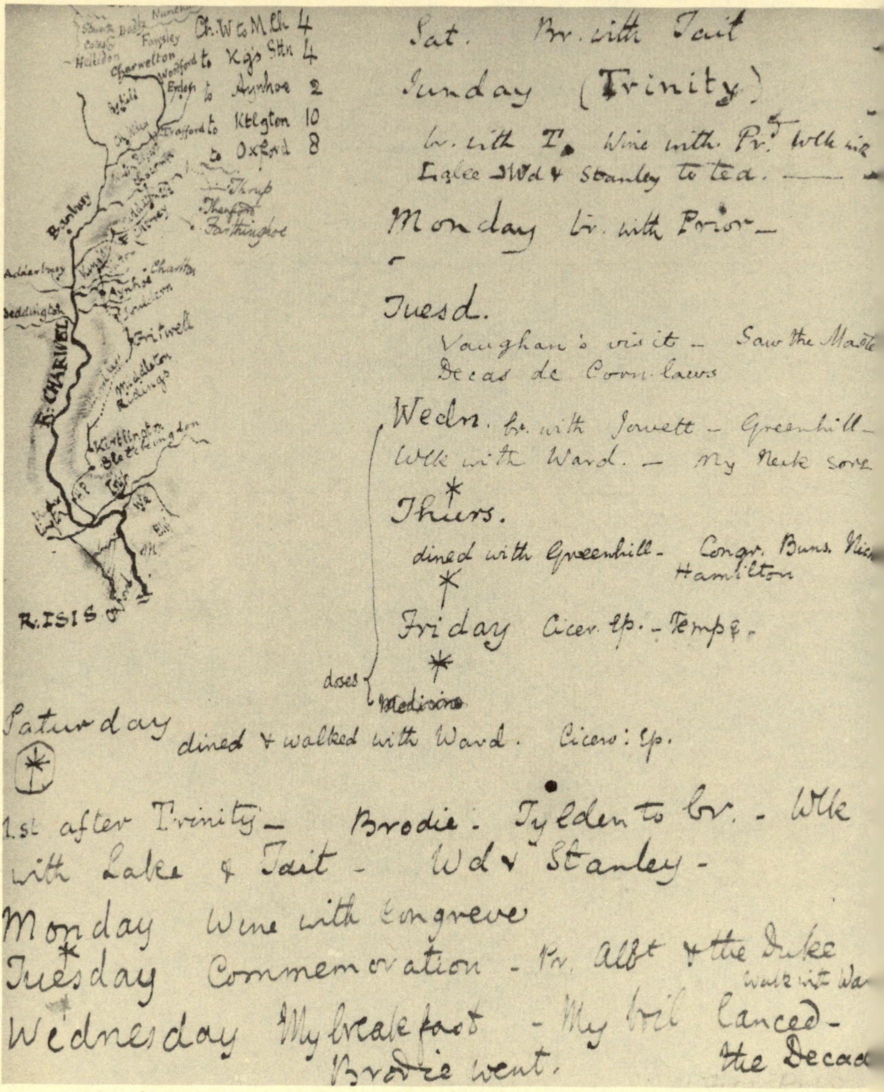

Sat.   Br. with Tait

Sunday (Trinity)
br. with T. Wine with Pr. Wlk. with
Eagles Wd & Stanley to tea. ———

Monday br. with Prior ——

Tuesd.
Vaughan's visit — Saw the Master
Decas de Corn laws

Wedn. br. with Jowett — Greenhill
Wlk with Ward. — My Neck sore

Thurs.
dined with Greenhill. Congr. Buns. Nic.
Hamilton

Friday Cicer. Ep. - Temp &.

Saturday dined & walked with Ward. Cicero: Ep.

1st after Trinity — Brodie. Tylden to br. - Wlk
with Lake & Tait - Wd & Stanley -
Monday Wine with Congreve
Tuesday Commemoration - Pr. Albt & the Duke
walk with War.
Wednesday My breakfast - My boil lanced -
Brodie went. the Decad

does Medicine

Ch. W to M. Ch. 4
Kgs Stn. 4
Aynhoe 2
Kelgton 10
Oxford 8

R. ISIS
R. CHARWELL

Fig. 4 After missing a First Class in Schools

Sunday [May 30] (Whits⟨un⟩day)
Ch⟨apel⟩ at Bilton—went to Braunston by 5.

Monday [May 31] Club-day at Br⟨aunsto⟩n Walked with the
L⟨am⟩bs in the evening.

Tuesday [June 1] Started about 3 & went by Staverton upp⟨er⟩
Catesby, Hellidon Mill, & Byfield to C⟨hipping⟩ W⟨ar⟩den
(little boy & girl)

Wedn⟨esday⟩ [June 2] by Chacombe, Middleton Cheney, King's
Sutton, Aynhoe, Souldern, Fritwell, Heyford leys & the Cottage,
to Kirtlington. wrote to T⟨homas⟩ B⟨urbidge⟩.

Th⟨ursday⟩ [June 3] By Bletchingdon, Hampton Poyle, Islip,
Woodeaten, to Parson's Pleasure & Holywell by ¼ to 5. dined, saw
Ward, went to Common Room, saw Tait.

Friday [June 4] Letters from home, Grenfell, Burbidge. Jowett &
Fanshawe's Prizes.

[neatly drawn map of his walking tour to Daventry]   fo. 23ᵛ

Sat⟨urday⟩ [June 5] Br⟨eakfast⟩ with Tait

Sunday [June 6] (Trinity) br⟨eakfast⟩ with T⟨ylden⟩ Wine with
Pr⟨ichar⟩d w⟨a⟩lk with Lake W⟨ar⟩d & Stanley to tea.

Monday [June 7] br⟨eakfast⟩ with Prior.

Tuesd⟨ay⟩ [June 8] Vaughan's visit—Saw the Master. Decas de
[*Decade on*] Corn-laws

Wedn⟨esday⟩ [June 9] br⟨eakfast⟩ with Jowett—Greenhill—
W⟨a⟩lk with Ward—My Neck sore   ✳

Thurs⟨day⟩ [June 10] dined with Greenhill. Congr⟨eve⟩,
Buns⟨en⟩ Nicholls Hamilton   ✳

Friday [June 11] Cicer⟨o's⟩ Ep⟨istles⟩—Tempe. ✳
[*'doses' marked against Wed. to Fri.*]

Saturday [June 12] dined & walked with Ward. Cicero:
Ep⟨istles⟩   ✳

[Sunday June 13] 1st after Trinity—Brodie. Tylden to br⟨eakfast⟩ W⟨a⟩lk with Lake & Tait. W⟨ar⟩d & Stanley.

Monday [June 14] Wine with Congreve ✳

Tuesday [June 15] Commemoration. Pr⟨ince⟩ Alb⟨er⟩t & the Duke [of Wellington] walk with Ward ✳

Wednesday [June 16] My breakfast—My boil lanced. Brodie went. The Decade Free Press.

fo. 24ʳ Thursday [June 17] Short walk with Stanley. Wrote to Burb⟨idge⟩ & Annie

Friday [June 18] br⟨eakfast⟩ with Blackett—Wine with Hobhouse. Heard of Merivale's death. ✳

Saturday [June 19] Tylden's trouble. What am I to do?

[Sunday June 20] 2nd after Trinity
Only W⟨ar⟩d to tea & only went to M⟨ornin⟩g Ch⟨urch⟩.

Monday [June 21] wrote to Tylden . . . Walked with Ward nearly to Abingdon & home by Bagley Wood. Went to Common Room. answered T⟨ylden⟩'s answer

Tuesday [June 22] Answered T⟨ylden⟩ again & ended it . . . saw him at 1 o'cl.

Wednesday [June 23] Br⟨eakfast⟩ with Goulburn.

fo. 24ᵛ Thursday [June 24] K⟨ir⟩tl⟨in⟩gton by the Spring to Souldern & Aynhoe, Charlton, Farthinghoe, Thenford, near Thrup to Ch⟨ipping⟩ W⟨ar⟩den. ✳

Friday [June 25] to Br⟨aunsto⟩n by ⅓ to Rugby by Dunch⟨urch⟩ by 9. slept at Mr Edmunds'

Saturday [June 26] Rugby Ch⟨apel⟩ The Prices. by [. . .] home by 9. Aunt M⟨artha⟩ & Marg⟨are⟩t letter fr⟨om⟩ T. W⟨alrond⟩

[June 27] Liverpool 3rd S⟨unday⟩ aft⟨er⟩ T⟨rinity⟩

Monday [June 28] Over the River with Annie

Tuesday [June 29] Nomin⟨ation⟩ day. Wrote to T. W⟨alrond⟩ etc. ✳

Wednesday [June 30] Election day. Pr⟨inces⟩ Parade

Thursday Mosley Hill. H⟨ear⟩d fr⟨om⟩ R. C⟨lough⟩—Very idle doing I don't know what. July the 1st

Friday [July 2] shopping.—//WORK// My Work my engagements & responsibilities.

(Westmoreland)   fo. 25ʳ

Saturday [July 3]—left, with Lucy & Emma Perfect as far as Lancaster. thence by coach to Ambleside   To Mrs Nicholson's & Mrs Aines. ✳

Sunday [July 4] to Stock gill force—to Ambleside Ch⟨urch⟩ to Patterdale.

Monday [July 5] by Grisedale & Seat Sandal to Grasmere & Ambleside—to Grasmere & back again. Heavy Rain. ✳

Tuesday [July 6] To Fox How with Cotton—to Grasmere & back & finally to Grasmere for dinner & bed   note fr⟨om⟩ Walrond.

Wednesday [July 7] Conic S⟨ectio⟩ns—to Easedale Tarn—to Ambleside & back

Thursday [July 8] ibid. dinner at ½ p. 4 to Langdale & top of Silver How.—Found Walrond here on my return at 9.

(Tuesday Getting up early. Going to bed at once after tea   fo. 25ᵛ

Friday [July 9] Lectures at 7 & 12. Walk towards Fox How—met & turned back with Cotton, Bunsen, Penrose.

Saturday [July 10] Walk into Langdale in heavy rain   Ovid Tristia translation.

Sunday [July 11] Grasmere Ch⟨urch⟩ over Loughrigg to Fox How. Conv⟨ersatio⟩n with Mrs A⟨rnold⟩. Rydal Church ✳

Monday [July 12] Walked separate. Stickle Tarn. Easedale Rocks. Conic Sections.

Tuesday [July 13] Wordsworth. Translation. Walked alone. B's dell & Alan bank rocks.

Wednesday [July 14] Conic S⟨ectio⟩ns Parabola. Went together on the lake.

fo. 26ʳ I do not doubt but that I am resting idly on Walrond; so as to be unable to do him any moral assistance; I fear so as to be doing him harm. It has been getting worse & worse: I think the great loss was on Sunday when I was very foolish.

Thursday [July 15] A foolish day—talked over much & vehemently at breakfast & at tea:—& was also idle. Walked alone in Easedale.

Friday [July 16] 5:—Walked together round Grasmere, fording the Rotha below it, having started for Ambleside:—Perhaps a little better today, but—

Saturday [July 17] 5 Began the early Mathematics. C⟨onic⟩ S⟨ectio⟩ns & transl⟨atio⟩n. Heard from B⟨urbidge⟩ Went on the lake in Mr Green's boat. [Aeschylus'] Agamemnon at 12 Thucydides ½9 to 10.

fo. 26ᵛ Sunday July 18th

Work my hardest—for next Sunday.

My dependence on T W⟨alrond⟩

2 miles tow⟨ar⟩ds Grisedale with Walrond. Sketching & writing to B⟨urbidge⟩ both before & after Church & reading Wordsworth till ½ p. 4 Went up to Easedale t⟨ar⟩n returned by 7. Went out again fr⟨om⟩ ¼ to 9 to ¼10. Butterlip How & Easedale. Laodamia.

Monday [July 19]—Walr⟨ond⟩ not down till 8 did not see him till b⟨rea⟩kf⟨as⟩t ½9 ran out into Easedale for a ½hr first. Still have been foolish thro⟨ugh⟩ the day: at breakf⟨as⟩t & returning from Ambleside & perhaps at tea. Called on Swainson.

Tuesday. [July 20] Walrond math⟨ematics⟩ & L⟨atin⟩ Pr⟨ose⟩ bef⟨ore⟩ breakf⟨ast⟩; ran out again into Easedale: lectures at ¼10

& 2½: Read 5 at most. Cotton & Bunsen came at dinner time. Not very well I think;—very much inclined to depend. Read Burbidge's two Sermons almost through ❋

Wedn⟨esday⟩ [July 21] Much floored in the Morning & indeed thro⟨ugh⟩ the Day. C⟨oul⟩d work very little—Bathed. Went on the Mount with Walr⟨ond⟩; to Langdale by Blind Tarn by myself thro⟨ugh⟩ heavy rain.

[*drawings of mountain scenery*]   fo. 27ʳ

Not back till 10 p.m.—tea & talk.—

Thursday [July 22]—Hardly set to till ¼ p. 7:—Tea & rhymes at Fox How.

Friday [July 23] 5 I suppose. To Easedale bef⟨ore⟩ b⟨rea⟩kf⟨as⟩t Over to Langdale by Silver How Crag & back the same way: found W⟨a⟩lr⟨on⟩d with a headache:—

Thought of writing to Burbidge to offer to go away if he f⟨oun⟩d on asking that W⟨a⟩lr⟨on⟩d was suffering fr⟨om⟩ my levity: but there seems no need.

[Had been much put out with thought of committal (I suppose) with Walrond; & was much relieved to find him quite unconscious]

Saturday [July 24] Bathed with W⟨a⟩lr⟨ond⟩ at ½ p. 3 with   fo. 27ᵛ Bunsen there. Charles arrived to dinner. Went with him to Patterdale.

Sunday [July 25] to the Ramp⟨ar⟩ts bef⟨ore⟩ br⟨ea⟩kf⟨as⟩t alone;—with Ch⟨arles⟩ after;—to Ch⟨ape⟩l; to Keswick by Aira Force 1½ to 8 to Friar Crag.

Monday [July 26] to Lodore by boat; by Watendlath alone to Thirlspot hence home to tea: Ought to have gone to the Swan. foolish at tea; exceedingly tired.

Tuesday [July 27] Verses at 4 & Easedale Tarn at 5 a.m; bathed;—was idle; walked up the Raise alone: in good health apparently, but p⟨assio⟩n for p⟨assio⟩n's sake: foolish at tea.

Wednesday [July 28] Idle again after b⟨rea⟩kf⟨as⟩t Mr Jeffreys

Called on Mrs Fletcher; went to Fox How; Simpkinson cum fratre [*with his brother*]; Boutrimer. ✳ I am resting in a false state.

> If when mid cheerless walkings dull & cold
> A scent of human kindliness hath found us
> We seem to have around us
> An atmosphere all gold
> Mid Darkest shades a halo of rich shine
> An element that while the bleak wind bloweth
> On the dry heart bestoweth
> Imbreathed draughts of wine
> Heaven guide the cup be not as chance shall be
> To some vain mate given up as soon as tasted
> No, nor on thee be wasted,
> Thou trifler, Poesy!

Thursday [July 29] Went up into Easedale fr⟨om⟩ 12 to 1 & to Ambleside to the Simpk⟨inso⟩ns & with them to Fox How—home by 10

Friday [July 30] The Simpk⟨inso⟩ns to breakfast (bathed at 9 up at ½ p. 7) at 10; we left with them at 12 and walked as far as Grisedale first farm; returned by 6 at Mrs Fletchers from ½ p. 7 to ½ p. 9 Prichard of Jes⟨us⟩ Coll⟨ege⟩

Saturday [July 31] Not up till 8; Walrond departed for Keswick at 6 after arrival of sketches from B⟨urbidge⟩:—felt in remarkably bad temper. Walked with W⟨alrond⟩ as far as Grisedale turning; then into Langdale by High Rise, but almost to Mill beck. 6 to 10

Have taken no Pills since this day week.

Necessity of Work for Walrond during the Coming Week

Shortness of my own time here.

Simpkinson's return.

August

1st Sunday. Not down till ¼ to 9:—Went to Church at Langdale & afterwards up & to Blea tarn; 10 a.m. to 6 p.m. & afterwards fr⟨om⟩ ½ p. 7 to ½ p. 9 into Easedale. Wrote to B⟨urbidge⟩ & to Annie.

Horace Virgil Transl⟨ation⟩ into English.

Alone

[Sophocles'] Ajax Philoct⟨etes⟩ [Aeschylus'] Agamemnon
Choephori.

Monday [August 2] Very foolishly lay in bed till 7½ Walrond
surprised me at ¼ to 8. Went into Easedale for 3/4 hr. In the
evening to Easedale T⟨arn⟩ & E⟨asedale⟩ T⟨ar⟩n high Man.
Horace 9 to 10 ✳

Tuesday [August 3] Wordsworth & Cicero. 4½ I suppose bathed,
called at Mrs Fletchers but went to Ambleside & Fox How & in all
these was I think very foolish. Carey 10 to 11

> Would that I were—O hear thy suppliant, thou   fo. 29ᵛ
>   Whom fond belief has ventured here to see
> Would that I were not that which I am now
>   Would that I be not that I wish to be
> What wouldst thou? Poor suggestions of today
>   Depart, vain fancy & fallacious thought
> Would I could wish my wishes all away
>   And learn to wish the wishes that I ought.

Wednesday [August 4] 4 ditto:—Mrs Jeffreys, bathed, went on
the lake: foolish with Walrond. letter fr⟨om⟩ B⟨urbidge⟩

Neglect of Pr⟨ayer⟩ & Consideration.

Thursday [August 5] Fox How dinner—Miss Roughsedge, Car-
ruthers, &c Boutrimer. Very tired & out of heart. A very kind
note fr⟨om⟩ B⟨urbidge⟩.

Friday [August 6] I am now all along resting on the fancy of
affection in Walrond; whereas I have no reason to believe he cares
for me, nor yet could be justified in expressing to him that I care
for him.

Letter from B⟨urbidge⟩—Walk up Bl⟨ind⟩ T⟨ar⟩n Ghyll &
across to E⟨asedale⟩ T⟨ar⟩n. Wax, I fear, expansive to
W⟨alrond⟩ at tea; have recovered all my spirits after the walk, &
lost I fear, my seriousness with the talk. ✳

Saturday [August 7] Not up till p. 8 having been up last night till
½ p. 12.—bathed; Mat⟨thew⟩ W⟨illiam⟩, & Bunsen to breakf⟨as⟩t

at 9, then on the Lake till 1: Walked again 8 to 9. Very wild & heedless.

Sunday [August] 8th

Rydal. Morning & Evening. The Arnolds. the Simpkinsons, the Fletchers, Hill, the 2 Randals: the Fletchers & Helm Crag 7–10:—Foolish bey⟨ond⟩ Measure.

fo. 30ᵛ Monday [August 9] Up late & off after 1st lecture to Fox How with Bunsen, Penrose & Simpk⟨inson⟩ 1 & 2, whence by Colwith Brow & Oxenfell Cross to Coniston Waterhead, & thence with Arnold to Fox How. Dinner & Wordsworth:

Tuesday [August 10] lect⟨ure⟩ at 8. 2 Simpkinsons to breakfast. Mrs Fletcher. Easedale Tarn. Sticklebarn, Dungeon Ghyll; Langdale; Fox How; the Salutation: home by 11.
Medicine. Straps. P. Off.

Wednesday [August 11] Patterdale—plan prevented by rain. Ambleside & Stock Ghyll.—Cicero.

Thursday [August 12] Not up till p. 8 Wordsworth—Langdale by Silver How Crag.

F⟨ri⟩day [August 13] ib. little or nothing. Thirlmere

Saturday [August 14] ib. Wordsworth. Fox How for ½ an hr letter from B⟨urbidge⟩ de C T A⟨rnold⟩ &c & from home with the bad news.

fo. 31ʳ Sunday Aug⟨ust⟩ 1⟨5⟩th

11 Grasmere M⟨orning⟩ S⟨ervice⟩ Grisedale Tarn 1–5 Easedale 6½–9

Monday [August 16] Not up till p. 8:—to Fox How ½ p. 12—½ p. 4 to Ambleside with Mrs A⟨rnold⟩ over Loughrigg with Arnold de re tutoria, de magistratu [*on tutorial matters, mastership*] &c &c to Easedale tarn, ½ p 6 to 9. Talked overmuch to Walrond—lecture at 11. E⟨nglish⟩ Essay. Exam Paper. Horace. Tylden E⟨nglish⟩ Essay. W⟨or⟩ds⟨wor⟩th letter to A⟨rnold⟩

Tuesday [August 17] ib. Thucyd⟨ides⟩ Ex⟨amination⟩

pass⟨ages⟩ E⟨nglish⟩ Ess⟨ay⟩ &c Bl⟨ind⟩ T⟨ar⟩n Ghyll 1–4; ib
Mountain 1–9 ✳

Wednesday [August 18] Bathed before breakf⟨ast⟩ & packing.—
Easedale, dinner ½ p 1, Bills & Latin, Off about ½ p. 4. Fox How;
Arnold de Anstey; walked to Milnthorpe arriving very tired at 11
p.m.

Thursday [August 19] Walk into the Park:—No Portmanteau— fo. 31ᵛ
letters to father & T B⟨urbidge⟩ dinner, after starting for Bowness
& returning—Walk on the Hill 4–8:—Supper.

Friday [August 20]—Not up till over late; st⟨ar⟩ted for
Lanc⟨aster⟩ at 9, walked as far as Bolton le Sands 10 miles; note
fr⟨om⟩ Walrond; railway home; Mother & Annie sad enough; the
rest cheerful—Anstey not coming.

LIVERPOOL

Saturday [August 21] Wrote to Ward & T. B⟨urbidge⟩ Saw Mrs
Clay, Mather, Corrie, Smith, Davidson:—& arranged for 9 or 10
pupils.—Heard from, Wrote to Dr A⟨rnold⟩. Father went off to
Old Mold.

Ward. T. B⟨urbidge⟩ Dr A⟨rnold⟩ Mather 12 o'clock.

Corrie Mather. 2 Whiteleys. Percival Clay Adams Hill IV
Davidson R.

[*Drawing of a church amid mountains*] fo. 32ʳ

To be alone when not engaged—   ✳

Monday [August 23] 9½ to 1½ cum pupillis [*with pupils*] 2
Whiteleys, Clay, Hill:—

Tuesday [August 24] 9½–3½ 7   ✳

Wednesday [August 25]—3½ 7

Thursday [August 26] 10–4 Went to Seaforth. The Hour & The
Man

Friday [August 27] 10–4 7 Called on Mr Smith. No Wine. Early fo. 32ᵛ
Dinner. ?

Sat⟨urday⟩ [August 28] to Rhyl & Rhydlan.   ✱

Sunday Aug⟨ust⟩ 29

to St Asaph & by Caerwys to Rhualisa for 2 hrs & so to King's
Ferry by 11

Monday [August 30] to Sutton by train—Smith

Tuesday [August 31] Invitation to B. Corrie's   A boy drowned at
Churchover

Wednesday [September 1] dinner at B. C⟨orrie⟩'s

Thursday [September 2] Hill's row. Friday finished Hour & the
Man

Sat⟨urday⟩ [September 4] Mr Greenall. 10–2 W⟨or⟩k 2–8 lunch,
walk dinner.

Going to Chester tomorrow to avoid Communion.

fo. 33ʳ   Sunday Sept 5

Told father I was not going to Commun⟨io⟩n. Went to Chester
by 9½ train. Cathedral. Walks & River—the Foulkes', dinner,
Cath⟨edra⟩l; Walked to Sutton & by train home by ½ to 9.

Monday [September 6] (Greenall) 9–4:–5¾ Walk
5¾–8 dinner &c. Letter from Ward & to B⟨urbidge⟩ ✱

Tuesday [September 7] 9–4 Examination ✱
Ward's offer of his dressing room:—

Wednesday [September 8] thought I detected Geo⟨rge⟩

Th⟨ursday⟩ [September 9] dined at 4 & went to Bootle
l⟨an⟩dm⟨ar⟩ks

Fr⟨iday⟩ [September 10] Wrote to B⟨urbidge⟩ a good deal tired.

Saturday [September 11] broke down in lesson. ✱ in consequence

fo. 33ᵛ   Sunday 1⟨2⟩th September

Monday [September 13] Aunt [. . .]　　Went to Childwall. letter fr⟨om⟩ B⟨urbidge⟩. early dinner

Tu⟨esday⟩ [September 14] to the Shore. Cazneau Street house.

W⟨ednesday⟩ [September 15] to Allerton

Th⟨ursday⟩ [September 16] H⟨ear⟩d fr⟨om⟩ Dr A⟨rnold⟩ A good deal tired. Walked b⟨e⟩y⟨on⟩d Mossley Hill 6–9

Fr⟨iday⟩ [September 17] Walked n⟨ea⟩r to Mossley Hill 6½–9

Saturday [September 18] Pup⟨ils⟩ till 3: left at 4 for Rh⟨uali⟩ssa Ch⟨arles⟩ & Geo⟨rge⟩ went to Braunston.

Sunday [September] 19th

At Mold *foolish* Slept at Queen's Ferry.

Monday [September 20] fr⟨om⟩ Q⟨ueen⟩sferry to b⟨rea⟩kf⟨a⟩st. Pupils 10–5:—A short walk.
wrote to Shairp to Foulkes & to Ward

Tu⟨esday⟩ [September 21] Mossley Hill wards bef⟨ore⟩ dinn⟨er⟩
Aunt Harriet

Wed⟨nesday⟩ [September 22]. d⟨itt⟩o.

Th⟨ursday⟩ [September 23] The Shore　dining early　wrote to Dr A⟨rnold⟩　the Rock-house　✳

Fri⟨day⟩ [September 24] Short walk after dinner. [✳ ✳ ✳]
Dr & Mrs F⟨oulkes⟩ Corrie & Mather's announcement of departure. ✳

Sat⟨urday⟩ [September 25] the Corries. [✳ ✳ ✳] £12　✳　　　fo. 34ʳ
Greenall—Clay—Whitely—Whitely—Davidson—Hill—Smith—[Corrie Mather]

Sunday [September] 26th

At home:—walked with Father to the Old Swan & by

Smithd⟨ow⟩n lane home. . . . had doubted very much whether I sh⟨oul⟩d not go by Rhyl b⟨oa⟩t, ½ p. 2 y⟨e⟩sterday, & so by Conway & Aber to meet the Snowdon at B⟨i⟩r⟨kenhead⟩ ferry at 4 today.

✱ an propter δουλωσιν Rhualissanam? [*because of the Rhyl enslavement?*]

Monday [September 27] discessus Matheri: [*departure of Mather*] walked to Childwall 4½–7½ letter from B⟨urbidge⟩ letter from Chas to Jr [?] Brownlow St prosp⟨ec⟩t.

✱ tho⟨ugh⟩ after a cold bath at ¼ to 11

9–11 Tuesday [September 28]—W⟨or⟩k 10 to 4 The Mount 9–10 11–12½ down Town bathed ¼ p 4 to ½ p 5. to Wavertree to Mr Pownalls ½ p 6 to 8.

Tomorrow fortnight:—

Wednesday [September 29]—W⟨or⟩k 9 to 3 Pownall's introduction—Went to Seaforth by the Shore, 4–8, beautiful sunset,—letter from B⟨urbidge⟩, & to him.

Slippers—Map—

Thursday [September 30]—Pownall's b⟨ro⟩th⟨e⟩r ½ p 2–½ p 4 Childwall fields ¼ p 4 to 8.

fo. 34ᵛ   October

1st Friday—Wrote to Simpkinson. dined at home.

From palsying self-mistrust, from fear
from doubting thoughts & heart's distress
I rose into a higher sphere
Of Action hope & joyfulness.
I rose. Not so: what fell then? Yes
from doubts which constancy had bred
to hopes on vagrant fancies fed
Vain motions clothed in Action's dress
Still varying, still convictionless.

Saturday [October 2] Unwell & made overmuch of it.
Mrs Newman's call. saw her from 4½ to 5½

[October 3]   Sunday

Skipped M⟨orning⟩ Serv⟨ice⟩ propter valet⟨udinem⟩ [*for health reasons*] tho⟨ugh⟩ unnecessarily walked in M⟨oun⟩t G⟨ar⟩d⟨e⟩ns. Wrote to B⟨urbidge⟩ & T W⟨alrond⟩

Monday [October 4] Greenall—Clay, D⟨avison⟩ Wh⟨itely⟩ Wh⟨itely⟩—Pownall [. . .] & dinner at home ✳ [✳ ✳ ✳]

Tuesday [October 5] letter fr⟨om⟩ Ward. Shopping.   fo. 35ʳ
Importance of reflection during this following week, while I have more leisure [✳ ✳ ✳]

Wednesday [October 6]—Went to Seaforth. Inv⟨itatio⟩n fr⟨om⟩ Mrs N⟨ewman⟩ Lodgings—Magisterium. [✳ ✳ ✳]

Thursday [October 7] Clay defecit [*Clay decamped*]. 2 Wh⟨iteleys⟩ & D⟨avidso⟩n. 11–2 dined with Mrs N⟨ewman⟩ at the Ironsides 6–9½: considerably tired.

Friday [October 8] Davidson defecit [*Davidson decamped*]
finished Philoctetes with 2 Whiteleys dined with the Clays at New Brighton—Mrs & Miss Sherard returned by Egremont 4 to 9½ Letter fr⟨om⟩ Simpk⟨inso⟩n ✳ foolishly took tea. [✳ ✳ ✳]

Saturday [October 9] Mrs N⟨ewman⟩—Atkinson—P⟨owell⟩. left for Rhyl at ½ p 1 Sick—arrived at Aberg⟨ele⟩ ½ p 6 supped & slept.

Sunday [October] 10th

To M⟨in⟩ y. d⟨on⟩ by 9¼ br⟨eakfast⟩ 10 ch⟨apel⟩ ½ p. 11 luncheon ch⟨apel⟩ dinner & conv⟨ersatio⟩n with Uncle Rich⟨ar⟩d. ✳

Monday [October 11] Off ½ p. 5 to Ab⟨ergele⟩ & fr⟨om⟩ Rh⟨yl⟩ fo. 35ᵛ
at 8 consid⟨era⟩bly tossed at L⟨iver⟩p⟨oo⟩l by ½ p, 11 [✳ ✳ ✳]
[*A list of names, mainly cancelled, including*:] Hill C B C⟨lough⟩ Dr A⟨rnold⟩ razors Calders Mrs Monk

Tuesday [October 12]

Wednesday [October 13] Called on Mrs Monk, & the Calders. went to bed very tired. ✳

Thursday [October 14] Off at 6 a.m. p⟨e⟩r 3rd class, at Rugby ½ p. I found B⟨urbidge⟩ away. Hill & Clay. Jane Arn⟨old⟩ Todo. the Prices. [* * *] A B C⟨lough⟩ the Arnolds, the Prices.

Friday [October 15] br⟨eakfast⟩ at Prices. Todo for 5′ Conybeare Pig with Hull. In at about 7; at Jones' ✳

OXFORD

Where the whole heart willeth a way will soon be found the insincere to begin with end in nothing, unpainstaking among the Mass the search for the truth still was, is yea & will be for ever while the race of man choose rather the harlot Fancy's charm than toil hope fear, the result of sober minded assurance.

fo. 36ʳ Saturday [October 16] Walked alone, but Ward twice. Began [Euripides'] Medea.

Sunday [October] 17th Walk with Ward & him to tea.

Monday [October 18] Bullingdon: the Statutes: E. S. F⟨oulkes⟩ & calls. Slept at the new lodgings.

Tuesday [October 19] Ch⟨rist⟩ Ch⟨urch⟩ 2½ hrs a.m. Migration. Stanley ✳
Heard of H. Walrond's death

Wednesday [October 20] Not at Chapel; Bullingdon. Union de re Christi

Thursday [October 21] ditto   Sunningwell   Common Room

Friday [October 22] Woodeaton by Elsfield. Union. B⟨ritish⟩ & F⟨oreign⟩ Rev⟨iew⟩ Ward at 10
I suppose about 5 hrs.

Saturday [October 23] Not up till ¼ p. 8 H⟨ear⟩d Fr⟨om⟩ B⟨urbidge⟩ Wrote to him & Simpk⟨inson⟩ called on Greenhill. Ch⟨rist⟩ Ch⟨urch⟩ Walk & paying bills. Union. Ward again.

Sunday [October] 24th

Congreve r⟨oun⟩d the Parks. Walk with Lake & his brother.
Shelley. R⟨oun⟩d the P⟨ar⟩ks after dinner. Ward &c ¼ 9 to 10 ¼

Monday [October 25] Magd⟨alen⟩ Walk. Tylden—at Temple's
& Prich⟨ar⟩d's

Tuesday [October 26] Tylden to br⟨eakfast⟩. Heywood's call.
Congreve. Mat⟨thew⟩ Arn⟨old⟩

Wednesday [October 27] Heywood with Ethics—Union—
Stanley.

Thursday [October 28] Matthie—called on Riddle.　　　fo. 36ᵛ

Breakf⟨ast⟩ [*list of names, some ticked & some cancelled, including:*]
Riddle M. Arnold. Vansittart. Conybeare Jones Doxat Moberley
Temple Goulb⟨ur⟩n Jowett Lake Blackett Stanley Congreve

Friday [October 29] Heywood iterum: Bagley wood. Tickell's to
wine: Ward fr⟨om⟩ 7½ to 9.

Saturday [October 30] Breakfast Party.

Not very well this week: though in high Spirits—a good deal *too*
high. Have read very little & seen a good deal of society this week.

Sunday Oct⟨ober⟩ 31st

Some verses to B⟨urbidge⟩ a little Butler's Analogy & some
Thucydides. Evening S⟨ermo⟩n. In Ch⟨rist⟩ Ch⟨urch⟩ Walk
solus. [*alone*] Ward ¼10–¼11

I seem to be utterly filled altogether with idle hopes that all will be
right and we may do as we please. Utterly careless in society &
ready to do anything there just as this time four years 1837 when I
first came up.—to be by myself.

Monday　　　　　November　　　　　fo. 37ʳ

1st H⟨. . .⟩d. Went to the Union instead of walking. Wrote to
B⟨urbidge⟩ & read Napier. Seymour's to wine. Emerson de
Historia et Self Reliance.

[Tuesday November] 2nd Bagley W⟨oo⟩d:—5 hrs work I hope

[Wednesday November] 3rd early to Horspath. 5 hrs but not good work, nor as work—very sleepy & heavy.—read another Essay of Emerson. Analogy.

Thursday [November] 4th Idle 1 or n⟨ear⟩ly. Not above 3½ work. walked alone Happy Valley & by Bagley cross.
The Probable Importance of this present interval of leisure
The use I may make of it.   ✳

Friday [November 5] 3½

Saturday [November 6] 2½ finished Emerson's Essays.

Sunday Nov⟨ember⟩ 7
Read Shelley's Ode to liberty. Skylark. Arethusa. Walked to Horspath alone. Ward.

Monday [November 8] Woodeaton. Coleridge's to Wine. 2 Cardens. Goulburns 2 Shadwells Farrer. Batt⟨ersb⟩y mi⟨nor⟩ Hawk⟨er⟩ minor, Johnson. 5 hrs ✳

fo. 37ᵛ   Tuesday [November 9] Walked n⟨ea⟩r to Horspath 8–10 met Hoskyns. Read fr⟨om⟩ 10½ to 3 to Horspath & Shotover 3 to 5¼ dined with Tom Davies—¼6 to ½ p. 9 Read 10 to 11. 5 hrs.
     Birth of the Prince of Wales.

Wednesday [November 10]—Horspath & Shotover. Gell to Stanley. Wrote to Gell. 6 Hrs or nearly.
                    [✳   ✳   ✳   ✳   ✳]

Thursday [November 11] 6½ Bagley Wood.
somewhat lazy work however, & with difficulty. Platonis Crito, Arist⟨otle⟩ de Pol⟨itica⟩ IV
                    [✳   ✳   ✳   ✳   ✳]

Friday [November 12] Not up till past 8 Not well in morning. Shotover. Union. 5½ [Plato's] Apologia. Heywood. Macculloch.

fo. 38ʳ   Saturday [November 13] With Stanley, cloisters.—5
     Average 5½   ✳

Hast thou seen higher holier things than these
And therefore must to these thy heart refuse?
With the true best, alack, how ill agrees
That best which thou wouldst chuse
The Summum Pulchrum is in Heaven above
Do thou as best thou canst thy duty do
What God allows thee be content to love
Some day thou shalt it view.

Sunday Nov⟨ember⟩ 14

br⟨eakfast⟩ with Conybeare 9½–11 with Congreve to 12 by myself
reading Shelley & Macculloch till dinner Ward 9–10 ✻

Monday. [November 15] after my long hesitation wrote to Ward
de Comm⟨unione⟩ [*about communion*] [Walk to Bullingdon, Snow]
W⟨ar⟩d in Evening.

Tuesday [November 16] Not at Ch⟨apel⟩ as I sh⟨oul⟩d have   fo. 38ᵛ
been—Walk to Bagley Wood. Ward again 8–9½   3½

Contempt. Whether I am not merely resting in Ward.

Wednesday [November 17] br⟨eakfast⟩ at Queen's. Walk with
Ward. Dinner (Mrs Hughes, Wynn & others) at Jes⟨us⟩
Coll⟨ege⟩ lodgings. foolish in all; how much so I cannot tell.

Thursday [November 18] br⟨eakfast⟩ with E. S. F⟨oulkes⟩
Lewis, Gilbertson, Green of Linc⟨oln⟩, Walk Ch⟨rist⟩ Ch⟨urch⟩
solus. Wine with Congreve. Lingan, Henderson, Lake & Blackett.
6 but only Goeller.

Friday [November 19] Arrival of Todo. Ward at tea

Saturday [November 20] 2 Arnolds Tickell, W⟨alrond⟩ &
Tristram to breakf⟨as⟩t. Ch⟨rist⟩ Ch⟨urch⟩ walk solo—to Matt.
after dinner.

About 5 each day.

[Sunday November 21]   last after Trinity.   fo. 39ʳ

Communion—Absent—with Walrond to Newman's ev⟨ening⟩
serv⟨ice⟩ & to Tristram's to wine Ward 8–9 Infidel Reports which
gave me a great fit of spirits.

Monday [November 22] with Walr⟨ond⟩ in Ch⟨rist⟩ Ch⟨urch⟩ walk—& at Conybeare's to wine. ✳

Tuesday [November 23] Fellowship   Latin Es⟨say⟩ & Gr⟨eek⟩ into English

Wednesday [November 24] [Fellowship] Engl⟨ish⟩ Ess⟨ay⟩ Eng⟨lish⟩ into Lat⟨in⟩
br⟨eakfast⟩ with Temple—On the River with W⟨alrond⟩ & Tom.

Walford & Palmer Scholars

Thursday   [November   25]—Philosophy—Greek   Pr⟨ose⟩ I⟨ambi⟩cs & Hex⟨amete⟩rs, & v⟨iva⟩ v⟨oce⟩.
br⟨eakfast⟩ with Morcom, on the river with W⟨alrond⟩ & Mat.

Friday [November 26] W⟨alrond⟩ & T A⟨rnold⟩ to breakf⟨ast⟩ Ch⟨rist⟩ Ch⟨urch⟩ walk. Cram. river solus. History & v⟨iva⟩ v⟨oce⟩ till 11

Saturday [November 27]—Not up till p. 9 Divinity. Bullingdon solus. After Chapel Ward with his news of Karsl⟨ake⟩ & Lingen & my own well-doing which excited me greatly & took the excitement with me to Greenhill's Christie Congreve Jane Arnold & others. ✳

fo. 39ᵛ Nov⟨embe⟩r 28th Advent Sunday

Very much tired after my bad night. Newman's M⟨orning⟩ S⟨ervice⟩;—Tickell's to wine;

Monday [November 29] Prichard's to breakf⟨as⟩t. Heawood Shotover 2–4 Hall at 9
      Karslake—Lingan—
Stanley & Ward
ψήφων ἀναλύσις [*analysis of the voting*]

M⟨aster⟩	K⟨arslake⟩	K⟨arslake⟩
O⟨akeley⟩	Pr⟨ichard⟩	Cl⟨ough⟩
T⟨ait⟩	Cl⟨ough⟩	
W⟨ard⟩	Cl⟨ough⟩	

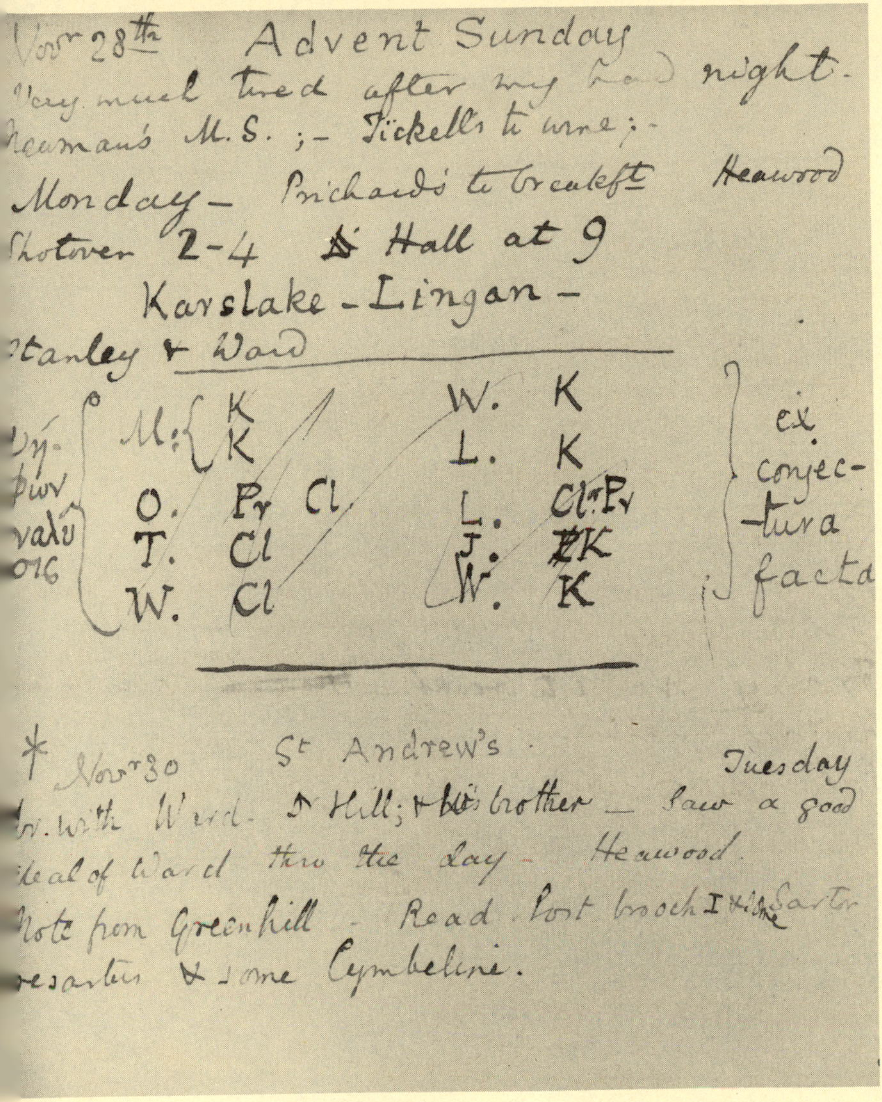

Nov. 28th   Advent Sunday
Very much tired after my bad night.
Newman's M.S. ;— Tickells to wine ;—
Monday —   Prichard's to breakfast   Heawood
Shotover 2-4   ☆ Hall at 9
         Karslake — Lingan —
Stanley + Ward _____

Dj- ⎧ M.⎧ K   W.   K   ⎫ ex.
pwv ⎪   ⎩ K   L.   K   ⎬ conjec-
valu ⎪ O.   Pr Cl   L.   Cl·Pr ⎪ -tura
016 ⎪ T.   Cl   J.   ℣K   ⎪ facta
     ⎩ W.   Cl   W.   K   ⎭

* Nov. 30   St Andrew's .   Tuesday
br. with Ward. ☆ Hill; + his brother — saw a good
deal of Ward thro' the day — Heawood.
Note from Greenhill — Read. Lost brook I think Carter
resartus + some Cymbeline.

Fig. 5 Clough's defeat in the Balliol election, 1841

W⟨oolcombe⟩   K⟨arslake⟩
L⟨onsdale⟩   K⟨arslake⟩
L⟨ake⟩   Cl⟨ough⟩ or Pr⟨ichard⟩
J⟨owett⟩   K⟨arslake⟩ ['P' *cancelled*]
W⟨all⟩   K⟨arslake⟩

ex conjectura facta [*made on conjecture*]

✱ Nov⟨embe⟩r 30   St Andrew's   Tuesday
br⟨eakfast⟩ with Ward. Dr Hill; & W⟨ard⟩'s brother—Saw a good deal of Ward thro⟨ugh⟩ the day—Heawood.

Note from Greenhill. Read. lost brooch. I r⟨ea⟩d some [Carlyle's] Sartor resartus & some Cymbeline.

Wednesday Dec⟨embe⟩r 1st   fo. 40ʳ

Walked a little with Lake—waiting for Cl⟨ass⟩ list from 3½ to 5. ⟨Pri⟩ma [*First class*] Prich⟨ard⟩ Rawst⟨orne⟩ Hutchins. Chase Wine with Goulb⟨ur⟩n mi⟨nor⟩:—Note in answer to Greenhill. Ward departed 11 a.m.

Thursday [December 2] Morning Chapel—idle mostly till ½ P. 12 Went to Greenhills saw the Arnolds. The Inaugural lecture 1–2½ with the Arn⟨olds⟩ till 4 when they started

Friday [December 3] Nothing particular. read about 4 hrs letter fr⟨om⟩ Annie & to her

Saturday [December 4]—Letter fr⟨om⟩ Geo⟨rge⟩. Wrote to Price & B⟨urbidge⟩—Ward's return. In college 9 to 10.—wined with him partly [?] with Karslake

[Sunday December 5]   2nd in Advent
Ch⟨apel⟩. letters from B⟨urbidge⟩. C T A⟨rnold⟩ ans⟨were⟩d & A B C⟨lough⟩ ans⟨were⟩d—Visit from Lowe—Walk with Lake 2–4 Left a card on B⟨attersb⟩y. dined with Lake & Carden. Ward 9½–¼11
talked about my Essay & overmuch about the fellowship.

✱ To write to Arnold de Comm⟨unione⟩ [*about Communion*]

Monday [December] 5 [6]th letter from Annie—& to her. Wet   fo. 40ᵛ
through.—A good deal reduced by the bad night. Ward 10–3¼

Tuesday [December] [7]th

Roused by importunate knocks
I rose & turned the key, & let them in
First one, anon another & at last
Trooping they came—for how could I who once
Had let one in nor looked him in the face
Show scruples e'er again; so in they came
A noisy band of revellers. Vain hopes
Light joys—Wild fancies—& there they sit
In my heart's holy place & through the night
Carouse—to leave it when the cold grey dawn
Gleams in the East & tells me that the time
(For fasting & for prayer bestowed) is gone.

fo. 41ʳ Walked alone. run the Shotover round in little more than an hour. dined with Stanley. Herm⟨an⟩ Merivale. S⟨i⟩r Fr⟨ancis⟩ Doyle, Cox, St. Denison &c. 5–7½ Ch⟨apel⟩ incl⟨uded⟩ then at E S F⟨oulkes⟩' Lonsdale Fraser Lloyd Dalgairns Haskins, Lewis

Wednesday's Party [*List of names, some cancelled, including:*] Coleridge Lloyd Johnson Seymour S Riddle Battersby—Congreve M. Arnold Walford 2 Foulkes.

Wednesday [December 8] Only 4th breakfast. P⟨hilosophy⟩ E⟨ssay⟩ & Lect⟨ure⟩ 10½–2¼ Stanley 3–5 Ward 9–10½ p⟨ar⟩tly here p⟨ar⟩tly round the Parks

Thursday [December 9] Six hours a day at least Ethics for next term. E⟨nglish⟩ E⟨ssay⟩ L⟨atin⟩ E⟨ssay⟩

Heawood's last. breakf⟨as⟩t with Johnson. called & had to dine at Jes⟨us⟩ Coll⟨ege⟩. [* * *] 6 to 11! 5 incl⟨uding⟩ lect⟨ures⟩.

fo. 41ᵛ Friday [December 10]—Not above 3 hrs reading I sh⟨oul⟩d think but wrote to Arnold. 1–2½ Battells to Ward; Haircutting &c. 7–8¼ Ward here; 9 called on Lonsdale & Tait.

Am I right with Ward—?—to write & put him off?

If help there is not but the Muse
Must needs the one or other chuse
I do prefer I must confess
The somewhat slovenly undress
Of slippered slip-slop sentimentals
To Philosophic regimentals.

Saturday [December 11] Mill's article. Called on Greenhill. Ward
again fr⟨om⟩ 8½–¼ 10. ? ? ?

✳ Very much vexed with myself.

Sunday December 12th   fo. 42ʳ

Laus Deo! [*Praise be to God*]   Laus Deo!

Stanley Lake Jowett & Woolcombe Ward

Monday [December 13] Up at ½ p. 6 Looked in at Balliol at 8
br⟨eakfast⟩ at Jes⟨us⟩ Coll⟨ege⟩ Off with Mrs Hughes per Pig;
left her at Southam, lunched & walked with Bunsen to the
Sch⟨ool⟩ House.

Tuesday [December 14] Davidson & Cothen to br⟨eakfast⟩. With
B⟨urbidge⟩ from 10 to 4, calling at Prices, lunch & walking. ✳

Wednesday [December 15] Skipwith & 3 others to br⟨eakfast⟩
with B⟨urbidge⟩ fr⟨om⟩ 10 to 1 Walk with Arnold solus. Prices to
dinner 5½ to 10½ Mat's return.

Thursday [December 16] This enjoyment since I left Oxford very
questionable indeed probably a very foolish & beastly business.

left R⟨ugby⟩ on Saturday [December 18] 3 arriving here about 9 fo. 42ᵛ
PM

[December 19] Sunday b⟨efore⟩ ⟨Christ⟩mas
On Tuesday [December 21] went off by mail to Chester & Min-y-
don arriving there about 1 AM—to spend Uncle R⟨ichard⟩'s
b⟨ir⟩thday
left on Thursday [December 23] about 4 walking to St Asaph, &
next day thence by Holyw⟨ell⟩ & the ferry to L⟨iver⟩p⟨oo⟩l.

[December 25–6] ⟨Christ⟩mas day—& Sunday
missed Comm⟨unio⟩n openly

Monday [December 27] The Whitleys & Mr Clay dined at
Corries

Tuesday [December 28] Clay Wh⟨iteley⟩ Sept⟨. . .⟩

Wedn⟨esday⟩ [December 29] Wh⟨iteley⟩ Sept⟨. . .⟩ dined at the
Clays Mr North etc.

Thursday [December 30] ✳ Haigh⟨primo⟩ Sept⟨. . .⟩

Friday [December 31] H⟨ai⟩gh ⟨secundo⟩ Cic⟨ero⟩

Saturday ✳

January 1st 1842

Sunday [January 2] to Childwall

Monday—Tuesday [January 3–4] at N⟨ew⟩ Br⟨ighton⟩ fr⟨om⟩ 2 pm to 12 H⟨ai⟩gh pr⟨ose⟩.

Wednesday [January 5] to Childwall H⟨ai⟩gh Cicero

Th⟨ursday⟩ [January] 6th dined at the Clays & b⟨rought⟩ young B⟨er⟩keley over   H⟨ai⟩gh d⟨itt⟩o

Friday [January 7] Wh⟨iteley⟩ Sept⟨. . .⟩.

Saturday [January 8] H⟨ai⟩gh Cic⟨ero⟩ dined at Mr Barbers— Malc⟨olm⟩ Corrie & Mr Crowder & 2 bottles of claret. ✳

fo. 43ʳ [January 9] S⟨unday⟩ after Epiphany
read a good deal of Kant. called at the Corries

Monday [January 10] only Haigh & Clay. dined at N⟨ew⟩ B⟨righton⟩ ret⟨ur⟩n⟨e⟩d by $\frac{1}{4}$6 & b⟨oa⟩t ✳

Tuesday [January 11]. Very much floored pr⟨opter⟩ malam noctem [*because of bad night*]. Whitleys 10 to 11$\frac{1}{2}$—& again 7$\frac{1}{2}$ to 9 pm left Clay at $\frac{1}{2}$ p. 3

Wednesd⟨ay⟩ [January 12] Still a good deal floored. Called on Mr Clay at $\frac{1}{2}$ p. 1 & went over at 2

Th⟨ursday⟩ [January 13]. Wh⟨itley⟩ Wh⟨itley⟩ H⟨ai⟩gh 10–1 & Cl⟨ay⟩ & fr⟨om⟩ 7$\frac{1}{2}$–9 Wh⟨itley⟩ Wh⟨itley⟩

Fr⟨iday⟩ [January 14] Wh⟨itley⟩ Wh⟨itley⟩ Cl⟨ay⟩. Ja⟨me⟩s Bateson.

Saturday [January 15] Wh⟨itley⟩ Wh⟨itley⟩ Cl⟨ay⟩ Wrote to H⟨owar⟩d & B⟨urbidge⟩

[Sunday January 16] 2nd After Epipany

Going out to dine at Mr Haigh's with Charles letter fr⟨om⟩ B⟨urbidge⟩

Monday [January 17]

Tuesday [January 18] Wh⟨itley⟩ Wh⟨itley⟩ Cl⟨ay⟩ Cicero exam⟨inatio⟩n. In high spirits & foolish. Notes to M⟨essrs⟩ Wh⟨itley⟩ H⟨ai⟩gh. Packing ✳

Wednesday [January 19] ✳ Journey to Braunston. Saw the Bier $1\frac{1}{2}$ to $2\frac{1}{2}$

OXFORD—LENT TERM

Thursday 20th Jan⟨uary⟩ Kant Ethics Pol⟨itical⟩ Ec⟨onomy⟩ Latin Ess⟨ay⟩ Econ⟨omics⟩ & Pub⟨lic⟩ Money ✳

Necessary superf⟨luity⟩ in soc⟨iety⟩. Clay, Min-y-don—Mr Barber G A C⟨lough⟩ etc

Friday [January] 21st. Read about 7 hrs I think.

Saturday [January 22] $5\frac{1}{2}$ (exc⟨luding⟩ Chapel) chiefly Kant.
Danger of being taken in by praise & my vanity.

[Sunday January 23] Septuagesima

Overslept myself. Newmans at 11 Ward to tea—at 9

Monday [January 24] Not read above 4 or 5 am in a bad way tho⟨ugh⟩ comfortable enough. ✳

Tuesday [January] 25th ⟨Christe⟩ning of Pr⟨ince⟩ of W⟨ales⟩
Robbins I, br⟨eakfast⟩ with Conybeare—wrote to B⟨...⟩ S⟨...⟩. & home. Not above 4 at most, lect⟨ures⟩ excl⟨uded⟩.
[*List of names, some ticked, some cancelled, including:*] Price Addington
Lawley Brodie Farrer Walford Riddle Johnson Coleridge Shairp Temple Seymour Jno W⟨illia⟩ms Dr Foulkes Stanley the Arnolds Tait T. Davies.

Wednesday [January 26]—called on the Arnolds—Tom Davies to dine ubi miser eram [*where I was wretched*] 4

Thursday [January] 27th Robbins II Arnold's 1st lecture—Ivory pup⟨il⟩ went to B⟨urbidge⟩ before Dinner.

That for the present in general there is no great need of being very decided & greatest need to avoid it.

That I am sure to be telling lies in all my intercourse, dealings & doings.

Necessity of not getting into half-ways from my conformity:—of doing *something* that *is* true:—

the quantity of beastliness that I have got in my heart—the Vac⟨atio⟩n follies:—I am gratified & satisfied with any filth:—

fo. 44ᵛ Can I go on tutorizing?—do not all my efforts here and elsewhere go upon lies & encourage me in the belief of them?

The utter folly of my venturing into society as I did. Mrs Hughes—the Arnolds—at home & then worse at Min-y-don:—the silliness of letting fancies work in me last term as they did.

Even this—

Even the finest—& plausiblest.

At work—simply because I am expected to do so—mere conformity.

fo. 45ʳ Give up pupils seems the nat⟨ura⟩l thing.

Friday [January 28]

A sort of vision about 2 AM a very strange influence at any rate. In over high spirits during the morning ending in Ivory's 1st lect⟨ure⟩—Abingdon road.

Farrer's to wine Coleridge Johnson 2 Farrers & Shadwell.

Stultissimus [*Most foolish*]

Saturday [January 29] Not in Chapel   Robbins III   called on Mrs A⟨rnold⟩ Shotover—Blackett   &   Cave   Brodie   in hall   Ward at 9 for ½ an hr.

fo. 45ᵛ Ward Sund⟨ay⟩ Wedn⟨esday⟩ Stanl⟨ey⟩ Mon⟩day⟩.

Sunday [January 30] Sexagesima

Shotover trespass   Met Cole & Others on M⟨agdalen⟩ Br⟨idge⟩. passed B⟨attersb⟩y & another   ✳

Monday [January 31] br⟨ea⟩kf⟨as⟩t P⟨ar⟩ty Ward in the P⟨ar⟩ks;—fields by the Marston road

Tuesday [February 1] To Shotover 8 to 10½ Ivory & A⟨ddingto⟩n 1–3

Wednesday [February 2] To Shotover again—Ivory & Addington

✻

Sat⟨urday⟩[?] My present scheme seems to be just taking in   fo. 46ʳ
enough false fancy to keep my head above water. Is this allowable?—Satisfying myself with the mere sense of its not coming at once from dependence on others—last night & this morning seized by a sort of fancy of God curing all which took complete hold of me. I think it has left some sediment or seed behind.

Tuesday [?]
The Wickedness of my Acts of yesterday Morning & after leaving Min-y-don.

Thursday [February 3] Vansittarts to breakf⟨ast⟩. Robbins.   fo. 46ᵛ
Add⟨ingto⟩n.

Friday [February 4] Shotover . . .
Filth of my heart—false hopes—quite ascertained. dinner. res⟨olution⟩.

Saturday [February 5] After a most happy night to Shotover. lectures to Robbins & Add⟨ingto⟩n floored me by some means or other—having begun to trust my heart for the 1st time.

Wedn⟨esday⟩ ✻

Sunday [February] 6th
Morning Chapel—Long Walk
Suppo⟨sitio⟩n that God loving & forgiving us Excuses us from debts to others . . .
Sunday (skipped Evening Chapel

Monday [February 7] to Shotover at 11. [half] comm⟨ons⟩

Tuesday [February 8] ibid. dinner-foolishness, wh⟨ich⟩ has affected my whole week.

Wednesday [February 9] night (Ash W⟨ednes⟩day

I seem to have got out of my difficulties by the worst possible way—est⟨a⟩blishing a new φαντασια [*fancy*], which being independent of other people I am not ashamed to stick to, but is wholly illegitimate all the same. Whereby Past things are all vanished away.

At any rate to be humble in this & not more proud & positive than I can help. [* * *]

fo. 47ᵛ Thursday [February 10] Arn⟨old's⟩ last lecture. Magd⟨alen⟩ Walk. Carey. folly. Greenhills—Arnold.

Friday [February 11] Shotover 11–1. Add⟨ingto⟩n & Ivory. the P⟨ar⟩ks at night

Saturday [February 12] Magd⟨alen⟩ Walk—common room. Pride again which had left me since Thursday pupils

fo. 48ʳ Sunday [February 13] morning

How far the past steps can be or ought to be recalled?

The Admission of a Forgiveness-Uberh⟨au⟩pt seems to let back all the past upon one—but how far is this admiss⟨io⟩n correct & ἐπὶ τίσιν [*with respect to whom?*]

Meditating, poking &c 7 to 10 Walking 11–5 Evening Chapel

Very foolish—sh⟨oul⟩d have stayed at home

Monday [February] 14th

Forgiveness at least implying Confession before all men.

Thinking on my Vac⟨ation⟩ follies quite right.

In a terrible mess from 7 to 9

That my old reserve was a folly—I seem to be taking for granted.

fo. 48ᵛ Tuesday [February 15] br⟨eakfast⟩ with Ivory. asked B⟨attersby⟩ to walk. H⟨erman⟩ Merivale's lecture 2–3

To go to Bagley Wood 1st thing tomorrow?

Wedn⟨esday⟩ [February 16] Tea with B⟨attersb⟩y

Thursday [February 17] Ward Stanley Arnold. M⟨or⟩ning Chapel. Walked to Garsington 9½ to 12. False hopes the Past—all gone?

χρεῶν ἀποκοπη [*cancelling of debts*] False positiveness again today 3–4½ walked with him.

Walked out as for K⟨ir⟩tl⟨in⟩gton 8 to 11

Friday [February 18] Another strange sort of influence 1 to 3 AM dissipated by B⟨attersby⟩'s note—refilling my as I seemed to see it, empty heart.

Walked out 4 miles H⟨ea⟩d⟨in⟩gton r⟨oa⟩d.

Saturday [February 19] Possessed today by Ward's morning visit:—& then the Master's Party 6 to 10 ✳?

Sunday 2nd in Lent Feb⟨ruar⟩y 20th. Newman's 12 to 1:—Not to admit idle fancies of B⟨attersby⟩ at any rate:—Consequence of connexions.

I seem to have filled my heart again which was as empty as possible on Sunday 6th, if no later, with idle fancies of him; with old recollections of all kinds admitted by the forgiveness fancy:— Shotover-fancies, & latterly I suppose with Burbidge & Ward committals. [Item Evangel⟨ica⟩l. Hopes]

Shakespeare's Sonnets: dinner but not Chapel.

Monday [February 21] walk to Bullingdon 11–11½ evening chapel—Ward's visit

Tuesday [February 22] Humility
Possessed by Goulburn, as last night by Ward. Very comfortable H⟨ea⟩d⟨in⟩gton R⟨oa⟩d 6–8½

Wednesday [February 23]
Humility—remembrance that I am waking in forgetfulness of a host of truths—my dependence & obligations—& the importance of connexions. Not to poke

[✳   ✳   ✳   ✳   ✳]

fo. 50ʳ Whatever else is true my conduct throughout since this time two years—especially since last term ended—has been most utterly contemptible for weakness &c &c

read hard fr⟨om⟩ 9 to 10 Ward with his Whately 10–½

Th⟨ursday⟩ [February] 24th Item that my turnings to God were so weak, foolish, temp⟨orar⟩y & mixed with falsehood that they are perhaps worse than none.

up at 7 Bullingdon 9½–11½

? Geo⟨rge⟩ here—Home at Easter

[*   *   *   *   *]

Ward for ¼hr   I seem to be daily fuller of vain hopes & of self-trust.

fo. 50ᵛ Friday [February 25] floored again by pupils Headington road doing penance 5½ to 9½

Sat⟨urday⟩ [February 26] fr⟨om⟩ 7½ to 10½ ruminating—filled with a fancy of writing a confession to Arnold which has freed me from all anxiety & tribulation about the Past for today. this also has done me harm. ✻

went without dinner. went to bed full of a fancy

Sunday [February 27]
Neither chapel nor Church morning or evening.
Short walk Bullingdon way   dinner in Hall
✽ Awake from 12 to 4 & again before 5 de C⟨. . .⟩o

Monday [February 28] Walked from 8¼ to 9½ Water Eaton. A very agreeable day. letter fr⟨om⟩ Dr Taylor.

Tuesday March 1st
lost again amid morning-fancies—False positiveness again as usual. Ch⟨rist⟩ Ch⟨urch⟩. Walk around the river.
B⟨attersby⟩'s note [Utter folly about 7 p.m.

Wednesday [March 2] Walk H⟨ea⟩d⟨in⟩gton r⟨oa⟩d 11–1

fo. 51ʳ Thursday [March 3] [Utter folly about 7½ AM] br⟨eakfast⟩ with B⟨attersby⟩. Hopes owing to him.

Friday [March 4] I seem to have now got Cave Cole, & the whole
Party into my heart　　Farringdon road 6–9

Humility—my beh⟨aviour⟩ to others　To leave him on the least　fo. 51ᵛ
symptom of ἀρεσκεια [*complaisance*] & go home. My hopes all for
him. [sketch of boy's face, twice]

Sat⟨urday⟩ [March 5].

To go home, nisi [*unless*]

I have no right to my hopes. what am I to do with them? Tuesday
night the worst instance.

I have not the least right in the World to my hopes, all built on
fancies of him.

To be alone wholly to-morrow　　　　　　　　　　　　fo. 52ʳ

Behaviour to others pretty sure to be wrong

I have no right at any rate to go and act upon my hopes

Sunday [March 6]

The 2nd Sunday's fancy was true

Go go home cert⟨ain⟩ly; I shall be resting on all kind of stuff—as
indeed I am.

στρυφνοι [sour ones]

Not into the world without him, nor to leave without forgiveness.
[*page covered with sketches of faces, ten male, one female*]

To write & tell all my foolishnesses to Burbidge.—　　　　fo. 52ᵛ

Caught by forgiveness-fancies both this night & again & worse in
the morning (Monday)

Monday [March 7]

[* * *] that I have been continually using help

—I took false hopes which have departed & disqualified me for the
true.

Addington 1–2

Called up a hope or φαντασια [*fancy*] of Walrond to help me　fo. 53ʳ
through Addington. ?

Confession-fancy br⟨ough⟩t on by rumination.
Not　to　stir　hence

Confession seems the only plan

Tuesday [March 8] morning.

The whole of these confession-feelings have now got salved over by love hopes, false for the most part;—& I seem to be returning to the Saturday's ideas.

fo. 53ᵛ That going to him ought to be accompanied if not preceded by:—

Obligations throughout

Sins throughout.

last Term's Acts were all Acts of Pride.

No right to let my hopes rest on any but him—& home I suppose.

How can I go out?

fo. 54ʳ danger of forgetting all before—Ward [* * *]

Necessity of keeping that sense alive.

Oh me $\sqrt{-1}$ This Presence

Possessed by a forgiveness fancy.

Temple? G. A. C⟨lough⟩

Stat Veritas quantumvis mutemur. [*Truth remains, however much we change*]

My hopes all the same [* * *] are most beastly, world-hopes, indiscriminate &c/

The Confession fancy still is upon me. I feel as if I had confessed

fo. 54ᵛ Ward's visit

Am now satisfied with the fancy of going to W⟨alro⟩n⟨d⟩ ✻

Wednesday [March 9] Morning. Possessed still by the forcing fancies & resting on hopes in accordance with it.

N o t   t o   g o   so as to exl⟨ude⟩ C⟨...⟩ & ⟨...⟩

καλλος κακῶν ὕπουλον [*beauty harbouring festering evils*] [* * *]

—evening

Possessed wholly by Walrond.

fo. 55ʳ Thursday [March 10] Went to Newman 6–8.

to trust oneself; to take the lowest place; [* * *]

Battersby M⟨athew⟩ Arn⟨old⟩ Lawley, Walrond to breakf⟨as⟩t

Friday [March 11] Walk to Beckley—dined. [*page torn*]

φρονησις [*wisdom*] phronesis phronesis φρονες φρον Christmas   fo. 55ᵛ
φρονησις chreesthai tee doxee [*to use opinion*]

That we cannot take without moral obligations.   ✳

Saturday [March 12] Full & quite possessed with vain hopes.

N A H Clough

Trusting my own heart.   ✳

[*sketch of two capitalled columns*]

Full

[✳   ✳   ✳   ✳   ✳]

Sunday [March 13]   fo. 56ᵛ

Humility &c.—false hopes & shallowness all worse than before.

divorcement of Action & H⟨ear⟩t.

fasting seems notwithstanding temporary fancies to have been
benef⟨icia⟩l on the whole (except the Beckley fancy).—these last 3
days just the reverse. The Thursday night's temper seems to me to
have been the truest, & that I have getting worse ever since

Humility—Acknowledgement of truth's unrecognised, & forgot-   fo. 57ʳ
ten Obligations—& Sins—Confession.

Everything salved over by vain world-hopes κάλλος κακῶν ὕπουλον

Have lost earnestness ἐγκρατεια [*self-control*] & have taken in false
hopes, forgetfulness of offences, coatings of pride, sand of
conformity . . .

have gained or sh⟨oul⟩d have knowledge that I must not trust my
heart, nor act after it & on it alone. To avoid positiveness &
disregard fancies.

Continual takings of help & love & then cutting them—✳   fo. 57ᵛ
Humility Universal

Whatever else   ✳

Ward. last night I rested wholly on the belief & acceptance of
B⟨attersby⟩'s love & then when I got to H⟨ea⟩d⟨in⟩gton hill
took in the idea of God's love wh⟨ich⟩ as bef⟨ore⟩ destroyed if cf
March 1st.

fo. 58^r Utter falsity of my present Heart as regards the way I came to it.

Yet impossibility of recall.

Necessity of Hope: yet where to be had?

danger of Ward

Confession.

DIARY 6

Si noles sanus, curres hydropicus—[*If you will not run in health, you* fo. 1ʳ *will run with the dropsy*: Horace, Ep. i. 2. 32–4]

Not to be positive

not to act upon my impulses

Saturday [March 19]—Went to Rugby—

Sunday [March 20] Workh⟨ouse⟩ Service—Confessio

Monday [March 21] Prices, Arnolds, & a party at B⟨urbidge⟩'s

Tuesday [March 22] to Oxford
To act as little as possible upon my imagination [* * *]

Wednesday [March 23]
Here I am with all my imagination truths utterly departed; and a
new false growth in their place; so that I cannot act rationally—
my affections utterly divorced from both im⟨agination⟩ & reason.

Humility— fo. 1ᵛ
Walking in forgetfulness of a host of truths & duties & past sins.

I believe in all my past & now rejected doctrines.

My imag⟨inatio⟩n utterly wrong; & my aff⟨ectio⟩ns out of
harmony even with it. Yet I am resting on my next neighbours,
& allowing myself to rest with satisf⟨actio⟩n on Rugby
conv⟨ersatio⟩n.

Th⟨ursday⟩ [March 24] called on Tuckwell in the morning

Fri⟨day⟩ [March 25] Tuckwell

Sat⟨urday⟩ [March 26] Geo⟨rge⟩ arrived. Oriel letters.

Sunday [March 27] Walk with Geo⟨rge⟩ fo. 2ʳ

Monday [March 28] I have as yet, th⟨an⟩k God, no connexions
here at any rate—Not to be positive tho⟨ugh⟩ I am so sadly—

from a false imag⟨inatio⟩n in St Mary's yesterday & from
George   Accepting sympathy without acknowl⟨edgment⟩
Oriel 1st day Spectator & E⟨nglish⟩ Ess⟨ay⟩. br⟨eakfast⟩ with
Lake

Tu⟨esday⟩ [March 29] I have now got a sort of misbegotten
imagination to rest upon, having helped myself by George &
perhaps yesterday's party
Latin Ess⟨ay⟩ & Math⟨ematics⟩   Geo⟨rge⟩ at Dr F⟨oulkes⟩'s

Wedn⟨esday⟩   [March   30]   L⟨atin⟩   into   E⟨nglish⟩   &
Phil⟨osophical⟩ Q⟨uestio⟩ns & V⟨iva⟩ V⟨oce⟩ wined at
Prichard's

Thursday [March 31] G⟨reek⟩ into E⟨nglish⟩ E⟨nglish⟩ into
G⟨reek⟩ & V⟨iva⟩ V⟨oce⟩ dined at home with Geo⟨rge⟩

fo. 3ʳ Friday April 1 Orielensis factus [*elected to Oriel*]
br⟨eakfast⟩ with Shairp.

[*list of names, some ornamented, including:*] Shairp Seymour, Prichard,
Temple, Hawker, Arnold, Stanley, Burbidge, Mrs Pr⟨ice⟩, Ward,
Aunt H⟨arriet⟩ Uncle Ch⟨arles⟩. Simpk⟨inso⟩n Tylden Lowe

Sat⟨urday⟩ [April 2] br⟨eakfast⟩ with Ch⟨arles⟩ Geo⟨rge⟩
departed. W⟨illia⟩m Tuckw⟨ell⟩   Walked alone seized with
fancy after dinner. verses.

Rules. Humility. Self-Mistrust. To be up to Chapel & as soon as I
awake always to keep to Work in all earnest. & (?) Society—
though as far as possible not to be positive in it.

Sunday [April 3] Not to Chapel but by accident.

fo. 3ᵛ To remind myself continually that I may be called upon to do
things in wh⟨ich⟩ I must not expect the sympathy of those about
me.

The less S⟨ermo⟩n [?] & less d⟨evotio⟩n [?] the better

dined at Oriel Walker—Chase—Cornish

Went to L⟨iver⟩p⟨oo⟩l on Monday [April 4] after calling on Mrs
Wynter. Slept at Birm⟨ingha⟩m

Tuesday [April 5] to L⟨iver⟩p⟨oo⟩l by 11½

Wednesday [April 6]—with Cha⟨rle⟩s to call on Fitzgerald Mr Barber—Old Curiosity Shop.

Thursday [April 7] to Oxford by 6 AM tr⟨ain⟩. B⟨irmingha⟩m 12–1 at Oxf⟨or⟩d by 9

Friday [April 8] W⟨illia⟩m T⟨uckwell⟩—Robbins—Ward—Common Room

[*list of names, some cancelled, including:*] Lytton Newman Church fo. 4ʳ Marriot [Daman] Eden Christie Cornish Fraser.

Saturday [April 9] Chapel. T. R. I⟨. . .⟩. Mrs Greenhill.—H. Coleridge, Seymour, M. Arnold—Hall—Stanley

I seem to know nothing except that I am wholly wrong within.—a hundred Carats of positiveness & false enjoyement.

Sunday [April] 10th   fo. 4ᵛ

    Humility—
    The filthiness & falseness of my imagination
    The superficiality of my likings
    My total ignorance of all beside.

read in chapel. br⟨eak⟩f⟨ast⟩ with Chase. alone till 2 & 3 to 5

Hall—Eden Corn⟨ish⟩ Chr⟨istie⟩ Fr⟨aser⟩ Ch⟨urch⟩

Chapel—the Provost's 7½–⁴⁄₉9

Ward 9 to 10 very foolish & communicative.

Reality extra-sensual has no ground but conscience—revelation or fo. 5ʳ necess⟨ary⟩ int⟨ui⟩t⟨ion⟩s of Morality.

Entia rationalia converted into Entia Realia.

Belying a false manner.

[*   *   *   *   *]   fo. 5ᵛ

Tuesday [April 12] Oriel dinner Corn⟨ish⟩. Barker Nicholls. Ivory

Wedn⟨esday⟩ [April 13] Eden w⟨ith⟩ Cockey & Barnes. Chace ma⟨jor⟩ & Northcote Swayne Daman staid till 8

Thurs⟨day⟩ [April 14] Congr⟨eve⟩ walk To Tait's room. Newman & others in Common Room.

[*   *   *   *   *]

Friday [April 15] Prichard Walk Nicholls & Froude

Sat⟨urday⟩. [April 16] dined at the Provost's

Sunday [April] 17th dined at Oriel—with Ivory & Temple fr⟨om⟩ 8½ to 9½

Monday [April 18] Walked with Robbins—Newman, Chace Ryder at dinner.

[*   *   *   *   *]

fo. 6ᵛ Tuesday [April 19] Prichard & Congreve to dine

Aristophanes—Livy—Logic

Wednesday [April 20] R. T. Ir⟨...⟩. Chapel. Breakf⟨ast⟩. Seym⟨our⟩ Temple B⟨attersb⟩y Sh⟨air⟩p Walf⟨ord⟩ Vans⟨ittart⟩ Ivory Prichard Seymour Temple Shairp

Livy .

Accounts in C⟨ommon⟩ R⟨oom⟩ Tuckwell Robbins. dinner at Balliol—with Lake Mr Cornish—Lake & Tait Moberly Blackett

Thursday [April 21] 9—R⟨obbins⟩, T⟨uckwell⟩, ✱ H⟨...⟩, A⟨ddington⟩—3 dinner at Oriel. Mr Cornish Prichard & Moberley with Church.

[*   *   *   *   *]

Friday [April 22] dinner at Oriel Fraser, Sheppard.

fo. 7ʳ Saturday [April 23]

To be, be thine
To work, to worship & to wish be mine,

Neither Chapel R⟨obbins⟩ T⟨uckwell⟩ H⟨ayley⟩ Al⟨stone⟩ R⟨obbins⟩ to walk dined at home. possessed by a false fancy R⟨obbins⟩ & H⟨ayley⟩ 12

Addington 1
Alstone

Ivory
Tuckwell

Sunday ⟨April⟩ 24th
Read in Chapel.
Logic—Ethics—[Aristophanes'] Knights

Monday [April 25] Marriott & Chace
My follies are increasing daily & hourly.

Tuesday [April 26] breakfast party 3 boys Lake G⟨ou⟩lb⟨ur⟩n   fo. 7ᵛ
minor Ivory. dined with Goulb⟨ur⟩n ma⟨jor⟩ Bigge &c.
Ward ½ p. 9 In Balliol fr⟨om⟩ 9 to 10 left a card on B⟨attersby⟩

Wednesday [April 27] both chapels dined at home waited
expecting B⟨attersby⟩ walked to Iffley meeting & returning with
Temple. greatly floored.

Thursday [April 28] after lectures went up to Lake's room. Met
B⟨attersby⟩ Stanley & Lake to dine.

Friday [April 29] an idle day—only Tuckwell—dined at Oriel—
Lytton Marr⟨iott⟩ Fr⟨aser⟩ Corn⟨ish⟩ Christie.

Saturday [April 30] T. Hayley, Add⟨in⟩gton. little todo.
B⟨attersb⟩y called.
If I had only gone on with my duty instead of going to Rugby—or   fo. 8ʳ
indeed this last fortnight
    Caliginosae noctis somnium suavissimum [*the sweetest dream of
darkest night*]

Sunday   May 1st

Inter vota vix amata
    Unicum amabile
Inter indies mutata
    Minime mutabile
Inter vana, foeda, falsa
    Verum vel simillimum
Noctis quam tumultuosae
    Somnium suavissimum.

With Newman 3–4

fo. 8ᵛ Monday [May 2] Went to Newman at 3 found him with company dined at home & went again so as to talk from ¼ to 8 to ½ p 9—

Tuesday [May 3] dined at home—full of fancy all day long.

Wednesday [May 4] Walked to Stowe Wood & Wood Eaton with Seymour & Richard. [* * *]

Thursday [May 5] Ascension Day
Bullingdonw⟨ar⟩ds before dinner—it being Ball⟨iol⟩ & Br⟨asenose⟩ match.
dined at Oriel, having Hall of Ch⟨rist⟩ Ch⟨urch⟩ with me.
Golightly, Eden.

Friday [May 6] Ivory & Alstone—exceedingly beastly at both. Eve⟨ning⟩ Chapel; Walk alone tow⟨ar⟩ds Bullingdon.

fo. 9ʳ Continually setting up sham relations.
I am so utterly exposed that I feel sure I shall fence my heart around with some false protection.
for Monday [Aristophanes'] Equites [Aristotle's] Ethics
for Wedn⟨esday⟩ Livy Ethics
for Tomorrow

Saturday [May 7] br⟨eakfast⟩ with Ivory dinner in Oriel, Stanley, Lake & about a dozen.
Felt myself driven into some exceedingly foolish & beastly step. & worse again this

fo. 9ᵛ Sunday [May 8] morning after reading in Chapel & foolishly let myself read & as good as finish [Goethe's] Goetz von Berlichingen—wherewith I am possessed.

Monday [May 9] dined at Oriel—Shephard. Mrs Curtis. Ran to Shotover.

Tuesday [May 10] br⟨eakfast⟩ with Chase dinner with Goulburn mi⟨nor⟩
Walked a mile or two with Casey.

Wedn⟨esday⟩ [May 11] dinner with Congreve walked with Prich⟨ar⟩d & Ivory
the Class list   very miserable.

Thursday [May 12] In better spirits   Bullingdon. saw B⟨attersby⟩ pl⟨ay⟩ cricket.

Friday [May 13] Went to Newman   fo. 10ʳ

Saturday [May 14] The Provost—The Pig—Southam—½way to Dunch⟨urch⟩ & back

Sunday [May] 15th at Southam & thence to Adderbury very tired

Monday [May 16] to Oxford—Tuckw⟨ell⟩ & Ivory to Shotover

Tuesday [May 17] Tuckwell—Shotover—Ward de rebus Cottonianis [*about Cotton's affairs*]

Wednesday [May 18] Tuck⟨well⟩ & Ivory. Evening Chapel Shotover.

Thursday [May 19] Crowder to dine. Ward fr⟨om⟩ 10 to 11
                                                           fo. 10ᵛ

Friday [May 20] Sh⟨otover⟩ 7–10 Bessie Gray

Saturday [May 21] M⟨orning⟩ Ch⟨apel⟩ Sh⟨otover⟩

Sunday [May] 22d Shotover fr⟨om⟩ 12 to 6

Monday [May 23] Shot⟨over⟩ 7–10

Tuesday [May 24] didnt walk—having read Othello

Wedn⟨esday⟩ [May 25] dined at Oriel—walked a little with Carden.

Thursday [May 26] Bevisioned at night after a weak fashion   fo. 11ʳ

Friday [May 27] bathed at P⟨arson's⟩ Pl⟨easure⟩
Temple—Waite double 1sts. Bullingdon 7–10

Saturday [May 28] B⟨urbidge⟩ br⟨eakfast⟩ with Ivory—So far as

I see now the Journey to Southam was rather an Evil than
otherwise.

I ought to have gone on with my Work then—as before in the two
previous journeys, and after I came back from L⟨iver⟩p⟨oo⟩l. *All*
acceptance of hope & sympathy ever since I felt I could not go . . . was bad.

fo. 11ᵛ Sunday [May] 29th Ought to have got up at 6 didnt till 9.

I have already set up a new heart founded on all sort of false
proceedings—if I was wrong in trusting my old heart which at any
rate had some truths mixed up with its positiveness, how much less
may I this.

I ought certainly, I suppose, to have let it take its chance when
regular duties came in the way, but for no other reason to have
sacrificed the least bit.

Was on Shotover & at Stowe wood from 2 to 9 skipping both
chapels.

fo. 12ʳ Friday

> Believe me lady,
> There's not a face in any crowded room
> No radish head fantastically carved
> Peeping above the Nature-hiding clothes
> Itself full oft more Natureless then they
> Not one in Church or Concert Room or Street
> But I could give you theory & tale
> Specious & mostly true, with subtilties
> Heart introspective-psychological
> With explanation, keen & delicate
> Of every class of fixed or moving eye.
> The passing smile, the pouted smile unmoving
> The twitchings & the lines about the mouth
> Could tell you that that each man rested on
> What was the figure of repose & hope
> And its proportion (many and many a time
> As thousands to a cipher) to his belief—
> This & much more than this.
>   And for no better reason

fo. 12ᵛ
> Than that I have within my belly (pardon lady
> So bold a word) within my stomach then
> A Papal Index Purgatorius

Of all the follies that in human shape
Walk & grimace it thro' the World.

Monday [May 30] Shotover 7–10   Fire

Tuesday [May 31] b⟨reakfast⟩ with Robbins. Called on the
Wagners. Oriel with Accounts. [Goethe's] Herm⟨ann⟩ & Dorothea after dinner with the Wagners in Ch⟨rist⟩ Ch⟨urch⟩ walk &
at tea 7–10 very foolish

June 1st Wedn⟨esday⟩ the Wagners to breakf⟨ast⟩ dined at Oriel

Thurs⟨day⟩ June 2 dined at Oriel   Church & Dr Trueton
br⟨eakfast⟩ party Addington & other pupils. after dinner the
Wagners

Friday [June 3] Shotover 7–10

Saturday [June 4] bathed with Prich⟨ard⟩—br⟨eakfast⟩ with
Ivory. Stanley's rooms. The Bodleian. Ward & Tait.
less Im⟨aginatio⟩n & Sympathy & Consciousness the better.
Meditation on *Truths*
Ignorance of Truths.

Sunday [June 5] both Chapels & dinner   saw B⟨urbidge⟩ at 2nd
Sermon or fancied it.

Monday [June 6] My evident tendency just now is to set up some
protection to build up hurriedly a new self upon hypotheses. Indeed
it seems to be already done—& if it were to be taken from under
me I sh⟨oul⟩d be left with nothing—& so it is clear enough I shall
stick to it

                    [*   *   *   *   *]

The best thing that could have been done w⟨oul⟩d have been a
sober connexion with Temple or Goulburn . . . such as I proposed
to myself last Term.

Tuesday [June 7] read some Faust—called on Mrs Greenhill
dined in Hall—walked in H⟨olywe⟩ll fields fr⟨om⟩ 10 to ¼4 pm
The Hampden Day

Wednesday [June] 8th reading Faust. Bathed & Chapel. Tuckwell with £35 [Commemoration]—saw Congreve—sent £66 home—walked about with Scott—dined at home—in College a little bit—Ward here.

Thursday [June 9] with Prichard & Seymour 7½ br⟨eakfast⟩ with Lloyd and in College a good deal—looking for Lawley.

Friday [June 10] Heard from Burbidge. The Master & the Provost. Ran up to Shotover.

Saturday [June 11] Tuckwell's last day—Took him on the River.

fo. 15ʳ Of course there can be no doubt that every act I did, every feeling I have appropriated against or without truth is an utter misery—item I suppose all this hope & sympathy. Especially the Oriel-folly;—the not getting up at once;—the reading Poetry, specially Goethe;—the Wagner-folly

Work—Work—Work—Not to be positive. Stat Veritas. [*Truth Remains*]

Every act done against truth or even phantasia of truth is of course a διαφθορα [*corruption*]

fo. 15ᵛ   [*   *   *   *   *]

fo. 16ʳ Sunday [June 12th]

Monday [June 13] Heard of Arnold's death Went to Birmingham

Tuesday [June 14] to Derby. Cromford & the Dog & Partridge

Wednesday [June 15] Isaak Walton & Dovedale.

Thursday [June 16] Cromford & by Coach to Buxton. Tickell &c

Friday [June 17] to Liverpool by Manchester

Saturday [June 18] to Rhyl at 3 p.m. Abergele & by mail to Bangor

Sunday [June] 19th to Cathedral, Carnarvon, Llantyfri

Monday [June 20] Clynnog to breakf⟨as⟩t—bathed. Nantlleread

Tuesday [June 21] to Dows-y-Coed & back to Clynnog—Pelham

Wednesday [June 22] to Tremadoc in the Evening

Thursday [June 23] to Tan-y-bwlch

Friday [June 24] With Shairp up Moelwyn—with him & Boyle & Farrer & Willock to dinner & tea & walk after.

Saturday—[June 25] read Wordsworth there Rhaiadr Du

Sunday [June] 26th both Services—Walk to T⟨an⟩ y B⟨w⟩l⟨ch⟩ L⟨ake⟩ & M⟨oe⟩lwynw⟨ar⟩ds.

W A L E S   fo. 16ᵛ

Monday [June 27] by myself Llyncwmdr. by the glen

Tuesday [June 28] the glen. Dolgellewards & to Brondanw

Wednesday [June 29] to Bethg⟨e⟩ll⟨er⟩t—Clynnog & Llantwrog

Thursday [June 30] to Carnarvon & Bettws Garnon

Friday July 1st at Bettws—& to Carnarvon

Saturday [July 2] Bettws & Bethgelert

Sunday [July] 3rd Bethgelert—neither service

Monday [July 4] [Bethgelert] Heavy Rain Llyn Gwynt

Tuesday [July 5] letters

Wednesday [July 6]—Morning Walks on the M⟨oun⟩t⟨ai⟩n. to Bettws

Thursday [July 7] at Bettws. Wrote to B⟨urbidge⟩ de . . .

Friday [July 8] to Carnarvon Testimonials.

Saturday [July 9] to Bangor & Aber

Sunday [July] 10th No service The Waterfall

Monday [July 11] the M⟨oun⟩t⟨ai⟩n side the Wood

Tuesday [July 12] [the Mountain side] [the Wood]

Wednes⟨day⟩ [July 13] to Bangor & at Bangor

Th⟨ursday⟩ [July 14] to L⟨iver⟩p⟨oo⟩l by St⟨eame⟩r Wrote to Goulb⟨ur⟩n

Fr⟨iday⟩ [July 15] at L⟨iver⟩p⟨oo⟩l the Crowders.

IRELAND

Saturday [July 16] at L⟨iver⟩p⟨oo⟩l

Sunday [July] 17th started p⟨e⟩r Medina at 6 AM in Dublin at 5 PM left d⟨itt⟩o at 9

Monday [July 18] 5 AM at Kilkenny—Waterford—Lismore, Younghall, Cork 9 PM

Tuesday [July 19] Cove—Carium—Passage—Calomel

Wednesday [July 20]—Bathed—the Gen⟨era⟩l & Miss C⟨arey⟩

Thursday [July 21] rode alone

Friday [July 22] rode with Carey

Saturday [July 23] Staid at home. John C⟨arey⟩ at breakfast.

Sunday [July] 24th Went over at 12 Capt Patey &c

Monday [July 25]

Tuesday [July 26] rode with J⟨ohn⟩ C⟨arey⟩. Mrs Mund & Miss Loyn & Capt Elr⟨in⟩gton at Dinner

Wedn⟨esday⟩ [July 27] By st⟨eame⟩r with Lady C⟨arey⟩ to Cove.

Thursday July 28—Price's test⟨imonia⟩l book

Fr⟨iday⟩ [July 29]

Saturday [July 30]

Sunday [July 31] Arrival of How   Tait's election.

Monday 1st August ap⟨ud⟩ Caros [*At the Careys*] Carey lamed

Tuesday [August 2] at home—Coolmore

W⟨ednesday⟩ [August 3] Raffeen ball. With How in Cork   fo. 17ᵛ

Th⟨ursday⟩ [August 4] The Field-day ap⟨ud⟩ C⟨aros⟩. 8 PM

Fr⟨iday⟩ [August 5] Austin's ball ap⟨ud⟩ C⟨aros⟩ 6–7½

S⟨aturday⟩ [August 6] H⟨ow⟩ & C⟨arey⟩ in Cork; bathed & walked by M⟨on⟩kst⟨ow⟩n Castle, alone

Sun⟨day⟩ [August] 7th Passage Church

M⟨onday⟩ [August 8] Called at Raffeen

T⟨uesday⟩ [August 9] Removed to Monkstown 9th

W⟨ednesday⟩ [August 10] The O'Grady's yacht

Th⟨ursday⟩ [August 11] How at Cork—Discovered the dell & the Osmunda.

Fr⟨iday⟩ [August 12] The O'Grady's ball. Rowed in Sir R. Hagans boat. called at Raffeen   ✳

Sat⟨urday⟩ [August 13] Party at the Caries

Sunday [August] 14th Monkstown Church.

Monday [August 15] The O'Grady's yacht. How ret⟨urne⟩d at ½ AM. The Old House.

Tuesday [August 16] Walked with How up the dell

Wedn⟨esday⟩ [August 17] Called on Mr Nash dined ap⟨ud⟩ C⟨aros⟩ How at home

Th⟨ursday⟩ [August 18]. dined ap⟨ud⟩ Caram [*with Lady Carey*] Sir R. Hagan's ball.

Friday [August 19]—Went up to Cork—Raffeen Wood.

Saturday [August 20]—dinner ap⟨ud⟩ Caros, the Arndn [?] & the Nashes

fo. 18ʳ To what purpose is it to act on a belief such as mine is—made up of a mess of false positivenesses & false concessions—continual closings upon anything true or false that seemed by comparison my own, continual surrenders of & fallings down to worship from the sense of obligation.

Tuesday September 6th

How September 13 to Oct 4   Carey Oct 10 to 31

Sunday [August] 21 Ch⟨urch⟩ at Monkstown. ap⟨ud⟩ C⟨aros⟩ fr⟨om⟩ 3½ to 7:—

Monday [August 22] Si noles sanus, curres hydropicus—si noles hydropicus, conabere hydropicissimus. to Coolmore with How. Inv⟨itatio⟩n [?] to Mr Saunders' Carey at home all day.

fo. 18ᵛ Tuesd⟨ay⟩ [August 23] ap⟨ud⟩ Careos. Spy hill. [*financial calculations*]

Wedn⟨esday⟩ [August 24] Regatta I.

Walked to Balybrickan with Howe. Swam home. M⟨on⟩kstown Castle

Thursday [August 25] ap⟨ud⟩ Caros. Luncheon: the Abbott: How at the ball.

Friday [August 26]—Lane above M⟨on⟩kstown Castle with How

Saturday [August 27] apud Caros—a dance—ret⟨urne⟩d with Gen⟨era⟩l Chenar.

Sunday [August] 28th M⟨on⟩kstown Church—the Caries—letter fr⟨om⟩ my Father

Monday [August 29] Rowed in the Harbour 4–5½PM

Tuesd⟨ay⟩ [August 30] Went up to Cork—dining at ½ p 7 at home—

Wedn⟨esday⟩ [August 31] Mr Percys to br⟨ea⟩kf⟨as⟩t Walked with Carey. Capt de Lancey—the Percy party.

Th⟨ursday⟩ September 1st Dr & W⟨illia⟩m to br⟨eakfas⟩t. How in Cork—no lectures. the O'Gradies at Carium where I slept.

Fri⟨day⟩ [September 2] [Dr & William to breakfast] Rowing fr⟨om⟩ 11 to 5. Cross haven. dinner at Carium.

Sat⟨urday⟩ [September 3] How & Carey dep⟨ar⟩ted. Bathed. & dined & jingled in Cork which I left at 6

[* * * *Two pages of detailed annotations of botanical names of plants.*]

journeying p⟨e⟩r Dublin Mail to Cahir, thence p⟨e⟩r Limerick fo. 20ʳ
Mail to Waterford arriving there on

Sunday (Sept⟨ember⟩ 4

morning, at ½ p 5, leaving p⟨e⟩r 'Adder' packet at 6¼ reached Milford at 5 PM, left it at 12 & reached Camarthen on

Monday [September 5] at 5 AM, left for Llandovery at 6, walked to Lampeter by 5 PM.

Tuesday [September 6] to Aberystwyth by Fal y Tarn & Llanrhysted

Wednesday [September 7] to Abergynolwy by Averdovey & Towyn   dined with Hessey.

Thursday [September 8] breakfast at Talyllyn, dined at Dolf-fuenos with Swayne of Wadh⟨am⟩ tea with Ivory & Temple's party at Dolgelle

Friday [September 9] Home by 9½ via Bala, Druid, Ruthin, Mold & Chester p⟨e⟩r Sir Watkin Coach.

Saturday [September 10] Started for Rugby at ½ p 7 PM arrived ab⟨ou⟩t 1 AM

Sunday [September] 11th

started at ½ p. 7 with B⟨urbidge⟩ for Leicester—acted as sponsor &c &c and ret⟨ur⟩n⟨e⟩d to Rugby by 10 pm

Monday [September 12] Walrond, Mrs Price, Lake, Vaughan, Cotton—Burbidge as far as Birmingham.

fo. 20ᵛ Tuesday [September 13]—to Bangor and at B⟨ango⟩r

Wednesday [September 14]—at ditto—along the shore

Thursday [September 15]—fr⟨om⟩ ditto by Llanberis & thro⟨ugh⟩ slate quarries to Bethgelert

Friday [September 16] to Maentwrog. How p⟨e⟩r Mail

Saturday [September 17] to Llandegwyn lake.

Sunday [September] (18th) to Llandegwyn

Monday [September 19] to Festiniog.

Tuesday [September 20] to Llyntrwstyllon with Pr⟨ichard⟩

Wednesday [September 21] to Bethgelert ⟨with Prichard⟩

Thursday [September 22] from Brondanw,—Lloyd

Friday [September 23]—to Llyndewyn with Prichard

Saturday [September 24] up Moelwyn & to Llyn Curmorthin with Prich⟨ard⟩ & How 1–6

Sunday [September 25] with Pr⟨ichard⟩ &c Bethg⟨e⟩l⟨er⟩twards. Pr⟨ichard⟩ Hawker & Willock dep⟨ar⟩ted

Monday [September 26] to Rhaiadr Du—with How

Tuesday [September 27] to Lowes fall

Wednesday [September 28] with Prichard to Dolgelle, & back

Thursday [September 29] the Consecration—Oakley, Tickell, Goldsmid

Friday [September 30] How's departure—with him to Festiniog, Rh⟨aiadr⟩ Cynfael

Saturday 1st October Rhaiadr du solus

'It is the trial and mystery of our position in this age and country, fo. 21ʳ
that a religious mind is continually set at variance with itself, that
its defence to what is without contradicts suggestions from within,
& that it cannot obey what is over it, without rebelling against
what was before it' Br⟨itish⟩ Cr⟨itic⟩ lxii 401

In this state of non adjustment, Obedience becomes conformity,
conventionality . . . and shame, while Non-conformity leads us
into Passion for Passion's sake, fancy for fancy's sake, that
perpetual semi-consciousness of rebellion which leads into rebellion

We are tempted at one time to give our faith in semblance, where fo. 21ᵛ
we do not feel it reality,—to . . . at another to fasten upon that
which we know to be an object of faith only by a proud
assumption of our own. Seeing nowhere extant the truly adequate
object, we attach ourselves to that which so far as we know is
inadequate, by an arbitrary assumption in the one case of pride, in
the other of cowardice. Desunt multa [*much is missing*]

Sunday October 2nd   fo. 22ʳ
to Bethgelert. John Ellis. to Caernarvon.

Monday [October 3] to Bangor & Liverpool

Tuesday [October 4] Father's departure

Wednesday [October 5] to Childwall with Annie
Ignatius Loyola. British Critic &c &c

Thursday [October 6] to Everton—to B. W⟨rench⟩ & Carey

Friday [October 7] to the Fire   Medwin's Conv⟨ersatio⟩ns

Saturday [October 8] Last of the Mohicans

Sunday [October 9] St Davids twice. The Irvingite Chapel. Mr
Barber

Monday [October 10] Mrs Butler. The Nunnery

Tuesday [October 11] [Mrs Butler] Meant to start but did not.
letter fr⟨om⟩ B⟨urbidge⟩

Wednesday [October 12] came off to

OXFORD

Thursday October 13th Ward from $7\frac{1}{2}$ to $10\frac{1}{2}$ quod grande malum erat [*which was a great evil*]. Louisa or the Bride.

Friday. [October 14]

Saturday [October 15] dined with Prich⟨ard⟩ Comm⟨on⟩ Room Balliol. Stanley

Sunday [October 16] dined at Oriel.

Monday [October 17] [dined at Oriel] Audit dinner

Tuesday [October 18] dined at Oriel—a large party

Wednesday [October 19] dined at Oriel   Balliol to meet Tait

Thursday [October 20] Heard from & wrote to Burbidge.

Friday [October 21]

Saturday   [October   22]   br⟨eakfast⟩   with   E.   S. F⟨oulkes⟩   Corrie—dined at Balliol. Ward.

fo. 22ᵛ   Sunday Oct⟨ober⟩ 23rd. wrote to Burbidge. Walked with Lake. dined at O⟨ri⟩el with Corrie. Lawley, Corrie, &c to tea

Monday [October 24]—Walked with Stanley

Tuesday [October 25] L⟨awle⟩y &c to breakf⟨ast⟩ dined at Oriel.

Wednesday [October 26] [*the following entry cancelled*:] br⟨eakfast⟩ with L⟨awle⟩y. Walked with B⟨attersb⟩y Carey. Sum turpissima bestia [*I am a most filthy beast*].

Thursday [October 27] br⟨eakfast⟩ wtih Lawley. Walked with B⟨attersby⟩ saw B⟨attersby⟩ at $\frac{1}{2}$10 Carey to dine here

Friday [October 28] S⟨ain⟩ts S⟨imon⟩ & J⟨ude⟩ Heard fr⟨om⟩ Price, & Burbidge. Dined at Oriel—walked t⟨oward⟩s Bullingdon.

Saturday [October 29]—Carey, Davies, Hayley,—dined at Oriel,—Farrer, Ward.

Sunday [October 30] Ch⟨rist⟩ Ch⟨urch⟩   Prichard in Holywell fields. at Prich⟨ar⟩ds to tea

Monday [October 31] dined at Jes⟨us⟩ Coll⟨ege⟩ lodgings.

Tuesday [November 1] All Saints—d⟨ined⟩ at Oriel. walked with Marriott.

Wednesday [November 2] breakf⟨as⟩t party

Thursday [November 3] dined with E. S. F⟨oulkes⟩ walked with Marriott

Friday [November 4] dined with Davies. tea with B⟨attersb⟩y

Saturday [November 5] dined at Oriel. Fraser.
[*list of names, some cancelled, including*:] Bennett Hayley Davies Carey   fo. 23ʳ
Shepherd Lytton Eden Marriott Church Fraser Cornish Christie Chace W Foulkes Shairp Boyle Farrer Willock Hawker Swayne Meade Burrows Moberley How Woolcombe Jowett Greenhill E. S. Foulkes. Tuckwell Principal Master Greenhill.

Shairp Boyle Farrer Burrows Mat. Tom. Richard Swayne How Carey

[*   *   *   *   *]

Sunday Nov⟨embe⟩r 6th Read [Schiller's] Wallenstein   fo. 24ᵛ

Monday [November 7] Walked with B⟨attersb⟩y to Bagley Wood.

Tuesday [November 8]

Wednesday [November 9] Rode with Carey to Bletchingdon— dined cum Praepos⟨ito⟩ [*with the Provost*]

Thursday [November 10] dined with Cornish

Friday [November 11] The Schools opened—dined here Stanley de re Liverp⟨olitana⟩ [*on Liverpool matters*]

Saturday [November 12] finished Ages⟨ilaus⟩ Carey to br⟨eakfast⟩ Jowett–Temple–Ward

Sunday November 13th Lake & Jowett. dined at Oriel.

Monday [November 14] tea with B⟨attersb⟩y. Uncle Alfr⟨ed⟩ arrived.

Tuesday [November 15] Rode with Carey—& dined with him Oakley?

Wednesday [November 16] finished Spartan Kings—tea with B⟨attersb⟩y Lawley

Thursday [November 17]—4 oar race, B⟨attersb⟩y & L⟨awle⟩y—dined here. Mend⟨icity⟩ Soc⟨iety⟩ Coleridge. Parks

Friday [November 18] br⟨eakfast⟩ & dinner at Jes⟨us⟩ Coll⟨ege⟩—Lawley, Sh⟨air⟩p, Ward.

Saturday [November 19] Walrond, Wingfield & Carey to dinner.

Sunday Nov⟨ember⟩ 20th br⟨eakfast⟩ with Conybeare. Communion. Walrond to dine. tea with Ivory & Temple, Ward.

Monday [November 21] br⟨eakfast⟩ with Prichard. the Charwell with Battersby

Tuesday [November 22] br⟨eakfast⟩ with Farrer & Addington. Carey's v⟨iva⟩ v⟨oce⟩ Walrond in Ch⟨rist⟩ Ch⟨urch⟩ d⟨inne⟩r at Oriel Hows to wine. The Decade—where I spoke.

Wednesday [November 23] to Littlemore.

fo. 25ʳ Carey Bradley Pigou Tom Lawley Mat. Mildmay.

Bennett—5 Carey—15 Hayley—10 Monday 12th Davies—15 Oakeley—15 Addington—7 Oriel collection Wedn⟨esday⟩ 15

Thursday [November 24] to Littlemore wrote to B⟨urbidge⟩ the Provost

Friday [November 25] Walrond announced—Corn⟨ish⟩ Fraser dinner

Saturday [November 26]

Sunday [November] 27th Walrond to breakfast—dinner Oriel

Monday [November 28] br⟨eakfast⟩ with Bradley—dinner Oriel. Murray. wrote to B⟨urbidge⟩ Montpelier.

Tuesday [November 29] br⟨eakfast⟩ with Hawker. Walk with Walrond

Wedn⟨esday⟩ [November 30] St An⟨drew⟩ Walrond 8 to 11— W⟨alrond⟩ & Carey to dinner 5–7

Thursday Dec⟨ember⟩ 1st Prichard to dinner

Friday [December 2] d⟨ined⟩ at Oriel wrote to B⟨urbidge⟩

Saturday [December 3] dined at Oriel Greenhills to tea. Pr⟨ichar⟩d to breakfast.

Sunday Dec⟨embe⟩r 4. Walked with Lake

Monday [December 5] in bed till 10—at Or⟨iel⟩

Tuesday [December 6] [in bed] till ½ p 9—[at Oriel] wrote to B⟨urbidge⟩

Wednesday [December 7] [in bed] till 10 Up Shotover—the Decade de Educatione Ecclesiastica [*On church education*]

Thursday [December 8] br⟨eakfast⟩ with B⟨attersb⟩y. walked with him & Lawley, dined with Fanshawe.

[*On this page and the next, pleasant drawings of mountains and lakes*]   fo. 25ᵛ

Friday [December 9] in bed till n⟨ea⟩r⟨ly⟩ 10 dined at Oriel tea with Ivory, Prich⟨ar⟩d & Temple ✳

Saturday [December 10] [in bed till nr 10 dined at Oriel] Ward fr⟨om⟩ 10 to ¼11 Balliol collections began
wrote to Conybeare Heard fr⟨om⟩ B⟨urbidge⟩ wrote to him

Sunday Dec⟨embe⟩r 11th Walked with Lake—called on Newman

Monday [December 12] H⟨ayley⟩ A⟨ddington⟩ dep⟨ar⟩t

A woman fair & stately
Yet pale as are the dead
Oft in the watches of the night
Sat spinning by his bed
And as she plied the distaff
In a sweet voice & low
She sang of great old houses,
And fights fought long ago
So sat she & so sang she
Until the east was grey
Then pointed to her bleeding breast
And shrieked and fled away

Tuesday [December 13] Heard from B⟨urbidge⟩ Carden & Trihten to dine Ward

Wednesday [December 14] dinner at Or⟨iel⟩. Coll⟨ections⟩ Fraser de re tutoria [*on tutorial matters*] ✳

Thursday [December 15] Bathed. Or⟨iel⟩ d⟨inner⟩ in Shepheard's rooms from 7 to past 9

Sumnerus Κεστριδης ὁ νεωτερος [*the young man of Chester*]

Friday [December 16] Oakley def⟨e⟩c⟨i⟩t [*decamped*] 1–2 & 7½– 8¼:—Aristoteles. Or⟨iel⟩ d⟨inner⟩

Saturday [December 17]. the Bodleian. Shotover 1½ to 4½ d⟨ined⟩ Or⟨iel⟩. Read Burbidge's article & one on Goethe in the Br⟨itish⟩ & For⟨eign⟩. Also some [Goethe's] Faust.

Bennett Carey Davies. Hayley 12th Addington ib. Oakeley 20th. [* * *]

fo. 26ᵛ Sunday [December] 18th. d⟨ined⟩ Or⟨iel⟩. Marriott & Coffin. Ryder & Murray major Lake ord⟨ained⟩.

Monday [December 19] Lawley dep⟨ar⟩ted:—Heard from Bur- bidge & Carey Wrote to B⟨urbidge⟩ & to Lawley—Oakley

Tuesday [December 20] Aristides—the Bodleian &c till 3. Lytton solus Oakley   Polybius lib⟨rary⟩

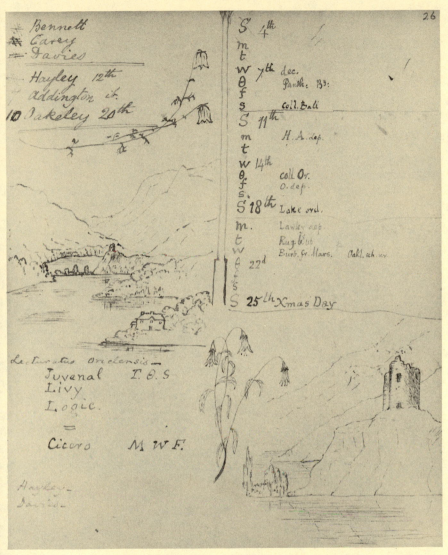

Fig. 6 Clough as illustrator: December 1842

Wednesday [December 21] br⟨eakfast⟩ with E. S. F⟨oulkes⟩ At Oriel & the Union. Aristides. Walked ½ an hr with Jowett. Article in the Standard. Heard from Simpkinson. Burb⟨idge⟩ fr⟨om⟩ Mars⟨eilles⟩ Oakl⟨ey⟩ sch⟨olarship⟩ v⟨iva⟩ v⟨oce⟩

Thursday [December 22] Wrote home to Ξ, & Carey, & Mrs Rose

Friday [December 23] Went to tea with Farrer Also saw Boyle Astyochus

Saturday [December 24] Farrer to breakfast. dined at 3 at Oriel— left for town at 5½, arrived at Golden Cross about 10

Sunday [December] 25th ⟨Christ⟩mas Day
Went to St Margarets Westminster for morning, and Westm⟨inster⟩ Abbey for evening S⟨ervice⟩ left for Brighton at 7 & arrived about ½ p 9

Monday [December 26] to Herstmonceux

Tuesday [December 27] Called on Hare. who also dined with us

Wednesday [December 28] Arrival of Cotton. Walk with him to the Castle

Thursday [December 29] Mr Wagner to dinner

Friday [December 30] Walked with Cotton to Dallington—dined ap⟨ud⟩ Wagneros [*with the Wagners*] Bunsen &c.

Aristeas W⟨ednesday⟩ Aristides M⟨onday⟩ Aristodemus Aristo- crates T⟨uesday⟩ Aristonymus Astyochus Th⟨ursday⟩ fo. 27ʳ

Livy 2 Niebuhr // Juvenal // Middleton's Cicero // Logic

[*   *   *   *   *]

Niebuhr I, II, III* Arnold I Livy I Whately Organon Outlines Trendelenburg Aldrich Lowe's notes [Saunderson] Arnold's L⟨atin⟩ P⟨rose⟩.

books to lib⟨rary⟩. Index to Plutarch. Aristocr⟨ates⟩ ⟨Aristo⟩dem⟨us⟩. Aristeas. Astyochus. Check at Parsons. Daman Eden.

[*   *   *   *   *]

fo. 27ᵛ Saturday [December 31] Returned with the Blacketts to Brighton: thence to town.

[*sketch of bluebells*]

1843

SUNDAY JAN⟨UARY⟩ 1ST

Went to Margaret Chapel. called on Smithius. left town for Rugby at ½ p. 8. arrived at 12.— ✳

Monday [January 2] br⟨eakfast⟩ & Dinner with the Prices. de multis rebus et quibusdam aliis [*about many things and some others*] Home [to Liverpool] by 3d class, arrived at ½ to 10

Tuesday [January 3] Mrs Hindley's

Wednesday [January 4]

Thursday [January 5] Athenaeum C⟨ollegiate⟩ I⟨nstitute⟩ tickets.—Mr Barber's to dine

Friday [January 6] Coll⟨egiate⟩ Inst⟨itute⟩ Gladstone & Conybeare

Saturday [January 7] Mail to Prices.

Sunday [January] 8th St Martin's in the Fields, & St James'

Monday [January 9] from Burbidge, 2 letters (to Jan 1st) and from Gell wrote to B. H⟨. . .⟩

Wednesday [January 11] to the Brooks'

Saturday [January 12] to Rhual is a Dora Annie Aunts J⟨emima⟩ & A⟨. . .⟩

Sunday [January] 13th Mold Ch⟨urch⟩

Monday [January 14] to Min y don

Tuesday [January 15] back

fo. 28ʳ   [*   *   *   *   *]

Stahr Aristotelia. Didot's Historici Graeci Minores

[*drawing of mountain scenery*]

Wednesday [January 18] to L⟨iver⟩p⟨oo⟩l W⟨ined⟩ with Moberly Called on the Conybeares and went to tea there.

Thursday [January 19] to Seaforth with Moberly. M⟨oberly⟩ also to b⟨rea⟩kf⟨as⟩t

Friday [January 20] the Corries' to luncheon—Moberly to the New Park—the dinner party Moberly. John Corrie & Susan & F. Corrie to tea

Saturday [January 21] to the Conybeares to tea. Cotton.

Sunday [Janaury] 22d St Judes with the Conybeares.

Monday [January 23] Macaulay de Mad⟨ame⟩ d'Arblay— fo. 28ᵛ Cotton about town

Tuesday [January 24]—Juvenal. Mr Barber. to Birmingham.

Wednesday [January 25]

to

OXFORD

dined at Oriel

Thursday [January 26] in the evening Walrond & Ward.

Friday [January 27]

Saturday [January 28]

Sunday [January 29] Walrond to b⟨rea⟩kf⟨as⟩t

Monday Jan⟨uar⟩y 30

Tuesday [January 31] Came into College—received 3 lectures, giving one

Wednesday [February 1] Rec⟨eive⟩d Cic⟨ero⟩ lect⟨ure⟩. W⟨al⟩r⟨on⟩d's to tea. wrote to B⟨urbidge⟩

Thursday [February 2] Newman's Sermon—the Panegyric, the Gaude Congreve

Friday [February 3] Cicero lecture—W⟨a⟩lr⟨on⟩ds to tea. Stanley

Saturday [February 4] three lectures. Calls Ward [?], W⟨. . .⟩ R⟨. . .⟩ G⟨. . .⟩ on Arnold.

Sunday Feb⟨rua⟩ry 5th Walrond to br⟨eakfast⟩ & Walk 9–1

Monday [February 6]

Tuesday [February 7] The Scholars' dinner at Balliol

Wednesday [February 8] Newman at dinner. Davies prox⟨ime accessit⟩.

Thursday [February 9] dinner with Congreve—tea with Greenhill—Shotover.

Friday [February 10] short walk with Walrond.

Saturday [February 11] br⟨eakfast⟩ Shairp, Ward, B⟨attersb⟩y. Walk with Temple. dinner with Marriott tea with Walrond.

fo. 29ʳ Write to Price Stanley de B⟨urbidge⟩. B⟨. . .⟩s f⟨. . .⟩l. Not to talk to Ward.

fo. 30ʳ Sunday Feb⟨ruar⟩y 12th. Walked with Walrond. Beckley, Woodeaton, Elsfield. 10–2½:—Wrote to B⟨urbidge⟩.

Monday [February 13]

Tuesday [February 14] Rode with Congreve. dinner in Hall:— Kay Linc⟨oln⟩ Crewe Mert⟨on⟩

Wednesday [February 15]

Thursday [February 16] dinner in Hall & Party

Friday [February 17] Walrond to br⟨eakfast⟩ & to tea

Saturday [February 18] Prich⟨ar⟩d to br⟨eakfast⟩ Walk with Temple & Prichard by Beckley, Stanton St J⟨oh⟩n, n⟨ea⟩r Wheatley, over Shotover: dinner at Temple's + M⟨atthew⟩ A⟨rnold⟩, Battersby, Shairp.

Sunday Feb⟨ruary⟩ 19th. W⟨alked⟩ w⟨ith⟩ W⟨ar⟩d 10 to 2 Besselsleigh.

Monday [February 20] Carey, Cross & others to breakf⟨as⟩t

Tuesday [February 21]

Wedn⟨esday⟩ [February 22]

Thursd⟨ay⟩ [February 23] Carey departed

Friday [February 24] My breakfast party, Twemlowe Kirkp⟨a⟩trick &c St Matthias

Saturday [February 25] dined with Daman

Sunday Feb⟨ruar⟩y 26th Walk solus

Monday [February 27] br⟨eakfast⟩ with Greenhill

Tuesday [February 28] [breakfast] with Stanley

Ash Wednesday March 1st Etc for S⟨er⟩m⟨on⟩ ran over Shotover fo. 30ᵛ (to B⟨urbidge⟩) Ward.

Thursday [March 2] W⟨a⟩lr⟨on⟩d's to tea

Friday [March 3] W⟨a⟩lr⟨on⟩d here—Over Shotover Cuddes-don G⟨ar⟩s⟨in⟩gton

Saturday [March 4] Temple & Prichard 2–4½ Mill's Logic

Sunday March 5
Communion Sunday Neither Chapel Bagley Wood 11–5

Monday [March 6]

Tuesday [March 7] Chiselhampton & Wheatley with Congreve riding. Spoke with the Provost Corrie to breakf⟨as⟩t.

Wedn⟨esday⟩ [March 8]

Thurs⟨day⟩ [March 9] dined with Congreve, Powles &c &c

Friday [March 10]

Saturday [March 11] Walk & dinner with Prichard. heard fr⟨om⟩ Burbidge. tea with Walrond, Henrietta Temple

Sunday March 12th Walrond to breakf⟨as⟩t Mannings Sermon Walr⟨on⟩d to Chiselhampton & Cuddesdon 12 to 5 *

Monday [March 13] Walked with E. S. F⟨oulkes⟩ bathed. dined in Hall all this week

Tuesday [March 14] ran up Shotover

fo. 31ʳ Wedn⟨esday⟩ [March 15]

Thurs⟨day⟩ [March 16]

Friday [March 17] Rode with Congreve tea with W⟨a⟩lr⟨on⟩d
*

Saturday [March 18] Walked with Temple—br⟨eakfast⟩ with Hawker tea with W⟨alron⟩d.

Sunday March 19th Solus 1½ to 5½ Rob⟨er⟩t Wilberforce. tea with W⟨alrond⟩.

Monday [March 20] s⟨en⟩t to B⟨urbidge⟩.

Tuesday [March 21] bathed solus 4 pm tea with W⟨alrond⟩

Wednesday [March 22] bathed with W⟨alrond⟩ 7½ AM H⟨ar⟩tf⟨or⟩d Sch⟨olarship⟩ tea with W⟨alrond⟩

Thursday [March 23] bathed with W⟨alrond⟩ 7¼ AM

Friday [March 24] bathed solus 7½ AM Saw the Comet. tea with W⟨alrond⟩ *

Saturday [March 25] br⟨eakfast⟩ with Prich⟨ar⟩d in Common Room. Walk with ditto:—dined with the Prov⟨ost⟩ Mat & others

Sunday March 26th Walk with Walrond.

Monday [March 27] Palmer Latin Scholar

Tuesday [March 28] walk with Walrond: the Brag:

Wednesday [March 29] Coll⟨ections⟩ br⟨eakfast⟩ with B⟨attersb⟩y, walked 6½–8½ tea with Walrond ✳

Thursday [March 30] Coll⟨ections⟩ Walk & tea with W⟨a⟩lr⟨on⟩d W⟨a⟩lr⟨on⟩d dep⟨ar⟩ted.

Friday [March 31] Coll⟨ections⟩

Saturday April 1st. Battersby & Temple to breakfast:—with Mat &c from 9 PM to 12 Palmer Ireland scholar.

Sunday April 2nd with Prichard from 12 to 4 Temple to dine in C⟨ommon⟩ R⟨oom⟩   fo. 31ᵛ

Monday [April 3] tea with Shairp

Tuesday [April 4] br⟨eakfast⟩ with Temple. Battersby, Stopford, Shairp—with Temple by K⟨ir⟩tl⟨in⟩gton to Chipping Warden thro⟨ugh⟩ much rain

Wednesday [April 5] by Daventry & Bragboro⟨ugh⟩ to Rugby to the School House. Agriandria[?] Stanley

Thursday [April 6] the Morning with Mrs Price de rebus Taitianis et B⟨urbidg⟩ianis [*about the affairs of Tait & Burbidge*]

Friday [April 7] walked to Braunston

Saturday [April 8] at Braunston ✳

Sunday [April] 9th returned to Rugby

Monday [April 10] br⟨eakfast⟩ with the Frau   Caena Episcopalis [*dinner with the Bishop*]

Tuesday [April 11] ret⟨urne⟩d to Oxford.

Wednesday [April 12]

Thursday [April 13] h⟨ear⟩d from B⟨urbidge⟩

Good Friday [April 14] wrote to B⟨urbidge⟩. [* * *]
Balliol plans

Saturday [April 15]

Sunday [April 16] Easter Day Communion

Monday [April 17] [* * * *notes on candidates for Oriel fellowship election*] dined with Temple.

Tuesday [April 18]

Wednesday [April 19] dined with Jowett (wrote to B⟨urbidge⟩ [?])
✳

Thursday [April 20] b⟨reakfast⟩ with E S F⟨oulkes⟩ Skiffed Temple—Jowett, Temple E. S. F⟨oulkes⟩ & C E M⟨oberley⟩ to dine. H⟨ear⟩d fr⟨om⟩ B⟨urbidge⟩

Friday [April 21] Chretien & Buckle fellows ✳
Admitted

Saturday [April 22] Wrote to B⟨urbidge⟩ & A B C⟨lough⟩ A J C⟨lough⟩ & T. W⟨alrond⟩

fo. 32ᵛ Sunday [April 23]—dined with Temple

Monday [April 24] Walked with [Temple] & him to dine

Tuesday [April 25] br⟨eakfast⟩ with [Temple]

Wednesday [April 26] Hall & Temple to dine

Thursday [April 27] [Carlyle's] 'Past & Present' solus with Eden at 3.

Friday [April 28]

Saturday [April 29]   TERM

Sunday. April 30th

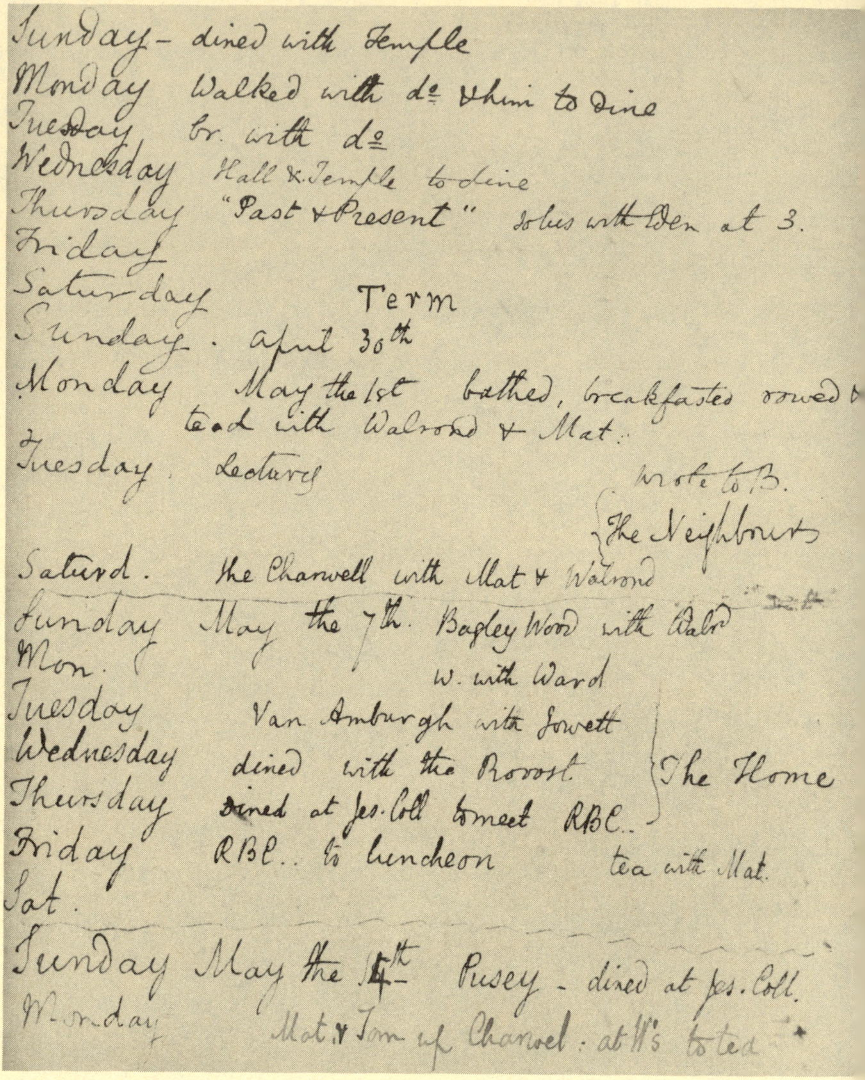

Sunday – dined with Temple
Monday   Walked with d⁰ & him to dine
Tuesday   br. with d⁰
Wednesday   Hall & Temple to dine
Thursday   "Past & Present"   solus with Ben at 3.
Friday
Saturday   Term
Sunday.   april 30ᵗʰ
Monday   May the 1st   bathed, breakfasted rowed &
            tead with Walrond & Mat.
Tuesday.   Lectures
                                    wrote to B.
                                    The Neighbours
Saturd.   the Charwell with Mat & Walrond
Sunday   May the 7ᵗʰ. Bagley Wood with Walr.
Mon.   W. with Ward
Tuesday   Van Amburgh with Jowett
Wednesday   dined with the Provost   The Home
Thursday   dined at Jes. Coll to meet RBE..
Friday   RBE.. to luncheon   tea with Mat.
Sat.
Sunday   May the 14ᵗʰ   Pusey – dined at Jes. Coll.
Monday   Mat & Tom up Charwel: at W's to tea

Fig. 7 Messing about in boats with Matthew Arnold: Trinity 1843

Monday May the 1st bathed, breakfasted rowed & tead with Walrond & Mat

Tuesday [May 2] Lectures   Wrote to B⟨urbidge⟩
The Neighbours

Saturd⟨ay⟩ [May 6] the Charwell with Mat & Walrond

Sunday May the 7th Bagley Wood with Walr⟨on⟩d

Mon⟨day⟩ [May 8] w⟨alk⟩ with Ward

Tuesday [May 9] Van Amburgh with Jowett

Wednesday [May 10] dined with the Provost

Thursday [May 12] dined at Jes⟨us⟩ Coll⟨ege⟩ to meet R B C⟨lough⟩
The Home

Friday [May 13] R B C⟨lough⟩ to luncheon tea with Mat

Sat⟨urday⟩ [May 14]

Sunday May the 14th Pusey—dined at Jes⟨us⟩ Coll⟨ege⟩

Monday [May 15] Mat & Tom up Charwel: at W⟨alrond⟩'s to tea.

Tuesday [May 16] Mat & W⟨alrond⟩ up Charwel here to tea   fo. 33ʳ
✳

Wednesday [May 17]

Thursday [May 18] Woodeaton

Friday [May 19] With W⟨alrond⟩ to the Fox & at tea, Tom & Mat Visio beatifica [*beatific vision*]

Saturday [May 20] Woodeaton way
M. A⟨rnold⟩ T. W⟨alrond⟩ Lawley [*cancelled*] Shairp Fanshawe Battersby Prich⟨ar⟩d Temple Hawker

Sunday May 21st Walrond unwell   wrote to B⟨urbidge⟩

Monday [May 22] walk with Lawley breakf⟨ast⟩ party Clarke &c.

Tuesday [May 23] walk with Cl⟨ark⟩e.

Wednesday [May 24] Walk. T⟨om⟩. M⟨at⟩. W⟨alrond⟩   heard fr⟨om⟩ B⟨urbidge⟩ May 9th

Thursday [May 25] Asc⟨ensio⟩n day d⟨inne⟩r party ut supra [*as above*] Races I

Friday [May 26] Solus d⟨ine⟩d

Saturday [May 27] solus d⟨ine⟩d. heard fr⟨om⟩ B⟨urbidge⟩ May 18th

Sunday May 28th Wrote to B⟨urbidge⟩

Monday [May 29] Holiday br⟨eakfast⟩ with Walr⟨ond⟩. br⟨eakfast⟩ with M⟨at⟩

Tuesday [May 30]

Wednesd⟨ay⟩ [May 31].

Thursday June 1st Lawly br⟨eakfast⟩ dined with Prichard

Frid⟨ay⟩ [June 2]

Saturday [June 3]

fo. 33ᵛ Whitsunday June 4th

Mon⟨day⟩ [June 5] br⟨eakfast⟩ with W⟨a⟩lr⟨on⟩d. Heard fr⟨om⟩ B⟨urbidge⟩ Mat lost his Watch.

Tues⟨day⟩ [June 6] wrote to B⟨urbidge⟩ br⟨eakfast⟩ with Shairp. d⟨inner⟩ with Lake

Wednesday [June 7] Punt upset. Pusey's row

Thurs⟨day⟩ [June 8]. br⟨eakfast⟩ with Nicholls. H. Bunsen cum pupillo [*with a pupil*]

Friday [June 9]

Saturday [June 10] br⟨eakfast⟩ with Hawker

Trinity Sunday [June] 11th Communion

Monday [June 12] Hickley Ormely Trinity   ✱

Tuesday [June 13]   ✱   ✱

Wednesday [June 14]—Exam⟨ination⟩ Scholarship L⟨atin⟩ E⟨ssay⟩. D⟨ivinit⟩y Q⟨uestions⟩ Prizes Mat. Walf⟨ord⟩ Ling⟨en⟩

Thursday [June 15] Viva Voce E⟨nglish⟩ E⟨ssay⟩—G⟨reek⟩ V⟨erse⟩

Friday [June 16] Viva Voce L⟨atin⟩ V⟨erse⟩ E⟨nglish⟩ [into] G⟨reek⟩. L⟨atin⟩ [into] E⟨nglish⟩

Saturday [June] 17th Elect⟨io⟩n Scholar⟨s⟩. Robinson Byrne, Robinson

1st [Sunday] after Tr⟨inity⟩ June 18th Moberly to dine—& wrote to B⟨urbidge⟩.

Monday [June 19]

Tuesday [June 20] the Accession—Holiday

Wednesday [June 21]

Thursday [June 22] Coll⟨ections⟩

Friday [June 23] [Collections]

Saturday [June 24] [Collections]

2nd [Sunday] after Trin⟨ity⟩ June 25th

Monday [June 26]

Tuesday [June 27]
Commemoration June 28th [✱ ✱ ✱]

[1846]

fo. 2ʳ Left Oxford Thursday June 25th. Brougham—L⟨or⟩d J⟨ohn⟩ R⟨ussell⟩ O'Connell—Peel.

Friday [June 26] Westminster Abbey—Exhibition—Turner's, Going to & Returning fr⟨om⟩ the Ball. The Erebus Whaler.
Ramsgate with young Buckland & a Mr Burns Graham.

Saturday [June 27] Ostend—Louvain—Hotel de Ville & Cathedral

Sunday [June 28] Cologne—. (Cathedral & Jesuit Church & (?) St Andreas). Rhine to

Monday [June 29] Coblenz 4 AM. Mannhein 9 PM

Tuesday [June 30] Heidilberg &c by Railway to Freyburg— Cathedral better than Strasburg—Diligence to Basle—pleasant road. Zurich people.

Wednesday [July 1] Dil⟨igence⟩ to Lucerne with rain—the Cottons—The Swiss Lion—Bridges.

Thursday. [July 2] Fluellen—Carriage to Andermatt & Airolo

Friday. [July 3] Giornico—Bellinzona—Magadino

Saturday [July 4] by Monte Cinere to Lugano, by Capo Lago to Como. Slept in the Borgo Vico.

fo. 3ʳ Sunday [July 5] Barca before breakfast under the Eastern Chestnuts towds Blevio;—Varese road in the evening.

Monday [July 6]. Varenna,—Bellagio—Villa Serbelloni,— Cadenabbia & Villa Somma Riva with the Contessa diavolessa [*she-devil of a Countess*] & her sister & a Venetian capitano.

Tuesday [July 7] Barca again. Como—Ice—the Domo—Passports &c &c.

Wednesday [July 8] 9 AM. Menaggio—Porlezza (6 miles) Lugano by barca. Barca on the lake 6–8 PM.

Thursday [July 9] 5 AM San Salvadore rather a failure. 5PM to Luino by Ponte Stresa–good.

Friday [July 10] Steamer to Baveno. Isola Madre & Isola Bella

Saturday [July 11]. The Monterone to Orta.

Sunday [July 12] San Francesco & by Omegna to Vocogna.

Monday [July 13] to Pestarena   fo. 4ʳ

Tuesday [July 14] Macugnaga

Wednesday [July 15] back to Vocogna

Thursday [July 16] Baveno (Bradley) // Milan

Friday [July 17]—the Duomo—the Brera—Como inter imbres [*between showers*].

Saturday [July 18] to Colico per boat, to Chiavenna per voiture [*by carriage*]. Mr & Mrs Taylor cum fratre [*with brother*]. Gordon

Sunday [July 19] over Splugen to Splugen // the Waterfall.

Monday [July 20] to Coire thro⟨ugh⟩ Via Mala

Tuesday [July 21] Pfeffers—Wallenstadt—Wesen

Wedn⟨esday⟩ [July 22]. Wesen

Thursday [July 23] to Zurich

Friday [July 24] at Z⟨urich⟩ & to Shaffhausen

Saturday [July 25] The Rheinfall & to Freyburg

Sunday [July 26] Heidelberg—the Castle

Monday [July 27] Rhine to Coln—Jansonia

Tuesday [July 28] Railway to Antwerp

Wedn⟨esday⟩ [July 29] Cathedral—Museum—St Jacques

Thursday [July 30] to London per Antwerp 1½ PM to 9½ AM
Arch⟨deacon⟩ Berens cum uxore et puellis [*with his wife and girls*]
Oxford

Friday [July 31] Liverpool.

fo. 4ᵛ Saturday [August 1] Commodore to

Sunday [August 2] Glasgow—Houstoun

Monday & Tuesd⟨ay⟩ [August 3–4] Edinburgh

Wedn⟨esday⟩ [August 5] Perth & Blair Atholl

Thursd⟨ay⟩ [August 6] Glen Tile. Linn of Dee. Castletown.

Friday [August 7] Br⟨aemar⟩ 8. dinner 4 subs⟨e⟩q⟨uen⟩tly 3½

Sat⟨urday⟩ [August 8] Corrymulzie & the Dee below.

Sunday [August 9] Invercauld bridge

Monday [August 10] Loch Callater. F⟨isher⟩ H⟨unt⟩ J⟨elf⟩
D⟨eacon⟩

Tuesday [August 11] Hill to r⟨igh⟩t of Craigkynoch (Craig Veek)

Wednesday [August 12] Mar-lodge by the ferry

Thursday [August 13] Fall of the Garawaltt & forest of Balloch
Bowie—H⟨unt⟩ W⟨inder⟩

Friday [August 14] Morven to the top F⟨isher⟩ H⟨unt⟩

Saturday [August 15] Cluny J⟨elf⟩ F⟨isher⟩ W⟨inder⟩

Sunday [August 16] Inverc⟨auld⟩ br⟨idge⟩ &c W⟨inder⟩
H⟨unt⟩

Monday [August 17] Platform C⟨lough⟩

Tuesday [August 18] Inverc⟨auld⟩ br⟨idge⟩ & l⟨och⟩. W⟨inder⟩ (F⟨isher⟩ H⟨unt⟩)

Wednesday [August 19] Glenquoich—halfway F⟨isher⟩ H⟨unt⟩ W⟨inder⟩

Thursday [August 20] Platform C⟨lough⟩

Friday [August 21] Linn of Dee & bathe F⟨isher⟩ J⟨elf⟩ H⟨unt⟩ W⟨inder⟩

Saturday [August] 22 Lochnagar by Balloch Bowie—Loch Muick. fall of Glenmuick—Ballater

Sunday [August 23] Ballater to Castletown. W⟨inder⟩ cum gigante [*with the giant*]. H⟨unt⟩ & C⟨lough⟩ on foot to Inver Inn F⟨isher⟩ by coach W⟨inder⟩ F⟨isher⟩ H⟨unt⟩

Monday [August 24] Behind Invercauld, going by Ferry, returning by bridge F⟨isher⟩ H⟨unt⟩ J⟨elf⟩

Tuesday. [August 25] Linn of Quoich & bath—W⟨inder⟩ F⟨isher⟩ fo. 5ʳ

Wednesday [August 26] Glenlui, glen Dearg, & across the hills into Glenquoich 3–9½ C⟨lough⟩

Thursday [August 27] Braemar Sports—Running ¾ mile—Running up Craig Coyash—Throwing the hammer—putting the stone—tossing the tree. Hammer 88 ft 10. Dinner 4½–9 Dance 9–4

Friday [August 28] Glen behind Invercauld W⟨inder⟩ F⟨isher⟩ H⟨unt⟩

Saturday [August 29] with Capt Buckle Benmacdhui Fr⟨om⟩ Linn of Dee to the top by Etichan 8–12. From the top by Green loch to Castletown 1½–7 Hunt by Mar bridge 6 25 πανδ⟨ημει⟩ [*en masse*]

Sunday [August 30] Glenquoich, with Capt. Buckle. πανδ⟨ημει⟩ [*en masse*]

Monday [August 31] Glen Clunie to the 2d fork W⟨inder⟩ F⟨isher⟩

Tuesday September 1 Slogan to the Hut. W⟨inder⟩

Wed⟨nesday⟩ [September 2] Hill E⟨ast⟩ of Invercauld F⟨isher⟩

Thursday [September 3] Hills between E⟨ast⟩ Cluny & Bal⟨loch⟩ Bowie W⟨inder⟩ H⟨unt⟩ C⟨lough⟩

Friday [September 4]—Dee side from ford of Jelf to Br⟨idge⟩ of Mar. C⟨lough⟩

Saturday [September] 5th. Over Culardoch to Glen Gairden & Loch Balg
Glen Bulg. Glen Avon. Inch. Tory. Lugnal(?) Gorgarff (18m?)

fo. 5ᵛ Sunday [September 6] Kirk in Strathdon. Forbes. Over hills across Gairden water to Monaltie Inver inn & so home. (18m.) W⟨inder⟩ [H⟨unt⟩ D⟨eacon⟩ J⟨elf⟩ at Shelter Stone of L⟨och⟩ Aven.]

Monday. [September 7] Anti Morven Craig Veck & Craig Cluny.

Tuesday [September 8] E⟨. . .⟩y Water F⟨isher⟩

Wednesday [September 9] Loch Cander (Cairnturk?) πανδ⟨ημει⟩ 5¼–9¾

Thursday [September] 10th (C⟨lough⟩ Cluny) Torch-dance at the Duffs.

Friday [September 11] Dee side W⟨inder⟩ F⟨isher⟩ H⟨unt⟩

Saturday [September 12] Loch Aven by Dearg & Alt dhu lochan. The Shelter stone

Sunday [September] 13th down Loch Aven, over a shoulder of Benamain to Etichan, up Benmaickdhui, & home by Dui beg F⟨isher⟩ W⟨inder⟩ (J⟨elf⟩ D⟨eacon⟩ Stalking, Salmon spearing, & Callater)

Monday [September 14] in Grewer's field—

Tuesday [September] 15th Invercauld bridge F⟨isher⟩

Wednesday [September 16] (dinner ½ p 7) the lower bathe at Inverey. F⟨isher⟩ W⟨inder⟩

Thursday [September 17] Loch Callater & by Balloch Bowie West F⟨isher⟩

Friday [September 18] Invercauld Hill F⟨isher⟩ W⟨inder⟩

Saturday [September 19] Invercauld Bridge W⟨inder⟩

Sunday [September] 20th Invercauld bridge W⟨inder⟩ F⟨isher⟩ Free Kirk Mr Macray

Monday ⟨September⟩ 21st J + Bathe in Callater F⟨isher⟩   fo. 6ʳ

Tuesday [September] 22d Inverey t⟨o⟩ b⟨reakfast⟩, East Upper bathe & back by pass of Craig Nick F⟨isher⟩ H⟨unt⟩

Wednesday [September 23] the Garawalt in flood W⟨inder⟩

Thursday [September 24] farmer (?) fr⟨om⟩ Charleston Aboyne. rents £2 p⟨e⟩r acre, farm labourers hired by 6 months at £6 or £8 & feed either in kitchen or store of meal p⟨e⟩r week & 2 pts of milk per day In P⟨er⟩thshire by the 12 mth. Many farmers never touch meat.
Corrymulzie and the Shambler's Fall C⟨lough⟩ [H⟨unt⟩ D⟨eacon⟩ at Geldie]

Friday [September 25] The Platform & Jeremy Duff's Cairn.

Saturday [September 26] The Shambler F⟨isher⟩ W⟨inder⟩ C⟨lough⟩

Sunday [September 27] The Garawallt W⟨inder⟩

Monday [September 28] Slogan F⟨isher⟩ stopped by Castlereagh's keeper H + 6 AM

Tuesday [September] 29th The Shambler F⟨isher⟩

Wednesday. [September 30] Exeunt Omnes. Spital of Glenshee 15 Blaigowrie, 20

Dunkeld 12 with Winder to Kenmore C⟨lough⟩ [F⟨isher⟩ D⟨eacon⟩ to Aberdeen]

Thursday 1st Oct⟨obe⟩r. Kenmore to Killin by falls of Acharn & S side, crossing by ferry halfway to N. side 16

Friday. [October 2] Uphill. back 3m. Loch Earnhead 5 King's house 3. Loch Lubngaig h⟨ea⟩d 2 ft 7—to Callender 4 21¾ M'Gregors.

fo. 6ᵛ Saturday [October 3] to Trossachs (10) to breakfast by Venna-char. N shore—discourse with woodcutter alias roadmender—home made cloth 3s yard Wool, carding &c 1/6 dying 1/2 weaving /4 spinning exclusive. 2 pecks of meal p⟨e⟩r w⟨ee⟩k (meal now 1/7 ordinarily 1/3) i.e. 6½ bolls (boll = 8 stone) per ann. & £14 wages is what a shepherd gets with house & washing besides. work abundant. Trosachs & foot of lake by moon.

Sunday [October 4] Aberfole by L⟨och⟩ Drumky—Loch Ard—Ledard—by Ledard-glen. W⟨est⟩ of Benvenue to Mouth of the river by Achray bridge home.

Monday [October 5] Up Loch Katrine by steamer. Up Glengyle & over the hills to Inverarne (7m but took above 4 hrs)

[*   *   *   *   *]

Tuesday [October 6] to Tarbet by Steamer. Arrochar.

Wedn⟨es⟩day [October 7] Up the loch & back—& to Glasgow.

[*   *   *   *   *]

fo. 10ʳ   SCOTLAND—JULY & AUGUST 1847

Wednesday evening—June 30th
From Skelwith bridge to Carlisle, thence per mail, 10 pm

Thursday July 1st
to Calder P⟨a⟩rk 7½ am.
to Glasgow.

Friday, [July 2] 6 a m to 8½ pm, Kyles of Bute Crinan Canal. Ballachulish. Bannarie. Hunt, Scratton.

Saturday, [July 3] 6 a m Caled⟨onian⟩ Canal Lochs Lochy, Oich, Ness.

Ft Augustus, Foyers, Miss S⟨an⟩dford, & the Rosses of Rossie. 'The inner Shrine'—Blacketts Inverness Road.

Sunday [July 4]—Free Kirk. Sacram⟨en⟩t. Lakefield. H⟨unt⟩ fo. 11ʳ B⟨lackett⟩ C⟨lough⟩ Castle Urquhart C⟨lough⟩

Monday [July 5] Jelf. Invercannich. 27 H⟨unt⟩ B⟨lackett⟩ J⟨elf⟩ C⟨lough⟩ Lawrence

Tuesday [July 6] Scott B⟨lackett⟩ S⟨cott⟩ J⟨elf⟩ C⟨lough⟩ 4 miles Inverness

Wednesday [July 7] Castle Urq⟨u⟩h⟨ar⟩t B⟨lackett⟩ H⟨unt⟩ L⟨awrence⟩ S⟨cott⟩ C⟨lough⟩

Thursday [July 8] Loch Letter S⟨cott⟩ H⟨unt⟩ J⟨elf⟩ C⟨lough⟩

Friday [July 9] Mealfourvonie B⟨lackett⟩ C⟨lough⟩

Saturday [July 10] Deacon Jelf+

by Corrymony to Gensachan J⟨elf⟩ C⟨lough⟩ 18?

Sunday [July] 11th Gensachan to Drumdregan down Glen Moriston 6½ to Invermoriston:—home, 13

[*   *   *   *   *]

Saturday [July 17]—Lloyd & Scott. and at ½ p 2 a.m. fo. 12ʳ

[July] 18th Sunday, T. W⟨alrond⟩ I. C. S⟨hairp⟩ T. A⟨rnold⟩. & Scott alter. Dhivach fall.

Monday [July 19] Invermoriston with T. W⟨arlond⟩. I. C. S⟨hairp⟩ T. A⟨rnold⟩ & Scotis, Foyers by the way.

Tuesday [July 20]—Inverness with Lloyd

Wednesday, [July 21] back p⟨e⟩r Steamer. Altsigh, five or six bedrooms, besides garrets.

✳

Friday [July 23] Inverfarikaig

Saturday [July 14]—to Foyers.

[July] 25th Sunday at Foyers. home with H⟨unt⟩ B⟨lackett⟩

Monday [July 26] to Glen coyltie over Balmacaan hill.

fo. 13ʳ Lloyd & τὰ καρδικά [*affairs of the heart*]

Wedn⟨esday⟩ [July 28] Sc⟨ott⟩ Bl⟨ackett⟩ Craig-ora?

Thursday [July 29] Mealfourvornie. Ll⟨oyd⟩ & Sc⟨ott⟩.

Friday [July 30] Ruisky by Upper road. Congreve.

Saturday. [July 31] Glen Coythie S⟨cott⟩ D⟨eacon⟩ R. C⟨ongreve⟩

[August] 1st Sunday The Glen with Congr⟨eve⟩ Invern⟨ess⟩ terrace.

[August 2–3] Monday Tuesday Invermoriston—Congreve, Bl⟨ackett⟩
✳ The Boat

[August 7] Saturday—General Cameron's C⟨lough⟩ B⟨lackett⟩ S⟨cott⟩

Sunday, [August 8] Kiltarlity, Beaufort, Kilmorackfall Hanassie ford. Aigas Inn. Struy.

Monday [August 9] fr⟨om⟩ Struy home. B⟨lackett⟩ C⟨lough⟩ across the hills S. S. E. by two large mountain lochs, & smaller ones. [*sketch follows*]

fo. 13ᵛ Elections—Gladstone—Cobden—F O'Connor

Tuesday—[August 10] abiit Scott [*Scott left*]
τὰ σηδικά

Saturday [August 14] μωφι

[August] 15th Sunday κρῶφι 'the Free'
At home L⟨awrence⟩ B⟨lackett⟩ C⟨lough⟩

Monday [August 16] the Otter. H⟨unt⟩ D⟨eacon⟩ C⟨lough⟩

Tuesday [August 17] Simpkinson. Corrymony fall

Wednesday [August 18] [Simpkinson] Mealfourvonie. S⟨impkinson⟩ B⟨lackett⟩ C⟨lough⟩ Lawr⟨ence⟩ & H⟨unt⟩ at L⟨ord⟩ Ruthven

Thursday [August 20] [Simpkinson] abit [*departs*]. L⟨awrence⟩ & H⟨unt⟩ return from [Lord Ruthven]

Friday [August 21] Canning

Saturday [August 22] abiit Lawrence [*Lawrence departed*]

[August] 22d Sunday at home—Hunt

Monday [August 23] Corrymony H⟨unt⟩ B⟨lackett⟩ D⟨eacon⟩ C⟨lough⟩ Back by Steuglie

Tuesday [August 24]
τα φωτοβάλια [*the football*]

Wednesday [August 25]

Thursday [August 26] to Inverness with Donald & Munro meeting Deacon.

Friday [August 27] Dinner at Polmailly

Saturday [August 28] Abeo cum Hunt [*I depart with Hunt*]— Invergarry Bannarie—GlenFinnan
Fitzclarence μετα βίγγων [*with the bigshots*]
Sunderlandensis et Transatlantici

[August] 29th Sunday By Lochs [Rannoch] Ailt, & Aylort, & Loch na Nuagh & Borradale to Arisaig.

Monday [August 30] Back again. [Evasit Deacon] [*Deacon left*]

Tuesday. [August 31] Blackett arrives. Craig Conachan. Malmesbury & Canning.

Sept 1st Wednesday The Storm, with Blackett to Loch Aylt, Glenalndale.

Thursday [September 2] The Deer-drive. Adolphus & his Men. Long John. John McDonald, Duncan Cameron etc etc. McKeon The Feast & the Carouse. The Song & the Dance. even unto 5 AM

Two young Englishmen found dead between Kinloch level & Ft W⟨illia⟩m.

Friday [September 3] Cool reflection & bitters—abeunt [*they go away*]. In the evening on the lake

Saturday [September 4] Fort William

Sunday [September 5] [Fort William] the Kinloch Levin road with Palmer & Graham Moir.

Monday [September 6] + Hunt 3.30 + Blackett 4.15 am. Loch Arkaig; Invermealy; Glen Mealy, Glen Lye ἡ ξένη [*the foreign woman*]

fo. 15ᵛ   [*a map of the area*]

fo. 16ʳ   Tuesday [September 7] Glenfinnan again at 8 pm.

Wednesday [September 8] Ben ewt?

Thursday [September 9] Glenfinnan [glen]

Friday [September 10] Hill E of Glenfinnan.

Saturday [September 11] Rain 4½ t⟨owar⟩ds F⟨or⟩t W⟨illia⟩m

[September] 12th Sunday [rain] 3 t⟨owar⟩ds Arisaig: Cranstoun

Monday [September 13] Young Cameron of Polmailly. Callop(?) by the Stepping Stones.

Tuesday [September 14] Loch Beoraick—by Kinloch Beoraik returning by Loch Aylt fort.

Wednesday [September 15] Rain At home.

Thursday [September 16] F⟨or⟩t W⟨illia⟩m; Oban. William Campbell:—Munro: Bridge of Roy School.—

Friday [September 17] Oban to Glasgow. Tontine.

Saturday [September 18] Glasgow. Calder Park.

[September] 19th Sunday Versificatio

Monday [September 20] Clydeside. Marg⟨aret⟩ Graham [Ball]

Tuesday [September 21] towards Bothwell. Glasgow. Pr⟨ince⟩ of Wales

Wednesday [September 22] to Killin—Bridge of Lochay. Lochay falls

Thursday [September 23] to Georgetown or Tynaline on Rannoch.
Cockneyus quidam [*some cockney*].

Friday [September 24] Ben Alder. Loch Ericht. Dallungart. Laggan.

Saturday [September 25]—Br⟨idge⟩ of Roy, avec une trampe Keppoch.

[September] 26th Sunday—F⟨or⟩t W⟨illia⟩m & back: Crichton:—Inveroy: Gillies, in re Loch Nevish.

Monday [September 26]—Loch Laggan; by Pataig, to Dallungart.

Tuesday [September 27] Dalwhinnie, Dalnacardoch Driver, Stewart.

Wednesday [September 28]—Auch⟨in⟩lecks. Tummel bridge. Kenmore

Thursday [September 29] Inveraranan—Arrochar—Loch Long. Mitchell & Barnet Harvey

October 1st Friday D M'Ph⟨erson⟩ Calder Park. Carlisle per Mail &c

Saturday [October 2] L⟨iver⟩p⟨oo⟩l p⟨e⟩r Rail fr⟨om⟩ J. B⟨. . .⟩.

Sunday [October 3] . . . St Aug⟨ustine⟩, C⟨onybeare⟩ M⟨artin⟩

Monday [October 4] Mrs Rose Tuesday, ye Swarry to T⟨homas⟩ B⟨urbidge⟩ etc

Wednesday [October 6] . . .

Thursday [October 6] . . . ye two Swarries Conybeare Martin

[October] 8th Friday . . . ye Bulley Swarry Thomas Mrs Roscoe

Saturday [October 9] Rugby. Shairp ye Match

Sunday [October 10] Congreve's Monday Arnold's Tuesday B⟨onamy⟩ P⟨rice⟩ & Oxford.
Explicit longa Vacatio [*end of Long Vacation*]

[*   *   *   *   *]

Friday [November 18]. Princess's. Richlieu M A⟨rnold⟩ T A⟨rnold⟩

Saturday [November 19] Lyceum. M⟨atthew⟩ T⟨homas⟩ E⟨dward⟩ A⟨rnold⟩. T W⟨alrond⟩

Sunday [November] 20th John Wicliffe; dinner in Oxford St T A⟨rnold⟩

Monday [November 21] to Oxford & back. Philip van Artevelde E A⟨rnold⟩

Tuesday [November] 22nd finally back to Oxford T A⟨rnold⟩ went on board.
Mr Brooke

Dec⟨embe⟩r 18 Sat⟨urday⟩ Brodie at Oxford with Maskelyne

Sunday [December 19] Brodie at Oxford

Monday [December 20] to Town. Tuesday J B B⟨lackett⟩ M
A⟨rnold⟩ Haym⟨ar⟩k⟨e⟩t Much Ado

Wednesday [December 22] J B B⟨lackett⟩ M A⟨rnold⟩ B C
B⟨lackett⟩ et francogalli [*and the French*] Adelphi Tipperary

Thursday [December 23] Chapman & Hall J B B⟨lackett⟩ M
A⟨rnold⟩, B C B⟨lackett⟩ Haym⟨ar⟩k⟨e⟩t School for Scandal.

Friday, Sat⟨urday⟩, Sunday [December 24–6] Rugby R. C⟨...⟩

Dec⟨ember⟩ 27 Monday L⟨iver⟩p⟨oo⟩l

[*　　*　　*　　*　　*]

Saturday, March 18th [1848] 3

Up to Town:—Chapman & Hall:—Blackett: With Matt at
Very's: Haymarket; Sweethearts & Wives, Miss Fortescue.—

Sunday [March] 19th. Bre⟨a⟩kf⟨as⟩t with Matt. & Bl⟨ackett⟩ to
Brodie's: Quo-usque Domine? dinner at Longs. Matt.

Monday [March] 20th to Oxford. The Daily News reports
Metternich's resignation, 13th?

These were the days (18th 19th) of the Prussian revolution: the
Declarations the Concourse in the Palace Square, the Charge of
Dragoons, whose col⟨onel⟩ was insulted: the Barricades & To
Arms, the Neufchatel rifles ... The King's night-missive the New
Ministry: the Funeral; the Amnesty & liberation of Poles. The
New Cockade.

March 30th　　　　　　　　　　　　　　　　　　　fo. 24ᵛ

Thursday 11½ Emerson arrived ... Walked in Magdalen
... Fourier ... Radcliffe.　Chapman　&　Neuborg. ...
Stanley Oriel: Ch⟨rist⟩ Ch⟨urch⟩ & Walk ... (dinner with
Neate, Burgess' sauce) He with Stanley

Friday [March 31] B⟨rea⟩kf⟨as⟩t with Jacobson. Williams, New
Coll⟨ege⟩ & Acland. de Rich⟨ard⟩ Owen. Carus? Oken, &
others ... New Coll⟨ege⟩ Chapel ...

at 4½ to Jacksons with him: at 5 Exeter. Tea here, Froude,

Palgrave &c. Swedenborg . . . His physics superior to Jacob [Boehme], a mere mystic. Bhavagadghita [*sic*]—after Plato. Purest Theism on the Intellectual Side. Double edged Hebrew & G⟨ree⟩k on the Ethical. Carlyle, utterly faithless, 'Jack' a great 'Whore'

[*   *   *   *   *]

fo. 26ʳ Saturday Apr⟨il⟩ 1st.

B⟨rea⟩kf⟨as⟩t in C⟨ommon⟩ R⟨oom⟩. Daubeny. Left about 12:30

Sunday [April 2] Shairp.

Tuesday. [April 4] Vaughan

Thursday [April 5] to Town. at Blackett's, Lowndes Sq. Stanley & M A⟨rnold⟩.

Friday [April 6]

Saturday April 8th. breakf⟨as⟩t at Chapman's with R W E⟨merson⟩
dinner with the Blacketts

Sunday [April 9] b⟨rea⟩kf⟨as⟩t with B C B⟨lackett⟩. Emerson with Matt. Oration de Republica, Holyoake, Hetherington, D. Nixon, Clarke, in John St Tottenham Court Road.

Monday [April 10] Feargus O'Connor. Reynolds & Co from the Convention Hall.—Penkridge.

*   *

Monday [April 17] Dawson chez the Bulleys

Tuesday [April 18] Morell chez Ja⟨me⟩s Martineau

Wednesday [April 19] Mrs Paulet.—

Friday [April 21]—to Town—Fraternization with a Repealer. Matt v. Walrond at Long's

Saturday [April 22]—Emerson

Sunday [April 23]—Hampstead.

[* * * * *]

Whether in the body, I know not or whether out of the body, I fo. 26ᵛ
know not [2 Cor. 12: 2]. 'tis all one.

Life is life undoubtedly, yet morality is also morality. The oak
spreads abroad its boughs, but the violet flowers where its root is.

The Improved Charter fo. 27ʳ

Universal Education & Educational Suffrage.
Universal Settlement—& relief by Labour of Able-bodied Poor.

—PARIS— fo. 27ᵛ

Monday to Friday [April 23–8] the fellowships 'Sellar—

Tue⟨sday⟩ Wed⟨nesday⟩ Th⟨ursday⟩ Fr⟨iday⟩ R H⟨. . .⟩ cum
sororibus [*with sisters*]
E S F⟨oulkes⟩ Magd⟨alen⟩ Jes⟨us⟩ chez moi

Saturday—Sunday—[April 29–30]

Monday May 1 Stanley & Palgrave with Emerson.
Carlyle with P⟨algrave⟩ & E⟨merson⟩

Tuesday [May 2] —to Boulogne.

Wedn⟨esday⟩ [May 3]. to Paris

Jeudi [May 4] Meeting of the Assembly. Place Vendome

Vendredi. [May 5] Lefevre. Service at the Invalides. Jerome &
others. the Club Blancqui

Samedi. [May 6] Notre Dame &c the Bureau Blanqui again—
Champs Elysees, Dentiste Ambulant

Dimanche. [May 7] Milnes. to Versailles with the Paulets. Miss
Jewsb⟨ury⟩—the Bey.

Lundi [May] 8 Pont aux Arts St Eustache

Mardi [May 9] Letters A. P. S⟨tanley⟩ & Vine St. No 4 Mont Thabor—Rachel in Phedre & La Marseillaise

Mercredi [May 10] Emerson Madame Lefevre

Jeudi. [May 11] J⟨ardin⟩ des Plantes. Colonne. Phedre Emerson. When the Duchess of Orleans went to the Chamber a great crowd of blouses passed along the Rue de l'Universite, they came into the court where M⟨adame⟩ Lefevre lives, & called out for Arms, but politely and turned fortunately to the left side, which is another house.

[*   *   *   *   *]

fo. 28ᵛ Vendredi [May 12]—the Paulets fr⟨om⟩ 10 fr 10 les Varietés

Samedi [May 13] Champ de Mars—le rappel—Paulets fr⟨om⟩ 4–$9\frac{1}{2}$

[*   *   *   *   *]

Dimanche. [May 14] Paulets fr⟨om⟩ 9 to 8. Coninghams—Milnes—Span⟨ish⟩ Gallery

LUNDI [May 15] Palais Royal. M⟨on⟩tm⟨oren⟩cy. La Madeleine. De Courtis

Champs Elysées. Palais Royal 3 pm
Café du Theatre . . . Hotel de Ville, Pont au Change & Notre Dame
. . . Maison Sobrier 8 pm
The Invasion $1\frac{1}{2}$
The Assembly fly 4 or $4\frac{1}{2}$
the Recovery 6
Lam⟨menais⟩ v. L⟨edru⟩-R⟨ollin⟩ $6\frac{1}{2}$ or 7
the return 8?

Mardi [May 16] b⟨rea⟩kf⟨as⟩t with Milnes. M'Carthy

Mercredi [May 17] Luxemburg, the bivouac, Pantheon—St Germain, St Sulpice, St Etienne, St Severin

Jeudi [May 18] Arc de l'Etoile [Racine's] Mithridate

Vendredi [May 19]

Samedi [May 20]

Dimanche [May 21] Fete 7 am–8½ representants.—the char. 12½ the balloon. Emerson [de sexualibus] [*about sex*]

Lundi [May] 22—Place Royale. Gymnase. [Corneille's] Horace & Catiline. (Lamartine de Polonia [*about Poland*])

Mardi [May 23] Bal—Mabille.

Mercredi [May 24] Geo⟨rge⟩ Sumner, Ker, Lucrece

Jeudi [May 25] [Schiller's]—Marie Stuart, 2 boxes.

Vendredi [May 26] Geo⟨rge⟩ Sumner cum Emerso Louvre N⟨otre⟩ D⟨ame⟩ des V⟨ictoires⟩ cum Henri; Mendicator
[*   *   *   *   *]

Samedi. [May 27] Luxembourg gardens. Jeanne d'Arc. Supposed arrest of Emile Thomas

Dimanche. [May 28] Hotel Cluny & Thermes;—Club de la Revolution

Lundi [May] 29th Rachel as Tullie & Lucrece: Dinah-Felix

Mardi [May 30] Club des Femmes. Mad⟨ame⟩ Niboyer. Divorce

Mercredi [May 31] Hotel Cluny—L'Abbaye Temple

Jeudi [June] 1st (Asc⟨ension⟩) Walking with Emerson who departed 10 pm

Friday [June 2]—Picture dealing—Geo Sumner.

Saturday [June 3] Vr⟨aie⟩ Republ⟨ique⟩ Democr⟨atie⟩ Pacif⟨ique⟩ Pictures. Domicile of Pierre Leroux

Sunday [June 4] chez P⟨ierre⟩ L⟨eroux⟩ iterum [*again*]. Hotel de Sens. Place des Vosges. St Gervais &c. Pont aux Arts.

Monday [June 5] to Boulogne—the Swede

Tuesday [June] 6th 3 a.m. to Dover & London—the Brasilian.

Marriage of T. B⟨urbidge⟩ the Blouse. Emerson ⟨pri⟩ma [*first lecture*] the Blacketts

Wednesday [June 7] Em⟨erson⟩ the Blacketts.

Thursday [June] 8th Em⟨erson⟩ ⟨Secun⟩da [*second lecture*] Frank

Saturday [June 10] Em⟨erson⟩ ⟨terti⟩a [*third lecture*] Oxford.

Tuesday [June 13] back Emerson ⟨quart⟩a [*fourth lecture*] & walk

Emerson's lectures
1
2 Mental & Physical laws
3 Religion
4 Politics & Socialism: anti-Social analysis & acknowledgement of individual right. Socialism.

Wednesday [June 14] Carlyle with Mat.

Oxford again—the Four days of June 23 F⟨riday⟩ 24 S⟨aturday⟩ 25 S⟨unday⟩ 26 M⟨onday⟩ heard on Sunday E. H. Palmer

London again for 2 nights

Rugby. chez C T A⟨rnold⟩ 28th [June]

Lichfield July 2d

Congreve—Liverpool July 8th

Friday July 14th Emerson arrived from Manchester Out at the Paulets. Julia & Emma Newton—Foster, Ireland.

[Saturday July] 15th . . . Dinner at the Waterloo. On board the Europa. Appleton—& another cum filio [*with son*] Sailed at ½ pas 6.—

Explicit liber Emersonianus [*End of the Emerson Book*].

[*   *   *   *   *]

Carlyle 52 in Apr⟨il⟩ T A⟨rnold⟩ in June 53

[*   *   *   *   *]

fo. 30ᵛ Father left Mother straitened—the brothers kept school: he for five years kept school, succeeding his brother W⟨illia⟩m; first in a girls' school established by W⟨illia⟩m at Boston; then very soon

(disliking that) at Cambridge . . . then went to the South, for
health: then was ordained age 25? to help Ware at the 2nd
Church, Boston—whom he succeeded, preaching 'But I preached
Paganism' but not entering into parochial work—for four years.
Then a dispute about Lord's Supper separated him they refusing
certain definite proposals made by him & after a negociation with
Quakers at Bedford. Went to Europe for a year (–33) then to
Concord.

Born in 1803?   London

[*   *   *   *   *]

The lonely Shepherd's life is best. Better is it idly to follow one's   fo. 31ʳ
own fancy, the leading of one's heart & the instinct of the inner
sense than in a seeming industry be respectable & fill one's purse,
do one's duty & eat, drink, & be drunken—the handle of a mill
that grinds no corn—and die the death of the theologian saying as
he said, Vitam perdidi operose nihil agendo [*I have wasted my life
busily doing nothing*] [*much crossing and rewriting here*]

Only, should one want to marry, and should one wish for children.
[The vagabond is homeless; and the prophet is a vagabond.]
Desolate old age is sad, and spiritual relation precarious, and
'male & female created *He* them'   fo. 31ᵛ

'Thus my heart was grieved and it went even through my reins. So
foolish was I and ignorant; yea even as a beast before thee. Never
the less thou art alway by me' [Ps. 73: 22–3]

At the last, if one cannot live, one can starve. Wherefore not? Or   fo. 32ʳ
present one self it may be some hungry morning to the druggist
fresh come to his counter—saying Sir, I have no bread, give me a
morsel of prussic acid.

'The Lord gave & the Lord taketh away. Blessed be the name of
the Lord.'

Truly indeed I believe that Moses & Isaiah & David, Paul & John   fo. 32ᵛ
& their Master, & with these moreover many that shall come from
the east & west, Zoroasht it may be and Socrates, Confutzee &
Zeno, Mahomet & the Teacher of Peru spake in old time as they
were moved of the Holy Ghost.

Yet spake they or spake they not, irrespective of critics &
historians & transcending all private interpretation, a reality I

fo. 33ʳ know I feel I see there exists of whom & in whom are all prayers and pieties & intuitions & inspirations of old . . . communicating indirectly it may be thro⟨ugh⟩ them, directly, I know, to me. Think of it I may if I will as the God of Abraham, Isaac & Jacob; the I am of Moses or the demon of Socrates. Conceive of it I can if I choose as of a Communion and company of the souls of just men

fo. 33ᵛ made perfect—One thing alone I know—that that which at sundry times & in divers manners spake in times past unto the fathers by the Prophets hath in these last days spoken [Heb. 1: 1] unto me. Yea of them I remain uncertain: of myself to myself I have assurance. [*much crossing and correcting*] Wherefore henceforth know we no man after the flesh; yea . . . though we have known ⟨Chris⟩t according to the flesh, yet henceforth know we him no more.

To some special want or weakness some special help may
fo. 34ʳ respond—a look of a friend, a sight of a great man a passage of a book may relieve this or that distemper the presence of — or — her voice & his eye, Emerson's talk, the discourse of Carlyle, a sermon from Arnold may dissipate this disease, heal this sore, is specific for one or another. But a Presence I acknowledge, I am conscious of a Power, whose name is Panacea—whose visits indeed are seldom & I know not where to bespeak them; but who itself is Prescription & Recovery & of whom though invisible I feel is about my path & about my bed & spieth out all my ways, [cf. Ps. 139: 3] and in such feeling will I if need be endure, & be without
fo. 34ᵛ stoicism more than stoical.

In comparison of this Art is rigid & factitious, Poetry dull, and love carnally voluptuous. The statue & the Picture are fixed and uniform; are superfluous & exaggerative in line and grace in contour & colouring. yea the human face itself so faithful a mirror as it is, we call mere potter's clay cunningly fashioned. Even music whose fugitive quick evanescent & renascent & ever variant profusion most repudiates common sense ignores matter of fact, transcends the sphere of actuality, even music becomes ear-tickling and tinkling of cymbals.

fo. 35ʳ And Nature too, in the bosom of whose loveliness we lay ourselves with a peculiar childlike confidence, Nature so unrigid, so unaffected, so natural—nature too overfeeding us with animal spirits & joyousness—Nature too will not remain supernatural.

Truly indeed the watched pot never boils. For four long hours of _{fo. 35ᵛ} God's blessed workday morning I am fain to write and cannot. Through the open windows pours the balmy air:—nor noise of aristocratic chariots or plebeian drays, nor yelping dog, no company or fears of company to distract—my existence is one jubilant alone—the sweetest securest undisturbedest solitude.

No headache or forecast shadow of headache—through the total _{fo. 36ʳ} frame no notice of one single misstrung nerve. Sleep, thro⟨ugh⟩ the blessed night, hath so, with adroitest ministers, with delicatest tuning key, renewed me, readjusted me, harmonized me that I seem to myself as it were some instrument of happiest unity, some harp of perfectest concord. There stands it on its golden pedestal, silent, expectant, as a rich land on winter's first departure, _{fo. 36ᵛ} teeming but as yet bearing not. It stands in the very air around it seems to search for motion & a touch, inquiring emanations, faint bashfully wooing thrills of petition pass from it, one believes, and tingle in human nerves that should be sympathetic, of distant, or unwilling or unskilful fingers.

Even so I wasting God's good morning—O fine concurrence of felicities, rarest conjuncture of rare prerequisites—in vain—the Muse far wandering in country by lanes or sitting lowly in city _{fo. 37ʳ} chamber gives this hour to some happier worshipper—one perchance not like thee prepared for her—one whom she findeth in disarray, peradventure, huddling hastily on his 'singing clothes' one whom ere ready, alas, she will quit. Silence there as here still brooding over chaos. O blind one, capricious one, wherefore—to the just and the Unjust—Rain or new hay; & dry sunshine on aftergrass; Wherefore (that electric spark whose transit should at _{fo. 37ᵛ} infinitesimal moment metamorphose into lustrous shapeliness solidify, intensify, crystallize, this muddly mess within thee—it is denied thee) Ante . . .

In vain, yet no, not in vain.

> It was perchance a bower beneath whose leaves
> The violets of five seasons reappear
> And fade unseen by any human eye

Yet in the sixth or tenth it maybe or twentieth came on happy moment one into whose soul entered as some spirit some woodnymph of Odour, as an Effluence, Potency, Divinity of pure

fo. 38ʳ   scent, those lost & dissipated sweets, in into his Soul they entered, in his Verses they are fragrant evermore.

Not in vain, O Poor Poetaster, not in vain though life's total be summed up in one seeming-vain expectancy! Thou in thy petty cells & vulgar tissue & miserable organism art collecting it may be what when thou & they with thee perish shall be soil for some truly noble growth, to whose nobility thy meanness was indispensable.

Not in vain, though kindred are angered & friends are dubious, &

fo. 38ᵛ   observers sneer and 'the public' are not even observers; yea tho⟨ugh⟩ thou thyself to thy own self-contempt & self-satire seemest as it were some portentously deluded Joanna Southcote, lying-in of a Messiah that is flatulence—hiding thyself five months to listen to thine own belly-rumbling, & interpreting into the leaping of a babe in thy womb (feeding on fantastic memories of angelic visitation that came to thee of green tea wholly unsexual [? *much crossing*]

Howbeit 'blessed is she that believed: for there shall be a performance of those things which were told her from the Lord' [Luke 1: 45]

fo. 39ʳ   The real, it is true, shades off into the factitious: yet the one may be known from the other: illusion, yea, delusion must be but through them we attain the Truth. The sincere man, most easily too in neglect & unobservance—will amongst the counters of vanity detect the ringing coin of self-knowledge—he will in the end, & ere the end, find his work & do it.

[Not in vain! for, exempli gratia, has not my own poor pot here boiled at last—even while I reviled it.

My morning's investment has brought me its humble profit: some finger, how unskilful soever, has relieved, running over at least a few octaves, the harps painful silence: and the Muse wheresoever absent herself has sent me compliments & a message by her half-livery prose-flunkey.

fo. 40ʳ   Windermere, August 15 chez Greg

Difficulties for operative partnership

The year 4000 gain; another 2000 loss: then the immediate sacrifice of wages: profits being only divisible at the years end. £10 house 3 bed 2 sit⟨ting⟩ r⟨oo⟩ms.

Keats I p. 36, 1. 5

And so grace us in the disgrace of death it is printed 'disguise'?

p. 169.4 pro Annan l⟨ege⟩. Arran.

205.20 pro Titians l⟨ege⟩. Titans

the Great Sewage Question   fo. 40ᵛ
Wipe it not
Beasts . . . & Israelites . . .
Homo sum . . .

Flagellation   fo. 41ʳ

The feet of God al⟨ways⟩ treading the wine press. Who will not that his choice grapes perish, but shall survive in generous wine . . .

To do without a mirror.   ·   fo. 41ᵛ

The first step towards modesty is not to be ashamed of one's vanity.

The Games & Dinner (& Dance?)
The Tour.
The bothie of Topernafuosich.
Oh if your high born girls only know the charm the attraction . . .
Or high kilted perhaps—interposed the   in anger
Or high kilted perhaps, as once at Dundee I saw them
Petticoats   to the knee or indeed a trifle over
Shewing their thighs were more white than the clothes they trod in their washtub.

More cattle & more care—saith a Yorkshire proverb.

[*   *   *   *   *]

NOTES

Annotations to entries noted by date of entry. Surnames of persons are not annotated, but are entered into the index.

1838

1 Jan. *Döring de Metris*: F. W. Döring edited various texts of Catullus and Horace between the years 1782 and 1824

1 Feb. The Oxford Union was the undergraduate political debating club of the University, still in existence, then as now regarded as a proving ground for embryo statesmen.

2 Feb. *Uncle Alfred*: Alfred Butler Clough, fellow of Jesus 1817–39.

3 Feb. *Arnold*: Thomas Arnold, the headmaster of Rugby, who had come to preach on the following day.

4 Feb. *St Peter's*: St Peter's-in-the-East, often attended by Balliol men as an alternative to the university church.

6 Feb. *Went to Tuckwell*: This was a consultation with a doctor: Tuckwell was a well-known Oxford surgeon, another of whose patients at this time was J. H. Newman, who had consulted him a few months previously after spitting blood (L & D vi. 109).

8 Feb. *Nicene Council*: The Council of Nicea held in 325 to affirm the divinity of Christ against the heresy of Arius. Ward had argued that the unanimity shown at the Council proved either the genuineness of the tradition going back to the Apostle, or some universal common element in the consciousness of the Christians at the time.

9 Feb. *The London University News*: On 7 February 1838 Arnold's motion requiring the imposition of a Scripture examination in the London university was overruled by a resolution that an examination should be set but should be non-compulsory. This led eventually to the resignation of Arnold from the senate of the university (Stanley, *Life of Arnold*, ii. 12).

10 Feb. *Have read Newman's*... Both these sermons were contained in the third volume of Newman's *Parochial and Plain Sermons*, vol. iii, first published in 1836: no. 6, 'Faith and Obedience' and no. 23 'Religious Worship a Remedy for Excitements'.

11 Feb. *Hamilton's Prayers*: the Revd. W. K. Hamilton, dean of Merton and vicar of St Peter-in-the-East, a former pupil of Arnold's.

12 Feb. *The Master*: Richard Jenkyns, Master of Balliol 1819–54. See Introduction, p. xi above.

15 Feb. *The Record*: a periodical founded 1828, the occasion of much religious controversy. The vote was presumably to decide whether the Oxford Union should subscribe to it for its library.

17 Feb. *Powell Scholar*: The Powell scholarship was a Balliol prize for English composition (A & C i. 60).

18 Feb. *Wilberforce*: See S. Wilberforce, *Sermons Preached before the University of Oxford . . . in the Years 1837, 1838, 1839* (London, 1839), Sermon 1, 'The Moral

Consequences of Permitted Sin'. It included an attack on the account of the effects of Baptism given by Pusey in nos. 67–9 of the *Tracts for the Times*.

19 Feb. *rusticated this day*: The Latin register of the college for this day notes that the two had given themselves over in their rooms to games unworthy of a gentleman, and were therefore admonished and rusticated. *Newman's Sermon*: PPS, iii. 11.

20 Feb. *The Examiner*: a Sunday paper devoted to politics, literature, and the arts, founded in 1808. *Froude*: Richard Hurrell Froude, a leading Tractarian who had died in February 1836. His *Remains* were just about to be published by J. H. Newman and John Keble; see entry for 26 Feb., below.

22 Feb. *Greenhill*: A schoolboy senior to Clough at Rugby, Greenhill was now a medical student at Trinity College, and later became a physician at Oxford; he married Thomas Arnold's niece.

26 Feb. *readings of Froude's Remains*: Ward and Clough must have obtained a copy immediately on publication. Newman wrote to Keble on the same day to announce publication: 'At last I send you a precious book. It was published in London on St Matthias's day [25 Feb.]—and came down here this evening' (L & D vi. 205).

27 Feb. *poor Jowett's loss of his Sister*: This conflicts with Abbot and Campbell's life of Jowett according to which one sister Agnes died in 1837 and the other Ellen in 1839.

28 Feb. *Pusey's Baptism*: Nos. 67, 68, and 69 of the *Tracts for the Times* were written by Pusey in 1835 and added up to a 300-page treatise on Baptism.

3 Mar. *De Jure Gentium*: Clough's essay, 'The Law of Nations', is preserved in the Bodleian Library (MS Eng. Misc. d. 513). It is marked by Jenkyns 'Good—but deficient in grace and neatness of style'.

4 Mar. *Newman's Communion . . . Newman dined with me*: Newman's diary for this day reads, 'Spranger read in morning. I in afternoon and preached Number 492 [*PPS*, vi. 1, 'Fasting a Source of Trial'] Spranger, Cornish and Marriott assisted me in Communion. Dined in Rooms' (L & D vi. 208).

6 Mar. *The Hartford*: a university scholarship awarded each Lent term on the basis of examination for proficiency in Latin.

8 Mar. *The Ministry in*: A parliamentary vote of censure on Lord Melbourne's government (concerning Canadian policy) was defeated by 316 votes to 287.

10 Mar. δίψυχος: = double-minded; the first appearance of a key word later to be used as the title of Clough's greatest religious poem.

14 Mar. *Buttmann*: P. C. Buttmann, an authority on Greek irregular verbs, wrote a Greek grammar in 1819 which was often reprinted.

16 Mar. *Ireland Scholar*: The Ireland scholarship was a coveted University prize in Classics. Among the disappointed candidates was Benjamin Jowett.

20 Mar. *Copleston's Praelectiones*: *Praelectiones academicae Oxonii habitae, Oxonii 1813, 1828*; logic lectures by Edward Copleston, Provost of Oriel.

30 Mar. *Arnold*: C. T. Arnold, a Balliol contemporary, no relation of Thomas Arnold, who was also competing for the Hertford scholarship.

2 Apr. *Oct. 35*: There is a blank in Clough's Rugby diary for this period. It was in the winter of 1835 that Clough became head of School House.

3 Apr. *root of bitterness*: Cf. Heb. 12: 15.

6 Apr. *Dr. Foulkes*: the principal of Jesus College.

8 Apr. *Writing to Gell*: The letter is preserved, and printed in M i. 67–9. Its light-hearted tone contrasts with the scrupulous self-examination of the journal: 'Do you not envy me my idleness now? You, who, I suppose, are in the miseries of entering the Trin. Sch. Examination. I have got through all my trouble, and am now fully at liberty to lie in bed, go to the newsroom, read reviews and novels, learn to skiff, or finally to insult you ...' *Newman*: Newman preached a sermon entitled 'Tears of Christ at the grave of Lazarus' (*PPS*, iii. 10).

10 Apr. *Stanley's Essay*: The English Essay prize for 1838 was on 'The tests of national prosperity considered'; 10 April was the final day for handing in the essay. Stanley's entry was not successful, and the prize was won by a fellow of Exeter.

11 Apr. *Two silent nights...*: from *The Christian Year*, Monday before Easter.

12 Apr. *The Pilot*: a Dublin periodical, published between 1828 and 1849

14 Apr. *At length...*: from *The Christian Year*, Easter Eve.

22 Apr. *Newman*: PPS, iv. 18.

23 Apr. δεκωραιος: An invented Greek word, meaning 'ten hours' time' or 'ten o'clock session'.

27 Apr. *2 letters*: One of them, to his sister Annie, is preserved and printed in C i. 69.   *the Decade*: a select debating club, first of ten and later of twelve members, which included Jowett, Stanley, Coleridge, and others; it is described in the Introduction, p. xxiii above.

5 May. The letter to Gell is printed in C i. 71. It discusses Newman in a rather detached manner.

15 May. *Newman's lecture*: This was the second of 12 lectures given by Newman in Adam de Brome's chapel in St Mary's, on 'The Scripture Proofs of the Doctrines of the Church'. They were later published as Tract 85. Clough attended further lectures on later Tuesdays of the term; he described them in a letter as being 'on the Mystical Power of the Sacraments'.

22 May. *Little Go*: university slang for the first public examination in Greek and Latin grammar and Logic or Euclid (officially known as Responsions) which Clough was due to sit at the end of the term, but which he postponed, a few days later, until the following term.

23 May. *Talboys*: a university bookseller.   *v.e.n.*: appears to be an abbreviation for 'varia eiusdem naturae' = 'various things of the same nature', an affected form of 'etc.'

1 June. *Burbidge's book*: *Poems, Longer and Shorter*, just published.   *the Six Plays*: Andria, Hecyra, Heautontimoroumenos, Eunuchus, Phormio, Adelphoe—Terence's entire output.

2 June. *Nicholas Nickleby*: Dickens' novel was published in monthly numbers in 1838–9.

12 June. *Heads of my last ten years*: These were written in the final pages of the diary.

16 June. *the Pig*: the coach which Clough and his friends used for travelling between Oxford and Rugby, known officially as The Regulator.

22 June. *Legend of Montrose*: a novel by Sir Walter Scott, published in 1819. *Maid of Perth*: another novel of Scott, published in 1828 with the title *Valentine's Day, or the Fair Maid of Perth*.

23 June. *Parkers*: an Oxford bookseller, in Broad St opposite Balliol.

24 June. ½ *commons*: half-rations, supplied on request by the college kitchen in lieu of the normal college fare.

9 July. *map-making*: A number of sketch-maps of ancient historical sites are to be found scattered through Clough's journals.

29 Sept. *Stoics*: a school of Greek philosophers founded about 310 BC, who laid emphasis on liberation from passion and indifference to suffering.   *Pyrrhonians*: a sceptical school, named after Pyrrho of Elis, who recommended suspension of judgement since certainty was unattainable.

2 Oct. *Prize Poem*: Each year Oxford University offered prizes for poems on set topics; the title set for the English prize in the academic year 1838–9 was 'Salsette and Elephanta'. See E. B. Greenberger, ' "Salsette and Elephanta": an Unpublished poem by Clough', *Review of English Studies*, 20 (August 1969).   *Coleridge*: Early and late, Coleridge placed great emphasis on human free will; thus, the section of *Aids to Reflection* entitled 'Elements of religious philosophy' begins 'If there be aught *spiritual* in man, the Will must be such.' See also the entry for 6 October.

8 Oct. *will-worship*: Clough uses, as an argument against Tractarian insistence on ritual and fasting, the passage where St Paul asks the Colossians 'Wherefore, if ye be dead with Christ from the rudiments of the world, why, as though living in the world, are ye subject to ordinances, (Touch not; taste not; handle not; which are all to perish with the using;) after the commandments and doctrines of men?' Paul goes on to describe this attitude as 'will-worship'.   *Marvellousness—bump*: Here as elsewhere Clough uses the language of phrenology, a discipline created by F. J. Gall (1758–1828) which alleged that character traits were associated with distinctive skull shapes or 'bumps'. Gall and his followers identified more than thirty traits associated with personality organs, such as amativeness and philoprogenitiveness, but marvellousness was not among them.

14 Oct. *Truth is a golden thread*: This is the only manuscript of this poem, which was first published after Clough's death in 1865. See M 656, where variant readings are noted.

17 Oct. *Real Presence*: The nature of the presence of Christ in the eucharist signified by the words 'This is my body' was a matter of dispute between Tractarians and other groups in the Church of England.

19 Oct. *works*: It was one of the major issues at the Reformation, and therefore between Tractarian and Protestant groups at the time of the Oxford movement, how far the Christian's salvation was mediated by faith alone, and how much by good works. An often cited Pauline text was Gal. 2: 16, 'A man is not justified by the works of the law, but by the faith of Jesus Christ.'

28 Oct. *Athanasian Creed*: a creed, doubtfully attributed to St Athanasius of Alexandria (*c.* 296–373), which sets out in detail the orthodox doctrine of the Trinity; it contains 'damnatory clauses' ('Which faith except every one do keep whole and undefiled: without doubt he shall perish everlastingly') which caused anguish to nineteenth-century Anglican clergymen, who were obliged by the eighth of the Thirty-nine Articles of religion to which they subscribed to endorse its contents. Arthur Stanley, in November 1839, refused to be ordained until he had been assured by his archdeacon that the endorsement did not apply to the damnatory clauses (Prothero, i. 225).

31 Oct. This is clearly an idealized programme for a working week, not a record of actual performance. *Vulgus*: school slang for a Latin prose composition.

17 Nov. *Lyra Apostolica*: This was a collection of sacred poems by Keble, Newman, and other Tractarians, reprinted from periodical publication in 1836.

18 Nov. *Milnes' first volume*: Richard Monckton Milnes (1809–85) published several volumes of poems, the first in 1838. A letter to Gell of this date is preserved, and printed C i. 84; it discusses the *Lyra* and Milnes's poems, defending Newman's contributions to the former and dismissing the latter as affected.

8 Dec. *Think not of rest . . .*: *The Christian Year*, 11.

9 Dec. *Williams . . . Sophocles*: This appears to be a list of books to be taken home for the vacation. 'Williams' may be *The Cathedral*, a volume of poems published in 1838 by Isaac Williams, one of the contributions to the *Lyra Apostolica*. Three volumes of Arnold's sermons had been published 1829–34. Julius Charles Hare, rector of Hurstmonceux (1795–1855), was a prolific writer on religious & historical subjects; but in a letter of 16 Jan. 1840 Clough reports that his sermons are 'still only in preparation' (C i. 99). The fourth volume of Newman's *Parochial and Plain Sermons* was published at the end of 1838.

1839

12 Jan. 'C.S.' This probably abbreviates the title of a novel. *The Old Curiosity Shop* had not yet appeared. Possibly Defoe's *Captain Singleton*?

26 Jan. *earnest money*: In 2 Cor. 1: 22 Paul says that God 'hath also sealed us and given the earnest of the Spirit in our hearts'.

17 Feb. *Zacchaeus*: see Luke 19: 1–10.

1 Mar. *English Verse*: the poem 'Salsette and Elephanta', M 139.

24 Mar. *i de rebus Newmaniticis ii Justification*: In April 1838 Newman had published *Lectures on Justification* in which he attacked the traditional

Protestant doctrine of justification by faith alone, and sought to set out the relationship between faith, grace, sacraments, and good works.

4 Apr. *arguing from principles*: In November 1838 Clough had been set to write an essay on a passage of Aristotle which read, 'Plato was rightly worried about this and inquired whether the path of philosophy should be away from first principles or toward them'. The essay was never written (see Greenberger, 185).

8 Apr. *Ward's father*: William Ward, Tory MP for the City of London from 1826–35, and director of the Bank of England; best known as champion batsman and proprietor of Lord's cricket ground (Ward, 1).

18 Apr. *Gell's letter*: The letter is preserved and printed in C i. 89; it concerns Gell's plans to go out to Van Diemen's land.

21 Apr. *Articles*: One of the subjects to be studied for the second public examination was the rudiments of religion, defined as including a competent knowledge of the thirty-nine Articles of the Church of England.

10 May. *Ivanhoe*: the earliest of Sir Walter Scott's novels, published in 1819.

19 May. This is the only manuscript of this poem, which was first published in 1974, in M 138.

11 June. There is one of Clough's circle whom he identifies, in his letters and his diary, by the Greek letter Ξ, sometimes followed by an omega. (See e.g. C i. 73) I have been no better able than Mulhauser to identify him.

8 Aug. *letter to Gell*: This has been preserved and is printed in C i. 92.

9 Aug. *Heard from T. B⟨urbidge⟩*: The content of this letter (about Burbidge's travels in Germany in company with a High Churchman named Ramsay) were passed on by Clough in a letter to Simpkinson two days latter (C i. 93).

18 Aug. *The School*: In a letter to Gell of 8 September Clough says that he has been teaching a class of about two dozen at a Sunday school 'belonging to our church here'.

3 Oct. *Bickersteth*: a surgeon at the Liverpool infirmary.

5 Oct. *Mrs Hemans*: a Liverpool poet (1793–1835), best known as the author of 'Casabianca', whose collected works were published in 1839.

20 Oct. *Laurence Sheriffe*: the founder of Rugby School.

27–8 Nov. *excursion to Braunston*: This was for the wedding of Clough's Uncle, Alfred Clough, who had left his fellowship at Jesus for the living of Braunston. Clough was groomsman, and describes the wedding—the first he had ever attended—in a number of letters, of which one is printed in C i. 97.

5 Dec. 'The Judgement of Brutus' was the title set for the English verse prize for the academic year 1839–40. Clough's entry for it is printed in M, p. 148; it was first published, from an MS sent to Burbidge in June 1840, in *Victorian Poetry* 8. (Summer 1970). The lines in this journal entry correspond to lines 149–57 of the final version, but there are considerable differences. These lines were published by Mulhauser (M 658) but the text contains a number of alternatives not noted by Mulhauser, namely: line 6: 'even steady rest' is

given as alternative to 'fixed unvarying rest'; line 7 'as oft benighted travellers' has been cancelled and replaced by 'as sudden benighted men'.

8 Dec. *Shuttleworth*: P. N. Shuttleworth, Warden of New College and a noted anti-Tractarian, was one of the Select Preachers in 1838–40.

9 Dec. *Collections*: the end of term examinations, imposed by the individual colleges rather than the university. The comments of the tutors on individual performance in these examinations were recorded termly in the Balliol College Examination Register, preserved in the college archives. In this term, Clough's exercises were judged 'improved and very good', his morals for the term were described as 'uniformly good & exemplary'.

31 Dec. *Heard from Simpkinson*: This letter was answered immediately, and the reply is printed in C i. 98.

1840

18 Jan. *Scott's life*: J. G. Lockhart, Scott's son-in-law, published his life of Sir Walter in 1838

1 Feb. This is the only manuscript of this poem, which was first published in 1974 (M 156). There are a number of alternatives offered in the text, which are noted by Mulhauser on p. 659. My text differs from Mulhauser's in that I have printed Clough's second thoughts, whereas Mulhauser has printed his first thoughts unless actually cancelled. In line 7 I have printed Clough's third thoughts, which are not noted by Mulhauser.

6 Feb. J. R. Currer, who came to Balliol in the year after Clough, was drowned in a boating accident. Paradoxically, the accident converted the Master of the College from an opponent into a supporter of boating, as recorded in the *Reminiscences* of William Rogers. 'One of the Balliol undergraduates, Currer, the brother of my friend Mr. Roundell, late M.P. for Grantham, was drowned in Sandford Lasher, and the Master was persuaded to go and see the scene of the calamity. He ambled to the place on his little pony, and by a preconceived arrangement was there met by the Balliol boat. We began to display our skill under his very eyes. He was absorbed in interest, and exclaimed "Beautiful! Beautiful! It is as the act of one man!" He was converted on the spot, and never backslided.' (p. 26)

8 Feb. Clough composed a long Latin inscription of 32 lines for a memorial to Currer. The actual memorial, extant in the college chapel, has a far briefer inscription.

9 Feb. *Arnold's Prophecy*: In 1839 Arnold published two Oxford sermons on the Interpretation of Prophecy.

10 Feb. *Wedding Day*: Queen Victoria married Prince Albert on this morning in the Chapel Royal at St James's Palace.

22 Feb. This is the first poem in the journals which Clough published himself, in *Ambarvalia*. Variants between the text of the journal and that later printed are noted in M 581.

7 Mar. *no fires*: According to Clough's widow 'His habits are said to have been

at this time of Spartan simplicity: he had very cold rooms in Balliol on the ground floor, in which he passed a whole winter without a fire; and he used to say that, now that he was working in good earnest, this was an excellent plan for keeping out visitors, as nobody else could stand it for more than a few minutes.' (*PPR*, i. 17).

8 Mar. *Jocelyn, Henry, & Edmund*: three members of different generations of the Foulkes family.

13 June. *The Prizes*: The English verse prize, for which Clough had submitted the 'Judgement of Brutus', was won by a fellow of Exeter; Tickell won the Latin verse prize, Lake won the Latin Essay prize, and Stanley the English Essay prize (for an essay on the topic 'Do States, like individuals, inevitably tend, after a certain period of maturity, to decay?').

16 June. *Arnold's Picture*: Arnold was painted by T. Philips and the portrait was exhibited in the Royal Academy in 1839; the portrait was engraved and published by Ryman in Oxford in 1840. A copy of it hangs in Oriel college.

8 July. These lines were first published, under the title 'Three Religious Quatrains' by Mulhauser in 1974 (M 156), noting alterations in the text on p. 659. It must remain doubtful whether the final lines are intended to be in verse.

22 Aug. *to their yards*: In a letter to Simpkinson of 27 August Clough said that he could not leave Liverpool for Oxford until shortly before term was due to begin, because 'my 2 brothers are going out to America together (and the younger for the first time) and will hardly be off sooner than October.'

28 Aug. *& J N Simpkinson*: The letter has been preserved and is printed in C i. 102; it speaks of the unsettling effect of Oxford life.

8 Sept. *Uncle Charles*: Charles B. Clough, the vicar of Mold, Wales.

26 Sept. *about degree*: Having completed three years studies, Clough would have been expected to take his final degree examinations (the second public examinations, or 'Schools') in the Michaelmas term of 1840. However, he felt himself unprepared and, as subsequent diary entries show, postponed submitting himself to the examiners until the second opportunity in the academic year 1840–1, which came in the Easter term of 1841.

31 Oct. *Bell*: William Lake in his reminiscences says that for several years a burning issue in private business at the Oxford Union was the question whether to subscribe to *Bell's Life in London*, a periodical favoured by the sporting element but regarded as questionable by purists like himself (Lake, 32).

7 Nov. *Whateley's Examples*: Richard Whately's *Elements of Logic* had reached its eighth edition by 1844.

11 Nov. *over my head*: Mrs Jones was the wife of Clough's landlord, a College servant, of 60 Holywell.

12 Nov. *Schools opened*: Public examinations are noted in the University Calendar for 1840 as commencing on 2 November.

17 Nov. Clough published this poem as the eighth of the 'Blank Misgivings'

sequence in *Ambarvalia*. Some of the differences between the text in the journal and the published text are noted by Mulhauser (M 584). Other differences, besides punctuation, are in line 8, where the published text reads 'yon bright stars'. In the text in the journal 'O kind protecting darkness' replaces 'O Mother darkness', cancelled, in line 1; and in line 13 'must not pay' replaces cancelled 'may not pay'. *Mueller's Eumenides*: C. O. Mueller's *Dissertation on the Eumenides of Aeschylus* was published in Cambridge in 1835.

19 Nov. *Viva Voce*: The oral examination of the candidates in the second public examination, following their written papers. Clough would have been among them had he not postponed his finals.

20 Nov. *Vox Populi*: Clough's essay, with the title 'Vox Populi—Vox Dei', submitted on 20 Nov. 1840 and initialled by R.J., is in the Bodleian Library MS Eng Misc. d. 515.

21 Nov. *his first*: Congreve was placed in the first class along with Arthur Hobhouse.

27 Nov. *Scholars*: Balliol scholarship examinations were always held in the last weeks of November; the official day for the election was 29 Nov. On 16 Nov. Clough had written to his sister, 'Our scholarship examinations are also just beginning—who are to get them, no one can guess at all. There are 2 candidates from Rugby, one of them Dr. Arnold's son, and he of the two has the best chance.' (C i. 104)

9 Dec. Ritter's *History of Ancient Philosophy* had been published in an English translation at Oxford in 1838.

11 Dec. Ellendt published a lexicon to Sophocles in 1835, written in Latin; an English version was to appear in 1841.

12 Dec. *useless row*: Collections were held this term in Balliol on 10–14 Dec. The Balliol examination register throws no light on the nature of the row; Clough's exercises were described as 'good—in matter' and his morals were certified as 'uniformly regular and respectable'.

17 Dec. *Removed to College*: In a letter written to Annie from his Holywell lodgings in November, Clough had said, 'I shall get into College rooms as soon as the men go away, which save me the expense of lodgings, and as I believe scholars are allowed 10/- for every week they stay up, I shall not spend much money by so doing.' (C i. 104)

21 Dec. *Master*: i.e. schoolmaster at Rugby.

1841

16 Jan. *Rhubarb*: presumably as a purgative.

25 Jan. *letter to Tylden*: A draft of the letter is preserved in the Journal (fo. 11ᵛ); see Introduction, p. xxxviii.

3 Feb. The verses are lines 22–30 of the poem 'Once more the wonted road I tread', the ninth of the 'Blank Misgivings' sequence which Clough published in *Ambarvalia*. In line 24 Clough here first wrote 'some far distant' and then

changed to 'distant happy'. Variants between this text and the one eventually published are noted by Mulhauser in M 585.

5 Feb. *Since so it is . . .*: Further lines from 'Once more the wonted road'. After line 37 in the Journal Clough inserted 'One glance from who makes all things fair'; then cancelled it, and offered two alternative couplets for insertion:

> How quickly may a glance descend
> From heaven to bid the darkness end
>
> How if one beam from heaven descend
> The darkness all at once shall end

Line 42 in the journal originally read 'That guilty sinful heart of thine'. Variants between this text and the published one are noted by Mulhauser, M 585; in addition we may note that the published text of line 35 reads 'in thine own' for 'in this thy'.   *Yet Marks*: lines for insertion earlier in the same poem. In the published text lines 16–21 read

> Of ploughed and fenceless tilth between
> (Such aspect as methinks may be
> In some half-settled colony),
> From nature vindicate the scene;
> A wide, and yet disheartening view,
> A melancholy world.

6 Feb. *Essay*: The essay, 'A comparison of the French with the Athenian character', had been written on the previous Saturday, 30 Jan. Initialled by R.J., it is Bodleian MS Eng. Misc. d. 515.   *Fairy Bower*: Harriet Mozley, Newman's sister, published 'The Fairy Bower, or the History of a Month' in 1841.

8 Feb. *The Anniversary*: The anniversary of Currer's death was 6 Feb. and that of his funeral was 12 Feb.

14 Feb. *Burbidge*: The letter survives and is partly printed in C i. 105. It contains lines from 'Once more the wonted road . . .'.   *George's arrival*: In a letter to Charles Clough on 7 Feb., addressed to Savannah, Georgia, Clough notes receipt of the news of Charles's safe arrival and adds, 'I only wish that the news would come of George's arrival' (C i. 104).

16 Feb. *letter to Simpkinson*: The letter is partly published in C i. 106, and speaks of Oxford as being 'in full enjoyment of the Carnival'.   *Vice Chancellor*: Dr Philip Wynter, President of St John's College.

19 Feb. *saw nothing of the Lions*: i.e. he did not go sightseeing with Uncle Alfred and his wife and her sister on whom, as he wrote in an unpublished portion of the letter to Burbidge of 14 Feb., he had been dancing attendance. $\frac{1}{2}$ *a letter to Gell*: The letter, partly printed in C i. 106, contained many lines from 'Once more the wonted road'. The letter was not completed and dispatched for another six weeks.

24 Feb. *Misopot*: a medical regime of uncertain nature; see the entry for 2 Mar.

21 Mar. *Todo*: Theodore Walrond.

6 Apr. *to London*: On 16 Feb. Clough had written to Simpkinson to say that he had some idea of going to London about Easter 'to get some lectures from Lowe, my tutor of Easter term, who is now established there'. It was on this visit that Clough wrote 'To the Great Metropolis', first published in 1951 (M 157, 659).

5 May. *Do duty . . .*: This couplet was published in 1974 (M 157).

8 May. *Logic*: On this day and on each of the first four days Clough sat two of his written papers for the final examinations.

13 May. *Like one . . .*: First published in 1974 (M 157, 659).

16 May. *I have seen . . .*: These verses were published, in a considerably altered version, as the first three stanzas of the tenth and final poem in the 'Blank Misgivings' sequence in *Ambarvalia*. In line 8, Clough tentatively interlined an alternative 'It is a fearful debt'; in line 9 he wrote first 'Yet must I work, my daily duties do', then altered to 'how will the heart whose voice' and finally to the text printed above. Other, uncancelled versions of the final line are 'Remember too the debt', 'Think of that fearful debt'. Variants between the final text of the journal, and the printed text, are given in M 585.

19 May. *Viva Voce*: Clough's oral examination; the names are those of the three examiners, two fellows of Oriel and one of Lincoln. Candidates went up for examination alphabetically and so Clough was one of the first examined; that was why he had to wait so long for the result to be announced (see C i. 108).

20 May. *Arnold's volume of Sermons*: *Christian Life, its course, its hindrances and its helps*, published in 1841.

21 May. *Wards Pamphlet*: This was the second of two pamphlets which Ward wrote in defence of Newman's tract (defending a Catholic interpretation of the Thirty-nine Articles) published earlier in the year. It bore the title 'A few words more in defence of tract 90' and was written in reply to a pamphlet of Robert Lowe's accusing Tract 90 of dishonesty.

23 May. *Collegii . . .*: This is clearly an inscription to be placed in a book to be given to the college library. The book, unfortunately, can no longer be traced there.

29 May. *Second Class*: It was unusual for a Balliol scholar not to obtain a first, and Clough and his friends felt very disappointed by the result. Tom Arnold recalled Clough on this day standing in front of the headmaster in the court of the School House 'with face partly flushed and partly pale, and saying simply "I have failed"' (*Nineteenth Century*, Jan. 1898).

3 June. *Parson's Pleasure*: a bathing place in the Cherwell near Holywell.

4 June. *Prizes*: Fanshawe won a prize for a Latin poem on English railways; Jowett won the Latin essay prize for a work on Etruscan religion.

9 June. *Neck sore*: It was a boil, which was lanced on 16 June.

12 June. *dined & walked with Ward*: On the following day Clough wrote to Annie, 'Ward, my friend and George's, has been turned out of his tutorship for ultra-Newmanism' (C i. 110).

30 June. *Election*: After an election fought on the issue of free trade, the conservatives were returned with a majority of 75, and Sir Robert Peel succeeded Lord Melbourne as Prime Minister.

18 July. *Laodamia*: a poem by Wordsworth.

28 July. *If when . . .*: These stanzas are the first three of a four-stanza poem published as the penultimate one in *Ambarvalia*. Variations between the text here and the published text are noted in M 592. Clough later told Burbidge (Mulhauser, letter 125) that he wrote the verses at 3 a.m. 'after my return from Keswick, almost in a morning dream, if not quite'. On reaching Easedale tarn, about 4, he wrote a further stanza, not printed in the journal but sent to Burbidge: 'Heaven grant the manlier heart, that timely, ere / youth fly, with life's real tempest should be coping; / the fruit of dreamy hoping / is, waking, black despair.'

3 Aug. *Would that . . .*: Clough described this poem as a 'wishing gate conceit' in a letter to Burbidge (Mulhauser no. 125). Over the fourth line Clough wrote an alternative 'Nor yet become the thing I wish to be'. In the last line, 'only' is suggested as an alternative to 'and learn'. The poem was first published, from a different version in another notebook, in 1951. For differences between the two versions, see M 660.

14 Aug. *the bad news*: the failure of Clough's father's commercial concern (see C i. 111).

21 Aug. *9 or 10 pupils*: Clough told Gell 'They are most of them Rugby fellows detained here by typhus fever fears' (C i. 112).

26 Aug. *The Hour & the Man*: a historical romance published in 1841 by Harriet Martineau, based on the career of Toussaint l'Ouverture, the black revolutionary leader in Haiti during the French wars.

20 Sept. *A short walk*: Clough gave a fuller description of his activities this week-end in a letter to Burbidge written this evening: 'Your last came just as I was going off by steamer into Wales; about 3 p.m. Saturday (half-holiday). I went to St Asaph cathedral to service, & walked on over some mountains, gorse-and-heath-tinted, windy, beautiful, to dine with some Aunts resident thereabout. Thence a few miles Liverpoolwards to bed and thence again this morning starting at ½ past 6 part by foot and part by railway train and part by ferry boat to home breakfast and pupils at 10.' In his post-pupillar walk, he told Burbidge, he composed the poem 'Thought may well be ever ranging . . .' (M 26) (the letter is Mulhauser no. 125).

1 Oct. *From palsying self-mistrust . . .*: This is the only manuscript of this poem, from which it was first published in 1974 by Mulhauser, who notes the alternative readings in the text. M 159, 660. Mulhauser prints as text Clough's first rather than his second thoughts, and prints as the last two lines of the poem 'Vague changeable ephemeral / Still varying, still convictionless' but it seems clear from the position of the lines on the page, as well as from the rhyme pattern, that these were meant to be alternative, not consecutive.

18 Oct. *the Statutes*: At the beginning of each Michaelmas term the Master read the statutes in the College Chapel.   *the new lodgings*: 99 Holywell.

20 Oct. *Union*: The motion for debate was that the Catholic Emancipation Act be repealed.

31 Oct. *Analogy*: Joseph Butler's *The Analogy of Religion, Natural and Revealed, to the Constitution and Course of Nature*, published in 1736, was a defence of Christianity against deism, taught as a set text in Oxford.

1 Nov. Sir William Napier's *History of the Peninsular War* was published in 1828–40 and won him a considerable reputation as a historian.   *Emerson*: The first volume of Ralph Waldo Emerson's *Essays* was published in 1841, containing one of his most important discourses, 'Self-Reliance'.

7 Nov. *Skylark*: The 'Ode to a skylark' and 'Arethusa' are, like the 'Ode to Liberty', poems of Percy Bysshe Shelley (1792–1822).

9 Nov. *Prince of Wales*: The future King Edward VII, Queen Victoria's second child, was born on this day, but did not become Prince of Wales until December 4.

10 Nov. *Wrote to Gell*: The letter has been published in C i. 113; it is an account of his summer, gossip about Rugby friends, and a record of the toast to the newborn royal heir.

13 Nov. *Hast thou . . .*: These are the two final stanzas of the poem published in *Ambarvalia* as the final one of the 'Blank Misgivings' sequence, of which the first three occured in the entry for 16 May 1841. Variations between the two texts are noted in M 586.

18 Nov. *Goeller*: Franz Joseph Goeller, author of commentaries on Livy and Thucydides in the first decades of the century.

19 Nov. *Arrival of Todo*: Walrond had come to sit for the scholarship examinations for which Clough had been preparing him in Grasmere. As the entry for 24 Nov. shows, he was unsuccessful.

23 Nov. *Fellowship*: Each day until 27 Nov. Clough sat the examinations for the Balliol fellowship.

27 Nov. *well-doing*: This must mean that these three candidates were short-listed. If Clough's conjecture of the voting on 29 Nov. was correct, it seems that Lingen was the unanimous first choice, and the electors split between Karslake, Clough, and Prichard for second place, with Karslake securing the majority. Prichard had only just taken his final examinations, in which he was about to be awarded a first.

2 Dec. *The Inaugural lecture*: Arnold's first lecture as Regius Professor of Modern History, held in the Sheldonian before, according to Stanley, 'such an audience as no professor ever lectured to before' (Prothero, 308).

5 Dec. *my Essay*: Clough's portrayal of the character of Saul in one of his fellowship papers was favourably remarked upon and remembered.

7 Dec. *Roused by . . .*: This became the seventh of the poems in the 'Blank Misgivings' sequence, published in *Ambarvalia*. Variants between this text and the published one are noted in M 584; the most significant change is the substitution for 'for fasting & for prayer' of 'for watching and for thought'.

10 Dec. *Battells to Ward*: Clough paid his Balliol bills (battells) to Ward in his capacity as Junior Bursar of the year.   *If help there is not* . . . This is the only text of the poem, first published in 1974 (M 159, 660).

1842

27 Jan. *Arnold's 1st lecture*: Arnold's lectures as Regius Professor continued to draw audiences of 300 or 400 during the Lent Term. His popularity was partly due to the reaction against Tractarianism (Stanley, in Prothero, 308).

9 Mar. The Greek quotation is from Sophocles, *Oedipus Tyrannus*, 1396.

28 Mar. *1st day*: On this and each of the three successive days Clough sat two papers of the Oriel fellowship examination. In the first one a passage of Addison's *Spectator* was set for unseen translation into Latin prose.

1 Apr. *factus*: This Oriel fellowship election is reported to have been the last one in which Newman took part.

6 Apr. *Old Curiosity Shop*. This fourth novel of Dickens was published as a complete volume in 1841, having appeared in parts in the serial 'Master Humphrey's Clock'.

10 Apr. *the Provost's*: Edward Hawkins (1798–1882), Provost of Oriel since 1828.

10 Apr. *Entia Realia*: i.e. abstract creations of the mind turned into concrete realities. The pseudo-scholastic terminology perhaps reflects Clough's recent reading of Kant.

23 Apr. *To be* . . .: These lines are published as a poem in M (159, 660).

1 May. *Inter vota* . . .: This poem in the medieval manner may be translated thus: 'Amid desires of mere half-love one thing is really loveable; mid things which daily change and move one thing is barely changeable; mid matters vain or foul or false one thing is true or truth it seems—even in the most tormented night, the silent sweetness of our dreams'.

7 May. *Goetz von Berlichingen*: a drama of 1771, which was translated by Sir Walter Scott, who made use of episodes from it in *Ivanhoe*.

11 May. *very miserable*: possibly because of the class list, in which Oriel's only score was two fourth classes.

27 May. *double 1sts*: Temple and Waite had been awarded firsts in Classics in the list of 11 May; the publication of the mathematics and science list this day showed they had won firsts in that honour school also.

29 May. *Believe me* . . . This is the only manuscript of this poem, which was first published in 1974; alternative readings in the text are given in M 660.

31 May. *Hermann & Dorothea*: This poem of 1797 was available in an English translation by Thomas Holcroft.

13 June. *Arnold's death*: Arnold's last hours are very fully described in a letter from Stanley to Clough, C i. 118.

15 June. *Dovedale*: In Cotton's edition of Walton's *Compleat Angler* (1655) the fishermen fish along the river Dove.

8 July. *Testimonials*: Probably the testimonial to Tait in support of his application for the headmastership of Rugby, which was successful, the result being announced on 28 July (Davidson & Benham, 113). Clough's letter is printed in C i. 120.

22 Aug. *hydropicissimus*: Clough repeats the tag from Horace which he quoted at the head of this diary, and adds, 'if you will not run with the dropsy, you will try to do so with extreme dropsy'.

25 Aug. *the Abbot*: more likely to be a reading of Scott's novel of 1820 than a meeting with a live abbot.

8 Oct. *Last of the Mohicans*: a novel dealing with American Indian life published by James Fenimore Cooper in 1826.

9 Oct. *Irvingite Chapel*: the Catholic Apostolic Church, founded in the 1830s by an excommunicated minister of the Church of Scotland, Edward Irving, a friend of Carlyle.

13 Oct. *Louisa or the Bride*: a novel by Harriet Mozley, published in 1842.

17 Oct. Audit dinner: a feast to mark the approval of the college's accounts and the distribution of dividends, held annually on or near the feast of St Luke (18 Oct.).

12 Nov. *Agesilaus*: Clough was writing a series of lives, of which this was the first, for W. Smith's *Dictionary of Greek and Roman Biography and Mythology*, which appeared 1844–9. In the end Clough contributed 77 biographies to this; a number of them, beginning with 'A', figure in later entries in this journal (see C i. 122).

16 Nov. *Spartan Kings*: see note on 12 Nov.

17 Nov. *Mendicity Society*: The full name of the society, founded in 1818 by Provost Copleston of Oriel, was 'The Oxford Society for the Suppression of Mendicity and Relief of Distressed Travellers'; it carried out social work in the St Ebbe's slums, and Clough helped with running the hostel and soup-kitchen. The fullest account is in Greenberger, 67.

22 Nov. *Carey's viva voce*: Carey was awarded a fourth class.

4 Dec. From 4–25 December there are two separate sets of entries; they are amalgamated in the text into a single series.

12 Dec. *A woman* . . . This is the only manuscript of this poem, which was first published in 1974 (M 160, 660).

15 Dec. *young man of Chester*: John Sumner (1780–1862), later archbishop of Canterbury, was at this time bishop of Chester; he attempted to be neutral between Tractarians and Evangelicals.

30 Dec. *Aristeas* etc. See note on 12 Nov. *Trendelenburg: Logische Untersuchungen*, by F. A. Trendelenburg (1802–1872). *Aldrich . . . Saunderson*: Henry Aldrich and Robert Sanderson were the authors of compendia of logic, first published in 1691 and 1618 respectively, which had been issued in a new edition in 1841.

1843

5 Jan. [Liverpool] *Collegiate Institute*: a newly founded experiment in educational extension, of which William Conybeare had just been appointed first principal (see C i. 124).

15 Jan. *Stahr*: Adolf Stahr published *Aristotelia* at Halle in 1830.

23 Jan. *de Madame d'Arblay*: This essay was published in the *Edinburgh Review* in January 1843, and republished later in the year in Macaulay's volume of collected essays.

2 Feb. *the Panegyric, the Gaude*: 2 Feb., the feast of the Purification of the Blessed Virgin, is the patronal feast of Oriel, celebrated with a special service in chapel and a banquet.

24 Feb. *Kirkpatrick*: an American tourist, whose visit is described by Clough in a letter to Annie on 26 Feb. (Mulhauser no. 142).

24 Mar. *the Comet*: Halley's comet, next to return in 1910.

27 Mar. *Palmer Latin scholar*: Edward Palmer of Balliol in this year won the Hartford scholarship and the Ireland scholarship (see entry for 1 Apr.).

27 Apr. *Past & Present*: an anti-democratic political tract, published in 1843.

5 June. *lost his watch*: The loss of Matthew Arnold's watch is described in greater detail in a letter of Clough to Annie of the following day (Mulhauser, 144).

20 June. *Holiday*: for the anniversary of Queen Victoria's accession to the throne.

1846

26 June. *Turner's*: At the Royal Academy Exhibition of 1846 there were exhibited three paintings of J. M. W. Turner, *Going to the Ball* (*San Martino*), *Returning from the Ball* (*St. Martha*), and *Whalers entangled in Flow Ice*, all now in the Tate gallery.

1847

2 Sept. *Adolphus*: the 'Fitzclarence' of 28 Aug., the natural son of King William IV.

20 Nov. *John Wicliffe*: the ship on which Tom Arnold was emigrating to New Zealand. See Bertram, 8–11.

22 Dec. *Tipperary*: J. S. Coyne's farce, *The Tipperary Legacy*, which had opened on 4 Dec.

1848

18 Mar. *Sweethearts & Wives*: a comic opera by James Kenney, first performed at the Theatre Royal in the Haymarket in 1823.

31 Mar. *Swedenborg*: Emanuel Swedenborg (1688–1772) was a Swedish philosopher and mystic, who claimed a revelation of a theosophical system; his followers organized into a church in London in 1778.

10 Apr. *O'Connor*: Since 1838 the Chartists, a working-class reform group, had agitated for universal suffrage by ballot and annual sessions of a reformed Parliament. 10 Apr. was the date fixed for an enormous demonstration to assemble on Kennington Common to convey a petition to Parliament signed by over a million; 150,000 special constables were enlisted, but the demonstration, addressed by Feargus O'Connor, turned out to be small and peaceable.

21 Apr. *a Repealer*: a supporter of the repeal of the protectionist Corn Laws, in the hope that free trade would bring down the price of corn and relieve the distress of the poor. The Laws were repealed by Sir Robert Peel in 1846.

9 May. Vine St. Liverpool was Clough's mother's address.

11 May. *Emerson*: In a letter written this day to his sister, Clough writes, 'The only events since [Tuesday] have been my visit to the Theatre de la Republique to see Rachel in Phèdre, and the arrival of Emerson . . . I have been to the Jardin des Plantes and the column erected in honour of the revolution of July 1830, on the site of the Bastille. It was here that the Republic was solemnly inaugurated in February . . .' (C i. 204).

13 May. *le rappel*: the order to mobilize the National Guard, because of fears of disorder in connection with a petition in support of the Polish revolution.

15 May. *The Invasion*: The events of this day were thus described in a later part of the letter quoted above: 'The Chamber was invaded and turned out by a mob—and the hall occupied by them for two hours. At last the Natl Guard turned them out . . . La Martine came with Ledru-Rollin and rode along the quays to finish the work, with dragoons and cannon. I was at his side for a quarter of a mile . . . The whole thing is put down for the present, and I am glad it is, on the whole. The cry was Vive La Pologne, but the object was to get rid of the Assembly and set up a more democratic set of people.'

21 May. *Fete*: The postponed fête, with the float full of girls wearing tricolours and oak-wreaths, and the tricolour balloon, was watched by Clough in the Place de la Concorde and was described in a letter to Stanley the next day, C i. 208.

28 May. *Club de la Revolution*: The meeting of the club is described by Clough in a postscript to his letter to Stanley, C i. 211.

30 May. *Club des Femmes*: Clough reported the meeting in a letter to R. W. Church: 'Last night I visited the Club des Femmes—presided over by a Madame Niboyer. Alas, poor woman! she has a terrific task—not to speak of having to keep women silent, she has to keep men, or say, beasts, in order . . . Perhaps it may be useful for Frenchmen to see a woman face them and present herself before them *not* for purposes of flirtation. I got disgusted with my male neighbours and came away before it ended. The subject was divorce.' (C i. 213)

6 June. *Marriage*: Burbidge married an Italian wife, described by Clough in a letter to Tom Arnold of 27 Nov. 1848 as 'a very nice simple, lively and affectionate little body' (Bertram, 123).

15 July. *the Europa*: the ship on which Emerson sailed to America. *Father*

left Mother straitened: These are notes by Clough on the account Emerson gave him of his life.   *The I am of Moses or the demon of Socrates*: When Moses asked God's name, the reply was 'I am that I am; thus shalt thou say unto the children of Israel, I AM hath sent me unto you' (Exod. 3: 14). In Plato's *Apology*, Socrates speaks of the supernatural voice or *daimon* which has warned him against evildoing.

Joanna Southcote: Joanna Southcott (1750–1814), a maidservant who claimed supernatural gifts and believed herself pregnant with a spiritual being called Shiloh.

15 Aug. *Keats*: The reference is to the *Life and Letters of John Keats*, just published by R. Monckton Milnes (London, 1848)   *wine press*: a reference to Revelation 19: 15.   *Topernafuosich*: This is the first reference to Clough's poem, now known as 'The Bothie of Tober-na-Vuolich', written and published in the last months of 1848. The lines which follow appear with little change as lines 11, 26 and 122–6; see Scott, 7.

Index of Persons